Communication
and
Community

Edited by

Gregory J. Shepherd
University of Kansas

Eric W. Rothenbuhler
University of Iowa

LAWRENCE ERLBAUM ASSOCIATES PUBLISHERS
2001   Mahwah, New Jersey   London

Lawrence Erlbaum Associates, Inc., Publishers
10 Industrial Avenue
Mahwah, NJ 07430

Cover design by Kathryn Houghtaling Lacey

Library of Congress Cataloging-in-Publication Data

Communication and community / Gregory J. Shepherd,
    Eric W. Rothenbuhler [editors]
        p. cm.
Includes bibliographical references and index.
    ISBN 0-8058-3138-X (cloth : alk. paper)
    ISBN 0-8058-3139-8 (pbk : alk. paper)
1. Interpersonal communication. 2. Community. I. Shepherd,
    Gregory J. II. Rothenbuhler, Eric W.
HM1166.C66 2000
302—dc21   00-086821
                                                     CIP

Books published by Lawrence Erlbaum Associates are printed
on acid-free paper, and their bindings are chosen for strength
and durability.

Printed in the United States of America
10 9 8 7 6 5 4 3 2 1

To the community of partners and friends:
Mary, Jamie, and each other

—GJS
—EWR

Contents

Preface

Concerns about community, the balancing of individual rights with social responsibilities, and the weighing of freedom and equality permeate nearly every aspect of American life. In marriages, neighborhoods, and workplaces, via face-to-face and mediated behaviors, we strive to "commune" and we long to separate; we make sense of our cooperative lives and we deny them; we bond and we break.

Throughout the public sphere, political leaders and citizens bemoan a slide in civility, express a fear that the will to cooperate has weakened, and worry about the decline of responsibility in social life. Recent years have witnessed a remarkable thematic resonance across political speeches, media commentary, citizen complaints, and scholarly writings: The problems of contemporary life (e.g., declining "social capital," loss of neighborliness, threats to the family, divorce, uncaring corporations, unstable jobs, faceless technology, exploitative movies, anonymous suburbs, unsupervised children) are collectively captured by the "problem of community." Often, certain types or practices of communication are identified as contributing to the problem (e.g., violent television programs and movies, nihilistic music, apathy-producing news coverage); more frequently, the hope of communication is offered as the solution (as witnessed by the daily talk shows and their incessant calls for "more" communication—sincere, open, and face-to-face—as the balm for life's many, and sometimes weird, wounds).

A book on *Communication and Community* would thus seem to fit the Zeitgeist of the 21st century's dawn; and given the intricate character of the relationship between these complex terms, communication and community, a collection of essays by both new and established voices from across the areas of communication studies seems the most appropriate form for such a book. In the few pages that follow, we preface this collection by suggesting a few themes readers might keep in mind as they go through the volume's essays, and offer brief overviews of the book's 14 chapters.

THEMES OF COMMUNICATION AND COMMUNITY

Whether at the individual or collective level, in relationships, organizations, towns, or nation states, community is an enduring concern. From ancient Greece to today the concern for community has attracted serious thought, and as the essays in this volume make clear, that thought has often been directed to communication and the part it plays in the accomplishment or experience of community.

Just below the surface of agreement in this general point, however, lies a stunning diversity of theoretical and empirical claims. Community is found in time or place, in networks or relationships. It is used to control; it is freeing. It is the basis for democracy itself, or a cover for repression. Although some see community entering a new age of access, growth, and vitality, many others see it withering away. Communication, too, can be this, that, and the other thing. Communication is conceived as the necessary symbolic base of community, and, in the form of mass-produced entertainment as the number one distraction from community. Communication can be understanding, empathy, and relation; it can also be propaganda, ideology, and manipulation. Communication can be the very model of democracy, or the very method of its subversion.

The task of summarizing and predicting from all this diversity is, then, daunting. Nevertheless, we believe that two broad themes arise in this collection and would most likely arise in any serious treatments of the topic. Together these themes help gather a few thoughts about past problems, future research, and continuing worries about communication and community. We offer them, at least, as possible thematic guides to the diverse collection of essays in this volume. The first of the themes concerns the material, or situated, character of communication and community; the second addresses questions about the goodness of communication and community.

Materiality

One theme that emerges in several of the chapters in this volume, and which we predict will be relevant to future work on communication and community, is the enduring importance of locality. This issue is treated explicitly by some authors, implicitly by others, but is always a conspicuous thread in the weave of communication and community. This enduring relevance of locality is itself based on the materiality of communication and community.

The material bases of community are often overlooked by communication scholars—they are not our professional concern, they are relative constants, and this easily taken for granted. But, no community and no communal relation exists without an enduring material base. That base provides the situation in which, and the conditions and resources of which, communally directed communication is constructed and engaged. It is important we remember that buildings to meet in, or telephones and computers to talk through, are community resources and settings for communication; without them, either other arrangements would have to be made, or communication and community forgone. And, of course, the nature of these material bases make a difference too. How "virtual" is the space of the computer mediated community? What constraints and opportunities apply to building an "electronic" community? How does sharing the same physical space with one group of workers affect the community of another group of workers?

Communication is also never without a material base. From the physiology of speech and hearing to the bandwidth of computer networks, material bases certainly condition and provide resources for communication. Although these bases do not typically draw much explicit attention from scholars of communication, they do appear more indirectly in acknowledgments of the situated character of experience. Thus, for example, the physiology of speech and hearing becomes the phenomenal experience of one body interacting with another. And we feel differences between embodied speech and disembodied writing. Similarly, the bandwidth of the computer network becomes the very particular experience of satisfaction or frustration with an interaction episode. It is important as well to remember that symbols themselves are substantial: The sounds we hear as words, and the letters we see as sentences are full of history and force. They come from someplace and are going somewhere; pitched by some body or bodies, caught by an other or others. Hence our analyses of communication and community are full of contingency, as we confront the seemingly limitless variability of experience in all its situated glory, in its very materiality.

Goodness

Whereas materiality is a plain, but often inexplicit, theme in work on communication and community, the goodness of communication and community is an obvious, but typically perplexing, focus. Should we assume either communication, community, or both to be inherently good? What is required for either or both to be experienced as good?

Since the 1920s, John Dewey (1916/1966, p. 83) proposed two criteria for judging the goodness of any community. The first was, "How numerous and varied are the interests which are consciously shared?" And the second, "How full and free is the interplay with other forms of association?"

It is hard to read the chapters in this volume without hearing Dewey's echo. Many writers are concerned, for example, with the way in which communities are defined by exclusion as much as inclusion. After all, it seems that communities are often defined by who is *not* a member. But the reader might wish to recall Dewey's sense of the "good" community when encountering such concerns. The sense in which good communities exhibit tolerance, and diversity of interest and association can be seen as a banal concern of liberal pluralism, or as a profession of meliorism. Most scholars in this volume (and again, we would guess in any similar collection) would seem to assume community to be good, but communities to be something less. That is, they follow Rorty's (1989) following of Dewey in wishing communities would enlarge their sense of community, and "extend our sense of 'we' to people whom we have previously thought of as 'they'" (p. 192). The interesting questions, of course, center on how to best achieve such goodness.

As by this point should be plain, *communication* is most often taken as the road to the good community. As with community, communication is most often assumed to be good, although communications are not. Thus, most writers investigate the communicative rules, practices, structures, and relationships that might lead to the experience of (good) communication, which, in turn, might lead to the experience of (good) community. However, unlike Dewey with his criteria for assessing the goodness of communities, few scholars seem willing or able to address what would be the criteria for the goodness of communication (but, see Habermas, e.g., 1979). It is here where communication and community tend to entangle themselves. Is good communication something or nothing more or less than the experience of community? If, when looking for the road to good communities, we turn to the experience of communication, do we also find ourselves turning to the experience of community when looking for good communication? If so, we turn ourselves round and around in the fashion of a fine hermeneutic circle. Perhaps that is as it should be, but questions, begged or confronted, on the constitution and achievement of *good* communication and *good* communities permeate the literature in general, and the chapters of this volume in particular. We now turn to a brief overview of those chapters.

OVERVIEW

The book is organized into an introduction and two major sections. The two major sections are devoted to *Interpersonal Relations, Organizations, and Community*, and *Media, the Public, and Community*, respectively. This division replicates conventional thinking, following apparent distinctions made between interpersonal and mediated, micro and macro, and between the issues of communal relations and of geographical communities. We hope the volume shows, rather, that communication and community can not be adequately analyzed in any context without reference to other contexts, other levels of analysis, and other media and modes of communication. We hope that this move toward conceptual integration will be completed by readers. We hope that this book will find an appreciative audience among students, teachers, and researchers concerned with communication across contexts, media, and modes.

The introduction offers a *tour de force* chapter by David Depew and John Durham Peters. Reviewing the intellectual history of the idea that communities are formed by communication, they review a range of contributors to this idea from Aristotle to the American progressives and the Chicago school of sociology. Along the way they review the presence of this idea in theories of democracy and theories of society, with examples from philosophy, literature, and history. Between Aristotle and the Chicago school, they provide efficient exposition of theories from France, England, Germany, and the United States, across several centuries. We know of no better exposition; this is the place for students to start.

The section on *Interpersonal Relations, Organizations, and Community* begins with two important conceptual pieces, and then is organized roughly by increasing level of analysis or size of reference, from face-to-face interactions, through various issues of organization, to consideration of a major social movement. Greg Shepherd's chapter outlines a conception of what he calls "pragmatic idealism," arguing that faith in the possibility of communication as something interpersonal, or transcendent, is essential to the realization of community. Whereas Shepherd's chapter traces the role of idealism in social practices, Carey Adams' chapter identifies problems that follow when ideals are left implicit in social analysis. He points to the ways in which current theories of communication competence presume a concern with communal relations. There are implications here for both theories of communication, and the contributions of communication scholars to the understanding of community. Sherianne Shuler's chapter is an analysis of the emotional labor of 911 dispatchers. Required to be calm in the face of all emergencies, to offer the appropriate help to whomever calls, and to maintain an efficient organization, these workers are also people who must maintain selves and relations officially irrelevant to their nevertheless emotionally demanding labor. Her compelling analysis identifies a number of paradoxes involved in community, emergency, helping, and modes of communication.

Karen Lee Ashcraft's chapter is the first of three devoted explicitly to organizations. She combines a review of theories of feminist organizing with an analysis of the communication practices in one feminist community. The important lessons of her study include the paradoxes and difficulties of putting ideas into practice—especially the difficulty of building a viable organization, with simultaneous commitments to community and to individual empowerment. Lori Gossett and Phillip Tompkins analyze the establishment of workplace communities as means of management control. The latter is an instrumental imposition on informal and autonomous social networks within the organization, giving rise to a variety of tensions, conflicts, and paradoxes. George Cheney provides an overview of his larger work on the Mondragón worker-cooperative movement in the Basque Country of Spain. His major theme is the various forms, and tensions among forms, of connection and severance in worker control, organization, community, and democracy.

The section on *Media, the Public, and Community* is organized by clusters of concern. It begins with two conceptual pieces, followed by two chapters on new communication technologies, followed by three chapters on mass media, community, and democracy. Eric Rothenbuhler's chapter is an essay in reconceptualization, growing out of frustration with the failure of the research literature on communication and community attachment to make any tangible contribution to the work of communities. Each of the chapters that follows is concerned, to one degree or another, with the actual problems of communities and democracies. Communities are usually conceived in geographical space and most of the chapters of this book are concerned with such primarily space-based phenomena as organization, distance, and mediation. Barbie Zelizer's chapter reminds us of the necessity for community to endure in time, and of the role of collective memory in that process. Interestingly, collective memory is sustained by symbols and artifacts that must have a presence in space—this being yet another dialectic out of which community is formed.

Howard Sypher and Bart Collins review current thinking and offer their own advice on how computer-mediated communication may change community processes, and how it can be directed to help communities. Their attitude is practical—computer-mediated communication is not going to go away, no matter what our traditional notions of community and the types of communication that sustain it. Let us work, then, they say, to understand the uses of the computer and make good choices. Teresa Harrison and her colleagues offer an excellent example of this practical attitude in action. Their chapter is a report on a collaborative project among university faculty and students and local community citizens to build a computer-based community network. As their work continues, this progress report already offers a number of practical lessons from which we can also generalize to conceptual problems.

The next three chapters form a group on mass communication, community, and democracy. Keith Stamm's research grows out of the same literature critiqued by Rothenbuhler, and though less explicit in his critique, Stamm's concerns are moving in the same direction. Here he brings what we know from research on newspaper reading and community attachment, and some of his own recent research, to questions arising in current discussions of public or civic journalism. One of the lessons of his work is that the laudable goals of civic journalism projects presume a level of community involvement among citizens that may seldom exist. In keeping with the spirit of putting our ideas and knowledge to good use in communities, he points to this as an opportunity as much as a problem. Chris Martin's chapter is a sobering reminder of the contradictions inherent when newspapers are simultaneously tools of democracy and of capital, simultaneously community resources and profit centers of corporate chains. Following a review of the ideals of public journalism, and some of the misfit of those ideals, with the conventions of newspaper reporting and the newspaper business, he analyzes the 19-month strike of the *Detroit Free Press* as a failure of public journalism. Calabrese's chapter is similarly based in analysis of the contradictions of the contemporary organization of communication and capital. His conclusions provide a fitting close to the collection, as they draw our attention back to the theme of a concern for the local; that is the place, he reminds us, where participatory democracy and healthy community can best be conducted.

ACKNOWLEDGMENTS

The history of this book goes back several years; there are many people to thank. Greg Shepherd organized panels on communication and community at both the 1994 and the 1996 Speech Communication Association Meetings (in New Orleans and San Diego, respectively). The present chapters by Adams, Gossett and Tompkins, Rothenbuhler, Shepherd, Shuler, and Zelizer had their origin at one or another of those sessions. The questions and suggestions from the audience at both events helped our thinking. John Dimmick and Laura Stafford of Ohio State University, Dennis Mumby of Purdue, Barbara O'Keefe, then of Illinois, now of Northwestern, and Lawrence Grossberg of North Carolina were at one time associated with the project and each made important contributions, though each needed to withdraw for other considerations. An anonymous reviewer of an earlier book proposal offered valuable suggestions, which we have followed. We also thank our chapter authors, each of whom contributed more than a chapter. From each we have also received suggestions about the shape of the book as a whole, and lessons for our own work. Each chapter author also deserves thanks for their cooperation. Some have been extraordinarily patient; others have joined us late in the game and produced excellent work on a short deadline. We hope the final product rewards the help of everyone.

One devoted scholar and colleague is no longer with us. Herb Dordick fell ill and passed away as this volume was being edited. Herb was a key member of that 1994 convention panel, and the first to suggest that we put together a book. Herb's paper was a provocative essay entitled *The Tyranny of the Majority, the Compartmentalization of Diversity, Information Technology, and the Problem of Community.* Herb was one of Eric's teachers, and in later years he had become a friend. He visited Iowa periodically—he had a son on the faculty there—and conversations that took place with him have had a lasting influence. Herb was a fundamentally humane man. He was cultured, with a passion for ideas, and for people, too. Originally an engineer by training, Herb never let an interest in ideas distract him from an interest in the uses of ideas. We hope this volume captures some of that same spirit; we know it has benefitted from our time with Herb.

REFERENCES

Dewey, J. (1916/1966). *Democracy and education.* New York: The Free Press.
Habermas, J. (1979). *Communication and the evolution of society.* Boston: Beacon Press.
Rorty, R. (1989). *Contingency, irony, and solidarity.* Cambridge: Cambridge University Press.

I

Introduction

1

Community and Communication: The Conceptual Background

David Depew
John Durham Peters
The University of Iowa

ARISTOTELIAN ROOTS OF THE BASIC IDEA

Before anyone ever attempted empirically to verify or falsify the claim that communities—relationships, families, neighborhoods, voluntary associations, municipalities, regions, or nation states—are held together by communication; before anyone had noticed that the increasing size and complexity of communities requires novel, more powerful means of communication to forge them into a unity; indeed before anyone had hypothesized that the newspaper paradigmatically performs such a function in modern nation states; before any of this someone had to have had the basic idea that communities are welded together by communication.

The basic idea goes back as far as Aristotle's *Politics*. Aristotle says that every state is a community (*koinonia*), which "makes something one and common (*koinon*)" (Aristotle, *History of Animals* 1.1.448a8) out of separate households (which are themselves construed as communities that are composed of functionally differentiated sets of relationships among husbands and wives, parents and children, and masters and servants). Aristotle says that it is speech (*logos*) that binds this nested hierarchy of communities together. Although the voice (*phone*) of animals can certainly reveal the pleasant and the painful, it is the speech (*logos*) of human beings that uniquely serves to "reveal the useful and the harmful, and the

---

3

just and unjust ... and it is community in these matters that makes both a household and a state" (*Politics* I.2.1253a15-19).

Aristotle hypothesized that community, in the rather strong sense that he assigns to that word, rises or falls with discursive interchange. For that reason he says that a state should be no bigger, either in territory or in population, than is required for all adult male citizens to participate in public affairs by responding to and judging the unamplified speech of deliberative, judicial, and apodeictic speakers. That is also the reason why he is contemptuous of large urban aggregations. In what passes for one of the professorial jokes that punctuate the immense *corpus* of his works, Aristotle remarks that the capture of Babylon (which is his stock example of urban sprawl) by an invading army of Persians "was not noticed in certain parts of the city for three days," concluding from this alleged fact that Babylon is not really a *polis* at all, but rather a sort of nation (*ethnos*) concentrated into a single, intensely unpleasant, and distinctly apolitical walled site (*Politics* 3.3.1276a26-30). What remains for him the normative shape of political community is an assembly in which all may hear and speak. This necessarily has a restricted scale.

Aristotle's communication-based political theory was explicitly a critique of Plato's. In his raging search for order, Plato (427–347 BCE) proposed to replace the autonomous practical rationality (*praxis*) of freely associated citizens with governance by technical rationality (*techne*). In proposing such, he reduced (at least in Aristotle's opinion) the status of the governed to herd animals, who are manipulated by a shepherd-like ruling class that knows what images to display to the untutored masses (see Plato's *Statesman*). Thus, when Aristotle proceeded to say that humans are political animals, he meant precisely that they are *not* herd animals (*zoa ageleia*), or even "social animals"(*zoa koinonike*). (As contended by Arendt [1958], Cicero's Latin mistranslation of *zoon politikon* as *animal socialis* blurred this distinction, setting afoot a long-lived misunderstanding of this point.) The distinction is this: Herd animals all do the same thing in physical proximity to one another; political animals are able to do different things by dividing roles in pursuit of the same end (*History of Animals* 1.1.488a8-9). Humans (as distinct from other political animals, like social insects) perform this function by using rational speech to constitute and deal with the objects that uniquely bind them together, namely the "useful" and the "just" (Depew, 1995).

DEMOCRACY AT A DISTANCE: AMERICAN DEMOCRATIC REPUBLICANISM

Aristotle's prescriptions for the relation between communication and community ruled political thought for more than two millennia: Communities must be both small and concerned with participatory deliberation about the just and the unjust. Both the size and the character of a community in the Aristotelian vision are defined by the dynamics of face-to-face communication. Whenever worries arose about the viability of republics, as they did both in the Italy of Machiavelli (1469–1527) and in the neo-classical France of Montesquieu (1689–1755) and Rousseau (1712–1778), usually arose from deeper worries about how to meet these conditions of interpersonal, as opposed to mass, communication. The issue of appropriate size and scale was raised anew, and with particular salience, by the democratic revolutions of the late 18th and early 19th centuries, the discussion of which formed a sort of climax to the renewed civic republican discourse that had been transferred from renaissance Italy to Northern Europe by way of the Calvinist diaspora (Pocock, 1975; Skinner, 1978). Nowhere was this more the case than in North America, where the issue was discussed in a way that actually produced novel results.

In contrast to Montesquieu, who had declared that only military empires could encompass large territories, and to Rousseau, who thought that political giantism bred nothing but monsters, Madison, Hamilton, and Jefferson, among others, were alive in their different ways not only to the difficulties that a vastly enlarged physical scale presented for a new age of republican politics (*a novus ordo saeculorum*), but also to the positive opportunities that just such an enlarged scale afforded. What traditional political theory might regard as monstrous and contrary to nature—the vast geography of the American republic—the generation of Founders regarded as blessed and exceptional.

It had long been an axiom among the educated that, in the light of the historical record, self-governing republican communities are fragile and evanescent. The main reason that this perception persisted was the alleged tendency of the democratic impulse inherent in republican communities to degenerate into mob rule, and ultimately into tyranny. Despite this common belief, it was precisely in this vast geography that the Americans saw their opportunity. For Madison, an extended republic would evade the combustibility and faction that face-to-face assemblies fostered; for Jefferson, the distribution of a farming population across a vast space would prevent the formation of urban mobs; for Hamilton, the representative system would make a new, wider spatial orbit of republican politics possible. For this entire generation, in fact, means of communication that were unknown among the ancients were thought to be able to compensate for the physical dispersal of the population. When combined with the moralistic self-control that Protestant habits of private reading had already so widely dispersed among the white population, new technologies of communication would indeed enable America to constitute a democratic republican community that would endure.

Accordingly, as James Carey has argued, the founding narrative of the United States was rooted in the possibility of creating a great community by means of communication (Carey, 1989). High on the list of the means of communication that would be required to forge a linked system of republican communities over these vast distances were rivers, roads, canals, and later railroads, which were overtly spoken of at the time as paradigmatic means of communication. (The tropological structure of this usage persists today in the notion of an "information superhighway.") But no less important among communicative means that help constitute political community was the medium of print, which, as Carey noted, conquers space by permitting the easy transportation of messages via material means of communication such as canals and roads.

From this perspective, it was a happy circumstance that by the turn of the 18th-century there were more printing presses in more cities in the American colonies than in all of England, and that the European population of these colonies was, far and away, the most literate on earth (Ferguson, 1997; Warner, 1990). Admittedly, these presses were not yet politicized in the late seventeenth and early 18th-centuries. They did not become a bountiful source of broadsides, pamphlets, and newspapers until the period just before the revolution. When, however, the deeply internalized and widely diffused Protestant myth that treated print technology as the privileged instrument of world liberation (because of the direct popular access to sacred Scripture that it afforded) did at last meet the revolutionary impulses of the mid-18th century, the newspaper acquired the iconic, almost numinous, role that it has never ceased to have in the United States.

The efforts of 20th-century Progressives like George Herbert Mead and Robert Park to formulate empirical research programs designed to explore the link between community formation and communication would take place against this deep, yet too often unthematized, conceptual background. It was, in fact, just in this mythic setting (but not, on that account, less true) that we should place Park's notion that the immigrant press is a means of integrating new populations into the American experience, as well as the hope, entertained by the young John Dewey, that a "people's newspaper" would undercut plutocratic monopolization of the means of information (Park, 1923; this emergence would take place in an encounter between Park and Dewey, while the latter was a young faculty member at the University of Michigan, and the crackpot journalist Franklin Ford, who almost induced Dewey to edit a newspaper to be called "Thought News;" see Westbrook, 1991).

These visions are not at all an oddity. For the cultural *topos* on which we have been insisting—that American democratic republicanism is predicated on the possibility of using advanced means of communication to forge democratic community over a distance—is an interpretive scheme that has been instinctively appealed to whenever new challenges have arisen on the scene of the American experiment. Each new medium of communication, from the telegraph to the Internet, has been greeted not only as a more efficient means of sending signals, but as reordering, for good and ill, the tissues of the democratic order itself. The question of communication and community in the United States is thus not only a fascinating theoretical issue; it is entangled in a long and deep history of political anxieties and wishes.

Perhaps the most intense of many challenges to this inherited narrative arose at the turn of the 20th century. The closing of the frontier, together with the explosion of the polyglot urban agglomerations that had been made inevitable by the demand for cheap, imported labor to fuel the post-Civil War industrial economy, was almost universally imagined among older strata of the population as threatening the very foundations of the American republicanism. Not only would unrestricted population growth unleash the law-like Malthusian dynamics that had thus far been deflected to Europe by the availability of cheap land, but, in threatening American "exceptionalism," it would undercut the legitimacy of American democratic republican ideology itself (Ross, 1991). Progressives (for the most part scions of these older strata who refused to become reactionary nativists) attempted to meet this challenge in many ways, some of which (such as their enthusiasm for eugenics) cannot help but appear to us as falling into the very stance they ostensibly resisted. The most important, and perhaps most enlightened, of their efforts were various attempts to deploy means of communication that had been used earlier to solve the problem of physical dispersal—means that by now had added the time-collapsing telegraph to the space-collapsing newspaper, and would soon include the telephone, cinema, and radio—to address problems of communication and community formation that had been posed by competing classes in a crowded, urbanized, industrial world that could no longer be physically dispersed.

The work of the Chicago School of urban sociology must be understood as part of an effort to structure both city and civic life in a way that ran counter to traditional understandings of the role of communication. Communication, a concept that had once largely meant the spiritual intercourse of remote individuals, now became redefined as a general principle of social order that described both intimate and national scales of association. According to just that definition, the community and neighborhood studies of the Chicago School were undertaken as exemplary of social dynamics that could be spotted in any work of social struggle and reintegration rather than as forays into isolated social worlds. We return to the work of the Chicago School in a later section.

AN ENGLISH ANALOGUE:
GEORGE ELIOT'S *MIDDLEMARCH*

Turn-of-the century American Progressives were not the first moderns to entertain the notion that the newspaper and related means of communication could provide solutions to the distinctively social problem of integrating classes into a "great community." The problem of urbanization and industrialization affected England before it affected America. Thus, it is no surprise that we find in mid-19th-century Britain a circle of intellectuals, most of whom were centered around the liberal *Westminster Review*, who dealt explicitly with this array of problems, and who, like their American Progressive counterparts some half century later, assigned the newspaper the same galvanizing role.

Consider *Middlemarch* (1872), which stands on any score as one of the greatest novels ever written, and whose author, Mary Ann Evans (who wrote under the name of George Eliot) was a member of the *Westminster Review* circle previously mentioned. *Middlemarch* is a fictional study of a provincial city on the eve of the first Reform Bill (1832). The Reform Bill was the first of a long series of attempts in England to forge a constitutional compromise between competing classes at a time when the landed aristocracy was clearly losing its grip on the levers of power to a rising middle class, who were, in turn, being pushed hard by the potential of revolutionary violence on the part of a growing industrial proletariat. The overt moral of Eliot's story is that people, when they are placed on the shifting grounds of a rapidly modernizing society, are forced to use good intentions as a principle of making life decisions, because they cannot reliably appeal to the old reservoirs of received opinion that are fitted for a stable system of hierarchically subordinated classes. Good intentions alone, however, are not a very effective tool. For acting

merely from good intentions can have unpredictable, even devastating, consequences for oneself as well as the others with whom one is interactively linked,
consequences that can in retrospect seem more deterministic than deliberative in
their causes.

The heroine of *Middlemarch*, Dorothea Brooke, niece and ward of a pleasant
enough, doddering old lord of the manor, marries the decrepit Biblical scholar
Casaubon (who is a symbol of outdated Medieval learning), whom she mistakes
for a genius to whom she will devote herself. In consequence of doing so she nearly
ruins her life. Another character, the ambitious Dr. Lydgate destroys a promising
career in medical research and clinical practice, which he brings to the town in the
name of progress, by making an ill-advised marriage to the vain, consumer-oriented daughter of a rising merchant. Amid all this destruction, things work out, at
least in a muted, reflective, Wordsworthian way. But they work out only for those
characters, notably Dorothea, who come to recognize that their safety lies in their
personal growth, and that their personal growth in turn depends on communicative
interaction with (and exposure of oneself to) all the members of the larger community in which they live (Graver, 1984).

This moral is reinforced by the contrast between characters who grow by interaction and exposure and those who do not. Among the latter is the icy and remote Casaubon, whose scholarship is undermined by his failure to interact with
other intellectuals, especially post-Hegelian German Biblical critics, whose
work, unbeknownst to him, has rendered his own irrelevant. Equally locked up
within his own egoism is Mr. Bulstrode, a self-important and evangelically
unctuous banker who tries to cover up a shady past which, when it becomes
known, destroys him mercilessly and justly. Given this conception of the relationship between community, communication, and self-stabilization, it is interesting and emblematic that when, at the end of the novel, Dorothea is
married again (Casaubon having conveniently died), it is to a young property-
less reformer and outsider named Will Ladislaw, who had lent his hand to the
Reform party in Middlemarch by editing a local newspaper, and who, we are
told, will be elected to Parliament. That a newspaper should be more effective
in solving the deepest questions of human existence than the *Key to All Mythol-
ogies* hermetically sought for by Casaubon is an irony on which George Eliot
wants earnestly to insist.

By the mid-19th century, it seems, journalism was taking over the function of
making a society transparent and visible to all, thereby increasing the rate of interaction which the full development of both individual personality and communi-
tarian connectedness would depend on. (The notion of social connectedness as a
route to personal salvation appears as the epigraph, "Only Connect," to E. M.
Forster's *Howard's End*. Appearing at a later period in the internal development of
the British novel, it is testimony to the failure to connect represented in his story
rather than to the "growing good of the world" that Eliot, writing in the high tide of
Victorian Progressivism, sees in society. Newspapers, it is worth noting, figure little or not at all in Forster's writings; if anything, it is the novel itself that is supposed to foster the less than inevitable good of the world.)

WHY COMMUNICATION CREATES COMMUNITY:
FRENCH THEORIES

If 19th- and early 20th-century modernists were agreed on the premise that new means of communication, if properly deployed, can enhance community formation, they were in considerably less agreement about why. Questions about why this happens (assuming it does) can be divided into two types. One type is empirical: It asks how communication actually makes communities. Another type is conceptual, philosophical, or theoretical: It asks how it is *possible* for communication to create community. The greatest, or at least the most prominent, social thinkers of the 19th- and early 20th-centuries—Hegel, Marx, Spencer, Mill, Durkheim, Dewey—all asked this "how-possibly" question. Moreover, they were divided on the answer to it, their differences depending for the most part on how the very notion of the individual's relationship to society is to be construed at the conceptual level. It will repay us to survey these differences. For, despite a considerable amount of cross-fertilization, divergent answers to the how-possibly question about why communication facilitates community correspond to distinct national styles of social thought—French, German, English, and American—that persist to this day.

Let us begin with France, which, thanks to the Revolution of 1789, was the first European country to be forced to deal with political modernity (even if its encounter with social and economic modernization lagged considerably behind). French social thought generally lies in the long shadow cast by Rousseau, who proposed a version of social contract theory according to which each of us remains, in his or her private life, a self-interested egoist, but, as a political agent, acquires a new identity as an undifferentiated part of a generalized, consubstantial body politic, a *citoyen*, or citizen. When a French citizen votes, or alternatively digs up paving stones to hurl at a government that fails to express the Rousseauian "general will," he or she is presumed to do so not as a private person who is trying to get the best deal possible from civil society, as in Anglo-Saxon countries, but as a synecdoche of the general will itself. Thus political identity as a *citoyen* does not individuate us. Rather, it is supposed to produce, in Rousseau's mind, a modern analogue of a distinctly unindividuated Roman or Greek citizen—Sparta being his preferred model.

The central problem of post-revolutionary French politics is to keep the egoistic monster that is presumed to lie within each of us well out of sight. This is to be done by devising rituals, symbolic public displays, collective myths, and performances that are so compelling that the egoistical beast inside stays where it is. This concern explains why the French realistic novel is so preoccupied with the persistence of the "old Adam" in each citizen: with Balzac's grasping old Goriot, with Flaubert's hypocritical, bourgeois pseudo-aesthetes, with Mauriac's moral monsters. To the extent that motives are reducible to egocentric self-interest, *la patrie est en danger*. It also explains why French political thought from Comte to Durkheim to Althusser is so concerned with the role of ritual and display in creating political community.

In recent times, Althusser's latter-day brand of totalizing Marxism is continuous with the Rousseauian-Jacobin tradition because it insists that the person interpellated into the subject position by political identification is not a person who gains his or her individual life, but who, on the contrary, loses it (Althusser, 1970). The same presumption goes back much further. Comte wanted to invent a successor civil religion to Catholicism, which would always remain a political threat precisely because its public dramaturgy and its conception of La France as the first daughter of the Church is quite up to the job of contesting civic republican forms of ritual interpellation into consubstaniality. Then, for his part, Durkheim, following the Belgian mathematician and astronomer Adolphe Quetelet, takes advantage of the statistical revolution (of which Comte was largely ignorant) to draw a distinction between the individual, who exerts free will in a very narrow sphere of life—a sphere that sometimes contracts to mere self-consciousness—while the public person postulated by Rousseau is constituted through statistical regularities (Quetelet, 1847). The turn-of-the-century French sociologist Gabriel de Tarde was as enthusiastic about the modernizing communicative functions of the newspaper as Eliot. But far from regarding it as a medium for public deliberation, he took it to be a mechanism for conducting an ongoing, continuous statistical survey of the consubstantial public body, a journal of record of the general will (Tarde, 1890). In this consideration, Tarde was typically French (although in later work [Tarde, 1901] he argued that the newspaper derived its relevance from the conversations it provoked, thereby himself provoking a more talkative model of the newspaper. This would make Tarde a forerunner of the media-conversation-opinion-action nexus that has been so important in the history of mass communication research (Katz, 1992).

WHY COMMUNICATION CREATES
COMMUNITY: GERMAN THEORIES

In any of these typically French views, communication creates community largely because it ignores, marginalizes, privatizes, or even suppresses individuality in the normal sense. It is quite otherwise, however, with the German tradition inaugurated by Georg Wilhelm Friedrich Hegel (1770–1831), whose views are in many important respects a critique of Rousseau's and were much more influential in Progressive America than was the French political tradition. (This is in large part because prior to World War I, American intellectuals sought advanced degrees in German universities, not in English or French ones.) German political thought about modernity is preoccupied not with how residual personal identity can be suppressed by mass communication, but with how socialization and communication can, on the contrary, create genuine individuals in the first place.

It was Hegel who, long before Eliot, Park, or Tarde had noticed it, remarked in his *Lectures in the Philosophy of History* that in modernity reading the morning newspaper takes the place of morning prayer. For one who lived in a society that would not undergo a real modernization crisis until about the time of the American civil war and would not get through it until the fall of Nazism, Hegel was, in fact, remarkably aware of modernity and wished (in spite of a reactionary reputation falsely inflicted on him by liberals) to accommodate it in a new political philosophy. To this end, Hegel conceived of himself as a latter-day Aristotle, who would complete his predecessor's philosophy by applying Aristotle's community-communication *leitmotiv* to the more functionally differentiated societies and more subjectively individuated persons that he saw emerging from the French Revolution. Hegel interpreted the Revolution, the defining event of his generation, as the bungled first fruits of an indefinitely protracted effort—the effort of modernity itself—to bring the Christian conception of a self whose individual worth is recognized, and thereby constituted, by God down from heaven into a mutually-recognizing, this-worldly political community like the Greek *polis*.

What Hegel's reflection on Aristotle produced was the claim that communication can lead to community precisely because communication creates the mutually recognizing and mutually respecting individuals whose relationships constitute communities in the first place. Prior to communicative interaction there are no individual; posterior to communicative interaction, there are only individuals who are members of communities (Depew, 1992; Peters, 1997).

For Hegel, the relevant community of mutual recognizers was the modern nation–state, not the Greek *polis*. Yet, for Hegel, it was Aristotle, the theorist of the Greek *polis*, who, in spite of his underestimation of the degree of social differentiation and mutual recognition needed to produce full individuation, was the first to postulate that the process of individuation—the process of becoming an autonomous human being—is fostered by the process of social differentiation and, in turn, that increasing differentiation of institutions and functions is a result of communicative interaction. The total conception remains a major theme of German social and political philosophy to this day. It is explicit, for example, in the work of Jürgen Habermas and Niklas Luhmann (Habermas 1984, 1986; Luhmann, 1984; Habermas & Luhmann, 1971). Currently, it has the advantage of providing assurances that modernization, with all its discontents, is not at odds with the flourishing of the individual. To liberals, however, it has the disadvantage of conceiving of the individual as more definitively enmeshed in social reality than their general theory, under any articulation of it, can allow.

What most intrigued Hegel about Aristotle was probably the latter's denial that associations, where they go beyond temporary military alliances or business partnerships, can lead to the formation of stable communities on the basis of a set of merely contractual agreements between already individuated rational beings. Hegel's *Philosophy of Right* is an extended critique of the modern version of this "social contract" or "natural right" reasoning (which is most familiar to Americans in the form given to it by John Locke). What Hegel noticed here is that for Aristotle, there is an implicit correlation between coming to be a fully developed, individuated, autonomous human being, capable of making political decisions, and one's socialization, since childhood, into the ways of households that are themselves functionally embedded within city–states. At the same time, Hegel was aware that Aristotle, under the spell of the "master–slave relationship," was unable to see participation in the larger world of market economies as playing a positive role in self-formation of this kind. Thus, Hegel's modernization of Aristotle assumes the significance of the delegitimation of slavery to be its transferring of the scene of productive wealth from the repressive household to a commercial market economy. In turn, he construes the market economy as a sphere of activity that will produce greater degrees of practical reason and autonomy in persons who must make their way through it on their own steam, but who can do so in a way that does not harm their personal projects of individuation. With its alienating effects on the individual, this can occur only if the market is buffered on one side by the stability of a loving family life and, on the other side, by the administrative rationality of a state that guarantees one's standing and welfare as a citizen regardless of what resources one is able to command through the sale of one's estate, talent, or labor. What is most distinctive about this approach is that the individual is seen not as a being who precedes social relationships, or even as a being who emerges from them, but as a being who, in Marx's Aristotelian and Hegelian formulation, "is in the most literal sense a *zoon politikon*—not merely a gregarious animal, but an animal that can individuate itself only in the midst of society" (Marx, 1973, p. 84). Far from impinging on an already constituted individual, socialization for Hegel is a necessary condition for becoming a person in the first place.

THE MARXIAN AND LIBERAL IDEAS OF THE SELF: BACK TO ENGLAND

The Hegelian theory of individuation by socialization affected discussion of this issue for over the next half century, not only in Germany, but in England and America as well. Recognizing this influence allows us to conduct an interesting comparison between George Eliot and Karl Marx, both of whom were post-Hegelians living and working in a Victorian London that was already becoming more deeply and problematically affected by industrial capitalism than Hegel had anticipated. There is, in fact, an odd affinity between these two thinkers. Eliot translated the works of Ludwig Feuerbach and other post-Hegelians (such as David Friedrich Strauss, the German Biblical critic whom Casaubon missed) into English. From them, she absorbed the view that shows up in her novels—that social connectivity and communicative interaction foster individual maturation. From Feuerbach she took up the claim, later radicalized by Freud, that people learn about themselves by first projecting unknown parts of themselves onto others, from which it followed that without close interaction with others one could never know oneself. Eliot probably knew German idealist thought better than most anyone in Victorian England. If there was anyone who did know it better, however, it would have been Karl Marx, who in his youth had learned from the same Ludwig Feuerbach how to retain a Hegelian conception of individuation by socialization while at the same time turning toward philosophical naturalism and away from idealism. *Capital* and *Middlemarch* were published within 5 years of each other.

Marx's complaint about Hegel is that, in his ignorance of the effects of industrial capitalism on craft-oriented market economies, he is far too sanguine about how easily a proper balance can be struck between family, economy, and state if full individuation by communicative interaction is to result. Marx insists that the industrial capitalist market will swallow these other institutions whole, leaving persons exploited, alienated, unhappy, and less than fully developed. He resolves forthwith to solve the problem in a single stroke by eliminating the market altogether, and with it the notion that people must be as highly individuated as bourgeois society (and Hegel) seems to demand if they are to be considered fully developed.

Marx's regression to seeing humans as mere "species beings" was a tragic mistake in every way. Born of the consubstantialist Rousseauian-Jacobin thought that Marx encountered in the Bohemian Paris of his youth, which he attempted unsuccessfully to introject into a Hegelian framework, this notion was inherited and exploited by the monsters who later ruled in his name. Its French origin helps explain the otherwise inexplicable persistence of orthodox Marxism in mid-20th century France: Marxist subversion of the self by public identity does not sound at all odd to Rousseauian ears.

For her part, Eliot retains a Hegelian conception of the individual as a product of communicative interaction in a functionally differentiated society, but she is careful to preserve the bourgeois conception of individuality that Marx so carelessly discarded. In this Eliot was problematically drawn to the thought of Herbert Spencer, another member of the liberal *Westminister Review* circle, to whom she was romantically attracted before she met George Henry Lewes, a liberal writer who would be her life-long companion. Spencer argued against socialists of all stripes that if you want true individuals to come out of the fiery trials of social and individual development that exist under the conditions of modernity, you had better not cushion them in familial and political institutions that deviate too far from the vigorous competition of the market. That is, because for Spencer, as for liberal English political economists before and after him, it was the market that was uniquely the source of social differentiation in the first place, and it was the market that, if left alone in its internal dynamics, will eventually produce a society wealthy enough and spontaneously ordered enough to make the burdens it places on individuals light (Richards, 1987). Individuals, for Spencer, are indeed socially created, as English natural rights theorists and their liberal followers, with their faulty appeal to a state of nature, failed to recognize. They are, moreover, developmental organisms that come to be in and through their social relationships. But, for Spencer, humans only become individuals when those social relationships are modeled on the very thing Marx despised: the *laissez-faire* market. In consequence, individuals, precisely when they are fully individuated, rightly regard themselves as independent of society, which they see merely as a sum of individuals.

Spencer, who was more than a little inclined to model the development of society on the ontogeny of organisms, found societal analogues for digestive, circulatory, nervous and motor systems. He denied, however, the existence of a "social sensorium" or center of consciousness, as there certainly is for individual human organisms (Peters, 1989). In denying this, Spencer was simply registering his view that society is, in the end, merely an aggregation of self-interested individuals who cooperate in and through market relationships. If Eliot—as well as John Stuart Mill, another member of the *Westminster Review* circle—drew back from the full force of this highly competitive and individualistic mechanism of individuation, it was only in order to qualify it by adding fellow feeling and imaginative sympathy to economic rationality as a mechanism for communication. For Eliot clearly holds that emotions are cognitive instruments.

In the liberal view, accordingly, communication creates community only because it allows the desires of individuals (even if they are not reducible to economic desires) to be formed, expressed, and negotiated by market mechanisms, such as competition and differentiation, and by value-neutral political institutions that protect these mechanisms. If 20th-century intellectuals fail to honor Spencer in the way they honor Hegel and Marx, it is probably because his vision of the social imaginary is, ironically, the one that actually seems to have come prosaically true. Intellectuals like their heroes to be gloriously tragic failures. Successful social thought, because it often becomes co-terminus with social reality, is almost always mundane.

BACK TO PROGRESSIVE AMERICA:
THE CHICAGO SCHOOL

Many well-educated, turn-of-the-century American Progressives were aware of these Continental and English discussions. Dewey, in particular, was trained in the Aristotelian–Hegelian tradition. Even after he abandoned idealism as a philosophical framework and became, in 1894–1895, a naturalistic pragmatist, he continued to be influenced by English Hegelian social reformers like T. H. Green, the intellectual light behind the Settlement movement that Jane Addams (with whom Dewey worked in Chicago) brought to the United States. Like Green in England, and the idealist Josiah Royce in America, Dewey tried to find the exact point of balance between the market and other social institutions that would allow individuals who are constituted as individuals by their social relationships to flourish. Like them too, Dewey rejected Spencer's solution on grounds not unlike Marx's: Spencer's stress on the role of the market was, especially in its American Social Darwinist form, little more than a justification for the destruction of communities and individuals by unfettered capitalism.

Dewey's own solution was to regard the democratic culture that was already deeply planted in America by its historical experience as the privileged (one might even say world–historical) medium for personal development and community-formation. If the mediating institutions of democratic culture—a free press, free inquiry, free public education, a regulative state apparatus, and labor unions—could be shored up or reinvented, Dewey was sure that a fully differentiated society would emerge with the capability to produce fully developed individuals. Even under conditions of advanced industrialization, Dewey was confident that America's democratic culture would keep the market under political control, making both its total elimination and its Spencerian hegemony unnecessary for progressive social development. The private self and the public self would be, for Dewey, one integrated person.

These teachings were imbibed by Dewey's students at the University of Michigan, where Dewey taught until leaving for the University of Chicago in 1894. Charles Horton Cooley and Robert Park were among these students. (In a sense the

Chicago School was born in Ann Arbor). Thus, when in 1904 Dewey resigned from Chicago and headed off to Columbia University in New York, he left behind a research community that was devoted to the view just summarized, as well as one that was committed to interacting with the city of Chicago to bring its social vision into effect (Feffer, 1993). Gradually, the views of this research community seeped through the University of Chicago, and especially through its Department of Sociology. They did so in large part through the pervasive influence of George Herbert Mead, who had been Dewey's colleague at Michigan as well. Mead's social-role theory of the self was a direct descendent of the Hegelian theory of individuation by socialization, a fact that made his work particularly ripe for reimportation into post World War II German social theory (Habermas, 1984, 1986; Joas, 1997), but was expressed in an idiom that opened it up to empirical methods of inquiry, verification, and, in the end, modification, as was done in the sociological theories and studies of Park, Thomas, Burgess, Blumer, Wirth, Riesman, Becker, Gans, and others (Kurtz, 1986).

When Robert Park, after a decade and a half of vagabonding as a journalist and scholar of race relations (including service as personal secretary to Booker T. Washington), arrived at Chicago in 1916, only to become the university's leader of sociology for well over two decades, he stepped into an intellectual environment that had already learned to turn how-possibly questions about individuation by socialization into empirical ones. Unlike the more militantly empirical forms of social research that it would both promote and eventually be displaced by, the founding generation of the Chicago School saw itself quite in the spirit of pragmatism in its discovering of the practical bearing of philosophy in action. Thus philosophy would not be abolished, but rather consummated, in the work of social reconstruction, a work in which social research played a privileged part.

A rich intellectual tradition shaped the first generation of Chicago theorists. Park remarked in an autobiographical text that it was the reading of Goethe's *Faust* that first made him want to take up sociology (Park, 1950). Emerson's *Essays*, Darwin's *On the Origin of Species*, Eliot's novels, James's *Psychology*, the long tradition of post-Hegelian idealism, as well as the negative, but thoroughly studied example of Spencer—all these and more played both softly and loudly in the background. More precisely, however, we may say that the Chicago School was an attempt to continue the Aristotelian–Hegelian vision that self and community are constituted through interaction even in conditions radically different from the ancient *polis*.

Aristotle's community, we recall, was both small and homogeneous; the forms of communication that sustained it were necessarily face-to-face. Slaves, women, and barbarians were *prima facie* excluded as participants in both the *polis* and the theory thereof. Hegel, for his part, required that communication extend more widely and deeply. Finally, Dewey demanded that the process embrace all of democratic America. It was the Chicago sociologists, however, who first faced up to the full consequences of that demand. They confronted uprooted Polish peasants, taxi-dancers, and street gangs, among other forms of social life, in a world in which space and time had exploded. The Chicago School would not skirt the sheer fact of human heterogeneity, nor the vast new scale of social intercourse. A city of immigrants and a world of industrialism were exerting special pressures on the faith in communication as the foundation of community. The conviction that the shoulder-rubbing of ethnic and other differences is ultimately good for social order is a distinctive hallmark of the Chicago social research into communication and community.

Although the interactionism of the Chicago School became programmatic only with Herbert Blumer's by now well-known rubric of "symbolic interactionism," Park, Thomas, Burgess, Wirth, and others all already believed in the spontaneity and serendipity of public interaction. They saw the mixing of strangers both as an education for citizens and as a laboratory of social order, believing that unanticipated encounters among diverse ways of life could be both dangerous and democratic. (Dewey's 1927 vision of the public as open discussion reflects this faith in the benefits of cross-border transfers.) The city of Chicago, with its pattern of settlement into ethnic neighborhoods that persists to this day, provided one example of abrupt social juxtapositions. From that, it was the calling of the sociologist to cross the borders of difference and to serve as a catalyst in the larger mix of American social life. The social researcher was, accordingly, conceived as a liminal figure, a Hermes shuttling across the borders of a stratified society, bringing messages from the other side. Like reporters, sociologists were to play a role in the integration of a society that had made the plight of fellow-citizens opaque to each other. It was Park who always insisted that sociology was a kind of super-reporting: the mechanism that would make the social body clear to itself. For Chicago sociology, in short, communication was not only the method of social research—communicative participation in the social worlds studied—but also its ultimate purpose: the creation of a democratically integrated, but socially heterogeneous and fully differentiated society.

At points, this fascination with human difference could verge on a kind of voyeurism into the lives of exotics. In his reporting days, for example, Park had gone into an opium den and even taken a couple of puffs, in the name, no doubt, of well-rounded reporting. (He judged it "nasty.") For Park fully agreed with Francis Bacon that the light of the sun enters the sewer as well as the palace. There was something defiantly unsqueamish about Chicago sociology in its willingness to venture where the prissier Protestant reformers of an earlier generation had not dared (Matthews, 1977). Park's school was confident that the science of sociology exempted one from the blinders of moralistic judgment and offered a deeper kind of sight: the ability to detect, even in the extremes of poverty and degradation, the incessant and irrepressible will to make bonds with others. From the wreckage of family breakdown, for instance, children could still manage to form primary groups such as gangs. The cumulative message that came from studying social life in all its rawness and diversity was not a call to rage against the machine of heartless capitalism, as it was for more radical Progressives, but the more reassuring news that humans, however miserable their conditions, are incessantly community-making animals.

Though fascination with exotic others may seem less innocent today, Chicago sociology was akin to the Progressive project of muckraking and the melting-pot ideology of the day. Though lacking the normative pathos of the muckrakers, Chicago sociology was a younger cousin to Jacob Riis' *How the Other Half Lives* (1890), with its photographic and narrative exposé of dispossessed immigrants in New York City. The revelation of the lives of hidden others aimed to bring about sympathy, reform, and ultimately, uplift into the American mainstream. Its sense of the intractability of human differences was weaker than is the norm in cultural studies today; for the broad framework in which Park operated was certainly assimilationist, as his association with Booker T. Washington immediately suggests. If the Chicago School did not quite grasp the long-range persistence of alternative forms of identity (subcultures), still it deserves recognition as following (despite its ultimate allegiance to Washington's vision) in the steps of W. E. B. DuBois' *The Philadelphia Negro* (1897), which was the first social-scientific effort to grapple with race and ethnicity as forms of difference in the United States.

Just as they refused moralistic glasses for viewing social life, so Park and colleagues sought to treat the newspaper naturalistically. Rather than as the "Bible of Democracy," as Walter Lippmann, in an echo of Hegel's wisecrack, had referred to it, Park treated the newspaper as an evolving form governed by the quest for circulation. His title, "The Natural History of the Newspaper," is meant, in a way, to shock. Both Cooley and Park referred to the modern newspaper as the organization of gossip, that is, the means of institutionalizing the informal information that once circulated from mouth to mouth into a larger medium. This phrase is precisely not an elitist lamentation about the low quality of the newspaper; it is a double-edged recognition of the role that the newspaper can play in the building of community spirit in modern conditions. When Park claimed, in "The Natural History of the Newspaper," that the modern newspaper is an attempt to recreate village conditions in the modern city, that is, to make everyone acquainted with each other and to inform everyone of all that is happening, he sounded the Progressive theme that communication might create a Great Community, great both in size and magnificence.

Cooley's *Social Organization* (Cooley, 1909) provides the most expansive frame in which to view this dream. Cooley argued that communication, which he defined as "the mechanism through which human relations exist and develop," "makes a free mind on a great scale conceivable." (For a comparison of Cooley with George Eliot, see Marcus, 1975.) In saying this, Cooley is rejecting Spencer's view that a central source of consciousness cannot be found in society. For Cooley, the social sensorium is nothing like a private organ. It is, rather, the newspaper and other means of forming relations at a distance.

It had been a universal complaint in progressive social thought that Spencer had made moderns into herd animals, who dwell in contiguity but not in community. (Mocking the stature of his progressive colleagues, Thorstein Veblen quipped that they stand on Spencer's shoulders and box him about the ears.) It follows for them that new powers of communication could arouse us into realizing our destiny as political animals, creatures designed for what Cooley called "fellowship in thought." For Cooley, modern means of communication introduce a radical change in the principle by which communities are constituted. According to him, in a traditional world, where transportation is laborious, the principle of individuation for communities and individuals is "isolation": Each village or person becomes an extreme version of themselves, rather like Darwin's Galapagos finches; being cut off from each other by steep valleys, they diversify into the wildest varieties. In a modern world of swift communication, by contrast, Cooley believes that a new principle of individuality and community is possible, one based on choice. A person whose birth and locality would have once limited him or her to just a few roles now has the option of associating with like-minded people around the world in what we have since learned to call "virtual communities." Because individuals, whether in a New England village or a North Carolina mountain, can now choose to belong to any community whose tokens of membership they receive by newer forms of communication, Cooley concludes that a new range of flexibility in socialization, individuation, and democratic participation is now possible. Thus, Cooley renders modern mass communication the medium of the Deweyan principle that full individuality comes via democratic socialization.

Dreams, however, often have parallel nightmares, and novel powers of mass communication were also feared as agents of deindividuation. From the notion that far-flung people would all be exposed to the same stimulus, the old fear of leveling, which preoccupied De Toqueville in his description of the American democratic experiment, took on fresh relevance. Noting William Randolph Hearst's role in fanning the flames of the Spanish–American War of 1898, Cooley observed that the newspaper can stimulate a crowd mind in its readers, even if they are not assembled as a crowd. He noted that sympathy the newspaper and literature evoked for the other (Cooley mentioned Riis' *How the Other Half Lives*) could also take forms other than benign humanitarianism. In the intimacy of his journal, Cooley confided that even he imaginatively identified with the blood thirst and lust he read about in the yellow press. He posited that expanded agencies of communication were enabling a new range of imaginative subject positions, even leading to the possibility of the "emotional possession" that Herbert Blumer had found in his study of young peoples' experiences of movie-going (Blumer, 1933). For whatever reason, the Chicago School seems to have regarded the movies as forms of communication less democratically fruitful than the newspaper, this opinion running from Jane Addams' 1909 study of urban theater-going to Louis Wirth's 1948 speculations about mass society (Addams, 1909; Wirth, 1948).

Perhaps a residual squeamishness was reserved for fictive forms of sympathy. Perhaps the movies did not seem to sustain serendipitous public interactions (beyond "movie-mashing"), but rather individually experienced fantasies or overwhelming assaults on the sensorium. In any case, the Chicago School's positive view of the newspaper is to some extent played off against their judgment of other media of mass communication as less fit than it to play the role that was assigned to them by the Aristotelian–Hegelian vision of socialization-as-individuation. In some sense, the program never recovered after it became clear that wave after wave of new media technologies would become available to the public.

Unlike their Michigan colleague Cooley, the Chicago sociologists rarely faced either a community of isolation tied to place or a virtual community formed by choice; their dance halls, churches, and neighborhoods are decidedly impure forms. In a way, they discovered an additional option: what we call *twice-born* communities. A community such as the large Polish settlement in Chicago was not quite based on either time-worn geographies or the free choice of its members. Its perpetuation rested not only in its newspapers, but in the exchange of letters so extensively analyzed by Thomas and Znaniecki, as well as routes of travel between new world and old. This was a modern, amorphous kind of social substance with redemption and tragedy woven through it, as anyone who dips into Thomas and Znaniecki's huge volumes will quickly discover (Thomas & Znaniecki, 1927). By the 1880s, 2 million people were living where only wild onion patches had grown 50 years earlier. Chicago, the great experiment, provided a gift for social thought by stripping away the traditional sources of community formation. Once everything had been removed—homeland, tradition, structure, institutions, norms—communities still managed to develop. The only principle of explanation left was communication. The sense that communication could substitute for institutions would have baffled Aristotle or Hegel; Chicago sociologists were able to assign it a role not only in the constitution of the self, but in constitution of the social order as well. Indeed, with its somewhat naive stress on the positive effects of diversity in forming individuals (a stress later to be called in question by communitarians with more direct connections to Hegel), the Chicago School pushes the Hegelian conception of individuation by socialization to its limits, differing from run-of-the-mill liberalism in little more than its conviction that it is the communicative process, rather than the hidden hand of the market economy, that spontaneously generates social order.

Mead wrote that science was the evolutionary process grown self-conscious. The Chicago School and its intellectual lights, such as Dewey and Mead himself, discovered something similar: Communication is the process of community formation grown self-conscious. In this statement, Dewey and his followers lighted on a term for the basic social process whose vision is shot through with the hope of a blending of diverse identities into a new order. It is a distinctly American vision, marked by a particular moment in the country's history, and unchallenged by the new technologies, but still full of resonance today. It is also, however, as we have attempted to show, a vision whose variations stretch back to the very beginnings of the attempt to understand social life in ancient Greece. Those who take up the study of communication and community are destined, in some way, to work in this long horizon, and so should be aware of it.

REFERENCES

Addams, J. (1909). *The spirit of youth and the city streets*. New York: Macmillan.

Althusser, L. (1970). *Reading capital*. London: New Left Books.

Arendt, H. (1958). *The human condition*. Chicago: University of Chicago Press.

Blumer, J. (1933). *Movies and conduct*. New York: Macmillan.

Carey, J. (1989). *Communication as culture*. Boston: Unwin Hyman.

Cooley, C. H. (1909/1993). *Social organization: A study of the larger mind*. New Brunswick, NJ: Transaction Publishers.

Depew, D. (1992). The *polis* transfigured. In G. E. McCarthy (Ed.), *Marx and Aristotle: Nineteenth-century German social theory and classical antiquity* (pp. 37–73). Savage, MD: Rowman & Littlefield.

Depew, D. (1995). "Humans and other political animals. In Aristotle's *History of animals*. *Phronesis, XL*(2), 156–181.

Dewey, J. (1927). *The public and its problems*. New York: Henry Holt.

Feffer, A. (1993). *The Chicago pragmatists and American progressivism*. Ithaca, NY: Cornell University Press.

Ferguson, R. (1997). *The American enlightenment*. Cambridge, MA: Harvard University Press.

Graver, S. (1984). *George Eliot and community*. Berkeley: University of California Press.

Habermas, J. (1984, 1986). *The theory of communicative action* (2 vols). Boston: Beacon Press.

Habermas, J., & N. Luhmann (1971). *Theorie der gesellschaft oder socialtechnologie* [Theory of society r social technology]. Frankfurt: Suhrkamp.

Joas, H. (1997). *G. H. Mead: A contemporary re-examination of his thought*. Cambridge, MA: MIT Press.

Katz, E. (1992). On parenting a paradigm: Gabriel Tarde's agenda for opinion and communication research. *International Journal of Public Opinion Research, 4*, 80–86.

Kurtz, L. R. (1986). *Evaluating Chicago sociology: A guide to the literature, with annotated bibliography*. Chicago: University of Chicago Press.

Luhmann, N. (1984). *Soziale systeme* [Social systems]. Frankfurt, Germany: Suhrkamp.

Marcus, S. (1975). Human nature, social orders, and nineteenth-century systems of explanation. *Salmagundi, 28*, 20–42.

Marx, K. (1973). *Grundrisse: Foundations of the critique of political economy* (N. Martin, Trans.). New York: Vintage Books.

Matthews, F. H. (1977). *The Quest for an American sociology: Robert Park and the Chicago school*. Montreal, Canada: McGill-Queens University Press.

Park, R. E. (1923). The natural history of the newspaper. *American Journal of Sociology, 28*, 273–289.

Park, R. E. (1950). An autobiographical note. In *Collected papers of Robert Ezra Park* (Vol. 1, pp. iii–ix). Glencoe, IL: The Free Press.

Peters, J. D. (1989). Satan and savior of American democracy: mass communication in progressive social thought. *Critical Studies in Mass Communication, 6*(3), 247–263.

Peters, J. D. (1997). The root of humanity: Hegel on language and communication. In D. Klemm & G. Zoeller (Eds.), *Figuring the self: subject, individual and spirit in German idealism* (pp. 227–244). Albany: State University of New York Press.

Pocock, J. (1975). *The Machiavellian moment: Florentine political thought and history*. Princeton, NJ: Princeton University Press.

Quetelet, A. (1847). De l'influence de libre arbitre de l'hommes sur les faits sociaux [Concerning the influence of human free will on social facts]. *Bulletin de la Commission Central de Statistique, 3*, 135–155.

Richards, R. (1987). *Darwin and emergence of evolutionary theories of mind and behavior*. Chicago, IL: University of Chicago Press.

Ross, D. (1991). *The origins of American social science*. Cambridge, England: Cambridge University Press.

Skinner, Q. (1978). *The foundations of modern political thought*. Cambridge, England: Cambridge University Press.

Tarde, G. (1890). *Les lois de l'imitation: Étude sociologique* [The laws of imitation: A sociological study]. Paris: Alcan.

Tarde, G. (1901). *L'opinion et la foule* [Opinion and the crowd]. Paris: Alcan.

Thomas, W. I., & F. Znaniecki. (1927). *The Polish peasant in Europe and America* (2nd ed.). New York: Knopf.

Thrasher, F. M. (1927). *The gang: A study of 1,313 gangs in Chicago*. Chicago: University of Chicago Press.

Warner, M. (1990). *The letters of the Republic: Publication and the public sphere in eighteenth century America.* Cambridge, MA: Harvard University Press.

Westbrook, R. (1991). *John Dewey and American democracy* Ithaca, NY: Cornell University Press.

Wirth, L. (1948). Consensus and mass communication. *American Sociological Review, 13,* 1–15.

II

Interpersonal Relations, Organizations, and Community

2

Community as the Interpersonal Accomplishment of Communication

Gregory J. Shepherd
University of Kansas

There are cases where faith creates its own verification.

Believe, and you shall be right, for you shall save yourself;

doubt, and you shall again be right, for you shall perish.

The only difference is that to believe is greatly to your advantage.

—William James (1997, p. 337)

In both tone and content, William James' remark (from a paper entitled "The Sentiment of Rationality") presages this chapter. This chapter is intended to be provocative, even as it serves to recall rather innocent ideas. I also exhort and evangelize, so the chapter is likely to seem as much sermon as study. The preaching is primarily directed toward encouraging adoption of a certain set of beliefs about communication and community in the knowledge that faith-filled beliefs often have large practical consequences. This might be called a chapter on pragmatic idealism.

Most people have some sense that communication and community are coterminous; perhaps simply because as words, they look a lot alike. As I discuss here, it is important that the words share a common etymology, but as in Sammy Cahn and Jimmy Van Heusen's *Love and Marriage,* saying "you can't have one without the other," is more an expression of wish than wisdom. That is not to say that there isn't something right, in both cases, about such wishing. As already suggested, one point of this chapter will be that wishing, to the extent it represents an underlying faith in some possibility, is often important to the realization of that possibility.

There is a conspicuous longing for communication and community at the close of the 20th century. This chapter might also be read as a definitional and conceptual account for that longing, one that is grounded in a certain reading of the relation between communication and community in modern and postmodern eras.

IDEAS OF MODERNITY: INDIVIDUALS, TRUTH, AND COMMUNICATION AS CONVEYANCE

The beginning of the modern era is generally marked by the move out of the Middle Ages and into the Age of Discovery near the end of the 15th century. Among the many accomplishments of modernity's subsequent reign, none are as significant to the scholar of communication and community as the invention of the individual and the rise of rationalism (see Boorstin, 1983, for an accessible account of the rise of modernity and its essential ideas and values).

In 1517, Martin Luther nailed his 95 Theses to the door of the All Saints Church in Wittenberg, Germany. One of his disagreements with the Catholic Church proved central to his subsequent theology: Individuals require no priestly mediation in their dealings with God. The notion that salvation is a matter of individual faith, that relationships with God are "personal," was part of an extra-religious reformation that was gathering momentum in modernity, having to do with the prioritization of individual experience and consciousness.

According to the *Oxford English Dictionary* (1971), the earliest use of the word *individual* to refer to "a single human being, as opposed to society, the family, etc." (p. 1419) does not occur until 1626. But it was within a very short time that modernity came to rest on the psychological being as the source of significance, the seat of knowledge, and the site of identity. Thus, by 1641, Descartes could make thought the very determinant of being: *cogito ergo sum.* One year after the publication of Descartes' *Meditations,* Isaac Newton was born. If Descartes can be given credit for helping to establish the primacy of the psychological being ("psychologism") in modernity, then Newton should be equally credited for abetting the institutionalization of "scientism" in the modern era.

Although Galileo, who died the same year Newton was born (1642), was a somewhat celebrated scientist, Newton was the man who popularized science through the application of what came to be known as the scientific, or experimental, method. Galileo studied by observing through his telescope; Newton investigated by design, through his *experimentum crucis.* Newton was instrumental in popularizing belief in discoverable truth and its verifiability through the application of method. The first and most famous association of scientists, the Royal Society, was founded in 1662 and led by Newton for a quarter century (1703–1727).

The Society's motto was *Nullius in Verba*: words mean nothing; verify; truth can and must be proven.

By the end of the 17th century, then, the Western world was armed with the faith necessary for the dawning Enlightenment: Individuals have access to verifiable truths. Missing only was a means for individuals to convey their individually held, but ultimately provable, truths. In 1690, Locke's *Essay on Human Understanding* provided the required mechanism.

Peters (1989) offered a detailed account of Locke's invention of "communication" as a vehicle for the transference of ideas (what we might here think of as individually accessed "truths"). Essentially, Locke faced a dilemma: How could he build a social theory ("liberal pluralism") that maintained his era's devotion to the primacy of the individual? What would make possible a *society* of *individuals*? His answer, of course, was "communication," a term that at the time typically referred to a process of physical transmission between separate entities. Communication, then, would be the mechanism by which ideas could be carried from individual to individual; truths could thus be verified and shared; a loose social whole could be woven.

These three ideas of modernity—that the individual is ontologically primary (psychologism), that truth exists and can be procedurally uncovered (scientism), and that communication is a vehicle for the transference of ideas (a particular manifestation of mechanism)—became entrenched in Western thought, and reigned without great challenge for 200 years. Together, these ideas worked together to allow for community building of a certain sort. In particular, scientism together with the mechanism of communication allowed for the possibility of a *social* psychologism—a community of authentic individuals, made possible because communication can convey from person to person the truth that necessarily will out in the end. Modern communities, thus, gathered around what people knew rather than who they were, as had been the case with premodern societies, where identity in a determined social order linked persons, one to the other (see, e.g., MacIntyre's 1981 characterization of heroic societies). In the modern world, truth set people free from the epistemological authority of others, but communication's power to convey verifiable truths kept them related as part of a community of knowers. By the tail end of the 19th century, however, this set of relations began to unravel.

THE RISE OF THE POSTMODERN ERA: TRUTH AS A HUMAN CONSTRUCTION

If there is an idea that seems to characterize the rise of the postmodern era (and its clash with modernism), it is one championed in the work of a couple of men, born 2 years and an ocean apart. William James and Friedrich Nietzsche were men of wildly different backgrounds and temperaments who reached a similar conclusion about existence at a proximate time (Nietzsche probably somewhat earlier than James, although there is no evidence that the former influenced the latter): Truth is a construction. Each coined memorable characterizations of truth that are now over a century old. For James (1907/1991) truth is what is best to believe, "only the expedient in the way of our thinking" (p. 98). For Nietzsche, truth is "a mobile army of metaphors" whose illusory status has been forgotten (1954, pp. 46–47). Both objected strongly to the Newtonian belief in verification (except to the extent that one understands that verity is accomplished rather than demonstrated—James, for example, stressed this point by underscoring the productivity attached to the meaning by the suffix "fication" in the word "verification," p. 89); both poked fun at science's claim to objectivity.

This challenge to modernity's take on truth (scientism, or more generally, rationalism) has, arguably, been largely successful. At the very least, indeterminacy, in the physical as well as the social sciences, seems to have taken hold, and most of us do seem unwilling to bet that many received wisdoms will be everlasting. This general Nietzschean sense that are no more "grand narratives" on which to hang everything for evermore is, I am arguing, what best characterizes a rising era. It is important to note, however, that this new era is not yet well determined or defined. It is telling that the label of this era is one only marked by chronology (and implicitly, by opposition): the *post*modern—whatever comes after modernity.

We live, then, in a blended time, on the cusp between a fading modernity and something "post." Old eras, of course, never end neatly, and new ones never cleanly begin. So, times on the cusp are, necessarily, unsettling, as the ideas that will eventually distinguish an intellectual era gain prominence at different rates, and live side by often-clashing side with ideas from the previous era holding on to different degrees. Consider our current condition: Whereas the constructionism of James and Nietzsche has taken hold in 20th century thought, the individualism and mechanism of an earlier era remain. This set of uncomfortable relations is key to understanding, not the *ideas* of postmodernity (or whatever era is to come after the modern), but the *passions* of our current condition (or what often seems our collective angst), including our sense of community lost.

LIFE ON THE CUSP: SOLIPSISM, RELATIVISM, AND NIHILISM

As previously noted, the modern era's psychologism still allowed for the development and experience of a certain sort of community, one gathered around evident knowledge, discovered truths, and conveyed ideas. But what happens to the possibility for community in this equation when truth is overthrown? How is community to be achieved when individuals reign in a world absent of universal truths? What good will the mechanism of communication now do?

If communication can only convey ideas—if it is only a vehicle running between autonomous entities; and if no idea represents an accessible truth, but rather only an individual significance; and if individual selves are ontologically primary and epistemologically definitive; then it seems to follow that solipsism, relativism, and nihilism abound.

Solipsism

Solipsism is, of course, the bugaboo of modernity. If individuals rule, as it were, then isn't all knowledge self-knowledge? If I am because I think, then is my mind the only existent thing? Locke's modern invention of communication can be seen as an effort to avoid the dilemma of solipsism in his social theory (cf. Peters, 1989), but note how it only serves such a function *given* a world of pre-existent and verifiable truths. That is, in modernity, individuals could know the *same* truths; those extra-individual truths could be verified and carried from person to person and so create something greater than the individuals, namely a society, or community. Without the possibility of given truths in this equation, the vehicle of communication fails to guard against solipsism.

Relativism

If solipsism is modernity's bane, relativism would appear to be postmodernity's scourge. Technically, relativism presents a doctrine of epistemology: All knowledge is relative. But its implications are moral: In a world where truth is relative, good is indeterminate. The most common critique of James' and Nietzsche's antirationalism is that it renders us incapable of making judgments of right and wrong, better and worse. If truths are constructions, and individual significances are the only significances, than every truth is as good as any other.

Nihilism

Among the passions that might characterize life on the cusp, nihilism is the most frightening, and ironic (as passions go). From the Latin *nihil*, the word literally translates into nothing + ism (Oxford English Dictionary, 1971, p. 1927). This nothingism, this deep skepticism about existence and strong sense of meaninglessness, is the nearly necessary result of the already reviewed passions of solipsism and relativism. The bane of the preceding era (solipsism) and the scourge of the following (relativism) combine to produce the curse of this time in between (nihilism).

As a result, sociology must conceive anomie. After all, individual significances are significances of the smallest order; gone are any larger ones. Philosophy, for its part, must invent situational ethics. If everything is relative, then all decisions are made ad hoc. In education, a leveling ignorance will seem the rule: If I know only what I know, I do not know much at all—But then again, neither do you, so "Who's to say?" And communication, of course, will account for the widespread sense of meaninglessness by theorizing itself out of existence: "Meanings are in people," thus, one person can never really know or understand another. Our individual meanings can neither be added nor multiplied; the sum of our significance and the product of our meaning is nothing.

It might be tempting to read this brief analysis of life on the cusp as a call to return to the comforts of full-blown modernity and its verifiable truth. But there is no going back. We live in a house under construction; it needs completion, not demolition. Thanks to James and Nietzsche, among many others, we now know that truth is made (just as we once knew it was found). That is not something we can forget. Rather, we will continue to build understandings of a new era. An after-modern understanding of communication is what should most interest those of us with concerns about community at the dawn of the 21st century.

Until this point in the chapter, I have been laying out a particular diagnosis of the "problem" of communication and community at the close of the 20th century that might be simplistically summarized thus: We are adopting with increasing conviction a postmodern conception of truth, even as we cling to a modern theory of communication and maintain modernity's devotion to the individual; this has resulted in a sense of community lost. Overcoming that sense of loss will require a theorization of communication quite unlike the vehicular one that served modernity. Ironically, building this postmodern conception of communication requires a premodern understanding of communication. We begin, then, by temporarily going back.

THE PREMODERN COMMUNICATION

According to the Oxford English Dictionary (1971, p. 700), the word *communication* first appears in 1382, and is used to reference the imparting of material things—vehicles of information, such as letters. And the term held this sense until Locke's use of it in 1690 to refer to the exchange of ideas. The word arose from the Latin *munia*, meaning gifts or services. Gifts, of course, are not conveyed, but conferred; services are not relayed, but rendered. Communication, then, might be understood in this premechanistic sense as an activity of mutual giving and servicing. (The prefix, "co-" implies mutuality; the suffix, "-tion" denotes an act or process.) Importantly, both voluntarism, or self-sense, and obligation, or other-directedness are implied in this conception. After all, a gift must be freely conferred for it to be a gift; there is no sense to be had from a notion of non-voluntary giving. I cannot steal from you and call it a gift. At the same time, services, to count as services, must be rendered unto others. In spite of the late-20th century's oxymoronic use of the term *self-service*, others in a collective order, and our responsibility toward those others, are implicated in the notion of service.

This is, of course, where the idea of community comes into play. Community arises from the same Latin root of *munia*, where the reciprocal giving and mutual service that takes place in communication works to make a common people, or *communis*, a community which is bound together through gifts of service. It is important here to note that commonality is given in this premodern equation. *Munia* (or communication) to the common group is required so that a community can be made and maintained. This set of relations is clear when examining the etymology of yet another related term, *immunity*. Eventually, those who felt inconvenienced by the obliged giving that was *munia* (no doubt the wealthy and the otherwise privileged) were granted "immunity" from what they might have called service *communis* (See Shipley, 1945, p. 187, for a discussion of the word origin of "immunity" and its relationship to *munia*).

As should now be clear, different eras have conceived communication differently in response to different needs. One such need has been the need for community. In both premodern and modern eras, community has been accomplished by communication, although communication of quite different senses. In hindsight, the accomplishment doesn't seem to have been terribly problematic in either era: Communication's task of binding people together in the premodern era required no miracle—the people to be bound were already deemed to share a common identity. So too in modernity, when Locke mechanized communication to serve as a transport system for ideas (and truth), was the accomplishment of community a rather mundane activity. After all, truth was then still truth. Carry it to people and they would be bound by their knowledge of it. Only on the cusp, between eras, when community must be accomplished while individuals, by definition uncommon, continue to reign, but where truth is indeterminate, does communication's task seem overburdened by the need to be divine. Now, in particular, does the possibility of sharing, of understanding, of experiencing community, of *communicating* seem "a wonder by the side of which transubstantiation pales" (Dewey, 1925, p. 138).

How is communication to accomplish community when individuals are sacrosanct and truth is under constant construction? Part of the answer, I think, lies in appropriating the self-sense and other-directedness implied in the premodern conception of *munia*, without purchasing the era's essentialism with regard to identity (i.e., given commonness). In other words, we should come to see similarity (and uniqueness) as resulting from communication and community rather than viewing communication and community as products of commonality (and thus reactions against difference). This will largely entail acknowledging communication's constitutive character as the maker of truths (shown to be plural and indeterminate by James & Nietzsche). I will not here write much about this part of the postmodern building project on communication (instead, see Shepherd, 1998, 1999). It is, plainly, well underway and reasonably well known. Rather, I turn to a second, less acknowledged part of the work needed to reconstruct communication for the 21st century, one that involves preaching a faith of transcendence, or belief in the possibility of communication as an interpersonal experience. This project will, in turn, "interpersonalize" the concept of community.

BUILDING A POSTMODERN COMMUNICATION

The prefix "inter-" has two somewhat different senses. It is often used to mean *between*, as in *intercede*. This is typically the assumed meaning of the prefix in the word *interpersonal* (i.e., "between persons"). But it is also sometimes used to mean "together" (one with the other), as in *intermingle* (see Barnhart, 1995, p. 393). Thus, *interpersonal* could be taken to mean something like persons that are together, or persons, one with the other. It is this latter sense of *interpersonal* that is key to understanding a useful postmodern sense of communication, one that returns to build on the premodern idea of communication as mutual giving and servicing.

What is conferred or rendered (*not* conveyed or relayed) in the act of communication? Given the still lasting influence of modernity's emphasis on individualism (and the waning of its commitment to the verifiability of truth), the answer must be something like "selves" (and not ideas). In all experiences of communication we give our selves. We render, each to the other, our uniqueness, our difference, our individuality (all of which is a product of earlier communication experiences). In so doing, we express our obligation to each other, and partake of one another; each is taken into the other and made a part of the other (hence another associated word, *communion*). We leave the communication then, in a sense, having been added to. Thus, the gifts that we always give and the services that we necessarily supply are interpersonal in nature. They are not interpersonal in some spatial (as when *inter* means "between") or situational sense (e.g., in the sense of interpersonal communication being face-to-face talk in dyads), but in the functional sense of interpersonal communication being the constant creation and recreation of relationships (as when *inter* means "together, one with the other").

In this way, "Interpersonal Communication" might become as redundant a collocation as "Rhetorical Communication" once was to many. That is, just as the rationalism essential to modernity led to the argument that all communication is about influence, the constructionism of the after-modern time suggests that all communication is interpersonal, in the sense of being about the realization of relationship (Shepherd, 1992, associated this view with the "feminine"). Again, this requires understanding "interpersonal" *not* as a context of communication, defined by numbers of participants, nor as a quality of communication, defined by how well the actors are acquainted, but rather as the defining feature of communication.

To say that communication is interpersonal is to say that when communication occurs, something communal is made. It is something of self and other, but not self and other. It is something synergistic. It is community. The conception of communication I am advocating turns the modern metaphor of "transference" into a postmodern one of "transcendence." *The simultaneous experience of self and other* might serve well as a definition of communication after the modern. The new, after-modern community that communication then accomplishes is one more personal than public, more of ontological growth than political structure. The postmodern community implies not the civic groups and fraternal organizations considered by de Tocqueville (1835/1956) to be so essential to American communal life, or even the local schools and neighborhood associations central to Dewey's (1927) analysis, but rather the postmodern community implies people-in-relation, as in the transcendence of individuality into something more, even as self-sense is maintained; knowing of the other, even as the other's particularity is overcome.

Again, it is important to underscore that the community of people-in-relation that I am defining is not one which is dependent on setting, numbers, medium, or knowledge. Even television and film characters, for example, might provide audience members a communal experience. I do not here mean that the film provides a medium for an audience's experience of togetherness (although that too can happen), but that characters on screen can be experienced through communication, and a sense of interpersonal community can thereby be built. The literalness of Woody Allen's *The Purple Rose of Cairo* is not here required: Ontological presence is necessary, physical attendance is not. What is key here is seeing others, whether in our homes, on the street, on the other end of a modem connection, or on the screen, not as performers to be observed, but rather as partners to be engaged. The experience of community as an accomplishment of communication in this interpersonal sense is indeed an *experience* in that it reeks of *personal* participation. The other here is not a spectacle, but a familiarity, either latent or realized. The "other" here is not an object, but an intimate, one either potential or actual. The other here is not ever one that is only other, but always conceivably, other-with-self. In other words, "the simultaneous experience of self and other" implies something more than self and other in its simultaneity: the possibility of community.

ON COMMUNICATION
AND THE POSSIBILITY OF COMMUNITY

I have suggested that premodern communities were identity-based, and that modern ones were knowledge-based. On what base, then, will postmodern communities be built? The answer is on a base of promise, or possibility, on what might be, rather than on what is. There is no other base in a world absent of given identities (what the premodern offered) and necessary truths (what the modern gave). The essential question then must become, "How will we identify what is possible?"

William James (1907/1991) noted that to say something is "possible," is to say "not only that there are no preventive conditions present, but that some of the conditions of the production of the possible thing actually are here" (p. 124). We come now to the rub of life on the cusp. Community has increasingly seemed an impossible achievement to us because we increasingly disbelieve the presence of the one condition required for its realization: the possibility of communication (i.e., communication in the interpersonal sense as it is here defined). If we are to believe that communication is impossible in this world of uncommon individuals and indeterminate truth, then so too is community. We are left, then, to wonder on the conditions necessary for the possibility of postmodern communication.

The first, and indeed, the essential, requirement for communication's realization is belief in its possibility. This is the anti-foundationalist foundation to which James continually returned, the ontological argument for belief in believing (as in his famous essay on "The Will to Believe"; James, 1977). That was the point of the epigraph to this chapter. I can think of no better example of faith creating its own verification than that with regard to communication. Believe in its possibility or not, in either case we will be proven right. The only difference, as James reminds, is that it would be much to our advantage to believe. We will not create community without allowing for faith in the possibility of intersubjective transcendence through communication.

A second requirement for the possibility of communication, and so for the realization of community, is subsumed by the first, but nonetheless worthy of mention. Remember that communication is, fundamentally, a gift. As such, it requires volition. We can not communicate without giving of ourselves; nor can we communicate if not served by the gifts of other selves. This requires action on our part, and faith in that of others.

We can *create* the conclusion, then. We can and we may, as it were, jump with both feet off the ground into or towards a world of which we trust the other parts to meet our jump—and *only so* can the *making* of a perfected world of the pluralistic pattern ever take place. Only through our precursive trust in it can it come into being. (James, 1977, p. 740)

CONCLUSION

Holding faith in the interpersonal vision of communication and community that is here advanced would prove consequential. We must work hard to preach this faith. We must give our students and fellow citizens the hope that they can connect with others, be known and understood by others, without sacrificing their individuality; that we can get inside one another and be forever changed in the service of our distinctness; we must give people hope in the possibilities of communication. To deny this hope is to accept with Nietzsche the nihilism that results from the hangover of the solipsism bequeathed us by modernity and by the newfound relativism resulting from the death of verifiable truth in the postmodern era. Without the possibility of communication and its promise of transcendence in community, "life itself *in its essence* means appropriating, injuring, overpowering those who are foreign and weaker; oppression, harshness, forcing one's own forms on others, incorporation and, at the very least, at the very mildest, exploitation" (Nietzsche, 1886/1998, pp. 152–153). And, of course, accepting that life is nothing more than "the will to power" only serves to guarantee its unhappy consequences. Let us better preach the optimism of what I earlier called pragmatic idealism—the promise that is communication and the possibility of community.

ACKNOWLEDGMENT

Thanks are due to Eric Rothenbuhler for his useful comments and help in working through some of these ideas. He is not, of course, responsible for any flaws that remain.

REFERENCES

Barnhart, R. K. (1995). *The Barnhart concise dictionary of etymology: The origins of American English words.* New York: HarperCollins.
Boorstin, D. J. (1983). *The discoverers.* New York: Random House.
deTocqueville, A. (1956). *Democracy in America* (R. D. Heffner, Ed.). New York: New American Library. (Original work published 1835)
Descartes, R. (1960). *Meditations on first philosophy* (2nd rev. ed.). Indianapolis, IN: The Liberal Arts Press. (Original work published 1641)
Dewey, J. (1925). *Experience and nature.* Peru, IL: Open Court.

Dewey, J. (1927). *The public and its problems*. Athens, OH: Swallow Press/Ohio University Press.

James, W. (1991). *Pragmatism*. Buffalo, NY: Prometheus. (Original work published 1907)

James, W. (1977). *The writings of William James: A comprehensive edition* (J. J. McDermott, Ed.). Chicago: University of Chicago Press.

Locke, J. (1975). *An essay concerning human understanding* (P. H. Nidditch, Ed.). Oxford: Clarendon Press. (Original work published 1690)

MacIntyre, A. (1981). *After virtue*. Notre Dame, IN: University of Notre Dame Press.

Nietzsche, F. (1998). *Beyond good and evil* (M. Faber, Trans. & Ed.). Oxford, England: Oxford University Press. (Original work published 1886)

Nietzsche, F. (1954). *The portable Nietzsche* (W. Kaufmann, Trans. & Ed.). New York: Penguin.

Oxford English Dictionary (Compact ed.). (1971). Oxford: Oxford University Press.

Peters, J. D. (1989). John Locke, the individual, and the origin of communication. *Quarterly Journal of Speech, 75*, 387–399.

Shepherd, G. J. (1992). Communication as influence: Definitional exclusion. *Communication Studies, 43*, 203–219.

Shepherd, G. J. (1998). The trouble with goals. *Communication Studies, 49*, 294–299.

Shepherd, G. J. (1999). Advances in communication theory: A critical review. *Journal of Communication, 49*, 156–164.

Shipley, J. T. (1945). *Dictionary of word origins*. New York: Philosophical Library.

3

Prosocial Bias in Theories of Interpersonal Communication Competence: Must Good Communication Be Nice?

Carey H. Adams
Southwest Missouri State University

It is true, doubt, that man is the most gregarious of animals, but it is nevertheless true that the thing of which he still knows the least is the business of carrying on an associated existence.

—Robert E. Park (1967, p. 99)

Let him who cannot be alone beware of community. Let him who is not in community beware of being alone.

—Dietrich Bonhoeffer (1954, p. 77)

Fundamental to all of the essays in this volume is the unavoidable tension between the individual and the social. It is in our nature to be social, yet our individuality often is at odds with our desire to be part of the group. Notions of communication and community are at the heart of this tension. In interpersonal communication theory and research, the pursuit of community is perhaps the defining characteristic of interpersonal competence. This assumed link dramatically influences how we understand both communication and community and the relationship between the two.

The decidedly prosocial bias of most interpersonal communication research (see Cupach & Spitzberg, 1994, for a detailed critique) indicates a prevailing concern for how interpersonal communication contributes to the creation and maintenance of community. This preoccupation may, however, limit our perspective on interpersonal communication (see Burgoon, 1995; Parks, 1982). Even more troubling is how the elevation of *community*, as the idealized goal of communication, has led to the establishment of community as the primary criterion for judging communication competence. We have moved from the claim that prosocial communication is more socially desirable to the assumption that it is more competent, or advanced, as well.

Failure to separate explanations of communication ability from these particular visions of community leads to three significant problems: First, we ignore the possibility that advanced or sophisticated communication can be antisocial. Second, we overlook the ways in which non-interpersonal, even antisocial, communication can serve the interests of community and even be necessary to its existence. Third, we isolate few of the potential disadvantages, both social and individual, that may be associated with more advanced social cognitive and communication abilities.

This chapter illustrates these problems through an examination of the prosocial bias in definitions of community and communication competence, as well as and in two prominent developmental communication theories, Constructivism and Message Design Logic.

COMMUNITY

Recently, the concept of community has received a great deal of attention in public discussions regarding democracy, participation, civility, and public welfare. Harvard University professor Robert Putnam received national attention for his article, "Bowling Alone: America's Declining Social Capital," published in the *Journal of Democracy*. Putnam (1995) argued that declining participation in social and civic membership has led to a loss of "social capital" and a deteriorating sense of community. Although some critics have argued against Putnam's thesis (Stengel, 1996), the health of "community" in our society continues to be of concern to a wide variety of social theorists and researchers (Rothenbuhler, 1991). For example, a growing number of authors are focusing on the workplace as a site for community (Cheney, 1995; Koonce, 1996; Naylor, Willimon, & Osterberg, 1996; Patterson, 1994; Powell, 1994; Zemke, 1996).

Definitions are important when considering the relationship between communication and community. Popularized conceptions of community tend to express it as a goal to be achieved: We speak of establishing a "sense of community," of "building community spirit," and of "feeling a part of a community," with the implication being that community is a qualitative state to which we aspire. Community in such examples tends to be viewed as characterized by supportive social ties, civility, and even intimacy. These definitions, sometimes explicit, but always implicit, have had an influence on theory and research about Interpersonal Communication. To this end, Burgoon (1995) argued forcefully that Interpersonal Communication research and theory historically have privileged collectivist concerns over and above those of individuals. Parks (1985, 1995) contends that an "ideology of intimacy" pervades the Interpersonal Communication literature, and a recent survey of college professors indicates this pervasiveness is reflected in the content of Interpersonal Communication courses (McNeilis, Craig, & Bauman, 1998).

Current Interpersonal Communication theory undeniably emphasizes politeness and cooperation as central features of communication competence. Why is this so, and what are the implications? The answers to both questions are tied closely to our understanding of the relationship between communication and community.

Although intimacy and close social ties may be desirable qualities for a community, they are neither necessary nor sufficient conditions for the structures and functions of communities. Early sociological definitions of community, principally from Robert Park and the Chicago School, were drawn from biological models of ecology (see Park, 1967; Park & Burgess, 1969; Park, Burgess, & McKenzie, 1925). Later conceptualizations focused on the role of institutions serving local needs and social structure, including socialization, interaction, and shared interests or goals (Park et al., 1925). Rubin (1983), drawing on the work of Emile Durkheim (1933/1964), argued that the function of community was to mediate the relationship between the individual and society. Even if we extend these definitions of community to include providing a sense of belonging and membership, there are still many ways in which belonging and membership may be expressed and experienced, and not all of them are characterized by supportive, intimate interpersonal relationships. Furthermore, although a community often is defined in terms of who is in it and what those people share, communities also are defined by who is not in, as any number of scholars from Burke to Durkheim have pointed out. A sense of community often is created out of explicit or implicit recognition of how members of the community are different from nonmembers. The achievement of communal spirit is frequently at the expense of fostering a larger, more inclusive community.

Community is *not* an interpersonal construct. Interpersonal relationships and interactions may be building blocks of community, but, more powerfully, they are the *products* of community. Therefore, we err when we treat community as a primary criterion for interpersonal communication. Most people are born into communities or join them rather than build them one relationship at a time. Even in circumstances where a community can be observed as springing from a few interpersonal relationships, once a community has formed, it no longer is simply the product of those relationships. As a community, it takes on the functional and structural characteristics described above, and those characteristics alternately shape the interpersonal relationships carried on in the context of that community (Giddens, 1979). A fascinating approach for interpersonal communication scholars might be the ways in which communities influence communication and relationships, as well as how new communities are, in fact, built out of interpersonal relationships.

Current theories of interpersonal communication competence are based on one of two models. The first model involves a functional approach, wherein competence is defined in terms of desired outcomes of communication. The second model uses the level of complexity as a basis for defining competence. Communication behavior that is more difficult to perform is considered to be more advanced, or more competent. Both of these models are biased in favor of prosocial communication as more being more competent and both are framed in the context of a particular vision of community. Neither of them allow for a full consideration of what might be the relation between communication and community. The remainder of this chapter addresses this prosocial bias in communication competence research and suggests potential areas for new research on interpersonal communication and community.

COMMUNICATION COMPETENCE

Definitions of communication competence tend to be contextualized and value-laden. What social actors perceive as competent is shaped largely by the standards of their communities, and the same is true of social scientists. Prosocial bias evident in most models of communication competence reflects our standards for successful and ethical relationships (Parks, 1985; Spitzberg, 1994;). For example, two widely cited measures of communication competence are Wiemann's (1977) Communicative Competence Scale and Duran and Kelly's (1988) Communicative Adaptability Scale. Wiemann's scale includes five dimensions of communication competence: general competence, empathy, affiliation/support, behavioral flexibility, and social relaxation. Duran and Kelly's scale measures six dimensions of communicative adaptability: social composure, social experience, social confirmation, appropriate disclosure, articulation, and wit. These definitions emphasize standards of intimacy (rather than distance), support (rather than confrontation), and appropriateness (rather than individual-based criteria). As Spitzberg (1994) concluded, there is a definitive consensus on the criteria of effectiveness and appropriateness. Although appropriateness may generally involve following social conventions for civility and politeness, this is not necessarily the case. As Spitzberg explained, "Behavior does not have to conform or be polite to be appropriate, because there are novel situations in which there are no norms to conform to," and, "appropriateness may subsume subordinate means. For example, in any given situation, clarity, deception, or ambiguity may be the most appropriate tactic" (pp. 31–32). However, Spitzberg also suggested that the idealized form of competence is communication that is both effective and appropriate.

In a provocative collection of essays titled *The Dark Side of Interpersonal Communication* (Cupach & Spitzberg, 1994), a variety of authors contend that significant aspects of interpersonal communication have been overlooked. These aspects include hurtful messages, equivocation, deception, physical and psychological abuse, and parental privacy invasion. The theme that connects these essays is that interpersonal communication research tends to focus on socially appropriate behavior and glosses over antisocial behavior and intentions. In the concluding chapter of that volume, editors Brian Spitzberg and William Cupach suggested that, "One of the ironies of these ideological assumptions is that they seem to be based on the notion that what is 'normal' is preferred, yet what is truly normal is far from the cultural ideal of good interpersonal relations" (p. 316).

Some authors have argued for definitions of interpersonal competence that are more specifically contextualized. For example, Monge, Backman, Dillard, and Eisenberg (1982) proposed a measure of communicator competence in the workplace that would focus on encoding and decoding skills that facilitate interaction between people in role positions. Of the 11 items in their scale, seven deal specifically with clarity and directness whereas only three appear to reference aspects of intimacy and sensitivity.

Other authors have argued with an "ideology of intimacy" (Parks, 1982), even our understanding of friendships and intimate relationships is limited. Parks (1985) favored placing personal control at the center of our conception of interpersonal competence. In Parks' view, "Communicative competence represents the degree to which individuals perceive they have satisfied their goals in a given situation without jeopardizing their ability or opportunity to pursue their other subjectively more important goals" (p. 175). Spitzberg (1994) questioned whether those dominant conceptions of competence that emphasize clarity, sensitivity, and politeness reflect the full spectrum of competent communication: "Competence is sometimes equated with the accomplishment of clarity, accuracy, and understanding. Yet, ambiguity, deception, equivocation, and tentativeness are often highly competent communicative tactics" (p. 33).

Shepherd (1992) argued that "personal control" always has been the defining characteristic of communication and communication competence and that this reflects a masculine bias. Shepherd asserted that viewing communication primarily as relational responsibility—drawn from a feminine perspective—rather than influence might dramatically alter our conceptions of competence. This may well be the case. Whether one views the primary function of communication as influence or relational responsibility, or both, competence still will be defined on the basis of desired outcomes. Having influence as the defining characteristic of communication does not preclude a definition of competence from having a prosocial bias. Even if social concerns are relegated to status as subsidiary goals, there is still a presumption that competent influence requires prosocial strategies, as demonstrated by the widespread agreement on effectiveness and appropriateness as essential dimensions of competence.

The prosocial bias in functional models of competence is understandable because they define the goals of competence for interpersonal relationships (e.g., intimacy, disclosure, cooperation) and then identify abilities, behaviors, and traits that promote those kinds of relationships. *Competency* is defined in terms of desired outcomes. In contrast, developmental theories of interpersonal communication abilities, similar to theories of cognitive development, attempt to explain how people's abilities progress from simpler to more complex forms, presumably without regard for ethical standards or personal motives. Developmental theories are similar to the functional theories already described in that complexity typically is defined in terms of the communicator's ability to pursue both personal control and relational goals. Complex situations are those that call on the speaker to reconcile or transcend goal conflicts. Because it is more difficult to construct and produce such complex messages and the ability to do so is dependent on mastery of earlier knowledge or skills, competence is therefore theorized in terms of development. Among the most sophisticated and empirically tested of all these theories are Constructivism and Message Design Logic. However, even these theories suggest an implied ethical dimension to development that only complicates our understanding of communication abilities and the interplay between communication and community. The prosocial bias inherent in these theories provides further evidence of how an idealized goal of community will prevent a full understanding of communication competence.

CONSTRUCTIVISM AND MESSAGE DESIGN LOGIC

Constructivism and Message Design Logic are chosen as examples for three reasons. First, both theories explicitly reference the importance of community in the development of social cognition and communication skills and dispositions (Applegate, 1990; O'Keefe, 1988; O'Keefe & Delia, 1982; O'Keefe & McCornack, 1987). Second, both theories claim to describe developmentally ordered abilities that are directly related to effectiveness in a wide variety of interpersonal contexts, rather than defining traits, specific skills, or highly contextualized competencies (O'Keefe, 1988, 1990; O'Keefe & Delia, 1982). Finally, both theories emphasize the abilities of speakers to transcend individual differences and achieve goals cooperatively through the skillful use of symbolic representation. In other words, these theories place communication in the context of community; they appear to describe the development of various abilities that transcend specifically contextual definitions of competence; finally, they both place integration of multiple goals at the top of their respective developmental hierarchies.

The extensive constructivist research program has been thoroughly reviewed (e.g., see Applegate, 1990; Burleson, 1989; Gastil, 1995) and is not described in detail here. Likewise, O'Keefe's Message Design Logic model is well documented and will also not be extensively defined (e.g., O'Keefe, 1988, 1990; O'Keefe & Lambert, 1995; O'Keefe & McCornack, 1987). The majority of research involving both theories has focused on their linking of social cognition variables with variations in message design, form, and functional effectiveness. Constructivist researchers have developed hierarchical coding systems for describing levels of sophistication in the messages designed to persuade, regulate others' behavior, comfort, and manage identities. Applegate (1990) summarized this research as an attempt to identify "person-centered" communication in a variety of interpersonal contexts. O'Keefe's (1988) Message Design Logic model similarly provides a hierarchical coding scheme for categorizing messages. She suggested there are at least three distinct logics, or sets of assumptions that guide reasoning about communication: expressive, conventional, and rhetorical. Both person-centeredness and Design Logic models will be described in greater detail as we proceed. For the moment, it suffices to say that all of these hierarchies describe progressions of message strategies from less to more complex and from less to more effective.

The hierarchical coding schemes in each of these theories describe the most sophisticated message strategies as prosocial and other-directed. For example, Applegate, Burke, Burleson, Delia, and Kline (1985) defined person-centeredness in communication as:

> the extent to which a message is responsive to the aims and utterances of the interactional partner, the extent to which a message is adapted or tailored to meet the specific characteristics and needs of a particular listener, the extent to which the topic or content of a message deals with persons and their psychological and affective qualities, the extent to which a message implicitly seeks to enhance interpersonal relationships or create positive interpersonal identities, and the extent to which a message encourages reflection by another about his or her circumstance or situation. (pp. 134–135)

O'Keefe (1988) described the three design logics as: *expressive*, in which communication is viewed primarily as a means of expressing thoughts, feelings, and desires; *conventional*, which views communication as a game played cooperatively in accordance with socially accepted or prescribed rules; and *rhetorical*, wherein communication is understood as the creation and negotiation of selves and situations. The development is from the least sophisticated level, where individual wants and goals are prioritized, to a second level where the individual recognizes that personal goals must be pursued according to social rules, and finally to the highest level, rhetorical, which O'Keefe described as "consensus-seeking."

In both Constructivism and Message Design Logic, the top levels of their respective hierarchies are characterized by: messages that are cooperative or consensus seeking, and messages that should be more difficult to produce because of complex goal demands. The former characteristic clearly is based in the particular view of community described earlier as emphasizing cooperation and concern for the other, ignoring the possibility that messages could be complex in ways other than being cooperative or consensus seeking. Both characteristics ignore the possibility that speakers might use cooperation and consensus seeking as manipulative tools. The following sections raise the question of how people might exploit rather than pursue community, and how both exploitation and pursuit of community might be understood as developmentally advanced, or competent.

Interpersonal Motives. The definitions of both person-centered and rhetorical messages appear to describe them as prosocial and to presume that speakers' motives in using these strategies are sincere. In all of the research in the Constructivist and Message Design Logic programs, either speakers are presumed to be sincere in their use of message strategies or the question of sincerity simply is never raised. Person-centeredness and rhetorical logic are described as facilitating behavioral flexibility and recognition of multiple goals (O'Keefe, 1988; O'Keefe & Delia, 1982), but whether behavioral flexibility might be employed in the service of deceit, manipulation, or equivocality has not been an issue.

Consider these contrasting definitions of the three design logics: Expressive design logic is described in clearly antisocial terms. For example, "When those who use expressive design logic are faced with conflicts among competing goals, they respond by producing *uncooperative messages, i.e., messages that withhold the problematic information or action by editing, distorting, withdrawing, etc.*" [italics added] (O'Keefe & Solowczuk, 1993, p. 9). Applying design logic to regulative messages, O'Keefe (1991) described expressive messages as "sparse, ineffectual, and highly affective in tone" and characterized by "failure to engage the immediate task" (p. 144). In contrast, conventional messages are those that "predicate some future goal-related action of the message target" and "often mention contextual conditions," whereas rhetorical messages are referred to as "sophisticated" and "consensus-seeking" (pp. 144–145). Clearly, the progression is from a logic that fails to appreciate the importance of cooperative facilitation of multiple goals to a more sophisticated logic that values cooperation as a means of goal attainment.

Clark and Delia (1979) proposed that task, relational, and identity goals represent the complexity of interpersonal situations. Complex situations demand and often elicit complex messages. Message complexity, according to Applegate (1990), "is reflected in the number and types of goals pursued, the variety of strategies employed, and the situational variables accounted for in the message" (p. 207). Most research appears to assume that relational and identity goals are prosocial, however, in many situations that call for a speaker to establish control or dominance, the speaker might use face threats strategically to accomplish his or her goals. Here multiple goals might also be accomplished, but the relational and identity goals might not be described as prosocial.

In summary, it seems that although prosocial strategies have not been considered as strategies that might be used insincerely or for antisocial purposes, neither have strategies that pursue multiple goals that are not characterized by cooperation and equality been examined as examples of advanced or sophisticated communication. This is not surprising given the types of situations studied by Constructivist and Message Design Logic researchers. These situations, including persuasion, regulation, comforting, and identity management, among others, have fostered a prosocial bias by creating the presumption of prosocial criteria. The demand characteristics used with message tasks alone tend to discourage antisocial responses. For example, in several studies employing Message Design Logic, the number of expressive messages elicited from participants has been quite low (Adams, 1991; Logan, 1992; O'Keefe, 1988; O'Keefe, Lambert, & Lambert, 1993).

Whether people are more likely to employ antisocial as opposed to prosocial strategies is an empirical question. Regardless of its possible frequency, most Constructivist and Design Logic research has not even investigated antisocial communication as advanced or sophisticated. For example, in the often-used Group Leader Problem (O'Keefe, 1988), speakers are not prompted by scenarios such as, "You don't really believe Ron's story, but the group needs his work," or, "You tend to believe that the time for being nice with Ron has passed." Such instructions might more accurately reflect what many people would actually think about Ron; they certainly would elicit messages based on very different assumptions. Furthermore, how do people with more advanced Design Logics respond when faced with a choice of whether to speak truthfully, or with an opportunity to deflect blame or responsibility? Until these and similar situations are studied we won't know what a rhetorical or person-centered lie would look like, for example, and we have no reason to believe that a rhetorical or highly cognitively differentiated speaker would be more or less likely to pursue selfish or even antisocial goals.

Both the Constructivist and Message Design Logic approaches claim to account for message variation by explaining the link between goals and message strategy or design, but the demand characteristics of the situations studied coupled with the implied prosocial motives of 'advanced' strategies completely sidestep the issue of ethics and moral intent. For example, O'Keefe et al. (1993) explained that, "in a rhetorical logic, the communicative situation is apprehended in terms of the ends being sought and the ways in which the interests of involved parties can be reconciled: expression is guided by the need to enact or create a social structure that is compatible with goal attainment" (p. 3). Meeting the interests of "involved parties" implies prosocial concern for others, but enacting or creating a social structure that is "compatible with goal attainment" conceivably could involve creating a situation where the other party only perceives that their goals have been attained. O'Keefe et al. (1993) went on to say that "rhetorical message design logic makes it possible for the speaker to present a positive image of the hearer and to represent the desired action as serving the interests of both speaker and hearer" (p. 5). Here it sounds as if a rhetorical logic could be used to "represent" a state of affairs rather than genuinely create a state of affairs. In fact, in a case study reporting its application of Message Design Logic in resolving an organizational conflict, O'Keefe, Lambert, and Lambert (1997) suggested that rhetorical communicators might be perceived as dishonest by expressives because rhetoricals "say what they think needs to be said to influence the hearer in particular ways" (p. 37). Although this would not necessarily involve deception, certainly it could. The issue of deception has not been raised much in Constructivist and Message Design Logic research, but recent developments in this area suggest that this would be a fruitful area for investigation.

Deception. A number of communication scholars have turned their attention to deception and deception detection (e.g., Buller, Strzyzewiski, & Comstock, 1991; Burgoon, Buller, Guerrero, Afifi, & Feldman, 1996; Kalbfleisch, 1992; McCornack, 1992; O'Hair & Cody, 1994). This research has focused on generating typologies of deception behavior, explanations of deception, and the abilities of perceivers to detect deception. A cursory review of this literature reveals a number of ways in which messages characterized as person-centered or rhetorical might be used to deceive. For example, speakers might insincerely express positive affect or concern, misrepresent personal beliefs or situational information, or mask actual intent. In fact, one could go back to definitions of person-centered and rhetorical and substitute the word "manipulation" everywhere the word "negotiation" appears.

A large body of research has documented that person-centered and rhetorical messages are perceived as more effective and lead to more positive impressions of speakers. If this is the case, and if communication ability and ethics are separate concerns, then there is every reason to believe that sophisticated communicators would be very good at deception and manipulation. Evidence suggests that most people are poor at detecting deception (Kalbfleisch, 1992), particularly in close, personal relationships (McCornack & Parks, 1986, 1990). And when deceivers detect suspicion, they have been observed to alter their behavior to mask deception (Buller et al., 1991). People with more developed social cognitive and communication abilities are particularly adept at relationship maintenance as well as monitoring situational demands and the feedback of partners, abilities that would seem to facilitate successful deception if that were their goal. But based on current Constructivist and Design Logic research, we are left with the presumption that "good" (i.e., skilled) communication is creative and honest.

Ironically, it's possible that those people with more differentiated interpersonal perceptions and/or more sophisticated design logics might also be especially susceptible to deception. Research by Wilson, Cruz, and Kang (1992) revealed that more highly differentiated individuals were more variable in making attributions based on what information was made that was salient to them, suggesting that they might be prone to attribution errors that would favor a deceptive speaker. Spitzberg (1994) suggested that abilities such as perspective taking and cognitive complexity might inhibit a person's objectivity or so overload him or her with possible interpretations that the ability to escape deception would be impaired. Finally, if rhetorical message producers are more likely to see redefinition as a natural process of mutual negotiation (O'Keefe, 1988), they may fail to be suspicious of someone using rhetorical strategies for the purpose of deception or manipulation.

COMPETENT COMMUNICATION AND COMMUNITY

The link between interpersonal communication competence and community is not made as easily as current theory would suggest. First, whereas intimacy may be the idealized goal of interpersonal relationships, it is not the defining feature of community. The ideology of intimacy (Parks, 1982, 1985) may prevent us from recognizing other ways in which interpersonal communication is both a product of and a contributor to community. A valuing of prosocial communication to the exclusion of other forms or motives also fails to acknowledge instances when prosocial forms or motives do not serve the needs of community. For example, in investigating responses to sexual harassment Bingham and Burleson (1988) found that although rhetorical messages were viewed as likely to protect the face of the harasser and maintain a working relationship with that person, they were not viewed as likely to be effective in stopping the harassment. Also, in a study of hospital supervisors' attempts to regulate the behavior of employees and volunteers, Adams (1991) found that rhetorical messages were not necessarily the most effective tactic. In fact, in some instances volunteers perceived that rhetorical messages were condescending. Finally, Burgoon (1995) cited health communication research showing that noncompliant patients are most responsive to verbally aggressive physicians. These examples point to instances in which concern for interpersonal politeness may work against other goals of community, such as those of protecting the rights of individuals or those of promoting individual behaviors that are in the best interests of the community at large.

A second problem with the assumed link between prosocial communication and community is the assumption that sophisticated or competent communication is necessarily prosocial. Functional definitions of competence present a rather one-sided view of what "good" communication is for. Not all skilled communicators share this view. Certainly, there are people who are very good at deceit, manipulation, and exploitation of others; they are highly skilled and knowledgeable; their communication performances may be as difficult as any act of consensus seeking; yet, how can we understand their accomplishments if they are not accounted for in our definitions and explications of competence? Developmental definitions imply that sincere concern for others and a desire for cooperation and consensus are inherent in more highly developed social cognitive and communication abilities. However, those same definitions state that much of what makes messages sophisticated is their ability to shape perceptions and redefine relationships, an ability that easily could be used for antisocial purposes.

A third problem in the link between prosocial communication and community is that although Constructivism and Message Design Logic clearly claim a relation between communities and the development of social cognitive and communicative abilities, research in these programs has not tapped the potential implications of this relation. Consider this discussion of Design Logic in Applegate's (1990) review of the Constructivist research program:

> People are socialized into communication systems with particular "logics for designing messages; logics which define the value and function of communication itself. Previous research has shown relations between cultural background and an orientation to person-centered communication. If people must accommodate to a system in which communication is valued as a means of bridging the gap between individual differences and negotiating individual realities, then these people will develop interpersonal schemata and strategic abilities designed to be successfully social within such a negotiation focused worldview. Other more traditional cultural communication systems might value conventions and rules as the basis for communication. Within such systems successful, competent communication is not that which best negotiates individual differences. Rather good communication is "appropriate" communication—communication which successfully enacts the correct cultural conventions. Value orientations such as these are central to the third most recent, and most provocative, account of the relation of constructs and communication. (pp. 224–225)

If we substitute the word "community" for "communication system," then this analysis suggests that different communities may have different standards for what constitutes competent communication. Recent studies by Peterson and Albrecht (1997) and O'Keefe et al. (1997) support this conclusion. In both studies, people's appreciation for rhetorical messages was mediated by their own design logics. O'Keefe et al. (1997) explicitly argued that "Every design logic provides a logically consistent and potentially satisfactory way for an individual to use language" (p. 49). O'Keefe's (1988) characterization of logics as developmentally ordered and in ascending order of competence makes a value connotation difficult to avoid. Taking seriously the claim that design logics are products of communities, we should examine the varieties of design logics that might be cultivated in different communities rather than assuming that a rhetorical logic or person-centered orientation are the desired forms for all communities.

At least one author (Logan, 1992) has suggested that O'Keefe's Message Design Logic hierarchy parallels models of moral development. Logan found that rhetorical design logic in individuals was associated more with a response and care orientation, whereas conventional logic was associated with a justice orientation. Interestingly, individuals with response and care orientations also were slightly more likely to produce expressive messages. As Gilligan (1982) argued, descriptions of moral development are inherently intertwined with ethical standards. Gilligan criticized Kolberg's stages of moral development for having a masculine bias such that masculine characteristics are equated with more advanced stages of moral development. Gilligan and others called for a more balanced view of moral development, one that recognizes different orientations as being neither superior nor inferior to one another. It is possible that developmental theories of communication competence also contain a bias that leads us to label as "advanced" something that is merely "different."

IMPLICATIONS FOR FUTURE RESEARCH

In the classic work, *The City*, R. D. McKenzie (1967) observed that the human community has its inception in the traits of human nature and the needs of human beings. As this statement implies, community is at the intersection of individual desires and collective action. These two drives are not always equal in guiding the actions of individuals or communities. At times individual needs are pursued at the expense of community, and at other times community is achieved by the sublimation and even the suppression of individual goals. Theories of interpersonal communication competence must take into account the full range of what might be defined as community and competence.

Our understanding of interpersonal communication is limited by approaches that imply a prosocial criterion for competence. As Spitzberg (1994) and others have pointed out, much communication that appears to be incompetent or antisocial is indeed functionally competent and may even be preferred in certain contexts. And developmental theories that imply a particular moral or ethical perspective obscure our understanding of the use of advanced communication abilities for antisocial purposes as well as presume that cooperation, intimacy, and negotiation are preferred standards for community. If we step away from these assumptions, a variety of new research questions emerge. First, do more advanced social cognitive abilities, such as cognitive complexity, self-monitoring, perspective taking, or message design logic, facilitate effective antisocial behavior? If so, in what ways are these abilities and outcomes related? Second, how closely related are moral development, social cognitive development, and communication abilities? If our models of social cognitive development and communication can define development without reference to moral judgment, then we are more likely to be able to answer this question. Third, what social disadvantages are associated with advanced social cognitive and communication abilities? Fourth, are people who are more competent according to the standards of current theories actually better at participating in and building community? In what ways and in what contexts might less "sophisticated" communication prove more effective in the interests of community? Exploring these questions will require that we continue to look for ways in which community is defined by communication, rather than assuming that competent communication is defined by the accomplishment of community.

CONCLUSION

What are the ingredients for the good community? Certainly the kinds of prosocial communicative abilities reviewed in this essay are an essential part of most people's ideal community. However, we must acknowledge there are many communities that are not characterized by the values implied in our interpersonal communication theories. Gangs, for instance, are an excellent example of communities that possess all the characteristics of a sociological community but which also are characterized by threats, intimidation, violence, and contempt for those outside the community. The question is not merely can we achieve community or not, but what *kind* of community do we want and how may we achieve it? Questions of ethics and morality must be a part of that discussion, but we must also recognize the wide range of values that might be advocated within the overall framework of community.

More than anything accomplishing the good community requires we understand the tools and processes that manipulate, destroy, and exploit community as well as those that help to create and sustain community. That understanding requires also that we not oversimplify the relationship between interpersonal communication and community. This relationship is better viewed through the long-term lens of community rather than the short-term lens of interpersonal encounters. In other words, while interpersonal relationships may be short-lived and interpersonal competence may be defined in even one-time encounters between strangers, community typically has a longer life span. How might short-term relationships be better understood in light of their community context? In what ways do interpersonal relationships over time help to define the communities in which they take place? How do individuals pursue the overarching goal of community in their relationships with many people over the long haul? Are long-term interests of community always consistent with short-term interests of relational responsibility? These are questions that deserve to be answered. They are questions that need to be answered if we are to understand either interpersonal communication or community.

REFERENCES

Adams, C.A. (1991). *Influences on the production and evaluation of regulative messages: Effects of social cognition, situational, and experiential variables in communication between hospital supervisors and volunteers.* Unpublished doctoral dissertation. University of Kansas.

Applegate, J. L. (1990). Constructs and communication: A pragmatic integration. In R. Neimeyer & G. Neimeyer (Eds.), *Advances in personal construct psychology* (Vol. 1, pp. 197–224). Greenwich, CT: JAI.

Applegate, J. L., Burke, J. A., Burleson, B. R., Delia, J. G., & Kline, S. L. (1985). Reflection-enhancing parental communication. In I. E. Siegel (Ed.), *Personal belief systems: The psychological consequences for children* (pp. 107–142). Hillsdale, NJ: Lawrence Erlbaum Associates.

Bingham, S. G., & Burleson, B. R. (1988). Multiple effects of messages with multiple goals. *Human Communication Research, 16,* 184–216.

Bonhoeffer, D. (1954). *Life together* (J. W. Doberstein, Trans.). San Francisco: Harper San Francisco.

Buller, D. B., Strzyzewiski, K. D., & Comstock, J. (1991). Interpersonal deception: I. Deceivers' reactions to receivers' suspicions and probing. *Communication Monographs, 58*(1), 1–24.

Burgoon, J. K., Buller, D. B., Guerrero, L. K., Afifi, W. A., & Feldman, C. M. (1996). Interpersonal deception: XII. Information management dimensions underlying deceptive and truthful messages. *Communication Monographs, 63,* 50–69.

Burgoon, M. (1995). A kinder, gentler discipline: Feeling good about being mediocre. In B. Burelson (Ed.), *Communication yearbook 18* (pp. 464–479). Thousand Oaks, CA: Sage.

Burleson, B. R. (1989). The constructivist approach to person-centered communication: Analysis of a research exemplar. In B. Dervin, L. Grossberg, B. O'Keefe, & E. Wartella (Eds.), *Rethinking communication: Vol. 2. Paradigm exemplars* (pp. 29–46). Newbury Park, CA: Sage.

Cheney, G. (1995). Democracy in the workplace: Theory and practice from the perspective of communication. *Journal of Applied Communication Research, 23,* 167–200.

Clark, R.A., & Delia, J. G. (1979). Topoi and rhetorical competence. *Quarterly Journal of Speech, 65,* 165–206.

Cupach, W. R., & Spitzberg, B. H. (Eds.) (1994). *The dark side of interpersonal communication.* Hillsdale, NJ: Lawrence Erlbaum Associates.

Duran, R. L., & Kelly, L. (1988). An investigation into the cognitive domain of competence II: The relationship between communicative competence and interaction involvement. *Communication Research Reports, 5,* 91–96.

Durkheim, E. (1966). The division of labor in society (G. Simpson, Trans.). New York: The Free Press of Glencoe. (Original work published 1933)

Gastil, J. (1995). An appraisal and revision of the constructivist research program. In B. Burleson (Ed.), *Communication yearbook 18* (pp. 83–104). Thousand Oaks, CA: Sage.

Giddens, A. (1979). *Central problems in social theory: Action, structure and contradiction in social analysis.* Los Angeles: University of California Press.

Gilligan, C. (1982). *In a different voice: Psychological theory and women's development.* Cambridge, MA: Harvard University.

Kalbfleisch, P. J. (1992). Deceit, distrust, and the social milieu: Application of deception research in a troubled world. *Journal of Applied Communication Research, 20*(3), 308–334.

Koonce, R. (1996). Workplace as community. *Training and Development, 50*(5), 25.

Logan, C. E. (1992, November). *Message design logics and moral orientations: "Justice" or "care" in constructing difficult messages?* Paper presented at the annual Speech Communication Association convention, Chicago, 1992.

McCornack, S. A. (1992). Information manipulation theory. *Communication Monographs, 59,* 1–16.

McCornack, S. A., & Parks, M. R. (1986). Deception detection and relationship development: The other side of trust. In M. L. McLaughlin (Ed.) *Communication Yearbook 9* (pp. 377–389). Beverly Hills, CA: Sage.

McCornack, S. A., & Parks, M. R. (1990). What women know that men don't: Sex differences in determining the truth behind deceptive messages. Journal of Social and Personal Relationships, 7, 107–118.

McKenzie, R. D. (1925). The ecological approach to the study of the human community. In R. E. Parks, E. W. Burgess and R. D. McKenzie, *The City* (pp. 63–79). Chicago: University of Chicago Press.

McNeilis, K. S., Craig, D., & Bauman, I. (1998, November). *Searching for an ideology of intimacy in basic interpersonal communication courses: A preliminary investigation of course content.* Paper presented at the annual meeting of the National Communication Association, New York.

Monge, P. R., Backman, S. G., Dillard, J. P., & Eisenberg, E. M. (1982). Communicator competence in the workplace: Model testing and scale development. *Communication Yearbook, 5,* 505–528.

Naylor, T. H., Willimon, W. H., & Osterberg, R. (1996, Spring). The search for community in the workplace. *Business and Society Review,* 42–48.

O'Hair, H. D., & Cody, M. J. (1994). Deception. In W. R. Cupach & B. H. Spitzberg (Eds.), *The dark side of interpersonal communication* (pp. 181–213). Hillsdale, NJ: Lawrence Erlbaum Associates.

O'Keefe, B. J. (1988). The logic of message design: Individual differences in reasoning about communication. *Communication Monographs, 55,* 80–103.

O'Keefe, B. J. (1990). The logic of regulative communication: Understanding the rationality of message designs. In J. P. Dillard (Ed.), *Seeking compliance: The production of interpersonal influence messages* (pp. 87–104). Scottsdale, AZ: Gorsuch Scarisbrick.

O'Keefe, B. J. (1991). Message design logic and the management of multiple goals. In K. Tracy (Ed.), *Understanding face-to-face interaction: Issues linking goals and discourse.* (pp. 131–150). Hillsdale, NJ: Lawrence Erlbaum Associates.

O'Keefe, B. J., & Delia, J. G. (1982). Impression formation and message production. In M. E. Roloff & C. R. Berger (Eds.), *Social cognition and communication* (pp. 33–72). Beverly Hills, CA: Sage.

O'Keefe, B. J., & Lambert, B. L. (1995). Managing the flow of ideas: A local management approach to message design. In B. Burleson (Ed.), *Communication yearbook 18* (pp. 54–82). Thousand Oaks, CA: Sage.

O'Keefe, B. J., Lambert, B. L., & Lambert, C. A. (1993, November). *Effects of message design logic on perceived communication effectiveness in supervisory relationships.* Paper presented at the Speech Communication Association, Washington, DC.

O'Keefe, B. J., Lambert, B. L., & Lambert, C. A. (1997). Conflict and communication in a research an development unit. In B. D. Sypher (Ed.), *Cases in organizational communication 2* (pp. 31–52). New York: Guilford.

O'Keefe, B. J., & McCornack, S. A. (1987). Message design logic and message goal structure: Effects on perceptions of message quality in regulative communication situations. *Human Communication Research, 14,* 68–92.

O'Keefe, B. J., & Solowczuk, K. (1993, November). *Effects of situation complexity and message design logic on responses to compliments.* Paper presented to the International Communication Association, Washington, DC.

Park, R. E. (1967). *On social control and collective behavior: Selected papers.* Chicago: University of Chicago Press.

Park, R. E., & Burgess, E. W. (1969). *Introduction to the science of sociology* (3rd Ed.). Chicago: University of Chicago Press.

Park, R. E., Burgess, E. W., & McKenzie, R. D. (1925). *The city.* Chicago: University of Chicago Press.

Parks, M. R. (1982). Ideology in interpersonal communication: Off the couch and into the world. In M. Burgoon (Ed.), *Communication yearbook 5* (pp. 79–107). New Brunswick, NJ: Transaction Books.

Parks, M. R. (1985). Interpersonal communication and the quest for personal competence. In M. L. Knapp & G. R. Miller (Eds.), *Handbook of interpersonal communication* (pp. 171–201). Beverly Hills: Sage.

Parks, M. R. (1995). Ideology in interpersonal communication: Beyond the couches, talk shows, and bunkers. In B. Burleson (Ed.), *Communication yearbook 18* (pp. 480–497). Thousand Oaks, CA: Sage.

Patterson, J. (1994, October). Welcome to the company that isn't there. *Business Week,* 86.

Peterson, L. W., & Albrecht, T. L. (1996, Fall). Message design logic, social support, and mixed-status relationships. *Western Journal of Communication, 60,* 291–309.

Powell, M. (1994). Quality and community in the workplace. *The Journal for Quality and Participation, 15*(5), 52–53.

Putnam, R. D. (1995). Bowling alone: America's declining social capital. *Journal of Democracy, 6*(1), 65–79.

Rothenbuhler, E. (1991). The process of community development. *Communication Monographs, 58*(1), 63–78.

Rubin, I. (1983). Function and structure of community: Conceptual and theoretical analysis. In R. L. Warren & L. Lyon (Eds.), *New perspectives on the American community* (pp. 54–61). Homewood, IL: Dorsey.

Shepherd, G. J. (1992). Communication as influence: Definitional exclusion. *Communication Studies, 43*(4), 203–219.

Spitzberg, B. H. (1994). The dark side of (in)competence. In W. R. Cupach & B. H. Spitzberg (Eds.), *The dark side of interpersonal communication* (pp. 25–49). Hillsdale, NJ: Lawrence Erlbaum Associates.

Spitzberg, B. H., & Cupach, W. R. (1994). Dark side denouement. In W. R. Cupach & B. H. Spitzberg (Eds.), *The dark side of interpersonal communication* (pp. 315–320). Hillsdale, NJ: Lawrence Erlbaum Associates.

Stengel, R. (1996, July 22). Bowling together: Civic engagement in American isn't disappearing but reinventing itself. *Time, 148,* 35–37.

Wiemann, J. M. (1977). Explication and test of a model of communicative competence. *Human Communication Research, 3,* 195–213.

Wilson, S. R., Cruz, M. G., & Kang, K. H. (1992). Is it always a matter of perspective? Construct differentiation and variability in attribution about compliance gaining. *Communication Monographs, 59*(1), 1–16.

Zemke, R. (1996, March). The call of community. *Training, 33,* 24–31.

4

Talking Community at 911: The Centrality of Communication in Coping With Emotional Labor

Sherianne Shuler
University of Alabama

"911, what is your emergency?" is a phrase that provides help and relief to citizens in more than 85% of communities across the United States. Nationwide, there are approximately 268,000 calls to 911 each day, and this number is expected to continue rising. Although this way of connecting to emergency services now seems natural and right to citizens of the United States, 911 systems were actually only developed in the late 1960s (Witkin, 1996). Before emergency services were centralized in this manner, a citizen needing assistance from the fire department, for example, would have to directly contact that particular agency. Indeed, one would not have to go back much further in U.S. history than this to find a time when citizens did not necessarily expect emergency services to be provided by professionals employed by an agency, but rather, by the collective effort of members of the community. In many communities, citizen volunteers still collaborate to provide at least some emergency services on an as needed basis.

When a 911 dispatcher answers a call in University City, the midwestern college town that serves as the setting for this case study, she or he does not do so as an individual. The 911 dispatcher represents an institution to that caller or more accurately, a collection of institutions that work together to provide various emergency services. In essence, in his or her talk, the dispatcher represents the community for that citizen in trouble. The citizens of University City rely on the 911 dispatchers to assist them in coping with problems. Most would never wonder, however, how the dispatchers cope with being invested with such a helping role in the community. This chapter addresses this question by examining how communicative coping constitutes community for dispatchers in a particular Emergency Communication Center.

Coping at 911 is enacted in both the public "front stage" and private "backstage" regions (Goffman, 1963). Teamwork and social support, retaliation against officers, "bitching," and the use of humor are all important back stage communicative strategies employed by communication officers to minimize the harmful effects of emotional labor. Participating in the use of these coping strategies is part of what it means to be a dispatcher.

In addition to the communicative coping strategies that are enacted in the back stage region, dispatchers also use some front stage coping strategies directly with callers and law enforcement officers. One means of coping is to creatively retaliate against those responsible for increasing the emotional labor burden. The retaliatory acts of questioning the callers and maintaining control by asking them to "hold please" if maintaining emotional neutrality becomes too difficult are examples of front stage coping strategies. Similarly, dispatchers can retaliate against officers by not helping them out, or by making them "standby." All four of these strategies are examples of emotional laborers seeking revenge communicatively, which Waldron (1994) urged scholars to examine. All of these front and back stage communicative coping strategies will be explored in detail in subsequent sections of this chapter. Presented first, however, are the theory and research that inform this project, as well as the methods used to construct the case study.

COMMUNICATION, ORGANIZATION, AND EMOTION

The job of the 911 dispatcher is fundamentally communicative. Dispatchers listen to, understand, and try to decipher requests from callers that they then must coordinate, prioritize, codify, and broadcast in institutionally appropriate messages. Although visitors to the emergency communication center would probably first note the technical equipment, and perhaps the somewhat quasi-military tenor that characterizes interaction, further observation reveals another side of work at 911: The job may be framed in rationalistic language, but being a 911 dispatcher also involves a great deal of intuition and emotion. Not only do dispatchers perform labor that is highly technical in a high-paced, sometimes frenzied environment, they also labor with their emotions. Although it is seldom recognized and valued to the same degree as other types of labor, emotional labor is difficult and requires considerable skill. In order to deal with the demands of emotional labor, dispatchers have developed an array of coping strategies in order to, essentially, talk their organizational community into existence. The assertion that dispatchers cope communicatively is undergirded by a social constructivist approach to communication, organization, and emotion.

The Social Constructivist Approach

In the American pragmatist and symbolic interactionist traditions, truth is created and sustained by communication that is not found either "out there" in the world or "in there" in the heads of individuals (e.g. Blumer, 1969; Dewey, 1958; Leeds-Hurwitz, 1995; Rorty, 1989). Rorty clarified and buffered this statement by arguing that it is not that there is no objective world, it is just that the objective world does not speak our language. Because reality must be interpreted through communication, the truths we seek and find are the truths that we actively participate in creating. One theoretical tradition that has been used in advancing this social constructionist perspective in organizational communication is Giddens' (1979) structuration theory. Structuration takes an interactional view of the production and reproduction of structure, positing that there is a centrality of communication in this process. Boden (1994) further argued that interaction is structure and, conversely, that the organization is talk. Thus, we do not just talk in an organization, or talk about an organization, we talk an organization into being.

This chapter takes a social constructivist approach to communication and organization, and this chapter also assumes that emotion is a socially constructed process. More positivistic approaches (e.g., Darwin, 1955; Freud, 1911; Zuckerman, 1988) assume emotion to be an internal and biological experience that is, "located in the bodily container" (Sarbin, 1986, p. 84). Contrary to such approaches, the interactional perspective views emotion as a social process that is consciously designed and managed by the actor (e.g., Denzin, 1984; Goffman, 1959; Harré, 1986; Sarbin, 1986; Shott, 1979). Denzin (1984) argued that, "emotions are not mere cognitive responses to physiological, cultural, or structural factors. They are interactive processes best studied as social acts involving interactions with self and interactions with others" (p. 61). For scholars of organizational communication, a social approach to emotion necessitates the examination of workplace communication as the site of the creation of emotion. Although the interaction between organizational and emotional meanings has not traditionally been a focus of organizational research, scholarship in this area has been increasing.

Emotion and Organization

The small amount of attention that has been given to the emotion-organization link is due, in part, to what Mumby and Putnam (1990; see also Putnam & Mumby, 1993) call the myth of rationality. This myth bifurcates emotion and reason and furthers the unfortunate assumption that emotion is somehow irrational. Several scholars have attempted to overcome the myth of rationality by exploring the ways in which emotion and organization intersect. Some of their research examined emotional display rules in various contexts (e.g., Albas & Albas, 1988; Rafaeli, 1989; Rafaeli & Sutton, 1987, 1990, 1991; Sutton, 1991; Sutton & Rafaeli, 1988; Zurcher, 1982), whereas other attempts to discern the congruence of felt and displayed emotion specifically at work (e.g., Fiebig & Kramer, 1996; Kassing, 1995; Waldron & Krone, 1991). Both of these approaches to emotion and organization are useful in that they recognize the importance of emotion in the organizing process, however, a third area, emotional labor, is what most informs this study (e.g., Hochschild, 1979, 1983; James, 1989, 1993; Stenross & Kleinman, 1989; Tolich, 1993; Van Maanen & Kunda, 1989).

Emotional Labor

According to Hochschild (1979, 1983), the expanding service sector in the American economy has created a new and potentially harmful means of alienation for workers. Whereas organizational members are aware of the ways their time, behavior, and physical labor are controlled by the organizations for which they work, organizational control over the emotional displays of employees, while just as pervasive, is not as commonly acknowledged. According to Hochschild, when rules for emotion management are dictated by one's job or employer, and the central aspect of a job is to manage one's own emotions for the good of the organization, such emotional labor is being performed. Depending on the profession, emotional labor may require the enactment of some emotions, or the repression of others. In their discussion of emotional display rules, Wharton and Erickson (1993) suggested that emotional displays can be characterized as positive, as with happiness, negative, as with anger or neutral. Using this category system, flight attendants and retail clerks, for example, do emotional labor by enacting positive emotions and suppressing negative emotions, and people like bill collectors do just the opposite. The 911 dispatchers who are the focus of this chapter strive to sustain emotional neutrality, which tends to be associated with conveying "dispassionate authority and status" (Morris & Feldman, 1996, p. 991). At least those dispatchers who talk to callers or officers over the radio, suppress fear, anger, sadness, and even happiness to portray themselves as calm and under control. This kind of emotion work, of course, takes its toll on those who must perform it every day.

Hochschild's (1979, 1983) work with flight attendants and bill collectors gives a poignant account of the harmful aspects of emotional labor. Certainly, at 911, dispatchers suffered physical, emotional, and relational consequences that seemed to be related to their performance of emotional labor. One way to alleviate these negative consequences would be to advocate more open expression of emotion and thus lower the emotional labor expectations. Whereas it might be possible to suggest that emotion rules could be relaxed somewhat in the case of retail clerks or flight attendants, it is harder to make that case for 911 dispatchers. Frightened and upset citizens who are accessing University City's emergency services via 911 expect dispatchers to help calm them down, not to scream and cry along with them. Instead of doing away with emotional labor, it seems preferable to explore and even celebrate the creative and heroic means by which people can cope with it. From a social constructionist perspective, this would mean looking not at how dispatchers individually cope, but how the organizational community copes together, through communication. Specifically, the questions that are explored in this chapter are: (a) What are the front stage strategies that dispatchers use to communicatively cope with the demands of emotional labor? and (b) What are the back stage strategies that dispatchers use to communicatively cope with the demands of emotional labor? Procedures for examining how 911 dispatchers cope with emotional labor are outlined in the next section.

THE CASE STUDY METHOD

The social constructivist approach to communication, to organization, and to emotion that undergirds this project necessarily leads to a focus on the role of communication in these processes. Sypher (1997) argued that a focus on participants' own voices, "helps us make sense out of their sensemaking" (p. 1). Indeed, the voices of dispatchers in interaction among co-workers, interaction between dispatchers and callers, and interaction between dispatchers and the researcher all contributed to the construction of this case. This chapter is derived from a larger case study of emotion and communication at 911, the results of which are reported elsewhere (Shuler, 1997). The methods employed for answering the two research questions being explored here are observation at the Emergency Communication Center and individual interviews with dispatchers. After a bit of background on the organization and the participants is provided, the methods used for constructing the case study are briefly described.

The Organization and Participants

The Emergency Communication Center serves University City, a prototypical midwestern college town, as well as the surrounding smaller communities. The communication officers in this study answer and dispatch 911 calls for University City Police, and County Sheriff, Fire, Ambulance, and Animal Control services. In addition, they answer and dispatch nonemergency calls for the City Police and County Sheriff. The 17 dispatchers are all county employees, and are trained to dispatch any type of call for service. Contrary to popular belief, the dispatchers in this county are not trained to be Emergency Medical Technicians (EMT), and are actually discouraged from giving advice of any kind to callers.

The Emergency Communication Center is located in a small room adjacent to the University City Police Department offices in the County Law Enforcement Building. The Center is actually a small room with four dispatch stations—two on the county side and two on the city side. The city and county sides are arranged to face each other, but are separated by radio and computer consoles, as well as large maps on each side. Dispatchers wear headsets with long enough cords that they can stand up and walk around the room, talk to their co-workers on the other side, or have access to shared equipment like the fax machine, printer, or copier. There is a television set that is always on, but only gets attended to in slow times.

Dispatchers work in three shifts, with a minimum of three dispatchers working at one time. The job requires a high school diploma or GED, and entry-level pay is approximately $11-$12 an hour, plus benefits. No background in law enforcement or emergency training is required, although many dispatchers at the Emergency Communication Center have worked in related fields. They range in experience from newly hired to over 30 years at the center, with most having been at the job for 9 or 10 years.

Multiple Methods

Yin (1994) and Merriam (1988) suggested that the use of multiple sources of evidence offers validity and adds to the overall quality of the case study. At 911, the overlapping use of observation and interviews worked to balance the strengths and weaknesses of each method, which Denzin (1970) argued is a benefit of triangulation.

Observation was conducted during all three shifts over a 9-month period. Because I was not a trained dispatcher participating in the work of the center, my presence was potentially obtrusive. The small size of both the room and the staff made it impossible to be inconspicuous in my observations. Therefore, until I adjusted to the rhythms of dispatcher interaction, I was quite concerned about disrupting important work. My awkwardness decreased as soon as I picked up an important dispatcher skill: understanding how to start and stop conversations according to the whim of the radio traffic and telephone. Observing work at the center was crucial to understanding the context in which dispatchers enacted and coped with emotional labor. This observation often included "plugging in" and listening to incoming calls with an extra headset. Brief field notes taken during visits to the center were elaborated on as soon after leaving the center as possible. The first few visits produced lengthy descriptions of the environment, the calls, and the actions of the dispatchers, but as observation became more routine, my notes tended to focus solely on key events and interactions. Observation provided me with first-hand accounts of the ways in which the dispatchers coped with emotional labor in 51 pages of text that referenced 91 hours and over 34 days of observation.

Interviews of approximately one hour in length were conducted with 16 of the 17 members of the dispatch staff, as well as with the director. Participants were paid for overtime, and interviews were scheduled for either before or after the shift. Standard practice was for me to additionally plug in an extra headset and observe the dispatcher on either the first or last hour of her or his shift on the day of the interview. This overlapping of interviewing and observation served to open up a dialog between the dispatchers and me. Listening to calls gave me a sense of how they labor emotionally that provided important contextual information for the examination of how they cope. An interview guide was loosely followed, but following Mishler's (1986) recommendations, emphasis was on achieving a jointly constructed dialogue with participants. Interview texts were interpreted as a means to tap into discursively displayed norms and values, rather than as an assumed window into the private worlds of individuals, as Silverman (1989) suggested. Interviews were audio taped and transcribed verbatim, yielding 267 pages of text.

The data were analyzed following the "open coding" techniques outlined by Strauss and Corbin (1990). Drawing a constant comparison between the three types of data served as a means of strengthening the findings, clarifying my understanding, and enriching the text of the report. The combination of observation and interviews would provide for a multifaceted account of how dispatchers cope with emotional labor. All 17 of the dispatchers who participated in the creation of this case study were competent at managing multiple tasks and bringing order to seemingly chaotic situations. As a group, they seem to successfully balance their dedication to helping people with sometimes cynical and suspicious attitudes about human nature. Their means of coping with the demands of their jobs were multiple and varied but also creative and seemingly actively constitutive of organizational community. Part of what it means to be a dispatcher includes communicatively coping with emotional labor. The harmful aspects of emotional labor, as well as the emotionalized zones that constrain expression contribute to the shaping of communicative coping strategies. Before turning to how the dispatchers cope, however, a discussion of the conditions under which they perform emotional labor is needed.

EMOTIONAL LABOR AT 911

"This is a highly stressful job" is a sentiment that I heard over and over again. Newton (1995) argued that, like emotion, stress should be seen as more of a collective than an individual phenomenon. Fineman (1996) pointed out that the rhetoric of stress management in organizations is simply a more socially acceptable way of talking about controlling emotions. The shared sense of stress discussed by dispatchers is certainly related to emotional labor. Although dispatchers may not specifically use the term emotional labor in describing the difficulty of the job, a similar rhetoric of stress management is embedded in the organizational language of the Emergency Communication Center.

Citing the high-stress level involved, one police officer told me that she would never want to be a dispatcher. In addition, two of the three former patrol officers who are now working as communication officers agree that the job of dispatcher is more stressful than the job of police officer. One reason for this is posited by a supervisor:

> You're able to do so much over the phone, but you can't prevent things from happening. When you get in a situation where you just, sort of like being a passenger in a car or on a train that is going to derail, maybe you're talking to somebody on the phone and they're thinking about committing suicide, or at the time they're talking to you, they need a police officer because someone is beating on them, that sort of thing. And you can't actually be there to intervene. It's the frustration of not being able to fully, to help these people in a way, to act it out.

Certainly, such a lack of control is one important contributor to the high stress level among dispatchers. This is not surprising, given that reduced personal control over work situations is commonly associated with higher stress (e.g., Albrecht & Adelman, 1987). It stands to reason, then, that this frustration would add to the costs of emotional labor, which are explored next.

The Costs of Emotional Labor

The work of Hochschild (1979, 1983) and others provides many examples of the harmful aspects of emotional labor, and 911 dispatchers are not immune to these problems. They specifically report three different types of problems stemming, at least in part, from their performance of emotional labor: physical problems, psychological problems, and relational problems.

Physical Problems. Ray (1987) reported that common physical symptoms of stress include ulcers, heart problems, back pain, headaches, high blood pressure, and chronic fatigue. Not surprisingly, dispatchers reported an array of similar physical problems that are experienced by themselves or their co-workers, including sleep disorders, the reactivation of chronic illness, bleeding ulcers, heart attacks, migraine headaches, and chronic neck pain. These physical problems range in severity from an occasional night of sleeping difficulty to the more serious chronic problems like ulcers or the propensity for heart attacks. Some individuals have attempted to decrease their own stress levels by such strategies as switching to a less busy shift, or by just trying to monitor their stress. As one dispatcher shared, in order to prevent reactivation of a chronic illness, "I try to keep myself as at peace as I can because I know that's [the absence of peace] what does it."

Psychological Problems. In addition to physical problems, some job-related psychological difficulties are also experienced by dispatchers. They reported built up anger, depression, desensitization, and burnout. One dispatcher described how upset she was about a call she received from the boyfriend of a woman who had a full-term baby and then left it to die in her toilet. The case was publicized locally and this particular dispatcher followed its progression quite closely, because, as she related: "I really—I hated her. I was just, you know, 'how could you do this?' You know, 'how could you actually have this kid and, you know, not try to show any kind of remorse?' … a lot of anger built up in me on her, and I didn't want to live like that, 'cuz, you know, I can't keep doing that." For this dispatcher, the anger continued to build up inside of her until she finally resolved it by attending some of the woman's trial to gain a sense of closure.

This sort of built up anger can also be paired with depression, another psychological problem that was reported by a dispatcher. Although she did not claim that her depression is solely job-related, she believed it to be a contributing factor. She linked it directly to the performance of emotional labor, saying that, when trying to help callers who are in personal danger, "I try to remain very calm, and that's probably why I'm on antidepressants right now."

Dispatchers agree that the ability to remain calm and not be fazed by the callers' tragedies, or becoming desensitized, is something that increases with job experience. This seems similar to Van Maanen and Kunda's (1989) finding that "willed emotional numbness" is both a coping strategy and a negative repercussion of emotional labor for Disney employees. Although some level of desensitization is probably needed to deal with the type of situations they encounter, several dispatchers expressed concern about the possibility that they have become, or might become, too desensitized. One of the more recently hired dispatchers said that the process of becoming desensitized to tragedy is not a conscious one, that it just happens, but that it is "not something I look forward to, becoming that desensitized," that crimes like murder seem commonplace.

Hochschild (1983) drew a distinction between surface acting and deep acting that is also helpful here. When dispatchers are surface acting, or just trying to act calm in the face of tragedy, it is difficult enough. When they are deep acting, however, and their need to take control and remain emotionally neutral causes them to cease all feeling for the callers, the personal consequences are perhaps even more grave. It stands to reason that the emotional numbness that Van Maanen and Kunda (1989) discussed could become more of a problem for long-time employees.

At this particular communication center, there are three employees who have been working in the job for more than 20 years. In addition, several employees have been there at least 10 years. Nevertheless, it is widely believed among dispatchers that "this is a burnout job." Maslach (1982) outlined three main components of burnout: emotional exhaustion, feelings of diminished personal accomplishment, and depersonalization. Several dispatchers have plans for what they might do when they reach the point that they begin to experience these aspects of burnout and are preparing now by taking college or vocational skills courses. They are quick to point to a few "fried" people and vow not to work at this job when they begin to feel and act as burned out as them. However, one dispatcher who identified herself as burned out remarked that with the decreased sense of accomplishment that is a component of burnout, "it's very hard to go find something else. It makes it very hard to go out and sell yourself and to even explore." In many ways, although she is unhappy, she sees herself as trapped in her current job.

The first two dimensions of burnout are experienced by some of the dispatchers, some of the time. The third dimension, depersonalization, however, has a curiously prominent place in the county emergency communication center. The tendency to see the public as rife with "stupid people" who have "no common sense" is indicative of this type of depersonalization. Although this perspective is often seen in a negative light, as an indicator of burnout, such labeling may also be a means by which employees deal with the difficulty of emotional interaction (Pacanowsky & O'Donnell-Trujillo, 1983). Although not all dispatchers are burned out, they all at least occasionally experience some of the forms of psychological difficulties. Built-up anger, depression, desensitization, and burnout all negatively impact the individual, and they also have strong relational implications. As Noe (1995) found in his study of paramedics, these individual problems can spill over to the employees' other relationships. Indeed, several communication officers reported general relational problems that they attributed, at least in part, to their jobs.

Relational Problems.   The performance of emotional labor at work can cause tension in personal relationships both at home and at work. Conflict among dispatchers is certainly sparked by emotional situations. Dispatchers agree that it is important to put aside personal differences in order to do this job well, but tension among some co-workers does exist and can make work seem more difficult. For example, one woman described a time in which she was having trouble in her marriage, but conflict among dispatchers meant that she did not, "have much support in the room" to help her deal with these personal problems. Her co-workers "looked at her funny" when she was openly crying about marital problems while on the job, and the department refused her request to be released from duty for the night. The relational sanctions of violating a feeling rule made an already painful situation that much more intense.

In addition to some difficulty in relationships with co-workers, problems in personal relationships outside of work are another consequence of emotional labor. With any job, relational and work success are somewhat intertwined. Dispatchers claim that, generally, those who have partners who are also in law enforcement enjoy more support and understanding in these relationships. Most partners and families who are not in law enforcement, however, do not have an understanding of the stressful nature of the work. Dispatchers whose loved ones "can't relate to what they go through" experience added strain on their relationships. Several dispatchers referred to the extraordinarily high divorce rate among workers in law enforcement as evidence of this strain:

> I think it's interesting to note, and I don't know if this is inherent to the profession of law enforcement or dispatchers in general, [but] out of our shift, there is one person who is fairly happily married, not for very long, meaning they are fairly newlyweds; two people that probably wish they could get divorced and can't figure out how; and myself, I'm on the edge of a divorce; and another one is divorced.

The relational consequences reported by communication officers, along with the physical and psychological costs, provide poignant confirmation of the claims of Hochschild (1983) and Van Maanen & Kunda (1989) who argued that emotional labor carries some serious negative repercussions for those who engage in it.

Given the emotional nature of their jobs, dispatchers have developed an array of both individual and communicative strategies to cope with the strain of emotional labor. Dispatchers individually engage in activities like escaping the room for a quick break, hitting the counter to physically release frustration, or rationalizing away difficult situations. Although individual strategies provide helpful means of coping and deserve mention, the focus of this study is communicative strategies. Not only do these more relational approaches help individuals cope with the demands of emotional labor, they seem to be important aspects of organizational community and thus contribute to the very structure of the organization.

One aspect of organizational life that shapes communication, and thus constitutes organizational structure, is the clear demarcation between the front and back stage regions. When a job produces emotional labor that takes place in a face to face manner, performers are fairly limited in the ways that they can deal with the strain that it produces. Communication officers, because they work over the telephone, have a wider variety of coping options available to them. In order to provide the proper context for the front and back stage communicative coping strategies used by dispatchers, it is first appropriate to discuss the differing emotion rules that guide interaction in each region.

Emotionalized Zones

Fineman (1996) argued that organizations have a number of emotionalized zones, each with different emotion rules. As has previously been discussed, when interacting in the front stage with callers or over the radio with officers, dispatchers attempt to achieve what Wharton and Erickson (1993) termed emotional neutrality. In their own words, dispatchers work to "take control" of each call by achieving an emotionally neutral demeanor. They suppress their emotions like sadness, fear, anger, and happiness, and consider this suppression a necessary component of "being professional." In addition, getting callers to "calm down" is an attempt to minimize emotional interaction.

As would be expected from Goffman's (1963) characterization of the back stage region, the emotionalized zone that is created among dispatchers or in nonradio conversation between dispatchers and law enforcement officers is more relaxed than is the emotional labor performed front stage on the phone or radio. Nonetheless, the preference for emotional neutrality, or at least for suppressing sadness or fear, still permeates the back stage region. With a few short observations of interactions in the communication center, it would be easy to conclude that the dispatchers do not empathize with callers at all. A dispatcher can, for example, be telling her partner about what she did on her day off, be interrupted for two minutes to take and dispatch a call from the spouse of someone having a heart attack, and then hang up and jump right back into her day off story. Even when dispatchers do seem to empathize with callers, they rarely voice this with their co-workers.

The preference for emotional neutrality in the back stage sometimes even turns to stringent enforcement. One dispatcher disclosed a story that captures the sense of emotional control that is expected. She had just dealt with a call in which a woman, about her age, had found her father after he committed suicide. The dispatcher mentioned her feelings about the call to a police officer who came to the Center, who then turned around and reported to a supervisor that the dispatcher was having a hard time. The supervisor then called the dispatcher to his office and recommended that she seek counseling. Of this incident, the dispatcher concluded:

> It wasn't, you know, I hadn't thought about seeking any counseling for that, because it was just a part of the job and I recognized it's bad and I think that it would be inhuman not to feel something, you know. This, I guess the problem that I had was discussing that with somebody around here where you couldn't feel that. You have to, you know, suck it in and take it all and not express any kind of regret or sorrow for anyone who calls in. And I think that, that doesn't seem natural to me, you know? I think that if I lose all of that, then, you know, where does that leave me as a human?

Although the supervisor's recommendation of counseling was intended to be helpful to the dispatcher, it worked to pathologize the use of emotional expressions within the organization. Notably, instead of offering his own support, or suggesting she share her feelings with other dispatchers, he recommended she seek help outside the organization. As the dispatcher pointed out, feeling something for certain callers is a normal part of being human, and especially, of working in a helping profession. Her experience of trying to share her sorrow at work and later regretting the effort demonstrates how a climate of emotional neutrality is perpetuated in this organization.

"Sucking it in," however strictly enforced for dealing with sorrow or fear, is not an act that is generally expected when the emotion being expressed back stage is either happiness or anger. Dispatchers express anger and frustration with officers and callers, help to energize each other during exciting calls, and share feelings of happiness or enjoyment about certain calls. However, they are careful, to maintain the boundary between the front and back stage regions. Although it is acceptable to make fun of callers and laugh at their situations back stage, dispatchers do not generally let this more relaxed environment leak into the front stage. I witnessed (and helped to provoke) the stringent protection of this boundary when a dispatcher, who had just disconnected from a call reporting a serious accident exploded at the other dispatchers and me because her caller could hear us laughing in the background.

Fineman (1996) argued that we need to focus our attention on these multiple and varied emotionalized zones that make up organizational culture. He suggested that safe settings provide places where employees can "drop their public mask, if they wish" (p. 556) and share "real feelings." Certainly, back stage at the Emergency Communication Center is a place where dispatchers drop the masks they use when dealing with callers, and the masks they use when communicating over the radio. As the following discussion of the ways in which dispatchers communicatively cope with emotional labor will demonstrate, a good deal of the kind of healthy catharsis that Fineman (1996) envisioned goes on back stage. That does not mean, however, that dispatchers are somehow completely unmasked in this setting. Safe back stage settings still have rules that govern the expression of emotion, and as the dispatcher who expressed sadness over a call discovered, violating these expectations is discouraged.

COPING AS COMMUNITY AT 911

Instead of openly challenging the stringent emotion rules, dispatchers rely heavily on the variety of ways they have developed to cope with the difficulty of emotional labor. Given the clear distinction between the emotionalized zones of the front stage and back stage regions at 911, it makes sense that the dispatchers have also developed separate coping zones for use in both the front stage and in the back stage regions of the emergency communication center. The more subtle and indirect coping strategies that dispatchers use in the front stage over the phone and radio are explored first.

Front Stage Communicative Strategies

The front stage coping strategies at 911 are those that are used directly with callers or with officers over the radio. Van Maanen and Kunda (1989) discussed how workers at Disneyland use covert strategies like the "seatbelt squeeze" to retaliate against problem guests, but Waldron (1994) urged scholars to examine the ways in which emotional laborers enact revenge against the public communicatively. The front stage strategies noted at 911 are examples of emotional laborers seeking revenge on either the public or on officers. Notably, the particular means of revenge or retaliation employed by dispatchers are, in fact, communicative in nature. Questioning the caller or putting the caller on hold, as well as not helping officers or asking them to standby, are four front stage ways that dispatchers communicatively cope with emotional labor.

Questioning.   Questioning is used as a means to indirectly communicate frustration to callers, especially those who make ridiculous requests. The story of the caller whose cat was stuck behind the water heater is one example:
"It's like 10:00 at night, she's now calling because she wants to take a shower and if the water heater fires up, it's gonna burn her cat. So this, "You said your cat had been behind the water heater all day, you know, why didn't you call someone then?"
Dispatchers are aware that this sort of questioning can be condescending, but as one dispatcher pointed out, there are times when "we really just want to say, or, or, at least give them a sense of how stupid they really sound."
Another dispatcher discussed the use of this coping technique and how it helps her to "feel better":

There are nights I'm like, "Why did you wait three hours to call us after this person was breaking into your house? Was there any particular reason why you didn't call us when your vehicle was hit and they drove off?" It's just, people are so stupid sometimes. And it's like, I feel like that is a fair question, even though that may be called badgering the reporting party. It's like, you know, "What reason did you have for not calling us when this was going on so we maybe could have done something?" And, you know, they usually don't have very good reasons. But I always feel better for at least having made them come up with one.

With the use of questioning, the dispatchers demonstrate the skillful use of an off-record, or indirect, face-threatening act (Brown & Levinson, 1978/1987). As was the case with Disney workers' use of the seatbelt squeeze (Van Maanen & Kunda, 1989), going off record by using the questioning strategy makes it more difficult for the dispatcher to be held accountable for the retaliation.

"Hold Please."   Another front stage coping strategy used by communication officers is a more direct form of retaliation than questioning. Because it is the dispatcher who controls the conversation, she or he can put difficult callers on hold. This technique might be used with a caller in a humorous situation, for exam-

ple, to prevent the dispatcher from inappropriately laughing on the phone. More commonly, however, it is the irate callers who get asked to, "hold please," while the communication officer takes some time to engage in an individual or back stage communicative coping strategy, like catching a breath or venting with co-workers. In addition to being a minibreak for the dispatcher, this technique may be used to serve the same function for the caller: "I put them on hold and say, "Oh my God. What am I gonna tell this person? How am I gonna make this person listen to me?" And I just sit there and think for awhile and then I pick up the phone and maybe at that point in time it was a break for this person, too. Maybe they've calmed down a little bit."

The extreme form of this technique, which can only be used with citizens who are not in emergency situations, is disconnecting completely from the call. Because dispatchers are permitted to disconnect from these types of uncooperative callers, this face-threatening act can be delivered on record (Brown & Levinson, 1978/1987). One dispatcher discussed how she uses this retaliation strategy, with an example of a caller who was overly irate over his car being impounded, "especially if they start using, um, expletives. I'll tell them, 'You don't need to use those, that type of language with me. It has nothing to do with me, I'm just telling you where it is.' And if they keep doing it, I'll tell them that 'I'm going to hang up now.' And I hang up."

This technique of putting the caller on hold or hanging up or both gives the dispatcher some control over the interaction that would not as readily exist in the face-to-face performance of emotional labor. In addition to these front stage strategies used with callers, dispatchers have also developed some front stage strategies for use in radio communication with law enforcement officers.

Not Helping.   When they have good relationships with officers, dispatchers often are willing to do them extra favors. Conversely, they punish those with whom they do not enjoy good relationships by not going out of their way to help them. As one dispatcher noted: "I think there's a little bit, a little bit of difference in if you're dealing with an officer who always treats you professionally as opposed to somebody who doesn't. You're, you don't really play favorites, you can't really play favorites, but you're more apt to help them out like in a way."

For example, dispatchers have the power to enforce the use of the 10-code system over the radio, and will sometimes feign a lack of understanding of officers' messages that do not conform to the system. One dispatcher's comments evidenced an understanding of the power of this strategy

> We will make you or break you, you know. I mean, we can make 'em stammer and stutter and not know what exactly or how to ask for something on the radio, and yet, we can know that they're having a problem and intercept it.

This unwillingness on the part of the dispatcher to help officers who are having difficulty is a particularly skillful off-record retaliation strategy because the dispatcher merely appears to be following proper procedure. Because offending officers do not know what is going on back stage at 911, they are not in a position to complain about dispatchers not helping or about being asked to standby.

"Standby." An officer who speaks to a dispatcher rudely over the radio is said to be "getting pissy," a violation that provokes a similar response to the hold please strategy used with callers. Dispatchers who are angry with police officers often ask them to standby when making unrealistic requests, as in the case when officers are, for example, "out there wanting to piddle around on the computer because they're curious about something, you know, or something that does not immediately affect any kind of investigation they are doing." Of course, the use of this front stage retaliation strategy with officers is confined to nonemergency situations. Like the hold please strategy that is used with callers, the standby strategy that is used with officers also serves as somewhat of an escape or route to back stage.

Although other studies of emotional labor have reported employees' various means of retaliating on the public to cope with the difficulty of emotional labor, they have not focused specifically on ways of doing this communicatively. Highlighting the front stage strategies that dispatchers use with both callers and officers demonstrates the centrality of communication in coping with emotional labor. In addition to the gap in our knowledge of front stage communicative coping, as Fineman (1996) pointed out, examinations of back stage emotionalized zones have not had a prominent place in the literature on emotional labor. Although several organizational studies have examined back stage contexts, they have not tended to focus centrally on the role of emotion, or on coping with emotional labor. The next section offers an attempt at combining these interests.

Back Stage Communicative Strategies

The fact that 911 operators do their emotional labor over the phone provides for some interesting contrasts between front stage and back stage communication. Dispatchers can, for example, make faces at their partners or complete other tasks back stage while holding an emotionally neutral front stage conversation with a caller. There are several communicative coping strategies that provide back stage relief from the demands of emotional labor. Some of these coping strategies are found outside of the organization, such as professional counseling or seeking support from friends and family members. The communicative strategies that are more germane to the present study, however, are those that are used at work, and that therefore help to constitute community in the organization. Teamwork and social support, retaliation against the officers, "bitching," and humor are all examples of these types of communicative strategies.

Teamwork and Social Support. Of the four types of social support that House (1981) delineated, workers at the Emergency Communication Center seem to provide each other with both emotional and instrumental support for coping with emotional labor. Instrumental support, in particular, is shared through teamwork. Dispatchers agree that they could not do their jobs very effectively without working as a team. Partners regularly listen to each others' calls, and as one dispatcher joked, "I think you have to have some sense of nosiness about you" to do this job well. This nosiness enables all of the dispatchers to know what their co-workers are doing and allows them to jump in and help each other out. For example, if one dispatcher is on the phone, getting information from a caller, the other will often intercept radio traffic and perhaps relay information to an officer who is handling that call.

Once they have worked together for a while, shifts develop patterns of interacting and get to know each others' work styles. One supervisor also spoke specifically about how well the people on her shift have worked together over the years, "It was always the three of us together, and it was, we were like a clock. It was kind of like tick and tock. And, we always knew what the other was thinking or doing or saying and if they asked for this, this one had already done it and, you know, vice-versa."

In some ways, this sense of teamwork may relieve the sense of personal responsibility for emotional labor. When dispatchers work together on calls, and share the burdens of emotional labor, they perhaps acknowledge or even create the sense of "being in this together." This group solidarity that comes with shared tasks is also due to the development of supportive relationships among co-workers.

Inevitably, when asked about the best aspects of the job, the vast majority of dispatchers said, "the people." Even those who do not count each other as friends outside of work attempt to create good rapport with their co-workers during their shifts. The role of social support in reducing work-related stress is well documented (e.g., Albrecht & Adelman, 1987; House, 1981). Ray (1987) pointed out that supportive communication with co-workers tends to buffer work stress. On the other hand, people who are socially isolated at work can suffer negative psychological consequences (Albrecht & Adelman, 1987), as seems to be the case with one dispatcher who complained of a lack of social support from her co-workers. Indeed, both she and others described her as socially isolated. Although she claimed that she tried to just "do her job," she knew that this isolation had taken its toll on her. By being cut off from an important communicative means of coping, this dispatcher was denied some important buffers against the negative repercussions of emotional labor. Perhaps this is at least part of the reason why she reported suffering from the largest share of the physical, psychological, and relational problems that come with emotional labor at 911.

Although the social support of friends and family is also important, it is the support provided by work relationships among dispatchers that contributes most visibly to the culture of the organization. Paradoxically, although dispatchers enjoy teamwork and social support among their co-workers, Van Maanen and Kunda (1989) suggested that close interaction with co-workers provides increased emotional labor requirements. At 911, this paradox was especially visible in the case of interaction with police officers, which provides both fun and frustration for dispatchers.

In addition to teamwork and supportive relationships among dispatchers, dispatchers enjoy the rapport they have built with law enforcement officers. Especially during slow times on the county side, officers and dispatchers sometimes call each other to chat privately, because they can not communicate informally over the radio. One night, on the county side, a deputy called the dispatcher to remind her that it was another deputy's last night "on the road" before his promotion to Sergeant, and asked her to "work out something to mess with him. Be thinking about a trick, something big, like we've been in an accident or something," he suggested.

Unfortunately, during the course of this study, the administration began discouraging officers from being in the dispatch room unless they could show they had official business there. This "crack down" was perceived by dispatchers to be quite a loss to the possibility of teamwork with officers. When rapport with officers instead breaks down due to the actions of the officers and not administrative policy, dispatchers use their available means of power to retaliate against offending parties.

Retaliation Against Officers. More than one dispatcher told me a story about a time when a training officer asked them to give a rookie police officer some advice. They both said, "Be nice to your dispatcher." If officers fail to do this by getting pissy on the radio, as has previously been discussed, dispatchers may choose to retaliate communicatively in the front stage by choosing not to help them out or by making them standby. One dispatcher said she prefers to confront the officer more directly, but off of the front stage radio, by calling the officer on the cellular phone and saying, "Listen, Buddy...." " Although it is important to remain professional over the radio, they have also developed some behind the scenes means of recourse for poor treatment by officers. Not only do the behind the scenes means of retaliation seem to be the most common choice for coping with pissy officers, the group collaboration that is needed to enact this particular strategy serves as a means of bonding dispatchers to one another, which also serves as a coping strategy.

One group means of getting even with officers was described similarly by several dispatchers, "If an officer gives us a hard time, we'll go, 'Well, you're gonna get barking dog calls the rest of the night.'" When a "bad call," like a noise complaint about a barking dog comes in and the officer assigned to that district is on another call, the dispatcher is permitted the discretion to choose what other officer to send.

Another means of collaboratively and communicatively retaliating against offending officers is described by one dispatcher as follows:

> There are some officers you just have to laugh at because they take themselves so seriously, that, you know, you can't help but laugh at people like that. Um, some

of them get on our nerves sometimes, and I guess to alleviate that then again we'll laugh at how they make a request or, or how demanding this person is and, you know … kind of make a running joke out of it the rest of the night kind of thing. You know, that way we don't risk the, the, uh, chance of snapping at 'em on the radio and saying we'd, uh, we'd regret later.

These various forms of the back stage coping strategy of retaliation against officers give the dispatchers some power and help them to continue dealing professionally with offending officers. This form of retaliating against officers is often used in conjunction with some amount of complaining, or bitching about the officers among dispatchers, which is the strategy that is described next.

Bitching. Another back stage coping strategy that pervades the culture of the emergency communication center is bitching or venting to other dispatchers about interactions with both callers and officers. As one dispatcher disclosed, after disconnecting from a frustrating call, dispatchers like to "have a little bitch session back and forth and we maybe play the tape back for the other person who is sitting next to us." Putnam and Mumby (1993) defined bitching as "a social construction that encompasses complaining, gossiping, joking, and friendly conversation" (p. 46). Although the dispatchers engaged in all of these activities, they seemed to define bitching more specifically as complaining.

Because they "know it's gonna stay there," dispatchers feel the freedom to "try to unload or vent, but, uh, and, you know, you tell it like you mean, you know, you bad mouth people, talk about your callers sometimes, but it's just human." These sort of bitch sessions usually arise from one dispatcher's spontaneous comment but tend to spiral into larger interactions. As one dispatcher pointed out, "If we have a real irritating call, I think that's another way we blow off steam, is that we tell others about it. Then it becomes fish stories. 'Oh, I had one!'"

Bitching among secretaries is discussed by Pringle (1988) as a means of subverting and resisting managerial conceptions of organizational rationality, and by Putnam and Mumby (1993) as a way of resisting emotional labor. Bitching is a key communicative strategy that dispatchers use to cope with and even resist emotional labor. As does the previous strategy of retaliation against officers, this type of bitching often becomes a source of humorous banter among dispatchers.

Humor. Far and away, humor seems to be the most relied on communication strategy for coping with emotional labor at 911. In general, humor seems to be combined quite often with all of the back stage communicative coping strategies. Humor at 911 goes beyond what might be considered typical officer banter, however. 911 humor involves dispatchers coping by joking together about situations that they know other people would not find funny. Like medical students who tell grotesque cadaver stories to other insiders taking anatomy lab (Hafferty, 1988), dispatchers tell stories that define who counts as an insider. Although I was often privy to this back stage humor, one dispatcher was reluctant to share any funny stories with me because, he said, "it's kinda sacred." In declining, he explained to me that "it's just that it sounds different. And, I don't know how you'll take it and I, I don't want to insult anybody. And that, it, it's kind of insulting humor." Dispatchers make fun of each other, of officers, of the administration, and of callers because they know that "it's gonna stay there," in the room. As Meyer (1991, 1997) demonstrated, sharing humorous stories provides a sense of cohesiveness and unity within organizations. This certainly seems to be the case at the Emergency Communication Center. Thus, an awareness of the problems with retelling dispatch jokes out of context is wise, because, as one dispatcher pointed out, they "joke about a lot of things that really aren't funny, but you turn them into a joke."

One such example that more than one person related to me, involves a humorous recollection by one dispatcher of a horrific 911 call from a man who wanted to know the name of a local funeral home:

So I gave him the name of the funeral home. And a little later the funeral home called [the police] and said, "Come out here." And he'd—she had died the week before. He'd beat her and before she was dead he made a wooden box and put it in metal, you know those metal sheds. They have a little metal shed, um, outside of his trailer. He, he, he made a little, basically a little coffin and she died when she was in there, but he was calling for a funeral home because she started to leak and it was summertime. And in a metal shed in a wooden box made of plywood, um, you know, instead of like Jack-in-the-box, you know, she was Judy-in-a-box.

After relating this story, the dispatcher pointed out that their 911 humor serves to help them "not to think about the reality of the situation." Perhaps this humor allows the creation of the sense of detachment that some have argued is necessary for coping with the emotional labor that comes with human service work (e.g., Miller, Birkholt, Scott, & Stage, 1995; Miller, Stiff, & Ellis, 1988).

The humorous stories that are told and retold among co-workers also seem to reflect the dispatchers' shared sense of organizational history. An illustration of this shared humor and history comes from a story that two dispatchers separately shared with me about a memorable and bizarre call that one claims was even mentioned on Paul Harvey's radio show, "The Rest of the Story." One dispatcher described the initial call he took from the woman reporting the unusual situation as follows:

Her husband was making the rounds of emptying trash out at the Lake at one of the, at like, Rock Haven Park. He heard this yelling coming from an outhouse. He said, "I couldn't figure out what it was." At first, she said that it was a woman yelling. And so I send officers out there. And so, Johnson gets out there, he's looking around and looking in the women's bathroom and there's nothing there. So he goes into the men's bathroom and it's quiet for a long time. He finally gets on the air and says, "We've got a guy down in it."

About this same situation, another dispatcher was a bit more graphic; his details had the dispatchers, the firefighters, and the deputies all laughing, but trying to help this man:

> I mean, it was a pathetic scene, I mean, the guy was just covered. He had it all over everywhere. He's lucky he lived, because of all the chemical stuff they put in there. And it wasn't really that full, and that was the only thing that saved him ... you've got a picture of these little porta johns and, inside, he just slung it all over the walls and got it all over and there was no way he could get a grip. And, like I said, he was just covered head to toe.

Even as they laughed, the man was rescued from his dangerous situation. Shared humor as a back stage coping strategy does not seem to impede their work and, in fact, dispatchers insist that having a sense of humor is a necessary quality for job success. As one dispatcher argued, "You gotta be able to turn things into interesting or amusing or funny, otherwise it would drive you nuts." The ability to joke about tragic situations helps the individuals from getting "nuts," and having people around who are witty also clearly helps the group to relieve the collective burden of emotional labor. Waldron (1994) suggested that humorous storytelling at work enlivens otherwise routine activities, which is certainly the case at 911. This use of humor as a means of coping allows dispatchers to become personally engaged back stage even though they are somewhat emotionally disengaged with callers, which is a definite benefit of the separation between the front and back stage regions. Humorous stories that are shared with co-workers create a banter that might continue for a whole shift, or as in the case with "Judy-in-a-box," for the duration of an entire investigation. And like Judy, if repeated often enough, the distinctive language of a humorous story can sometimes make its way into the group's sense of history and help to shape the culture of the organization (Meyer, 1997), including shaping the feeling rules to which members will be held accountable (Hafferty, 1988). More than any of the other coping strategies, the use of humor seems to encapsulate what it means to work at the emergency communication center.

SUMMARY AND DISCUSSION

Being a successful dispatcher means not only learning how to perform the technical tasks required, but also learning how to cope with the demands of emotional labor. Although dispatchers do enact various means of individual coping, this case study demonstrates the importance of coping as a community effort. Through communication, dispatchers share the burden of emotional labor with such backstage strategies as humor, bitching, retaliation against officers, and teamwork and social support. They also assert some control over their enactment of emotional labor by employing some front stage means of coping. Through the questioning, hold-please, not-helping, and standby strategies, dispatchers communicatively retaliate against callers and officers and thus diminish their own frustration while still attaining the emotional neutrality that their organizational community supports and enforces.

This case study offers the possibility to start new conversations in the areas of emotional labor, organizational theory, and the social construction of community. First, this examination of both the front stage and back stage regions at 911 provides a view of emotion and organization that places communication as central to coping with emotional labor. This case also demonstrates the role of emotion in the social construction of organization. Examining emotion rules and shared emotional resources provides another application of the structuration of organization. That dispatchers choose to cope with rather than challenge the culture of emotional neutrality speaks to the strength and power of socially constructed organization.

Wouters (1989) argued that the elimination of emotional labor is an unrealistic and unattractive possibility, and this certainly seems the case at 911. A better approach would be to broaden the ways we think about emotional labor, which would involve understanding the variety of creative ways that people cope and the outlets that they find to display emotion. Instead of falling into the common trap of assuming that emotional labor is inherently alienating and harmful, this case study calls us to further examine the ways that coping with its demands can constitute community. In discussing coping, it is important to reassert that I am not simply arguing that individuals must be pressed to develop the skills necessary to cope with emotional labor. As Fineman (1996) argued, this sort of individualistic approach unduly burdens individual employees, which has been the tendency of research efforts in the area of coping with job stress. Newton (1995) noted that instead of viewing coping with stress as an organizational or communal responsibility, organizational theory and practice has traditionally characterized it as an individual and privatized problem. Consequently, the responsibility for stress management rests with individual employees, rather than being dealt with at the organizational level. By assuming a more community-oriented approach to coping with emotional labor, this chapter attempts to avoid the sort of individual blame game that functions to hide the possibility of communal solutions.

Highlighting the ways in which employees enjoy coping with emotional labor should not lead practitioners or scholars of organizational communication to dismiss the harmful aspects of laboring emotionally. Although the dispatchers have creatively found ways to cope, some of their supervisors have not been so open to creativity. Not only have some not done much to help, others have actively worked against dispatchers' efforts to create healthy community. The new policy to keep officers out of the dispatch room is one such example. Given that radio interaction is characterized by emotional neutrality and brief, codified messages, the possibility of developing rapport with officers is in jeopardy under this new policy. Although many veteran officers seem willing to resist the rules by sneaking in to the Emergency Communication Center to visit their friends, it is doubtful that rookie officers and dispatchers will develop the kind of supportive relationships that help employees in both jobs buffer the effects of emotional labor.

The availability of counseling for dispatchers through an employee assistance program is an encouraging sign of support for the health of employees. However, when used to try to "cure" employees of experiencing emotion, or as an attempt to keep healthy emotional expression away from the workplace, offers of counseling are perhaps more repressive than empowering. The recognition that coping with emotional labor is a social and community-building function, rather than an individual responsibility, is crucial in the effort to decrease its harmful effects.

This case study also calls us to consider the paradox of community. In the wake of natural disasters, community members often bind together to help their neighbors. News accounts of a recent deadly tornado in Alabama, for example, contained multiple references to the "good coming out of the bad," and produced reports of the extraordinary kindnesses demonstrated by both neighbors and complete strangers. Likewise to the responses in Alabama, sharing the burdens of emotional labor at 911 encourages a sense of organizational community that makes being a dispatcher fun and interesting. Thus, emotional labor at 911 includes this irony: What makes emergency communication work difficult and harmful is also what facilitates the construction of community. As members continuously work to create and recreate organization, they produce and reproduce rules that govern emotional labor. Dispatchers at University City create an organizational community, in part, by coping together with emotional labor. Clearly, their easy access to the back stage region facilitates their ability to create a healthy coping community. While some emotion rules may be restrictive to individual members, they also aid in the development of a civil organizational community.

The lessons learned through the creation of healthy and civil organizational community can be tentatively translated to other arenas of community interaction. The paradox of community at 911, that people tend to bind together when facing adversity, is certainly not a new idea, although its implications for communication and community have been under theorized and studied. Scholars of communication would do well to focus on the roles of communication, emotion, and coping as sites of the growing edges of community.

In the seemingly most rationalistic of situations, such as University City 911 with its expectation of emotional neutrality, aspects of human experience that connect people occur in the creation of emotion in and through communication. Community, in its broadest sense, is a rather abstract notion. Although we sometimes speak of "the community" in concrete ways, using it as a noun, it is better expressed as a verb. As Giddens (1979) reminded us, social structures do not have goals or intentions, only people do. It is in communication that the structure of community is produced and reproduced. Just as dispatchers at 911 create their sense of place in the broader community through their interaction with each other and with citizens, so do we in our own corners of the world. This case study offers a look at University City 911's corner, and shows some of the rich and diverse ways that communication is central to the creation of community.

Members of the broader community who have come to rely on accessing emergency services through 911 depend on the dispatchers' doing of emotional labor, although its role in emergency work is not as visible as the role of the flashing lights and sirens that signify the arrival of help at the scene. That the dispatcher managed her or his emotions as well as those of the caller typically goes unnoticed, but is nevertheless crucial to the community's ability to work together to provide emergency services. Dispatchers' willingness to undergo some personal harm for emotional labor demonstrates a sort of altruism and commitment to helping make University City a safe community. By focusing on the ways that 911 dispatchers communicatively cope with emotional labor, this chapter attempts to demonstrate the difficulty and value of emotional labor, at the same time highlighting the centrality of communication in fostering healthy organizational community. It is, at least partially, this construction of community through coping with emotional labor, by 911 dispatchers, that makes civility possible in the wider community of University City.

REFERENCES

Albas, C., & Albas, D. (1988). Emotion work and emotion rules: The case of exams. *Qualitative Sociology, 11*, 259–274.

Albrecht, T., & Adelman, M. (1987). *Communicating social support.* Beverly Hills, CA: Sage.

Blumer, H. (1969). *Symbolic interactionism.* Berkeley, CA: University of California Press.

Boden, D. (1994). *The business of talk: Organizations in action.* Cambridge, MA: Polity Press.

Brown, P., & Levinson, S. C. (1987). *Politeness: Some universals in language usage.* Cambridge: Cambridge University Press. (Original work published in 1978).

Darwin, C. (1955). *The expression of emotions in man and animals.* New York: Philosophical Library. (Original work published in 1872).

Denzin, N. K. (1970). *The research act: A theoretical introduction to sociological methods.* New York: McGraw-Hill.

Denzin, N. K. (1984). *On understanding emotion.* San Francisco: Jossey-Bass.

Dewey, J. (1958). *Experience and nature.* NY: Dover Publications. (Original work published in 1916)

Fiebig, G. V., & Kramer, M. W. (1996). *The process of emotions in organizational communication.* Paper presented at the annual meeting of the Speech Communication Association, San Diego, CA.

Fineman, S. (1996). Emotion and organizing. In S. R. Clegg, C. Hardy, & W. R. Nord (Eds.), *Handbook of organization studies* (pp. 543–564). Thousand Oaks, CA: Sage.

Freud, S. (1911). Formulations on the two principles of mental functioning. In J. Strachey (Ed.) *Standard Edition, 12* (pp. 213–226). London: Hogarth Press.

Giddens, A. (1979). *Central problems in social theory: Action, structure, and contradiction in social analysis.* Berkeley, CA: University of California Press.

Goffman, E. (1959). *The presentation of self in everyday life.* New York: Doubleday.

Goffman, E. (1963). *Behavior in public places.* New York: Free Press of Glencoe.

Hafferty, F. W. (1988). Cadaver stories and the emotional socialization of medical students. *Journal of Health and Social Behavior, 29*, 344–356.

Harré, R. (1986). An outline of the social constructionist viewpoint. In R. Harré (Ed.), *The social construction of emotions* (pp. 2–14). New York: Basil Blackwell.

Hochschild, A. R. (1979). Emotion work, feeling rules, and social structure. *American Journal of Sociology, 85*, 551–575.

Hochschild, A. R. (1983). *The managed heart: Commercialization of human feeling.* Berkeley, CA: University of California Press.

House, J. S. (1981). *Work stress and social support.* Reading, MA: Addison-Wesley.

James, N. (1989). Emotional labour: Skill and work in the regulation of feelings. *Sociological Review, 37,* 15–42.

James, N. (1993). Divisions of emotional labour: Disclosure and cancer. In S. Fineman (Ed.), *Emotion in organizations* (pp. 94–117). Thousand Oaks, CA: Sage.

Kassing, J. W. (1995, April). *"Don't take it out on me!": Examining the suppression, displacement, and direct communication of emotional messages in the organization.* Paper presented at the annual meeting of the Central States Communication Association, Indianapolis, IN.

Leeds-Hurwitz, W. (1995). Introducing social approaches. In W. Leeds-Hurwitz (Ed.) *Social approaches to communication* (pp. 3–20). New York: Guilford.

Maslach, C. (1982). *Burnout: The cost of caring.* Englewood Cliffs, NJ: Prentice-Hall.

Merriam, S. B. (1988). *Case study research in education: A qualitative approach.* San Francisco: Jossey-Bass.

Meyer, J. C. (1991). *Values and narratives in organizational messages.* Unpublished doctoral dissertation, University of Kansas, Lawrence, KS.

Meyer, J. C. (1997). Humor in member narratives: Uniting and dividing at work. *Western Journal of Communication, 61,* 188–208.

Miller, K., Birkholt, M., Scott, C., & Stage, C. (1995). Empathy and burnout in human service work: An extension of a communication model. *Communication Research, 22,* 123–147.

Miller, K. J., Stiff, J. B., & Ellis, B. H. (1988). Communication and empathy as precursors to burnout among human service workers. *Communication Monographs, 55,* 250–265.

Mishler, E. G. (1986). *Research interviewing: Context and narrative.* Cambridge, MA: Harvard University Press.

Morris, J. A., & Feldman, D. C. (1996). The dimensions, antecedents, and consequences of emotional labor. *Academy of Management Review, 21,* 986–1010.

Mumby, D. K., & Putnam, L. L. (1990). The politics of emotion: A feminist reading of bounded rationality. *Academy of Management Review, 17,* 465–486.

Newton, T. (1995). *Managing stress: Emotion and power at work.* Thousand Oaks, CA: Sage.

Noe, J. M. (1995). *A communication rules perspective of emotional expression: An ethnography of impression management in an emergency medical facility.* Unpublished doctoral dissertation, University of Kansas, Lawrence.

Pacanowsky, M., & O'Donnell-Trujillo, N. (1983). Organizational communication as cultural performance. *Western Journal of Speech Communication, 46,* 115–130.

Pringle, R. (1988). *Secretaries talk.* London: Verso.

Putnam, L. L., & Mumby, D. K. (1993). Organizations, emotion, and the myth of rationality. In S. Fineman (Ed.), *Emotion in Organizations* (pp. 36–57). Thousand Oaks, CA: Sage.

Rafaeli, A. (1989). When cashiers meet customers: An analysis of the role of supermarket cashiers. *Academy of Management Journal, 32,* 245–273.

Rafaeli, A. & Sutton, R. I. (1987). Expression of emotion as part of the work role. *Academy of Management Review, 12,* 23–37.

Rafaeli, A. & Sutton, R. I. (1990). Busy stores and demanding customers: How do they affect the display of positive emotion? *Academy of Management Journal, 33,* 623–637.

Rafaeli, A. & Sutton, R. I. (1991). Emotional contrast strategies as means of social influence: Lessons from criminal interrogators and bill collectors. *Academy of Management Journal, 34,* 749–775.

Ray, E. B. (1987). Supportive relationships and occupational stress in the workplace. In T. Albrecht & M. Adelman, M. (Eds.), *Communicating social support* (pp. 172–191). Beverly Hills, CA: Sage.

Rorty, R. (1989). *Contingency, irony, and solidarity*. Cambridge: Cambridge University Press.

Sarbin, T. R. (1986). Emotion and act: Roles and rhetoric. In R. Harré (Ed.), *The social construction of emotion* (pp. 83–97). New York: Basil Blackwell.

Shott, S. (1979). Emotion and social life: A symbolic interactionist analysis. *American Journal of Sociology, 84*, 1317–1334.

Shuler, S. (1997). *Emotion 911: Communication And Emotion At A County Emergency Communication Center*. Unpublished doctoral dissertation, University of Kansas, Lawrence, KS.

Silverman, D. (1989). Six rules of qualitative research: A post-romantic argument. *Symbolic Interaction, 12*, 215–230.

Stenross, B., & Kleinman, S. (1989). The highs and lows of emotional labor: Detectives encounters with criminals and victims. *Journal of Contemporary Ethnography, 17*, 435–452.

Strauss, A., & Corbin, J. (1990). *Basics of qualitative research: Grounded theory procedures and techniques*. Newbury Park, CA: Sage.

Sutton, R. I. (1991). Maintaining norms about expressed emotions: The case of bill collectors. *Administrative Science Quarterly, 36*, 245–268.

Sutton, R. I., & Rafaeli, A. (1988). Untangling the relationship between displayed emotion and organizational sales: The case of convenience stores. *Academy of Management Journal, 31*, 461–487.

Sypher, B. D. (1997). *Case studies in organizational communication 2*. New York: Guilford Press.

Tolich, M. B. (1993). Alienating and liberating emotions at work: Supermarket clerks; performance of customer service. *Journal of Contemporary Ethnography, 22*, 361–381.

Van Maanen, J., & Kunda, G. (1989). "Real feelings": Emotional expression and organizational culture. *Research in Organizational Behavior, 11*, 43–103.

Waldron, V. R., & Krone, K. J. (1991). The experience and expression of emotion in the workplace: A study of a corrections organization. *Management Communication Quarterly, 4*, 287–309.

Waldron, V. R. (1994). Once more, with feeling: Reconsidering the role of emotion in work. In S. A. Deetz (Ed.), *Communication yearbook 17* (pp. 388–416). Thousand Oaks, CA: Sage.

Wharton, A. S., & Erickson, R. J. (1993). Managing emotions on the job and at home: Understanding the consequences of multiple emotional roles. *Academy of Management Review, 18*, 457–486.

Witkin, G. (1996, June 17). "This is 911: Please hold." *U.S. News and World Report, 120*, 30–38.

Wouters, C. (1989). The sociology of emotions and flight attendants: Hochschild's *Managed Heart*. *Theory, Culture and Society, 6*, 95–123.

Yin, R. K. (1994). *Case study research: Design and methods* (2nd ed.) Thousand Oaks, CA: Sage.

Zuckerman, M. (1988). Behavior and biology: Research on sensation seeking and reactions to media. In L. Donohew, H. E. Sypher & E. T. Higgins (Eds.), *Communication, social cognition, and affect* (pp. 173–194). Hillsdale, NJ: Lawrence Erlbaum Associates.

Zurcher, L. A. (1982). The staging of emotion: A dramaturgical analysis. *Symbolic Interaction, 5*, 1–22.

5

Feminist Organizing and the Construction of "Alternative" Community

Karen Lee Ashcraft
University of Utah

Feminist perspectives pose increasingly influential critiques of traditional organizational community. Much of this important work exposes and critiques the gendered character of modern organizations that normalize patriarchal orientations to community. However, few communication scholars have published accounts that clarify what it might look like to actually organize differently (Buzzanell, 1995). By further engaging the practice of feminist community, communication scholars can complement critique with the study of viable alternatives. Lessons gleaned from feminist organization can inform and transform traditional ways of thinking and doing community; concurrently, they can illuminate obstacles and tensions that constrain "alternative" organizing.

Across various disciplines, studies of feminist organizing tend to highlight key pressures that eventually compromise the integrity of feminist practice. Few scholars have examined how members cope with these antagonistic forces at the level of daily interaction (Morgen, 1990). The tactics through which members manage the tensions of feminist organizing are ripe for exploration, and communication scholars are particularly equipped to investigate them. Ultimately, the study of how alternative visions of community can be constructed through discourse may challenge mainstream organization theory and practice with emancipatory alternatives.

This chapter moves a step in that direction by exploring the efforts of one feminist community to translate ideology into practice. More specifically, the chapter examines a feminist ethic of organizational communication through which members sought to preserve their pledge to empowering community. The first section of the chapter evaluates traditional conceptions of feminist community and advances a different communicative approach. The second section analyzes the situated, semioppositional discourse of one feminist community. Finally, the third section assesses implicit member assumptions about competent organizational communication and considers the implications of my analysis for the theory and practice of communication and alternative community.

CREATION FROM CONTRADICTION: CONCEPTIONS OF FEMINIST COMMUNITY

Traditional Views of Feminist Organizing

The precise features that distinguish feminist communities are contested. This chapter takes interest in service organizations that confront more traditional forms of organizing with what members perceive as feminist alternatives. The pursuit of alternatives follows feminist critiques of the gendered logic of many Western workplaces. For example, such entrenched organizational features as hierarchical relationships (e.g., Acker, 1990; Ferguson, 1984); sexual harassment (e.g., Bingham, 1994; Clair, 1993; Gutek, 1989; Strine, 1992; Taylor & Conrad, 1992); the strict separation of public and private (e.g., Acker, 1990; Ferguson, 1984; J. Martin, 1990; Mills & Chiaramonte, 1991; Morgen, 1983; Mumby & Putnam, 1992); and male-biased norms of expression, conflict, decision making, self-promotion, and humor (e.g., Loden, 1985; Marshall, 1993; Murphy & Zorn, 1996). Feminist communities that challenge these and other oppressive conditions seek oppositional structures and practices that reflect feminist empowerment ideology (Acker, 1995; Morgen, 1990; Rodriguez, 1988; Schlesinger & Bart, 1982; Spalter-Roth & Schreiber, 1995).

In general, feminist use of the term *empowerment* entails at least two interrelated meanings: the development of individual autonomy to enhance a woman's consciousness of, and resistance to, gendered oppression (Ferraro, 1981; Leidner, 1991; Morgen, 1990; Rodriguez, 1988); and the development of mutually influential relationships (Ahrens, 1980; Maguire & Mohtar, 1994; Mansbridge, 1984; Mueller, 1995; Riger, 1994; Rodriguez, 1988). To cultivate empowerment, feminist communities often adopt such strategies as offering "options, not advice" to clients, minimizing rules that restrict personal choice, implementing consensual decision making or other forums for member participation, and distributing knowledge and authority widely among members (Ferree & Martin, 1995). Generally understood as promoting self-reliance in the service of interdependent relations, feminist empowerment ideology permeates the missions and structural choices of most feminist communities. It fuels the drive toward egalitarian relations.

Although alternative organizing may assume various forms, most scholars connect feminist patterns of doing and being to egalitarian, democratic, or participatory templates (Harvey, 1985; Schechter, 1982; Staggenborg, 1989). Certainly, egalitarian models of community are not the exclusive terrain of feminists, but they assume feminist flavor when applied to confront and correct an enduring legacy of organizational injustice toward women. Feminist scholars debate the necessity, intensity, and purity of the connection between egalitarian organizing and feminist community. Some authors staunchly advocate collective models that abolish hierarchy as antifeminist and maximize full-member participation through shared authority (e.g., Ferguson, 1987; Pahl, 1985; Peterson & Bond, 1985; Tierney, 1982). Others adopt a more inclusive, pluralistic approach concerned with extracting the best from multiple organizational models (Eisenstein, 1995; Leidner, 1991; Mansbridge, 1984; Martin, 1990; Riger, 1994; Ristock, 1990; Sirianni, 1984). Despite increasing summons for such pluralist perspectives, few have actually theorized "impure" feminist forms (Gottfried & Weiss, 1994; Mayer, 1995). The bulk of current research accents a fundamental contradiction of feminist community: a persistent pull between the ideals of feminist empowerment ideology and the practical demands of organizing. As I explain next, much of this scholarship serves to substantiate myriad forces that impede empowering feminist community.

Interpreting the Ideology–Practice Relationship

Practical barriers to the enactment of egalitarian feminist alternatives arise from complex intersections of external and internal pressures. Increasing formalization constitutes one key force. Feminist communities may develop formal structures in an effort to prove the organization's legitimacy to relevant external agencies (e.g., Ahrens, 1980; Bart, 1987; Mueller, 1995; Reinelt, 1994, 1995; Ristock, 1990). Formal hierarchy may also accompany choices regarding growth and change (Riger, 1994). For example, many domestic violence shelters formalize in an effort to systematize and expand client services (Staggenborg, 1988). Although the growth of increasing hierarchy and professionalization typifies the development of traditional Western organizations (Edwards, 1979; Gray & Ariss, 1985; Mintzberg, 1994), such features often pose serious ideological dilemmas for members of feminist communities, threatening their ability to define their community as oppositional (Maguire & Mohtar, 1994). Many scholars concur that formalization subverts the potential for egalitarian relationships (e.g., Mansbridge, 1973; Morgen, 1990). Although members may agree to treat formal distinctions as merely "on paper" or "in name only," even conscientious moves to preserve equality are difficult to sustain in the midst of formal hierarchy (Newman, 1980). Formal distinctions between staff and volunteers endanger egalitarian relations with practical differences in salary, experience, influence, and knowledge that may squelch self-direction and dissent from subordinate members (e.g., Mueller, 1995; Ristock, 1990). Member–client relationships also tend to suffer as "the institutional structure that puts some people in the position to empower undermines the act of empowerment" (Riger, 1994, p. 293). Community rules that apply only to client members provide one example of this problem (Maguire & Mohtar, 1994; Murray, 1988).

Certainly, feminist communities are not inherently destined for formalization. And should formal systems develop, they may be strategically employed to name and minimize some informal inequities (Morgen, 1990; Riger, 1994). However, as countless organizational studies caution, formal structures do not necessarily eradicate informal communication networks and corresponding hierarchies (e.g., Freeman, 1972–1973). Several mainstream and feminist scholars mark the potency of informal power structures, based on such personal attributes as communicative skill, personality, expertise, and physical appearance (Donnellon, 1993; Gottfried & Weiss, 1994; Mansbridge, 1973, 1984; Newman, 1980; Pfeffer, 1992; Raven, 1993; Ristock, 1990; Rodriguez, 1988; Zaremba, 1988). Informal ideological hierarchy can also undermine egalitarian relations: Although homogeneity of belief enables control in many egalitarian communities (e.g., Freeman, 1972–1973; Rodriguez, 1988; Rothschild-Whitt, 1979), this focus on similarity may elevate particular feminist views, identities, and forms of oppression over others (Gottfried & Weiss, 1994; Mansbridge 1986; Riger, 1994). Ideological hierarchy tends to suppress diverse perspectives and disagreement, ultimately intensifying and personalizing conflict (Barker, 1987; Mueller, 1995; Morgen, 1988, 1990; Reinelt, 1995; Sealander & Smith, 1986). Moreover, informal ideological power structures may pose a new qualification to formal selection and evaluation criteria: the "good feminist" resume (Leidner, 1991; Ristock, 1990). With such implicit conditions of eligibility, members may experience pressure to fit a feminist "script" for interaction; that is, tacit rules may sketch confining boundaries of appropriate communication topics and styles for "real" feminists or "empowered" battered women (Ferraro, 1981, 1983; Murray, 1988).

Most scholars emphasize how the formal and informal pressures reviewed here eventually collide with empowerment ideals to erode the integrity of feminist community (e.g., Calas & Smircich, 1996). This dominant focus implicitly privileges "pure" theoretical models of egalitarian feminist community, valuing theory over practice (Gottfried & Weiss, 1994; Mayer, 1995). As P. Martin (1990) explains,

> An assumption is often made in the literature that to be truly feminist, an organization must live up to an ideal type. Inconsistencies of goal and practice; the decoupling of structure and activity; conflicting values, goals, practices, and outcomes—circumstances that characterize practically all ongoing organizations—are depicted as fatal or disqualifying flaws. (p. 189)

The elevation of theory over practice carries several consequences: (a) it favors particular structures and procedures (e.g., minimal hierarchy, consensual decision making) to the exclusion of process and outcome considerations (Gottfried & Weiss, 1994; Martin, 1990; Mayer, 1995; Riger, 1994); (b) it promotes the rather bleak view that contradiction is inevitably disabling; (c) it depicts any form of power imbalance as an antifeminist development, thus equating feminist empowerment with absolute equality; (d) it counters feminist commitments to know and act in context (Marshall, 1993; Reinharz, 1992; Steiner, 1989); (e) it offers a feeble response to pragmatic concerns for alliances and diversity (Eisenstein, 1995; Ristock, 1990); and (f) it neglects agency, or member efforts to preserve empowering interaction amid power imbalance. At best, theoretical bias bounds our understanding of feminisms-in-practice (Mayer, 1995). At worst, it brands feminist community an impossibility—an endeavor inherently destined for compromise (e.g., Calas & Smircich, 1996).

Why depict the impurities of practice as flawed instances of feminist community? Given the empirical unlikelihood of pure forms, instead, why not challenge the abstract, exclusive nature of traditional models of feminist community? A more adequate framework would acknowledge a fundamental contradiction between ideology and practice, situate that tension in its local forms, and avoid deterministic accounts of its debilitating effects. Although pluralist scholars have begun to affirm an interactive link between feminist theory and practice, their perspectives have not yet enjoyed much empirical application. To extend their work, I propose a communicative approach that engages feminist community from a provisional stance.

Feminist Organizations as Alternative Discourse Communities

Toward a pluralist communication theory, feminist communities may be conceptualized as "alternative discourse communities" that contest "prevailing understandings of the ways in which gender, identity, power, and politics intersect" (Mumby, 1996, pp. 281–282). Rejecting dominant preoccupation with nonhierarchical arrangements, this view redresses the tension between ideology and practice to restore the significance of member agency in local contexts. It emphasizes the routine, discursive practices of everyday organizational life. The model advanced here builds on this shift in perspective.

As a point of departure, Fraser (1989, 1993) provided an important theoretical elaboration of alternative discourse communities. She explained how deliberation can disguise domination when members of marginalized social groups attain mere presence, rather than meaningful voice, in dominant arenas. In response, Fraser (1993) favored the development of multiple competing publics, or "parallel discursive arenas" that allow participants to "invent and circulate counterdiscourses" toward the construction of "oppositional interpretations of their identities, interests, and needs" (p. 14). According to Fraser, alternative spheres of discourse facilitate social transformation of patriarchal meanings and practices by providing subversive "spaces of withdrawal and regroupment ... bases and training grounds for agitational activities directed toward wider publics" (p. 15). Similar arguments support the claim that separatist feminist organizing is an empowering transitional strategy for women (e.g., Freedman, 1979). Fraser (1993) conceded the nonrevolutionary nature of counterdiscourses, as complex pressures enable only partial, tactical, incremental transformation of dominant meanings.

Maguire and Mohtar (1994) applied Fraser's model to one feminist organization for survivors of sexual and domestic abuse. These authors describe how the agency transformed into a community in search of a counterdiscourse of domestic violence, sexual assault, and organizing. Maguire and Mohtar noted the challenges roused by such specific issues as "the tension between the need for hierarchical structure and the desire for egalitarian relationships" (p. 241). Difficult but not disabling, these tangled tensions were maneuvered by organization members in an ongoing effort to "maintain a complex set of ideals, obligations, regulations, and desires all within a social world that continuously makes demands upon them" (p. 239).

When feminist organizations are cast as "alternative discourse communities," a distinctive approach to empirical inquiry surfaces. The fundamental ideology-practice contradiction becomes a situated mesh of dilemmas experienced by concrete members and discursively and materially navigated toward multiple and potentially competing ends. Thus, feminist organizing entails improvisation and invention through interaction.

Importantly, my emphasis on the emergent does not relinquish minimal requirements for a feminist discourse community. Feminist organizations may be loosely understood as communities that confront dominant gendered meanings and organizational patterns; they seek to develop counterdiscourses of gender, power, and organizing that approximate empowering relations. Consistent with my critique of theoretical bias, this provisional definition marks distinguishing norms and goals of feminist community yet avoids presumption of how counterdiscourse should unfold in local structure and practice. It highlights member tactics for coping with contradiction.

The proposed model may enrich the study of feminist organizing on several counts. It supports a fluid understanding of feminist community as oppositional meanings and identities constructed through the (counter)discourse of situated groups. Departing from dominant fixation on egalitarian structures, the framework depicts feminist communities as "tenuous, precarious, and founded primarily in the ability of the group to articulate their marginality in the face of powerful discursive and nondiscursive hegemonic forces that shape the 'will to truth'" (Mumby, 1996, p. 282). It invites attention to feminist agency, probing the largely understudied, undertheorized question: How do people apply ideology in everyday practice and accounts thereof? (Craig & Tracy, 1995). By treating tension as a starting point, it revises a pervasive view of organizational contradiction as inescapably disabling. Finally, my conceptual framework identifies an important theoretical and practical role for communication scholars in the study of alternative, and specifically feminist, communities. The remainder of this chapter applies the proposed approach to an empirical case. I examine the efforts of one feminist community to counter the practical pressures reviewed above previously—to "do" empowering relationships in the face of imposing inequalities.

APPROXIMATING EMPOWERMENT: NEGOTIATING FEMINIST COMMUNITY AT SAFE

Research Methods

The data reported here are part of a larger dissertation project with "SAFE," a feminist agency for battered women and their children (Ashcraft, 1998). Over two years of research, I logged nearly 300 research hours. I conducted approximately 230 hours of participant observation, distributed among shelter life, member training, volunteer support meetings, various staff meetings and retreats, and social events. My general interest in member experience of tensions between feminist ideology and practice honed my attention, and I recorded my observations of organizational interaction in detailed field notes. Beyond my role as researcher, I occupied the formal volunteer positions of shelter and crisis-line worker, outreach counselor, and training group facilitator. My active involvement in the SAFE community reflects the premise that research can be strengthened when inquiry blends with activism, when the ethnographer minimizes scholarly detachment and seeks to "know with" participants (Dervin, 1987; Fine, 1988; Hawkins, 1989; Mies, 1983; Reinharz, 1992; Spitzack & Carter, 1988). As researcher and volunteer, I experienced a dual consciousness that enabled a unique perspective—both outsider and insider, expert and subordinate. Although my observation of several SAFE forums required intense levels of personal participation, my contributions tended to decrease dramatically in staff meetings.

In addition to participant observation, I conducted 41 interviews with staff, intern, and volunteer participants, at least 4 of whom self-identified as former SAFE clients. These sessions ranged in length from 45 minutes to 3 hours, with an average of 1.5 hours. With the exception of a few participants who requested otherwise, the interviews were recorded on audio. Based on initial months of observation, I developed a standard interview guide with which I entered each session. A first set of questions explored general aspects of participant experience at SAFE (e.g., "Compare and contrast your experience at SAFE with that at other organizations"). A second category addressed philosophical issues (e.g., "If and how is SAFE a feminist organization?"). The next three question sets probed relations between and among staff, volunteer, and client members. Finally, each interview concluded with broad inquiries (e.g., "What do you see as the greatest strength and weakness of SAFE?"). Although the interview guide supplied a basic agenda, I often improvised to explore issues that emerged during the session. As such, most SAFE interviews approximated a blend of ethnographic and respondent genres (Lindlof, 1995).

I followed a general pattern of data analysis throughout the SAFE project. I began with preliminary data readings. Sensitized by theoretical concepts and research, I identified and described recurring observations in analytic memos (Jorgensen, 1989). In these memos, I collected examples from various data sources to support and elaborate potential patterns. These early memos pushed me to further investigate a SAFE strategy for cultivating empowerment that I analyze in this chapter: *ethical communication*. Based on these initial and often-repeated efforts, I developed inductive coding categories (e.g., the 3 themes explained later in *participant meanings*) and added, refined, and revised these through repetitive, comparative applications to data (Glaser & Strauss, 1967). The coding included cross-checks between data sources (e.g., interviews, meetings) and accounted for discrepancies (e.g., when interviews conflicted with observations) with a sort of negative case analysis (Lincoln & Guba, 1985). Following these efforts, I constructed descriptive and evaluative claims about SAFE practice, supporting these with exemplars identified through coding. Although this account reconstructs a coherent system for data analysis, the actual process reflected the often cyclical nature of ethnographic work (Lindlof, 1995).

Grounded practical theory supplied a basic structure for the analysis that follows (Craig & Tracy, 1995). This analytic framework reconstructs communication practice at three levels: (1) *problem* (i.e., dilemmas experienced by members), (2) *technical* (i.e., member strategies for managing dilemmas), and (3) *philosophical* (i.e., situated ideals implied by member strategies). In my description of the SAFE community, I address the problem level of analysis by considering how tensions between feminist ideology and practice manifest at SAFE. Turning to the technical level, I describe SAFE's strategy for preserving empowering relations in the midst of power imbalance: *ethical communication*. The concluding section engages the philosophical level by identifying and evaluating tacit SAFE premises about empowering workplace community. As this preview suggests, grounded practical theory complements my conceptual model with an analytical approach that allows for normative reflection without accepting fixed, a priori norms for critique. By revitalizing the theory–practice relationship, grounded practical theory cultivates a critical standpoint grounded in, and responsive to, feminist practice.

About SAFE: Persistent Problems of Feminist Community

Founded in the early 1970s, SAFE is an organization by and for women. As stated in the volunteer training manual, the agency's mission "is to provide safe shelter, support, and advocacy for battered women and their children, and to work toward an end to domestic violence through educating the wider community and networking with other community agencies." Toward that end, SAFE offers emergency shelter and preventative services to women and children, as well as community education and outreach programs. These services are provided from three locations. The most recently constructed site serves as a sort of administrative headquarters for the agency, simultaneously housing the majority of SAFE staff and hosting community education programs and events. Situated in a nearby suburb, a smaller second location extends similar counseling and educational services to women, children, and the community in areas outside the primary city that SAFE serves. SAFE also operates one emergency shelter, the location of which is maintained in strict confidentiality to preserve its status as "safe." Here, women (and their children) in acute crisis are offered transitional residence for a flexible, 6-week maximum stay, during which they are encouraged to "process" their situation and exercise control in rebuilding their lives. With an annual budget of $740,000, SAFE serves more than 1,200 women and children and speaks to some 8,000 community members about domestic violence each year. The success of SAFE services receives wide recognition. Recently, a prominent committee on alternative policy selected SAFE from 500 similar agencies nationwide as a model program for coping with domestic violence. But SAFE is by and for women in ways beyond explicit purpose. By design, all 20 board and 23 staff members are women, and an overwhelming majority of the approximately 100 volunteers are also women. This disproportionate gender constitution was recently challenged by a funding institution that threatened to remove its support due to SAFE's alleged discriminatory stance toward men. The dispute was resolved in SAFE's favor after staff members compiled a detailed report that depicted SAFE's position as essential to providing an empowering transitional space for women. The gender consciousness of SAFE is further reflected in member efforts to construct a policy regarding the "special case" of male volunteers; the policy describes a specific need for male volunteers to recognize and reject their male privilege. Although most members are White and middle-class, SAFE explicitly embraces a diversity of women. As shelter resident "screening forms" illustrate, the pledge to diversity must be at least verbally shared by those who wish to receive SAFE services. Substantial variation exists in member age, education level, marital status, and lifestyle or sexual orientation.

SAFE adopts a consciously feminist orientation to both domestic violence and organizing—a commitment encouraged in the agency's socialization practices and beyond. For example, the intensive 50-hour volunteer-training program provides detailed coverage of various forms of social oppression (e.g., sexism, racism, heterosexism, able-ism, etc.) and connects them to violence in society; simultaneously, the program critiques traditional organizational power arrangements and instructs volunteers how to enact more ethical organizational relationships.

Despite these efforts, SAFE structure does not reflect an absolute rejection of hierarchy and its accompanying features. Although power structures are kept to a minimum—and often attributed to external pressures and demands of efficiency—the formal organizational chart reflects clear status and labor distinctions. Position titles are not unlike those of traditional organizations; "directors," "managers," and "administrative assistants" delineate a familiar system of power asymmetry. Although the 20-member board of directors is a remote governing body, the executive director closely observes organizational staff and processes. Three supervisory figures further splinter the organization into three distinct programs: shelter, outreach (or, counseling and support), and educational services. However, dominant SAFE discourse seeks to minimize the potency of such power arrangements.

In a limited sense, SAFE embodies an "in name only" strategy for managing formal distinctions between staff, volunteer, and client members. For example, an informal organizational chart graces the wall of the shelter office that houses crisis line volunteers, women's counselors, and the shelter director. In contrast to the traditional layout of SAFE's formal chart, the informal display includes staff and volunteer photos arranged on a large slab of poster board. Although the positions are still arranged hierarchically, as much as they appear in the formal chart, the large print at the top reads as follows: "The path to empowerment ... " Following this "path" to the volunteer pictures at the structure's base, the phrase is completed: "... and some of the women along the way." Power distinctions between staff or volunteer members and clients are "debunked" through such explicit strategies as limiting rules to essential safety concerns, privileging client knowledge, or collectively dwelling on how to frame decisions to clients.

Countering these conscious efforts are the systematic practical differences between SAFE member experiences. Staff members are structurally designated as volunteer "supervisors." To meet efficiency and performance demands, staff members are often recruited, at least in part, on the grounds of some professional or experiential qualification. Their structural and professional positions tend to interact with their increased level of organizational contact to offer them greater informational control, greater organizational knowledge, greater access to informal communication networks, and greater influence in decision-making processes. For example, weekly staff meetings and social activities are generally understood as "for staff only" unless otherwise specified. Separate staff and volunteer communication logs, carefully kept from the eyes of clients, further reflect significant differences in access to the organization's inner workings. Moreover, rules governing participation and behavior exist in an inverse relationship with hierarchical level.

Thus far, the discussion of life at SAFE reflects a general contradiction between feminist ideology and practice; that is, competing pulls arise from the drive for empowering relations and the urgency of pragmatic demands. According to members, the most agonizing dilemmas stem from such forces as formalization and informal power structures. Put simply, how can SAFE construct and maintain an empowering system of interaction when formal and informal hierarchies lend greater weight to particular voices? The words of one staff member illustrate the dilemma:

> It's hard to be a good, empowering feminist when you're checking off chores, but that's a reality, even though it creates a sort of weird dynamic.... All we can do is just keep asking ourselves, "What does that mean or bring up for us; what does it mean for the women [clients]? ... We're not equals. No matter how we try to create conditions for not hoarding power, this is the reality. The women—and us—have learned to understand ourselves in these terms. It's the reality.

To reconcile that reality with feminist community, SAFE depends on an explicit system of organizational interaction known to members as "ethical communication."

Empowering Through Ethical Communication

Ethical communication (EC) is the pride and joy of the SAFE community. This section provides an in-depth, descriptive account of EC as an organizational innovation. First, I discuss the local history and logic of EC. Second, I present the formal principles that comprise SAFE's EC policy. Finally, I explore participant meanings, reconstructing an implicit system of member obligations that enables the practice of EC.

Background

Few participants know or remember precisely when SAFE adopted EC. But many understand why and where it originated. Several members identified indirect conflict management and rampant rumors as problems that commonly plague battered women's shelters. Many participants experienced these difficulties firsthand in their previous work with other agencies; their tales of widespread dissension and "backstabbing" confirm SAFE's need to guard against such ills. EC is designed as both prevention and cure. At the 1980 meeting of the National Coalition Against Domestic Violence, Kit Evans (1980) presented a paper entitled, "A feminist perspective on the ethics of communication, explored in the context of an ongoing group of women with decision-making responsibility." When SAFE members later encountered this work, they attempted to implement the ethics it described. "Ethical communication" soon emerged as a nickname for the program. Seasoned SAFE participants report that EC's centrality in the SAFE community—and member commitment to it—dramatically increased over the few years before I joined the organization.

SAFE participants routinely cite EC as the central, distinctive, enduring feature of SAFE's collective identity (Dutton, Dukerich, & Harquail, 1994). When asked to compare her experience at SAFE with that at other workplaces, one member succinctly replied, "Ethical communication—that's the difference." Another participant described EC as the "biggest difference" between SAFE and other organizations: "[EC] is what makes us unique, and actually makes us good; I think it's our key to success." Time and again, members posed similar contrasts. One director explained the importance of teaching EC to volunteers during training: "I think that that's a real strong value, that that's really the starting place for the whole program. And there's a belief that if somebody comes into the agency … and doesn't get that kind of fundamental piece that it follows them through their experience here and makes it kind of difficult." Clearly, members identified EC as a fundamental, unique dimension of SAFE life. They also characterized EC as a uniquely feminist communication system that enables SAFE's oppositional stance. The latter claim begs the question: How is EC feminist? SAFE discourse supplies three answers.

First, many SAFE members maintain that EC provides an alternative to violent, coercive, and ostensibly masculinist ways of managing difference. In colorful accounts that range from general indictments of society to disdain for modern corporate life, they contrast EC with interaction in masculine or male-dominated organizations. Specifically, participants name violence and power abuse as the primary mechanisms through which the patriarchal world resolves conflict; rife with war imagery, these dominant methods "set up a system where one has power over the other because one's lost and one's won." With EC, SAFE seeks a more gentle, peaceful path toward social change, allegedly derived from women's experiences. EC departs from the pervasive, presumably patriarchal model of managing conflict by denouncing relations built on dominance and submission. As the executive director explained:

> So that if we really want to bring an end to violence or bring an end to power over dynamics, we have to find gentle ways of creating change. And so we go to ourselves—what allows us to create change within our own lives and find that the best way to do that is when our own experience is respected and validated.... So we try to do that in all of our, in the way that we work with everybody.

Second, members depict EC as feminist because it turns SAFE's philosophy of empowerment toward all organization members. Many participants employ EC to distinguish SAFE from social service agencies that seek to empower clients but fail to empower themselves. As mentioned previously, members explicitly recognize in-fighting and failure to cope with conflict directly as common plagues that debilitate domestic violence shelters, and perhaps more generally, women's organizing (Ashcraft & Pacanowsky, 1996). One participant described how, "at the [SAFE] training, more attention was paid to ethical communication and process stuff ... making the connection between, sort of, how we do this stuff with clients also reflects how we relate to each other. So there's much more kind of overt discussion about feminist philosophy and ethical communication and all of that kind of stuff."

Her account hints a key SAFE assumption: Across hierarchical levels, relationships reflect one another. This firm belief in "mirrored relationships" insists that the empowerment of clients necessarily demands the empowerment of all members. Thus, members mark EC as a response to the poor communication habits of other shelters. Specifically, they declare EC "feminist" because it redresses the failure of other agencies to adequately account for difference, and thus, extends empowerment to all organization members.

Finally, a few members depict EC as feminist because, at a minimum, it represents a noble effort to organize differently. As one participant explained, "We are trying to change the way things are traditionally done.... Actually, I would say we learn more about what it means to be feminist, to be a feminist organization, by what it is not." Another noted that, "we're pretty good about marking shifts that don't seem to fit with the way we do things." When an interview respondent referred to EC as a feminist communication style, I asked her to explain in what way EC was feminist. After some thought, she replied, "I don't know quite, but I really do love the challenge of encountering the process of working some of these things out." These and similar reflections echo Rothschild-Whitt's (1976) claim that the practice of mutual and self-criticism, or an organization's basic capacity for critical reflection and thoughtful adjustment, constitutes a key feature of "alternative" organizing. Put simply, "at least we're trying."

Thus, in the eyes of members, EC is a uniquely feminist alternative because it rejects masculinist ways of managing difference, cultivates empowerment in all organizational relations, and, at the very least, endeavors to do differently. To assess if and how EC achieves these goals, we must first understand the formal and informal features of this local organizational communication system. The next two parts of my analysis address the simple question: What is EC?

Formal Principles

For volunteer and staff members, the interview typically constitutes the initial formal contact with SAFE. It is usually at this meeting that a prospective member will first encounter EC. For example, my own interview for a volunteer position began with a direct request for clarification about my personal experiences with abuse. At two points during the interview, the coordinator emphasized that the agency valued a particular form of open communication, a style of interacting that had surprised her during her early work with SAFE: "We try to train people to approach problems directly and through the appropriate channels, and I'll help you do that…. None of this resentment and indirect attacks you might find at other agencies." Participants from multiple positions report similar experiences of interactional surprise or discomfort during their initial interview, often describing the event as "intense" or "emotionally draining."

On the first day of training, members are introduced to EC in greater detail. The following points summarize the basic principles of a "feminist communication ethic" as described in the SAFE training manual:

1. *Open communication is ethical.* Hidden agendas, mis- or underinformation, and other forms of manipulation preclude egalitarian relationships, arouse subtle and eventually explosive hostilities, and block the possibility of change.

2. *Because different perspectives enrich the group process, every member's views are important.* Rather than asserting superiority or encouraging conformity, the goal of communication is to reach a "mutually acceptable balance" between equal voices.

3. *"Oppression is silencing."* Power-seeking squelches the voices of some, discouraging true consensus and decreasing long-term commitment to decisions. Individuals have a right to feel that their voice has been truly heard.

4. *Our climate should encourage members to raise opposing views.* Members should negotiate their positions openly until they arrive at a "mutually comfortable place." Though members may hold singular viewpoints, "it is the group's responsibility to make sure that no one is alone."

5. *Members should deal with a situation as directly as possible.* Each member has an obligation to "get/be/stay clear with each other." That "clearing" should occur directly with the individual in question, not with uninvolved others.

6. *If necessary for feedback, a member may discuss a situation involving a particular person with others, provided those "others" are "clear about their role as facilitators, not validators."* The person who engaged the discussion then assumes the burden to follow through and update the group on the outcome. Others involved agree to keep the discussion "in the group."

7. *Conflict does not always have to be engaged, but it must always be named.* Unspoken conflict contributes to negative communication, damaging member capacity to work collectively. In an effort to recognize the "whole person," each member bears the responsibility of "naming what is going on."

8. *Because personal relationships affect the group as a whole, they are not necessarily private.* Interpersonal relations impact the total group; they are a source of affiliation, power, and conflict.

9. *"The means is the end."* How we communicate determines the product of our interaction and "what, if any, value it will have in our communities."

As these guidelines suggest, EC establishes an explicit system of corresponding individual and group responsibilities and rights. It mandates authentic expression, declaring the group's right to know individual agendas. It asserts the group's duty to make room for all voices, affirming the individual's right to be heard. It demands mutual accountability for prompt, direct attention to conflict.

According to most staff members, EC is a feminist strategy designed to cultivate open expression, reduce the formation of coercive power alliances, and minimize the potential for covertly divisive communication, or "backstabbing." In everyday terms, members characterize EC in numerous though consistent ways: "honesty till it hurts," "having a process," "being straight up," "clean communication," "mutual respect," "learning and growing about ourselves and together," "keeping a tight container around communication ... not a lot of loose talk," and "you don't have to agree with everyone, but you need to be direct and straightforward."

Staff participants view EC as a collective commitment, necessarily embraced by all members at all hierarchical levels. One member described how at SAFE, "it would be worse to not be ethical and do the back-stuff and start all that crap and get called on the carpet than it would be to go to that person ... cuz you will get called on it." Other members explained that EC works precisely because "everyone's committed ... it's so exciting." In the reflections of one staff participant, "The key is not just offering it as an option or isn't it nice that we have this thing called ethical communication. We're requiring it, demanding it.... I think people have to buy into it. And people buy into it by being able to get through an experience of it." Consistent with her description, interviewees routinely volunteered their first encounter with the practice of EC as evidence of the system's success. Most depicted their initial experience as difficult and challenging yet liberating—surmounting a difficult hurdle to find a new world of relational freedom. Like numerous others, one participant recounted how "I talked with her and she talked to her supervisor, and it was like a happily ever after ... and that was the hard one ... I got to take responsibility for what was bothering me and in the end, it felt really good." After that instance, she recalled, she was "sold" on EC.

Beyond formal training and the initial "buy-in" encounter, other socialization processes also support the pledge to empowerment through EC. For example, facilitators of small consciousness-raising groups that follow each training session are responsible to encourage new members to practice EC by voicing their frustrations about the training, receiving support from the group, and following up with the appropriate person. Hypothetical conflict scenarios and "role-plays" enforce EC at volunteer support meetings and staff forums. These and other lessons generate visible results. In interview sessions and everyday member conversation, both new and more seasoned members measure their interactions with the "yardstick" of EC. Coupled with my own observations of practice, their accounts construct an implicit web of obligations that facilitate the transformation of a formal communication ethic into a pragmatic relational practice.

Participant Meanings

In this discussion, I clarify three themes that characterize how participants understand EC: "process" as precursor, "process" as relationship sense-making device, and power asymmetry as "modeling." As I explicate these themes, I reconstruct an intricate, informal, binding system of mutual obligation that enables the enactment of EC.

Every Woman's Burden: "Process" as Precursor. As described previously, EC entails an ongoing responsibility to "get clear" with one another. To accomplish this personal and relational duty, each woman should develop increasing awareness of herself—her comfort zones, her "trigger" issues, her motivations for particular communication choices, and her frame of reference. One participant tersely described the "biggest" yet "less obvious piece" of EC as "being responsible for identifying my own feelings and my own personal stuff and how that affects my interactions with other people." Although a woman may seek support from others along the way, it is her personal burden to pursue a developing consciousness of self. Members described this sense of individual duty as a need for each member to "have a process" and for other members to respect her place in that process.

For members, "process" precedes empowering organizational participation. Without personal process, communication is assumed to be inauthentic, one-sided, and thus, unethical. In tune with other participant accounts, the volunteer coordinator identified failure to process as grounds for dismissal from SAFE:

> And so what I learned was that I needed to get there right up front and start her [a volunteer's] process, because then I give her the feedback and get back to her in a week and see how she's worked with it. There is that point where we say, "Wow, if you're not working on it at all, or if you don't show any sign of movement, then we need for you to leave."

Her account suggests how the SAFE notion of process locates a context, or continuum, for personal empowerment. Each member is considered to "shift and move" between numerous "spaces" or "places" of self-awareness in a dynamic and personal course. The concept of process provides members with a fluid understanding of empowerment. It situates empowerment as an ongoing and individualized "journey"; simultaneously, it avoids exclusion by providing a space for those apparently not seeking empowerment. Consider one member's description of a client who repeatedly mourned her helplessness and victimization: "I think she just needs to be in a place of grieving right now." But why is there such force behind the SAFE mandate to process?

The implicit obligation to process presumably cultivates honest, open expression; that is, evolving knowledge of self enhances personal empowerment and growth, ultimately facilitating authenticity in interaction. One participant described this enabling function of process:

> So if something's gone on ... what it requires is that I spend some time figuring out how I got to that place. What's going on for me that I'm needing more of her [SAFE member] attention, or that getting that feedback from her threw me for a loop for a whole week? ... She can trust that I do that work. And it's just sort of enriching, I think, in our relationship.

If a member does not "get clear in her head," she cannot adequately know and express her needs, stunting the potential for individual, relational, and organizational learning and growth. More specifically, members reference the consciousness aroused by process as a necessary step toward establishing and articulating clear personal "boundaries"—borders that enable members to identify, understand, and voice interactional discomfort. One member explained boundaries this way: "It's my responsibility to decide what's gonna work for me—what I can accommodate and what I can't." The therapeutic concept of boundaries pervades SAFE talk, which depicts these borders as physical and symbolic. Volunteers are taught to decide and communicate what tasks they are "OK with." When requesting volunteer assistance, staff members routinely ask if "that's comfortable for you." All members learn to ask permission to play with a resident's child or touch a resident in any way. Staff decisions regarding clients and their children (e.g., the rule that crisis-line workers should not touch resident children) routinely rotate around the premise of safety concerns, implicitly defined as the preservation of personal boundaries. In sum, SAFE discourse insists that ethical interaction requires rational internal knowledge and external expression of a lucid, consistent self and its separation from and relation to other selves. Attributions of EC failure yield additional support for these twin burdens.

The relational importance of fulfilling one's personal responsibility to engage the process—and the communicative consequences for failing to do so—are illustrated as members account for EC difficulties. When describing a failure of EC among residents, one staff member explained that:

> We'll keep giving them [some residents] the ethical communication advice, you know, to go to the woman and talk with her directly about it. And they go, but nothing happens. The other woman maybe doesn't hold up her part of the bargain. This happened not too long ago.... They [some residents] were doing their side of the ethical communication, but the woman [another resident] wouldn't listen.... So we had to ask her to leave, and I think we should have caught that sooner. She was really threatening the women's safety.

Similarly, another staff member offered the following interpretation of volunteer departure:

> I had a volunteer do an exit interview with me and she was telling me how she felt that the interns were so rude and they didn't treat her well at all and so that pushed her over the edge and she's leaving. That to me meant that she didn't learn ethical communication. Because ethical communication is when you say to that person, "Wow. This is how I feel right now, but your tone seems really condescending. What is that all about?" Or to say, "I feel like you're angry with me" or whatever at the time rather than take it home with you and feel like, "Wow. What a jerk that person was." And you think it blew over but then you come back into the shelter and you see this person again. You're a little bit uptight the next time and there's some undercurrents."

While addressing distinct structural relationships, both accounts ground the possibility for ethical interaction in mutual fulfillment of the individual responsibility to "know and express thyself."

Individual process may serve many functions. One member described the mandate to process as the key to an informal system that renders otherwise uncertain decision-making dynamics coherent:

> It seems to maybe be our system that things are mulled over a lot and if it is still a priority a week or month or whatever later, then it eventually will happen.... I think coming from the outside, it would appear to be ambiguous. But coming from the inside, I think it is clear because of the presumed responsibility for oneself.... If something is a priority for me, then it's part of my responsibility to raise it and keep raising it.

Beyond its service to personal development, process ultimately serves a mediating function, as implied in the following account:

> If there are personality clashes, that's where the ethical communication comes in. Because what we've been taught and what we've practiced is if you have a feeling in your body ... when you come into work that something is wrong, you go internal, see what it's about, see who, what, where, and then get back to the source and iron it out.... And then it's all of our responsibility to allow and respect diversity.

Next, I probe how "process" evokes relational responsibility.

"What's Going on for Her": Relational Sense-Making and Process

Engaging one's individual process, or the development of self-awareness toward the authentic articulation of personal boundaries, provides a prerequisite for EC.

But process also entails an ensuing relational duty. Describing the departure of one night manager, a staff member reflected on a previous conversation in which the manager's central problem was identified:

> She [the night manager] knew we just weren't working right together.... I was talking to [another staff member] about this at one point and she said, "How do you teach a woman to recognize the boundaries of others when she has none herself?"

Consider how her account complements another participant's reflections: "Because you set your boundaries, and you respect that about yourself, you can also respect somebody else's boundaries. And theirs might look very different from yours."

As these excerpts suggest, consciousness of one's own relational needs serves as a bridge to understanding those of others.

At SAFE, all boundaries are presumably created equal. As they supersede the authority of formal or informal power distinctions, boundaries are a precious resource held sacred by members. For example, one staff member described the "incredible feeling" of confronting the executive director. In particular, she reported feeling silenced and humbled by the director during a meeting with the board. Although she originally hoped to "let it go," she realized her inclination to avoid was unethical. Instead, she approached the director at a later time and explained her discomfort. She described their conversation as constructive and personally exhilarating—"something you could never do anywhere else." The same participant also shared an instance in which her disagreement with other members led her to consider leaving SAFE. When she finally fulfilled her responsibility to name her concern, she explained, other members were bound to consider her voice, and the conflict was resolved through "honesty ... no ugly feelings or sabotage." In both examples, her faithful expression of boundaries obligated other members to integrate "what's going on for her" in their responses or decisions.

In this sense, "getting clear" becomes a relational responsibility; that is, each woman is bound to consider how her process intersects with that of others—how her frame of reference interacts with that of other women in distinct organizational and life situations. As one member explained, "We don't tend to treat each other like one is right and the other's wrong.... We try to have respect for people for being wherever they are in their process." At all structural levels, SAFE members explicitly disdain, "imposing my own framework on what she's saying." During one case review meeting, for example, shelter counselors discussed the possibility that one resident's decisions reflected racist assumptions. A few participants denounced her actions; one asked, "If this is clearly about racism, why does she need to be with us?" The conversation quickly transformed into a consideration of whether the resident recognized her choices as racist. Finally, any decision about the resident was postponed, as all members agreed that "we have to get more information on this before we decide what's OK .... We can't get so far into this without knowing what was really going on for her." Other case review conversations similarly conclude with consideration of how certain events and interactions are experienced by clients. This SAFE habit cultivates a view of clients as a legitimate knowledge source; it may even allow members to contend with frustrating clients yet avoid the classification of battered women as "bad" or "trouble" (Ferraro, 1983).

Extended to all member relations, the responsibility to weigh each other's process presumably encourages reflection on difference, enriching the diversity and quality of SAFE interaction. The individual importance of having a process assumes relational potency here, as members employ a woman's process as a device to assist relationship sense making. In this sense, process becomes a sort of equalizer; it challenges the inegalitarian force of formal and informal power structures by functioning as a mediator between divergent life situations and perspectives. Rather than treating difference in knowledge, skill, or (feminist) perspective as disabling the possibility of egalitarian communication, the notion of process creates an alternative context for interpreting interaction. As members urge the fundamental premise of a woman's process—"what was really going on for her"—differences are construed as demanding hearing, reflection, and negotiation. One staff member illustrated the relational function of individual process in her description of another staff member's explicit recognition of communication discomfort:

> The piece about focusing on our inner selves and who we are is really important here. Recently, in one of our staff meetings, one of the minority women raised a concern about the diversity training discussion we had a while back being dropped. She really hadn't felt like there was any sort of resolution on the issue, and it was disturbing her that we had just let it go. So we started talking about it, and another woman agreed with her, and some of the other women started saying stuff about things they had wanted to see happen with this, and it reopened the issue and things happened. And it's just that piece about the way we can work with each other to iron out any woman's glitch with the way she's feeling about things until she is comfortable with us again. You know, you get that peaceful feeling where things are OK, things are at rest and comfortable, and until she feels that kind of peace, we're not through.

Here, the participant enforced an individual responsibility for articulating boundaries and a relational burden to honor the process of others; she illuminated the benefits of conceptualizing individual difference as grounds for interpersonal or collective growth. Put simply, individual differences are neither neglected nor filtered through a hierarchical lens. Instead, they are reframed as potential for individual and interpersonal empowerment through egalitarian negotiation. Members insist that most organizations bypass "process," opting for the "easy way" out. As the volunteer coordinator explained:

> Ultimately, you know, we deal in a world of power, and people, I think, respond differently to that. And the easy way to do it is to stir the shit underneath so something erupts and that's so unfair to people because it doesn't provide them the

opportunity to learn, grow, and defend themselves and say, "That's not what I intended at all. This is where I was at." It's a lot of learning; I've learned a lot about how people think and function and not to make a lot of assumptions before I have the facts. Because people come from different walks of life and you have to give them that.

Because of the individual and relational obligations encompassed by SAFE's concept of processing, members believe they can "communicate around power." It is in this sense that "the means is the end": The practice of weighing each woman's process is thought to enable empowering outcomes.

Relationships on Parade: Power Asymmetry as Modeling.   Beyond absorbing "what's going on for her," EC entails a final relational responsibility: facilitating the self-awareness and expression process of others and thus, enabling EC. Recall the staff member who insisted that EC necessitates each member's obligation to the organization: "We're requiring it, demanding it ... part of it is that everybody holds everybody else accountable." Most participants resolutely concurred that every SAFE member bears the burden to enforce EC and its accompanying system of member obligations. In the words of another member: "We try to be really sensitive to these things. And that everyone in the agency is, so I think there is a lot of confrontation that happens.... If people perceive that somebody is starting to get their hackles up about something, we start talking to them about it. Like 'What and, what is the root of this?' 'What's going on with you?'"

In practice, members enact this "sensitivity" in various ways. A more subtle example emerged in the research process. When one counselor forgot her appointment to meet with me for an interview, she apologized to me via telephone. That evening, as we worked at the shelter together, she asked if I was angry about the missed appointment. In a friendly tone, I explained that all was well; I had met a friend and had lunch with her, so the afternoon was no loss at all. After a brief pause, the counselor replied, "Oh, c'mon. You weren't pissed? I would have been. It wasn't very considerate of me. Were you pissed?" Finally, I confessed some concealed frustration. In this example, the counselor assumed the responsibility to encourage my self-investigation process. Ultimately, this move served to facilitate the interpersonal practice of EC (e.g., "get/be/stay clear").

In principle, SAFE participants maintain that all members bear responsibility to be and hold one another accountable to EC. Even as it asserts the ideal of mutual accountability, the following interview account at once seconds the shared burden and confesses its occasional failure:

Q: And does everyone around here carry that responsibility?
A: Well, yeah, they should. I'm not saying that everybody does, but honestly, they should, because that's how it works.... It's everybody's responsibility, no matter who they are, to challenge people to take care of their own stuff

... so it doesn't grow.... That's what kills agencies ... other shelters, nonprofits, you see it all the time.

This excerpt identifies mutual accountability as a checkpoint for individual failure that ensures the survival of EC, distinguishing SAFE from other agencies. But it also admits that the sense of shared duty breaks down on occasion. In response, participants assign more of the burden to facilitate each member's process, and EC in general, to supervisory members. According to members, formal power exists in a positive relationship with accountability (Martin, 1993). In the words of one director, this enhanced accountability requires:

The commitment by the supervisors to provide process ... I do see it as my responsibility, and I think everyone does, on a different level because I'm a supervisor, to make sure that the process happens, to provide an arena, because that's my responsibility.... I think ultimately the leadership in the agency carries a lot of responsibility to make sure that the power differential, although it's there, is not played upon.

In remarkable harmony, members who act in anything resembling supervisory capacity note their increased burden to cultivate the conditions for EC (e.g., to encourage personal process, to remind all to consider "what's going on for her"). Accordingly, nonsupervisory members expect SAFE leaders to perform this function; they frequently report how supervisors seem magically able to couch critique in terms that encourage personal reflection and development: "But [education director] is the master of that sort of thing [facilitating EC], really, and so is [executive director] and [shelter director] too. I would say the rest of us are probably learning." Yet such accounts of awe may also spark concern.

The SAFE premise that formal power entails enhanced responsibility may be accompanied by the assumption that those who exercise legitimate power better enact EC. As the account of revered supervisors suggests, particular individuals might systematically facilitate the process of others, cultivating informal superior–subordinate relationships on the grounds of EC expertise. This condition may feed the growth of informal hierarchy. Because some are likely to better enact EC, their voices are likely to gain a systematic hearing, whereas those who lack such skill may be effectively silenced. For example, the volunteer coordinator recounted how some volunteers had reported self-censorship of their concerns, explaining their inability to ethically express themselves. Other staff and volunteer members cite numerous reasons for their occasional failure to express interactional boundaries. In the words of one participant:

It's difficult to do, though, when you're with so many personally powerful people.... Maybe it's just my own insecurities sometimes, but I don't always feel up to the ethical communication stuff.... I don't know, I just don't want to get in trouble.... Maybe I'm just conditioned that way, but I still worry about that and that makes ethical communication hard a lot of times.

As this member implied, EC may be experienced as another face of tyranny by those who lack the energy or skill to practice its principles. Yet most members emphatically resist this interpretation, careful to contrast traditional supervising with the empowering SAFE style.

Here again, the context of personal process cushions the impact of hierarchy, as the reality of formal and informal distinctions (including that of EC skill) are absorbed as an aspect of each woman's process. That some will emerge as superior and some as subordinate is not contested; that these are fixed relationships is unequivocally refuted. For instance, on a formal level, expectations for staff member performance exceed those of volunteers. Although staff members assume intense levels of responsibility, coupled with greater degrees of experience and qualification, volunteers are primarily expected to display an eagerness to learn. Rather than simply bolster power imbalance, these distinctions heighten a staff member's duty to nurture EC by consciously encouraging volunteer expression and development. As one staff member explained:

> If a volunteer's sitting there on crisis line and a woman comes up to me and says, "Wow, you know.... So and so told me this and that," then the volunteer's right there, so she has to see me. She has to watch what I do.... I'm in a position of trying to model stuff because I know that everybody hears everything that I say and I wanna try to put out good things.... Like on the phone, I know people hear me talking on the phone. I know they hear me talking to residents, so I'm always in a position of modeling something.... It makes me real conscious ... I'm consciously there thinking, "OK, this is my work but there are other people watching what I do, so I wanna put out good messages".... I'm very aware of that, because I think a lot of volunteers don't know a whole lot, and they're always asking for help with things ... I'm aware as much as I can be of what people are saying out there on the phones ... so that I can give feedback.

This account points to a pivotal SAFE belief: The visibility of everyday interaction renders it a productive stage for member observation and growth. For supervisory members, organizational relations serve the twin goals of *content* (i.e., "OK, this is my work ... ") and *display* (i.e., " ... but there are other people watching what I do"). The latter emphasis on display may assist member efforts to navigate empowering relationships in the presence of inequality. In particular, the power-over component of superior–subordinate relationships transforms into fluid relations founded on modeling, or tacitly teaching by example. Shifting away from a formal model of command and reprimand, members may observe and mimic ongoing performances of EC. SAFE's commitment to a positive link between one's formal power and accountability for modeling of EC coheres with the assumption of mirrored relationships mentioned previously. That is, participants believe that relationships at the top of a hierarchy build patterns that seep into relationships all the way down. Thus, members described EC as "a top down thing.... It has to be the standard from that place forward."

At all structural levels, examples of SAFE modeling abound. On one occasion, another volunteer and I struggled to provide support to an angry resident. Overhearing the fumbling conversation, the shelter director joined our uncomfortable threesome. After listening for a few minutes, she began to ask the resident a few questions, offering possible "names" for her feelings and allowing her space to vent. Eventually, she asked what action the resident wanted to take. By soliciting our input as well, the director avoided dominating the discussion. Following the incident, the other volunteer mentioned to me how much she had learned without feeling patronized or threatened. An example of modeling for clients emerges in member efforts to display a link between EC and parenting strategies. When one resident attempted to discipline her child, a nearby counselor quietly interjected words of support for her authority, while offering numerous other choices for disciplinary tactics. As these examples illustrate, SAFE modeling provides an alternate framework for power distinctions. Although such distinctions are not eliminated, they are crafted to more closely approximate feminist empowerment ideology. Members are bound in a fluid network of mentor–apprentice relationships that enhance the possibilities for personal growth and mutual influence.

Grounded in the salience of personal process, the preceding analysis identifies three dominant themes of SAFE talk that construct a complex web of reciprocal obligations. In the view of members, this web enables EC to approximate empowering relationships amid inegalitarian pressures. First, development of self-awareness nourishes authentic and mutually influential interaction through the articulation of personal boundaries that supersede formal structure. Second, member responsibility to consider the process of others provides an egalitarian tool for navigating through the inequities aroused by formal and informal difference. Finally, formal power asymmetry is reconceptualized as conditions for modeling empowering interaction. Thus far, I have assumed a largely descriptive tone to reconstruct the logic of communicating ethically at SAFE. In the final section, I evaluate the significance of EC for the theory and practice of feminist community.

EXTENDING "ETHICAL COMMUNICATION": IMPLICATIONS FOR THEORY AND PRACTICE

Many scholars of feminist community privilege pure, abstract egalitarian models and, in turn, mourn the emergence of power imbalance as an unfortunate, yet inevitable failure to preserve truly empowering feminist community. To address this conceptual problem, this chapter theorized feminist organizations as alternative discourse communities that develop semioppositional representations of gender, power, and organizing through communication practice. I explored SAFE's efforts to translate feminist ideology into pragmatically empowering community. In what follows, I examine EC through a critical lens and signal implications for our understanding of feminist community.

As a local discourse of empowering community, EC offers considerable contributions to communication theory and practice. For example, EC bridges interpersonal and organizational dimensions of research on communication and community. In an exploratory study, Zorn (1995) noted that most scholars who examine interpersonal relationships in organizational settings assume traditional models of the superior–subordinate relationship. Whereas Zorn added friendship to the mainstream equation, EC suggested a radical revision of superior–subordinate relationships that may mitigate coercive power imbalance. My analysis of SAFE's efforts to alter hierarchical relationships also responded to Lannamann's (1991) concern for the ideological contexts in which interpersonal relationships are embedded. Emphasizing the link between feminist ideology and everyday interaction, this chapter suggests the transformative potential of understudied communities and relational strategies (Wood & Duck, 1995).

For feminist communication theory and practice, EC may embody a pragmatic strategy for resisting one aspect of the socialization of many White, middle-class women. Many have noted cultural expectations for some women to avoid conflict and practice deference in interpersonal relationships (e.g., Cline & Spender, 1989; Todd-Mancillas & Rossi, 1985; Vollmer, 1986). In some women's organizational relationships, this subordinate orientation may become a site for the development of manipulative communication characterized by intense conflict undercurrents and backstabbing (Ashcraft & Pacanowsky, 1996; Madden, 1987; Rich, 1979). As SAFE members suggested, the assertive practice of EC may be partially said to oppose these divisive practices and destructive images.

Moreover, EC speaks to feminist critiques of mainstream organizational theory and practice. Although this work has long scrutinized the gendered contexts and practices that constitute many modern corporations, few communication scholars have asked what a feminist theory of workplace community might look like (Buzzanell, 1995; Trethewey, 1997). Moving beyond critique to the enactment of alternatives, this chapter suggests the potential for a grounded theory of feminist organizational communication. For example, EC may be understood as a local manifestation of the largely theorized notion of *bounded emotionality* (Mumby & Putnam, 1992; Putnam & Mumby, 1993).Bounded emotionality refers to an alternative organizing pattern that reclaims marginalized elements of organizational experience, including "nurturance, caring, community, supportiveness, and inter-relatedness" (Mumby & Putnam, 1992, p. 474–448). In such a system, members seek to reconcile individual tasks and interests with community building by implementing relational responsibilities. Certainly, EC yields a communication system that seeks to honor each individual's work feelings," or "spontaneous and emergent" responses to "relationships and interpretive schemes" (Mumby & Putnam, 1992, pp. 447–448). In particular, SAFE's pledge to process evokes feeling rules that encourage members to engage the responses of self and other, while member commitment to modeling builds a collective burden to uphold feeling rules in the midst of apparent inequities.

Yet there is also much cause for caution. EC does not appear to definitively resolve the tension between empowering relations and practical inequalities. Despite its professed interest in feeling, EC presumes the presence of an authentic, consistent, rational self with accessible motives that may always be known and expressed (Strine, 1992; Weedon, 1987). This premise mirrors a general difficulty in feminist thought and activism. Specifically, the feminist commitment to self-reliance as a form of empowerment counters the feminist challenge to liberal individualism (Ferraro, 1981; Leidner, 1991; Morgen, 1990). The former assumes an autonomous self and accents independent, rather than collaborative, action. We might then ask how collaborative community can emerge from such individualistic origins. For SAFE members, the answer stems from the social subordination of women. That is, relationships of equality will likely seem foreign to those who have internalized relationships of dominance and submission. Thus, most members must learn—if not invent—how to participate as equals. SAFE maintained that resocialization requires a woman to value "self" before she can engage mutually influential interaction. As such, her capacity to know and express herself precedes the growth of egalitarian community relations.

Beyond its implications for general feminist tensions, EC brings a local spin to the enduring conflict between empowerment and the practical demands of organizational community. Although it aspires to honor each authentic voice, it privileges a rational form of expression that values articulate, assertive members with advanced analytical and conflict skills. In addition, EC's demand for rational articulation may ironically encourage members to practice inauthentic expression. For example, SAFE members often stress the need to carefully couch concerns. The following participant account affirms this need across hierarchical relationships. Concurrently, it demonstrates how the drive for delicate discourse may invite inauthenticity:

> That's the same thing like when we approach the mom. It's the same dynamic. We just walk in there and say, "Hi, looks like things are stirring up, can I help?" Not, "What are you doing?!" Or, "You shouldn't be talking to Tommy that way!" Even though that's what's going on in your head. Yeah, that's the really neat thing about ethical communication.

Moreover, EC's rational norms for community reflect its cultural roots. Its embrace of open dialogue, reciprocal self-disclosure, process over outcome, feeling factors, and collaborative conflict resolution reflects competent organizational and interpersonal communication as theorized by most Western scholars (Eisenberg & Witten, 1987; Wood & Inman, 1993). However ironic, EC also resembles the interaction principles of such varied programs as parliamentary procedure (Robert, 1989) and "t-groups" (Appley, 1973; Cooper, 1971). Ristock (1990) cautioned against feminist models of nonviolent communication that privilege Western, White, middle-class norms of rational expression. Similarly, Uttal (1990) questioned the politics of support in many Anglo-feminist communities:

> The major disagreement I have with the practices of Anglo feminist groups is the strong message they send out that our discussions need to be smooth, orderly, efficient, and supportive. The idea is that we are not going to do to one another what men have always done to us—we are not going to silence one another nor be competitive. Instead, we are going to provide a space which is supportive and respectful of different opinions .... So we tell ourselves to make space for everyone to talk. Nod supportively .... These groups seem to gain their strength from a collectivity of women who are generally in agreement with one another. Those are the ones who come back again and again.

These reflections suggest that EC simultaneously rejects and invites the elevation of one voice over another. The discussion hints at the plight of members who lack introspection and self-monitoring capabilities; express anger, defensiveness, or hostility; pursue multiple goals; or remain uncertain of their motives for action. EC's specific tenets of good communication raise additional problems. Its fondness for unfettered self-disclosure, or open communication, yields a starting point. Eisenberg & Witten (1987) critiqued the pervasive scholarly presumption of openness as a desirable norm for organizational interaction. Likewise, they challenge the value of unrestrained, confessional disclosure of feelings. Speaking to feminist organizations, Morgen (1994) reminded us that copious self-disclosure often cultivates more than community. It tends to foster highly personalized conflict, introducing emotional charge and strain. EC also appears to discourage critical examination of its own premises. Consider Stohl's (1995) paradox of commitment in which members who question certain participative efforts are deemed resistant to participative ideals. A system labeled *ethical communication*—a moral matter, not merely good practice—compounds the likelihood that members will avoid critical analysis of EC.

SAFE's program for empowerment provokes several unanswered questions. For example, what if some disclose too much, or monopolize group time? What if some disclose too little, or detach from the group? How much energy should members devote to framing concerns in ethical ways? Do these efforts undermine authenticity? When do authentic expression and support become gossip? What happens when members fail to enact EC—when they choose a less ethical approach or lack the energy or ability to know and express themselves? What if members disagree on what EC prescribes or they take issue with the system itself? Who will manage these dilemmas and enforce EC? These and a host of other quandaries suggest the nagging uncertainties of building community through EC. In particular, they signal a general dilemma that implicates the enactment of power at SAFE: What happens when "authentic" expression endangers EC?

It is not my intent to dismiss the integrity of feminist community with observations of its conflicted character. Rather, I concur with many critical theorists that contradiction pervades nearly all communities; the partial, enabling, and confining nature of counterdiscourses does not disable their viability (Alvesson & Willmott, 1992; Bell & Forbes, 1994; Jermier, Knights, & Nord, 1994; Mumby, in press). I applied an approach that adopts contradiction as a point of departure and examines emergent discourses through which members seek to approximate feminist ideology. This conceptual framework contributes to a revitalized relationship between theory and practice in feminist organizational studies. The alternative discourse community model facilitates a fluid understanding of feminist organizing as partially oppositional meanings and identities constructed through the counterdiscourse of situated groups (Fraser, 1993; Mumby, 1996). With its interest in emergent, innovative discourse, the model encourages scholars to look beyond structural arrangements—to approach feminist community as a set of loose norms and goals (e.g., gender-conscious empowerment) that find articulation in particular contexts, as opposed to fixed normative principles (e.g., empowerment as egalitarian, antihierarchy) with uniform application. My analysis answers recent calls for research on how members creatively transcend tension between preserving participative ideals and accomplishing essential tasks (Cheney, 1999). My analysis extends pluralist theories of feminist organizing by demonstrating how members may enact empowering community without realizing "pure" egalitarian relations (Gottfried & Weiss, 1994; P. Martin, 1990; Sirianni, 1984). Toward the improvement of feminist practice, I also comb through SAFE premises for good communication and related potential dilemmas. Future research can explore how members preserve empowering elements of such premises yet cope with the local tensions they raise.

The preceding analysis suggests how the SAFE case informs the relation between communication and community. From a feminist stance, the quality of community is enhanced by the quest for empowering relations, understood as participative, collaborative, and mutually influential, if not egalitarian. But SAFE reminds us that this view of empowerment constitutes an ideal that cannot be fully realized in actual community practice. Empowering community does not necessitate fixed structural arrangements among community members; it does not rest in particular formal principles. In short, empowering community does not require pure egalitarian relations. Through emergent, situated discourse, concrete members improvise and invent meanings and tactics that approximate, counter, and/or transform feminist visions of community. Members negotiate precisely what constitutes "alternative" community: formal, theoretical principles and structures assume meaning as members construct, interpret, and enact them in everyday interaction. More specifically, SAFE members proposed that alternative community can merge individualistic beginnings with group authority and accountability to approximate empowerment.

Much scholarship catalogs the forces that subvert the potential of feminist organizing. As this work affirms, feminist communities are not adequately conceived as utopian sanctuaries, but neither are they inherently destined for demise. They merge transformative potential with lived contradiction—conditions that at once enable and constrain. This chapter advances the study of alternative communication and community by investigating interactional innovations through which members struggle to enact ideological commitments.

REFERENCES

Acker, J. (1995). Feminist goals and organizing processes. In M. M. Ferree & P. Y. Martin (Eds.), *Feminist organizations: Harvest of the new women's movement* (pp. 137–144). Philadelphia: Temple University Press.

Acker, J. (1990). Hierarchies, jobs, bodies: A theory of gendered organizations. *Gender & Society, 4,* 139–158.

Ahrens, L. (1980). Battered women's refuges: Feminist cooperatives vs. social service institutions. *Radical America, 14,* 41–47.

Alvesson, M., & Willmott, H. (1992). On the idea of emancipation in management and organization studies. *Academy of Management Review, 17,* 432–464.

Appley, D. G. (1973). *T-groups and therapy groups in a changing society.* San Francisco: Jossey-Bass.

Ashcraft, K. L. (1998). *Assessing alternative(s): Contradiction and invention in a feminist organization.* Unpublished doctoral dissertation, University of Colorado, Boulder.

Ashcraft, K. L., & Pacanowsky, M. E. (1996). "A woman's worst enemy": Reflections on a narrative of organizational life and female identity. *Journal of Applied Communication, 24*, 1–23.

Barker, D. (1987). Anatomy of working with a white collective. *Our Lives, 2,* 12–13.

Bart, P. (1987). Seizing the means of reproduction: An illegal feminist abortion collective—How and why it worked. *Qualitative Sociology, 10,* 339–357.

Bell, E., & Forbes, L. C. (1994). Office folklore in the academic paperwork empire: The interstitial space of gendered (con)texts. *Text and Performance Quarterly, 14,* 181–196.

Bingham, S. G. (Ed.). (1994). *Conceptualizing sexual harassment as discursive practice.* Westport, CT: Praeger.

Buzzanell, P. M. (1995). Reframing the glass ceiling as a socially constructed process: Implications for understanding and change. *Communication Monographs, 62,* 327–354.

Calas, M., & Smircich, L. (1996). From "the woman's" point of view: Feminist approaches to organization studies. In S. R. Clegg, C. Hardy, & W. R. Nord (Eds.), *Handbook of organization studies* (pp. 218–257). Thousand Oaks, CA: Sage.

Cheney, G. (1999). *Values at work: Employee participation meets market pressure at Mondragon.* Ithaca, NY: Cornell University Press.

Clair, R. P. (1993). The use of framing devices to sequester organizational narratives: Hegemony and harassment. *Communication Monographs, 60,* 113–136.

Cline, S., & Spender, D. (1989). Assertiveness is not enough. In N. Bernards & T. O'Neill (Eds.), *Male/Female roles: Opposing viewpoints* (pp. 227–233). San Diego, CA: Greenhaven Press.

Cooper, C. L. (1971). *T-groups: A survey of research.* New York: Wiley-Interscience.

Craig, R. T. & Tracy, K. (1995). Grounded practical theory: The case of intellectual discussion. *Communication Theory, 3,* 248–272.

Dervin, B. (1987). The potential contribution of feminist scholarship to the field of communication. *Journal of Communication, 37,* 107–120.

Donnellon, A. (1993). Power, politics, and influence: The savvy and substance of action in organizations. In A. R. Cohen (Ed.), *The portable MBA in management* (pp. 113–146). New York: Wiley.

Dutton, J. E., Dukerich, J. M., & Harquail, C. V. (1994). Organizational images and member identification. *Administrative Science Quarterly, 39,* 239–263.

Edwards, R. C. (1979). *Contested terrain: The transformation of the workplace in the twentieth century.* New York: Basic Books.

Eisenberg, E. M., & Witten, M. G. (1987). Reconsidering openness in organizational communication. *Academy of Management Review, 12,* 418–426.

Eisenstein, H. (1995). The Australian femocratic experiment: A feminist case for bureaucracy. In M. M. Ferree & P. Y. Martin (Eds.), *Feminist organizations: Harvest of the new women's movement* (pp. 69–83). Philadelphia: Temple University Press.

Evans, K. (1980). A feminist perspective on the ethics of communication, explored in the context of an on-going group of women with decision-making responsibility. Paper presented at the 1980 National Coalition Against Domestic Violence Conference.

Ferguson, K. (1984). *The feminist case against bureaucracy.* Philadelphia: Temple University Press.

Ferguson, K. (1987, August). Women, feminism, and collectives. Paper presented at the Annual Meeting of the American Sociological Association, Chicago.

Ferraro, K. J. (1981). Processing battered women. *Journal of Family Issues, 4,* 415–438.

Ferraro, K. J. (1983). Negotiating trouble in a battered women's shelter. *Urban Life, 12,* 287–306.

Ferree, M. M., & Martin, P. Y. (Eds.). (1995). *Feminist organizations: Harvest of the new women's movement.* Philadelphia: Temple University Press.

Fine, M. G. (1988). What makes it feminist? *Women's Studies in Communication, 11*, 18–19.

Fraser, N. (1989). *Unruly discourses: Power, discourse and gender in contemporary social theory.* Minneapolis, MN: University of Minnesota Press.

Fraser, N. (1993). Rethinking the public sphere: A contribution to the critique of actually existing democracy. In Robbins, B. (Ed.) *The phantom public sphere* (pp. 1–32). Minneapolis: University of Minnesota Press.

Freedman, E. (1979). Separatism as strategy: Female institution building and American feminism, 1870–1930. *Feminist Studies, 5*, 512–529.

Freeman, J. (1972–1973). The tyranny of structurelessness. *Berkeley Journal of Sociology, 17*, 151–164.

Glaser, B. G., & Strauss, A. L. (1967). *The discovery of grounded theory: Strategies for qualitative research.* Chicago: Aldine.

Gottfried, H., & Weiss, P. (1994). A compound feminist organization: Purdue University's Council on the Status of Women. *Women & Politics, 14*, 23–44.

Gray, B., Ariss, S. S. (1985). Politics and strategic change across organizational life cycles. *Academy of Management Review, 10*, 707–723.

Gutek, B. A. (1989). Sexuality in the workplace: Key issues in social research and organizational practice. In J. Hearn, D. Sheppard, P. Tancred-Sherriff & G. Burrell (Eds.), *The sexuality of organization* (pp. 56–70). Newbury Park, CA: Sage.

Harvey, M. (1985). *Exemplary rape crisis programs: A cross-site analysis and case studies.* Washington, D.C.: National Center for the Prevention and Control of Rape.

Hawkins, K. (1989). Exposing masculine science: An alternative feminist approach to the study of women's communication. In K. Carter & C. Spitzack (Eds.), *Doing research on women's communication: Perspectives on theory and method* (pp. 40–64). Norwood, NJ: Ablex.

Jermier, J. M., Knights, D., & Nord, W. R. (Eds.). (1994). *Resistance & Power in Organizations.* London: Routledge.

Jorgensen, D. L. (1989). *Participant observation: A methodology for human studies.* Newbury Park, CA: Sage.

Lannamann, J. W. (1991). Interpersonal communication research as ideological practice. *Communication Theory, 3*, 179–203.

Leidner, R. (1991). Stretching the boundaries of liberalism: Democratic innovation in a feminist organization. *Signs, 16*, 263–289.

Lincoln, Y. S., & Guba, E. G. (1985). *Naturalistic inquiry.* Beverly Hills, CA: Sage.

Lindlof, T. R. (1995). *Qualitative communication research methods.* Thousand Oaks, CA: Sage.

Loden, M. (1985). *Feminine leadership, or how to succeed in business without being one of the boys.* New York: Times Books.

Madden, T. R. (1987). *Women vs. women: The uncivil business war.* New York: Amacom.

Maguire, M., & Mohtar, L. F. (1994). Performance and the celebration of a subaltern counterpublic. *Text and Performance Quarterly, 14*, 238–252.

Mansbridge, J. J. (1973). Time, emotion, and inequality: Three problems of participatory groups. *Journal of Applied Behavioral Science, 9*, 351–367.

Mansbridge, J. J. (1984). Feminism and the forms of freedom. In F. Fischer & C. Sirianni (Eds.), *Critical studies in organization and bureaucracy* (pp. 472–481). Philadelphia: Temple University Press.

Mansbridge, J. J. (1986). *Why we lost the ERA.* Chicago: University of Chicago Press.

Marshall, J. (1993). Viewing organizational communication from a feminist perspective: A critique and some offerings. *Communication Yearbook, 16*, 122–143.

Martin, J. (1990). Deconstructing organizational taboos: The suppression of gender conflict in organizations. *Organization Science, 1,* 339–359.

Martin, P. Y. (1993). Feminist practice in organizations: Implications for management. In E. A. Fagenson (Ed.), *Women in management: Trends, issues, and challenges in managerial diversity* (pp. 274–296). Newbury Park, CA: Sage.

Martin, P. Y. (1990). Rethinking feminist organizations. *Gender and Society, 4,* 182–206.

Mayer, A. M. (1995, May). Feminism-in-practice: Implications for feminist theory. Paper presented at the annual convention of the International Communication Association.

Mies, M. (1983). Towards a methodology for feminist research. In G. Bowles & R. D. Klein (Eds.), *Theories of women's studies* (pp. 117–139). London: Routledge and Kegan Paul.

Mills, A., & Chiaramonte, P. (1991). Organization as gendered communication act. *Canadian Journal of Communication, 16,* 381–398.

Mintzberg, H. (1994). The fall and rise of strategic planning. *Harvard Business Review, 72,* 107–114.

Morgen, S. (1983). Towards a politics of feelings: Beyond the dialectic of thought and actions. *Women's Studies, 10,* 203–223.

Morgen, S. (1988). The dream of diversity, the dilemma of difference: Race and class contradictions in a feminist health clinic. In J. Sole (Ed.), *Anthropology for the nineties* (pp. 370–380). New York: Free Press.

Morgen, S. (1990). Contradictions in feminist practice: Individualism and collectivism in a feminist health center. In C. Calhoun (Ed.), *Comparative social research* (suppl. 1, pp. 9–59). Greenwich, CT: JAI Press.

Morgen, S. (1994). Personalizing personnel decisions in feminist organizational theory and practice. *Human Relations, 47,* 665–684.

Mueller, C. (1995). The organizational basis of conflict in contemporary feminism. In M. M. Ferree & P. Y. Martin (Eds.), *Feminist organizations: Harvest of the new women's movement* (pp. 263–275). Philadelphia: Temple University Press.

Mumby, D. K. (1996). Feminism, postmodernism, and organizational communication studies: A critical reading. *Management Communication Quarterly, 9,* 259–295.

Mumby, D. K. (in press). Power, politics, and organizational communication. In F. Jablin & L. L. Putnam (Eds.), *The new handbook of organizational communication.* Newbury Park, CA: Sage.

Mumby, D. K., & Putnam, L. L. (1992). The politics of emotion: A feminist reading of bounded rationality. *Academy of Management Review, 17,* 465–486.

Murphy, B. O., & Zorn, T. (1996). Gendered interaction in professional relationships. In J. T. Wood (Ed.), *Gendered relationships* (pp. 213–232). Mountain View, CA: Mayfield.

Murray, S. B. (1988). The unhappy marriage of theory and practice: An analysis of a battered women's shelter. *NWSA Journal, 1,* 75–92.

Newman, K. (1980). Incipient bureaucracy: The development of hierarchies in egalitarian organizations. In. G. M. Britan & R. Cohen (Eds.), *Hierarchy & society* (pp. 143–163). Philadelphia: Institute for the Study of Human Issues.

Pahl, J. (1985). Refuges for battered women: Ideology and action. *Feminist Review, 19,* 25–43.

Peterson, P. & Bond, M.A. (1985). Grassroots feminist organizations: Issues for consultants. *Community Psychologist, 13,* 15–17.

Pfeffer, J. (1992). *Managing with power: Politics and influence in organizations.* Boston: Harvard Business School.

Putnam, L. L., & Mumby, D. K. (1993). Organizations, emotion, and the myth of rationality. In S. Fineman (Ed.), *Emotion in organizations* (pp. 36–57). London: Sage.

Raven, B. H. (1993). The bases of power: Origins and recent developments. *Journal of Social Issues, 49,* 227–251.

Reinelt, C. (1995). Moving onto the terrain of the state: The battered women's movement and the politics of engagement. In M. M. Ferree & P. Y. Martin (Eds.), *Feminist organizations: Harvest of the new women's movement* (pp. 84–104). Philadelphia: Temple University Press.

Reinelt, C. (1994). Fostering empowerment, building community: The challenge for state-funded feminist organizations. *Human Relations, 47,* 685–705.

Reinharz, S. (1992). *Feminist methods in social research.* New York: Oxford University Press.

Rich, A. (1979). Women and honor: Some notes on lying. In A. Rich (Ed.), *On lies, secrets, and silence: Selected prose 1966–1978* (pp. 185–194). New York: Norton.

Riger, S. (1994). Challenges of success: Stages of growth in feminist organizations. *Feminist Studies, 20,* 275–300.

Ristock, J. L. (1990). Canadian feminist social service collectives: Caring and contradictions. In L. Albrecht & R. M. Brewer (Eds.), *Bridges of power: Women's multicultural alliances* (pp. 172–181). Philadelphia: New Society.

Robert, H. M. (1989). *Roberts rules of order.* Modern edition by D. Patnode. Nashville T. Nelson.

Rodriguez, N. M. (1988). Transcending bureaucracy: Feminist politics at a shelter for battered women. *Gender and Society, 2,* 214–227.

Rothschild-Whitt, J. (1976). Conditions facilitating participatory-democratic organizations. *Sociological Inquiry, 46,* 75–86.

Rothschild-Whitt, J. (1979). The collectivist organization: An alternative to rational-bureaucratic models. *American Sociological Review, 44,* 509–527.

Schechter, S. (1982). *Women and male violence.* Boston: South End Press.

Schlesinger, B. B., & Bart, P. B. (1982). Collective work and self-identity: The effect of working in a feminist illegal abortion collective. In F. Lindenfeld & J. Rothschild-Whitt (Eds.), *Workplace democracy and social change.* Boston: Porter Sargent.

Sealander, J., & Smith, D. (1986). The rise and fall of feminist organizations in the 1970's: Dayton as a case study. *Feminist Studies, 12,* 321–341.

Sirianni, C. (1984). Participation, opportunity, and equality: Toward a pluralist organizational model. In. F. Fischer & C. Sirianni (Eds.), *Critical studies in organization and bureaucracy* (pp. 482–503). Philadelphia: Temple University Press.

Spalter-Roth, R., & Schreiber, R. (1995). Outsider issues and insider tactics: Strategic tension in the women's policy network during the 1980's. In M. M. Ferree & P. Y. Martin (Eds.), *Feminist organizations: Harvest of the new women's movement* (pp. 105–127). Philadelphia: Temple University Press.

Spitzack, C., & Carter, K. (1988). Feminist communication: Rethinking the politics of exclusion. *Women's Studies in Communication, 11,* 28–31.

Staggenborg, S. (1988). The consequences of professionalization and formalization in the pro-choice movement. *American Sociological Review, 53,* 585–606.

Staggenborg, S. (1989). Stability and innovation in the women's movement: A comparison of two movement organizations. *Social Problems, 36,* 75–92.

Steiner, L. (1989). Feminist theorizing and communication ethics. *Communication, 12,* 157–173.

Stohl, C. (1995). Paradoxes of participation. In R. Cesaria & P. Shockley-Zabalak (Eds.), *Organizzazioni e comunicazione* [Organizations and communication], (pp. 199–215). *Rome: Servizio Italiano Publicazioni Internazionali.*

Strine, M. S. (1992). Understanding "how things work": Sexual harassment and academic culture. *Journal of Applied Communication Research, 20,* 391–400.

Taylor, B., & Conrad, C. (1992). Narratives of sexual harassment: Organizational dimensions. *Journal of Applied Communication Research, 20,* 401–418.

Tierney, K. J. (1982). The battered women movement and the creation of the wife beating problem. *Social Problems, 29,* 207–220.

Todd-Mancillas, W. R., & Rossi, A. N. A. (1985). Gender differences in the management of personnel disputes. *Women's Studies in Communication, 8,* 25–33.

Trethewey, A. (1997). Resistance, identity, and empowerment: A postmodern feminist analysis of clients in a human service organization. *Communication Monographs, 64,* 281–301.

Uttal, L. (1990). Nods that silence. In G. Anzaldua (Ed.), *Making face, making soul: Creative and critical perspectives by women of color* (pp. 317–320). San Francisco: Aunt Lute Foundation Books.

Vollmer, F. (1986). Why do men have higher expectancy than women? *Sex Roles, 13,* 351–362.

Weedon, C. (1987). *Feminist practice and poststructuralist theory.* Oxford, England: Blackwell.

Wood, J., & Duck, S. (1995). Off the beaten track: New shores for relationship research. In J. Wood & S. Duck (Eds.), *Under-studied relationships: Off the beaten track* (pp. 1–21). Thousand Oaks, CA: Sage.

Wood, J., & Inman, C. C. (1993). In a different mode: Masculine styles of communicating closeness. *Journal of Applied Communication Research, 21,* 279–295.

Zaremba, E. (1988). Collective trouble. *Broadside, 10,* 5.

Zorn, T. (1995). Bosses and buddies: Constructing and performing simultaneously hierarchical and close friendship relationships. In J. Wood & S. Duck (Eds.), *Under-studied relationships: Off the beaten track* (pp. 122–147). Thousand Oaks, CA: Sage.

6

Community as a Means of Organizational Control

lLoril M. Gossett
Phillip K. Tompkins
University of Colorado, Boulder

> The idea of community is born of demographic imperatives, changing personal
> and social values, the desire for stability in an ever-changing and increasingly
> threatening world.
> —*Zemke* (1996, p. 24)

Workplace communities have long been of interest to communication scholars. It is in these informal networks that information is exchanged, organizational norms are established, ideas are shared, and individuals form a collective identity. Workplace communities are especially interesting sites to examine the ways that control works within organizations: Organizational communities are not only inviting places for workers to interact; they can also be an effective management tool. In this chapter, we will examine the ways in which workplace communities have been and continue to be used as a means of controlling organizational members. First, we will contrast community-based management strategies with rationally based management techniques. Next, we examine the ways in which communities function as a means of organizational control. Finally, in response to a changing economy and workforce, we consider alternate ways of creating community based control in organizations.

TECHNIQUES FOR ORGANIZATIONAL CONTROL

Historically, changes in organizational control practices have corresponded to changes in technology and the economy. Barley and Kunda (1992) reviewed managerial discourse from 1870 through 1980 and found two basic premises had guided control practices. They determined that control could best be differentiated between *normative* and *rational* managerial approaches. Their research demonstrated that managers alternated between the use of these two philosophies when designing organizational structures and control techniques. Over time, as the work environment changed, the dominant approach would fail and managerial strategy would shift to the alternate paradigm.

History of Control Strategies
Berley & Kunda (1992)

1870–1900	1900–1923	1923–1955	1955–1980	1980–1992
Industrial Betterment "YMCA" (*Normative*)	Scientific Management "Taylorism" (*Rational*)	Welfare Capitalism "Hawthorne Studies" (*Normative*)	Systems Rationalism "Management by Objectives" (*Rational*)	Organizational Culture "Teams" (*Normative*)

Normative versus Rational Approaches to Control

Normative approaches to organizational control are designed to improve efficiency and worker productivity by increasing communication in the system. The formation of personal relationships between workers and managers is considered an important aspect of control because these bonds create a strong organizational culture. This sort of management strategy emphasizes the importance of social groups and horizontal communication. Barley and Kunda's (1992) study shows that such strategies, "blurred the boundaries between work and non-work and between managers and workers. Because advocates of each [control strategy] envisioned cohesion and loyalty as the ultimate source of productivity, they exhorted managers to be leaders: to set an example, to inspire, to motivate, and to provide for the employees welfare" (p. 384). Identification with the organization and interpersonal communication is encouraged in order to stimulate more fluid interaction patterns in the system. The normative perspective on control focuses on the communal and social aspects of work in order to gain greater productivity and organizational success. As we will later discuss, the normative philosophy is the basis for community based control strategies.

In contrast to the normative model, *rational* approaches to control center on organizational design and structural issues. The personal needs of the employees are not the primary concern of management. Employees are considered to be machines that can be regulated and programmed in order to perform in an organizationally appropriate fashion. Vertical communication (top down) is privileged in this model. The rational managerial rhetoric argues, "that productivity stem[s] from carefully articulated methods and systems" (Barley & Kunda, 1992, p. 384). Rational managerial models (e.g., Taylorism) see managers as experts who are able "to bring rational analysis and a body of empirical knowledge to bear on the firm's problems. Furthermore, [rational models] assume that employees are calculative actors with instrumental orientations to work. Employees [are thought] either to understand the economic advantages of an efficient system or to be powerless to resist a well-designed structure" (p. 384). In this system, workplace social groups are broken up and informal interaction is seen as a detriment to organizational efficiency. The rational management strategies replace the "soft and fuzzy" management principles of normative control with "rigid and scientific" rational techniques that are designed to maximize organizational productivity.

Recent approaches to organizational control have been based on the normative model. The organizational culture movement of the late 1970s and 1980s was grounded in the normative idea that highly involving and cohesive workgroups would enable organizations to be more efficient and effective. This strategy resulted in a focus on "productive" work cultures and the proliferation of self-directed work teams as means of managing work and achieving organizational success. Management writers such as Peters and Waterman (1982) and Deal and Kennedy (1982) encouraged firms to form strong cultures and communities in their organizations. Establishing mission statements and a highly participatory management system was thought to be the new, best way to control workers.

This type of participatory management is designed to let the workers communicate openly in order to create and sustain their own nurturing and rewarding work environment. Participation in the decision-making process allows workers to form connections, identifications, and a sense of ownership in their work environment. In keeping with normative principles, participatory management increases communication between workers and managers and reduces the organizational hierarchy. In this system, members of the organization are empowered. The belief is that increased involvement and self-control leads to greater worker satisfaction, and satisfied workers, according to the normative model, are seen as more productive and committed workers. In the end, the idea was to create a work community that would both enrich the membership and serve managerial goals.

The success of the culture-based control strategy relied heavily on the effectiveness of the workplace community. More so than any of the other control strategies, the workers were largely responsible for controlling themselves. Rather than developing the work community as a part of the management effort (as previous normative strategies had), culture-based control relied heavily on communication and peer pressure that arose from within the system. In the next section, we will discuss the nature of work communities and explain how they have been used as a means of organizational control.

ORGANIZATIONAL COMMUNITIES

We need to have some sort of identity in order to function with others. The workplace is one site where people can establish membership, form a sense of self, and interact with others in a meaningful way. Nisbet (1988) believed that there is, "a great sense of vacuum even among the most ardent of the new individualists, the most consecrated of yuppies, rebels, and escapists. Otherwise why the craving for 'community' wherever it might be found?" (pp. 119–120). People want and need to be "in communion" with others. Ironically, we need to interact and form connections with other in order to have an individual sense of self. Burke (1937) stated that our individual identity is little more than a "combination of corporate 'we's'" (p. 264). We form bonds or identifications with others because it is a necessary component of filling a role in society. We fill various positions in different social "scenes" as the opportunities present themselves and as a result of these numerous roles, we develop a unique sense of self—a unique "I" that is a combination of all the various identifications that we hold. Communication is the tool that we use to forge the gap between each other, and communities are sites where this interaction can occur. If communities are not readily available to us, we create them within whichever system we are operating—including the workplace. Therefore, it is in the best interests of organizations to ensure that workplace communities support (or at least do not interrupt) managerial goals.

Nature of Work Communities

When we think of "community" we often idealize it as an inclusive, safe, and enjoyable environment, a place where we can feel like we belong. Communities are systems where (to paraphrase the "Cheers" theme song) "everybody knows your name" and where you can be accepted as yourself. Novak (1997), following Oakeshott (1975), distinguished two different types of communities and cautioned against confusing them with each other. He noted that there are key differences between "civic" communities and what he called "associations of enterprise." As Novak explained, "Civic association aims at something larger than any particular end, interest, or good; the protection of a body of general rules and a whole way of life; in other words, the larger framework within which, and only within which, the pursuit of particular ends becomes possible, peaceable, and fruitful" (p. 89). This is the sort of community (or civic association) that a neighborhood or social group might fall into. It enables members to attain their own goals. The purpose of this type of community is simply to be a safe place for communion and membership.

The workplace community (or enterprise association) has a different set of objectives: " The enterprise association is built to attain quite particular purposes, often purposes that tend to come around again quite continuously .... Enterprise associations are focused, purposive, instrumental, and executive: they fix a purpose and execute it" (Novak, 1997, pp. 89–90). The organization is a goal-driven, task-focused system. Its reason for existing is to perform some set of predetermined tasks. Organizations are designed to manage communication within their systems. The purpose of their structure is to direct the focus and efforts of people and other resources. Additionally, "people have specific roles to play within the structure. Some people serve as authority figures that make the decisions for the group, while others carry out commands and work to achieve the common organizational goals" (Gossett, 1993, p. 42). There can still be feelings of fellowship, society, and belonging in these systems, but there is also a specific collective purpose for which people join.

The workplace community is a specifically designed type of system and it would be inappropriate to try to extend its purpose to fulfill all of our community needs. In other words, we should not attempt to make enterprise communities into civic communities as their purposes are distinct. Nevertheless, as we spend more and more time in the organizational environment, the workplace community becomes an increasingly important part of our daily lives. The organization provides a natural place for modern workers to search for some sense of community, especially for those who have difficulty finding it in other areas. According to Reich (1991), "in real life, most Americans no longer live in traditional communities.... Most commute to work and socialize on some basis other than geographic proximity to where they sleep. And most pick up and move every five years or so to a different neighborhood" (p. 277). In the past, people were born, raised, and died in the same town or county. People formed bonds and relationships that provided them with the sense of belonging and stability.

With economic and demographic changes, Americans seem to have become a nation of nomadic individuals, who fail to maintain a fixed location or long-term relationships. Instead, we travel across the country and globe, staying only as long as it serves our purpose or our particular skills and services are useful. Nisbet (1988) criticized our modern society by claiming that the only reason we form any sort of bond with others is in order to meet some monetary objective. In such a system every act of service, responsibility, protection, and aid to others is an act presupposing or calling for monetary exchange, for cash payment. What individuals do for their spouses, for their children and kinsman, for neighbors and all other common partners in the business of maintaining family, job, citizenship, and even personal identity itself, rest upon the *cash nexus* [italics added] and nothing else. (p. 86) Although the situation may not be a dark as Nisbet painted it, if he was at all correct, the workplace may be one of the few places that workers can form some sense of community.

The Structure of Organizational Communities

If we seek to create communities within the workplace, it is important to understand how they function with the rest of the system. Barnard (1968) indicated that organizations are made up of two basic structures. There is the "formal" organizational structure, which dictates the chain of command, assigns tasks, and sets out the organizational goals. The formal organization is what we think of when we look at an organizational chart and focus purely on the task functions of the system. Equally important and necessary to the running of an organization is the "informal" structure. The informal organizational structure defines the norms, values, rules, and ways of doing things in the system. These are the typical day-to-day interactions that people experience within the organization. It is through the informal organization that workers are able to give meaning to their work life and form some sort of commitment to the organization as a whole. The formation of work communities typically takes place in the informal organizational structure because this is where members interact. The community shapes and is maintained by the informal structure.

Barnard (1968) stated that the informal structure has three basic functions. The most important function of the informal structure is to facilitate communication among members. The informal structure enables workers to interact with each other in a code that they understand and can relate to. Whereas the formal structure might indicate official reporting relationships, the informal structure illustrates how information really gets transferred in the system. The informal structure also maintains, "cohesiveness in formal organizations through regulating the willingness to serve and the stability of objective authority. A third function is the maintenance of a feeling of personal integrity, of self-respect, or independent choice" (p. 122). Through interaction within the informal structure/workplace community, individuals form their organizational identifications. These identifications can, in turn, be reinforced by the formal structure. According to Wolf (1982), "Barnard says, formal organization cannot exist for long without informal. The formal organization provides the skeletal structure. It is impersonal. In contrast informal organization provides the energy and driving force and is personal" (p. 72). Ideally, the informal and formal structures compliment each other and work together to achieve the organization's goals. Neither one can work alone and be effective. Organizations need to have effective and vibrant workplace communities that work with (and not against) the formal system. Orchestrating the agreement between these two structures enables workplace communities to be used as a means of organizational control.

Communities as a Means of Organizational Control

Organizations that capitalized on the informal communication structure in order to manage their workers created a new type of organizational control under the normative model. The community-based management system was based on what Tompkins and Cheney (1985) called "concertive control." This system of control has been widely accepted as an effective method of managing workers in more participatory organizational structures. Concertive control relies largely, but not entirely, on Burke's (1957) notion of "identification." As noted earlier, Burke argued that humans are social animals and have a basic need to form connections with others. Thus most workers willingly seek to identify with others in the system and form a sort of cohesive bond or "community" with one another. The enactment of a shared identity is accomplished through communication within the informal organizational structure. Members of the identified group or workplace community explicitly accept a set of shared values, decision premises, symbols, and codes that serve to define them as a collective unit. According to Carbaugh (1996), "For shared identities like these to be forceful, a common code for so being, acting, and feeling must be presumed, realized, or conversed in the scene. When so, this demonstrates ... the communal function of communication, an enactment of shared identity" (p. 199). Organizations can use this identification to facilitate "organizationally appropriate" communication within the informal structure. Through careful member selection, training, socialization, and other programs, managers seek to orchestrate a highly identified and tightly bonded workgroup who will communicate effectively and do their best for the organization.

The theory of "concertive control" also relies on Simon's (1976) theory of the "decisional premise" to transform the organizational identification into a method for controlling worker behavior. Simon explained that organizations can control workers by limiting their decision-making options to those that are organizationally acceptable. Organizations can carefully select and train their members and inculcate the workers with specific values and decisional premises so that they behave appropriately. Tompkins and Cheney (1985) again used Burke's notion of "identification" to explain why members willingly select the organization's decisional premises rather than use other ones. Adopting a common set of decisional premises gives the workers a feeling of ownership and connection with others in the system. To maintain their identity as community members, workers choose the organizationally appropriate premise and then enthymemically deduce the best conclusion. Tompkins and Cheney defined the end result of this process to be "organizational identification." This is a situation in which, "a decision maker identifies with an organization when he or she desires to choose the alternative that best promotes the perceived interests of that organization" (p. 194). Control is "unobtrusive" in the system because the workers are managing themselves for the organization. There is the perception of greater freedom and flexibility in the system without a loss of managerial control. More importantly, involvement in a work community or work team allows workers to control each other. As predicted by Tompkins and Cheney and confirmed by Barker's fieldwork (1993), this sort of concertive control means that everyone in the system is managing and controlling everyone else, thus increasing the total level of control in the system.

Benefits of Community-Based Control

From the perspective of management, the community-based control strategy has provided numerous benefits. Because communication is more fluid and open, more members can take part in the decision making process. Additionally, people have a sense of camaraderie that allows them to work together more effectively. David Henderson, an organizational consultant, noted that workplace communities, "enhance decision making. It speeds it up, and gives higher-quality decisions because people can be more frank. You talk about the unwritten rules. They do less editing. It creates safety" (Zemke, 1996, p. 24).

Communication flows through the workplace community: The interactions between members enable information to be transmitted throughout the system—outside of the strict formal communication channels. These informal structures within the organizational framework also enabled members to learn from each other and improve in their own skill areas. People who feel comfortable and connected to each other work together more effectively. There is less need for managers to watch over people if they can work together on their own. Additionally, if all members are organizationally identified, they have a "short-hand" or easier way of communicating that might make it easier and faster to work together. Informal, social interaction provides a way for workers to share ideas and find new ways to solve problems.

From the perspective of workers, community-based control systems seem to be a more acceptable and rewarding way to interact with fellow workers and managers than other control options. Heckscher (1995) noted that workers want a sense of community in the workplace as a way to, "maintain a sense of teamwork and avoid the pure dog-eat-dog environment of a totally disconnected workforce" (p. 153). Workers want community "to facilitate cooperation and working together," (p. 152) especially in a society where this experience is increasingly hard to find. Workers also want to interact more freely, in order to learn from each other and grow in their positions. As Stamps (1997) described:

> At the core of the new thinking is the notion that work and learning are social activities. As people work together, they not only learn from doing, they develop a shared sense of what has to happen to get the job done. They develop a common way of thinking and talking about their work. Eventually they come to share a sort of mutual identity—a single understanding of who they are and what their relationship is to the larger organization. It is in these groups where some of the most valuable and innovative work-related learning occurs. (p. 34)

To get the most out of the work experience; workers appear to prefer the opportunity to interact in a workplace community.

The workplace community is a very powerful means of control because it becomes so natural and internalized in the individual members that it doesn't seem like a control system—it is unobtrusive and invisible, yet ubiquitous. However, this sort of control system can also be difficult to "manage" because it requires that the individual workers internalize the organization's goals and act appropriately. Organizational leaders must work to ensure that their workers are highly identified and then must allow workers to make decisions and participate in the organizational leadership. Recent changes in the economy and business practices have threatened the organization's ability to rely on having highly identified workers who will manage themselves in the best interest of the organization.

CHANGE IN SOCIETY

Just as in the past, changes in contemporary society have posed significant challenges to existing organizational control strategies. Although the organizational culture/community-based control system seemed to be very successful in the 1970s and early 1980s, the 1990s have problematized this normative form of control. Community-based control strategies rely on a sense of trust, identification, and camaraderie among the organizational membership. If a firm is going to rely on identified workers to make organizationally appropriate decisions, then the source of identification cannot be threatened. Unfortunately, a variety of factors have worked together to create a situation in which the worker is no longer a committed, stable part of the organizational structure. New challenges posed by international competition, technology, and the vary nature of organizational membership have all caused the workplace community to diminish as a means of effective control.

Downsizing

Increased globalization and foreign competition in the late 1980s prompted U.S. firms to engage in large-scale organizational downsizing. U.S. organizations underwent massive reorganization efforts in an attempt to reduce their overhead expenses and become more flexible for the fast-paced global economy. A significant part of this effort was downsizing permanent workers in order to give the appearance of becoming "lean and mean" to stockholders. Cutting full time employees and overhead expenses often provided companies with better stock prices and more immediate cash reserves. However, downsizing usually also meant that remaining workers had to take on the responsibilities of those who had been laid-off, in order to meet the organization's needs. Whereas blue-collar workers were subject to lay-offs for years, this period was significant because it impacted a large number of white-collar workers. White-collar workers had traditionally been protected by organizations. However, the growth in administration and "middle management" over time had left organizations with a great deal of overhead expense in the late 1980s. This was the layer that suffered the greatest cuts during the recent downsizing efforts.

An increased reliance on temporary employees was another way that organizations cut their overhead expenses and increased their flexibility (Butterfield, 1995). Although the temporary workers were unlikely to have the same kind of commitment or skills that permanent employees possess, the flat-cost savings and short-term stock price increases seemed to be sufficient to motivate organizations to replace permanent staff with temporary labor. The number of temporary workers in the U.S. doubled from 1989 to 1994 (to approximately 1.9 million). It is estimated that this population of workers might grow to 3.5 million by the turn of the century (Rose, 1994). Some estimates calculate the temporary labor pool to be one-fourth of the total workforce, forcing organizational scholars and managers to consider that, "the long-standing assumption that employees ... are regular or permanent members of their organization is no longer valid" (Sias, Kramer, & Jenkins, 1997, p. 3). This change in the workforce seems to require a reconsideration of organizational control strategies.

The use of temporary workers and large-scale downsizing efforts changed the nature of the organizational environment. At the same time that managerial discourse was advancing the participatory and culture management ideals of the 1980s, managerial practices were eroding the trust and security needed to realize these goals. Workers began to realize that organizations would no longer provide a stable environment for them to work within. The old "workplace community" that demanded loyalty and created a sense of organizational commitment and identification was severely diminished by downsizing. According to Zemke (1996):

> The '80s and '90s have exploded the image of the workplace as a village, delivering the unmistakable message: The company for which we work is owned by someone not us. Its purpose is to satisfy somebody's budget–profit expectations. Anything and everything not currently facilitating those expectations is expendable. (p. 24)

Workers began to develop a new attitude about work and their role in organizations. They no longer had the same sense of commitment to their firms. As Deetz (1996) explained it:

> Throughout the workplace, you hear the talk of a new social contract. The old contract was, 'I will give you loyalty and commitment and you will take care of me and my family.' Big companies broke that contract .... A new debate started. It isn't just the people who left. It is also the people who stayed who said, 'I must negotiate a better deal.' (p. 20)

As organizations failed to reward worker loyalty and increasingly used contingent forms of labor (Butterfield, 1995; Miller, 1995; Parker, 1994), the trust and loyalty of their workforce diminished. This created difficulties for some firms that had come to rely on concertive control strategies. Heckscher (1995) indicated that firms that rely on a community-based control system (e.g., having identified workers control themselves in the interest of the organization), have to foster an environment of trust within the system: "Trust, in these systems, is intertwined with loyalty; people trust others who, they believe, are oriented to the basic good of the company and who will be around long enough to bear the consequences of their actions" (p. 123). Additionally, Pearce (1993) found that firms that hire temporary or contingent labor to supplement their permanent workforce, fostered a sense of organizational "distrust" in their permanent staff. In an era of downsizing and temp workers, permanent employees cannot ensure that the people they work with will be there in the future; long-term planning and interpersonal connections are likely to diminish as organizational membership becomes more short-term in nature. The decrease in trust is likely to make the previously popular concertive control methods difficult for some firms to maintain.

For workplace community to be an effective control system, the permanent employee must be loyal and committed to the goals of the organization. Organizational identification is crucial to maintain worker control. However, with these new management strategies (downsizing and temps), the process by which identification is created is damaged. Authentic organizational identification must be a mutually involving relationship. Both parties have a vested interest in ensuring that the other's needs are met. Identification is therefore a two-way obligation, "with the corporation providing protection to the subordinate and the subordinate providing fealty to the corporation" (Burke, 1937, p. 265). In order to sustain identification, a sort of social contract is created in which both parties give up a bit of autonomy to gain the benefit of group cooperation. With the "social contract" between workers and organizations brought into question, identification and organizational control may be difficult for some firms to count on. Firms that have undergone the workforce changes described previously may need to reconsider their reliance on a pure concertive control system.

Technology

Technological advances have also had an impact on the contemporary organizational environment. Access to the Internet and the widespread use of home computers are allowing people to work in a wide variety of locations. Many workers no longer need to be on-site in an office or organization to do their work. Telecommuting is growing so popular that fully 15% of workers are expected to be working outside the traditional office space by the turn of the century (Gould, Weiner, & Levin et al., 1997, p. 158). These technologies allow what Taylor and Trujillo (in press) called "fluid" organizational memberships, ones in which employees can affiliate with groups for brief periods of time and operate in virtual work spaces that are physically moveable to nearly any place on the globe. Although telecommuters may be permanent organizational members, the access to this technology makes it easier for firms to use nonmembers (e.g., contingent labor) to perform organizational functions (Miller, 1995). Workers who can telecommute do not take up office space and take care of their own equipment, allowing the overhead cost to the organization to be virtually eliminated. If the telecommuter is also a contingent and nonidentified worker, the organization pays for nothing but the worker's time—a significant cost reduction, as well as incentive to use technology as a means to reduce organizational memberships and organizational expenses. With the global competition and economic challenges noted previously, this sort of system is increasingly attractive to contemporary firms.

The increasing use of this technology seems to further weaken the work community. Although the physical space of the organization is no longer required for work, some sort of shared location is necessary to sustain a sense of fellowship. Communities typically require a shared geographic space to help define membership—but technology is challenging the boundaries of organizations and workplace communities. Barker, in her 1998 study of virtual communities noted, the "territory" of communities might better be defined by analyzing interaction patterns within a system, rather than a specific location. Technological advances have enabled people to interact via computer or some other mechanized device. The sites for telecommuters are contained in the communication devices that connect them to other organizational members, and thus they operate in a cyberspace, rather than a physical space.

Although the technology makes virtual work communities possible, organizations still need to make sure that remote workers feel connected to the rest of the system. Remote workers may feel isolated by the lack of personal contact with other members of the organization. Although not every worker may be bothered by this lack of contact, others can miss the feeling of camaraderie that traditional organizational structures provide. As Gould (1997) pointed out, when working at home they miss the bonds and sense of community that they had. One remote worker, "admits that the one thing he longs for is 'just standing around shooting the breeze. It's not the same thing with e-mail'" (Gould, p. 160). Mulgan (1991) noted that the increase in technology, organizations can keep workers more separate and disconnected from others in the system. Likewise, the technology enables the workers to be more independent. This structure might provide the organizations with more flexibility and less expense, but it may also come at the expense of organizational control. The same technology that connects remote workers to the organization might also help to isolate them from the workplace community. The day-to-day, informal interactions that sustain a workplace community may be difficult to translate to the remote worker. If organizational leaders want to rely on concertive control, they must find some way to integrate remote workers into the rest of the organization and ensure some sense of common experience, informal interaction, and community. Whereas technological devices might provide workers with some sense of connection, the fact remains that this is a different type of work relationship than we have seen in years past, one that creates new challenges for the maintenance of workplace communities and concertive control systems.

Free Agency and Knowledge Workers

In light of the changes previously discussed, the modern worker has adapted and become an entirely different force for organizations to reckon with. The contemporary workforce is increasingly being dominated by what Drucker (1994) called *knowledge workers* and Gould et al. (1997) called *free agents*. Before the industrial revolution, most people in this country were farmers. After the turn of the century, the number of industrial laborers eventually surpassed agricultural workers. Currently, the number of traditional industrial workers is on the decline and the new *knowledge workers* are becoming more prevalent. *Knowledge workers* now represent a significant plurality and are increasing in number. These workers are specialists who rely on their educational background, experience, and basic intelligence to operate and work in society. Many of them are former white-collar workers who were unable or did not want to go back into a traditional organizational structure after being downsized.

Drucker (1994) argued that we are becoming a nation of *knowledge workers*, with people who are no longer reliant on the traditional skills and manual dexterity required in years past. Drucker stated that our society will be, "the first society in which not everybody does the same work, as was the case when the huge majority were farmers or, as seemed likely only forty or thirty years ago, were going to be machine operators" (p. 62). This new type of worker is focused on developing skills, products, and services that can then be turned around and marketed to customers. "They understand that their only security is being able to offer and sell the skills and services the market needs" (Gould et al., 1997, p. 9). The specialization of the *knowledge worker* ensures his or her value to the organization. Braverman (1974) argued that organizations attempted to control workers by "de-skilling" them. *Knowledge Workers/Free Agents* resist this type of control by holding on to their professional secrets—specialization allows them to retain some power in the organizational environment.

This kind of worker creates a society where people are distinct individuals rather than members of a greater whole. Similar to their experience in general society, the new knowledge workers are not connected to each other in the workplace. "The essence of a knowledge society is mobility in terms of where one lives, mobility in terms of what one does, mobility in terms of one's affiliations. People no longer have roots" (Drucker, 1994, p. 74). Although the modern worker is a participant in the organization, he or she no longer has the same sort of commitment that was known in years past. Gone are the days of the "organization man" working for the gold watch. As Drucker argued, knowledge workers "own" their tools and can take them wherever they want to go. Knowledge becomes a commodity that individual workers can package and sell to the highest bidder (Mulgan, 1991).

Although, this type of worker can become a specialist in his or her field, this specialization comes at a cost. They are forced to compete against each other in a free-market, labor free-for-all. Workers can become more isolated as they attempt to differentiate their services from their "competition." Durkheim (1933) warned against the dangers of over-specialization.

If public opinion sanctions the division of labor, it is not without a sort of uneasiness and hesitation. While commending men [sic] to specialize, it seems to fear they will specialize too much…. "It is sad commentary," said Jean-Baptiste Say, "That we have come to the state where we never do anything more than make the eighteenth part of a pin." (p. 43)

The disconnected worker loses his or her relationships with others and the ability to learn and grow as a result of those sustained interactions.

Alexis de Tocqueville (1966) also recognized the danger of extreme worker specialization and noted that under such specialization the art advances but the artisan recedes. The independent, free agent worker is usually separate and distinct from others—in a word, the person is "loose." Applying de Tocqueville's analysis to our present situation may indicate that this new breed of worker is improving in his/her specific art (job, discipline, etc.) but not advancing individually as an artisan because he/she is not open to outside influences that are realized through community and other external involvement. As previously discussed, the workplace community provides much more than a sense of belonging to workers. Membership in such a system provides individuals with a network of others with whom they can interact and from whom they can learn. A permanent worker in a supportive environment can learn and grow within the organization, becoming multi-skilled and able to work in a variety of areas, whereas the disconnected free agent might be limited in professional as well as personal development.

Change in Control Process

Barley and Kunda (1992) noted that they anticipated "the current emphasis on normative control to be followed by a resurgence of rationalism. Moreover, this surge should occur in conjunction with a long-term expansion in the economy and the rise of a new paradigm of automation" (p. 394). As we previously discussed, the U.S. economy has been strong for the past few years, with inflation and unemployment at record lows. Additionally, technological advances are transforming the workplace and creating new organizational opportunities. According to their theory, the situation seems ripe for a move back toward the rational model of control. However, we would argue that organizations do not seem to be swinging back to the rational forms of control that we have known in years past. That is not to say that there is not a change in organizational philosophy; rather, there may be a new form of organizational design that can merge elements of both normative and rational strategies in order to provide organizational leaders with a way to control their workers in the modern organizational environment.

Problems With the Normative Model for the Current Workforce

The traditional normative approach to control would have organizations focusing on their employee's needs and fostering open communication throughout the system. Unfortunately, in today's era of *free agent* workers and downsized organizations, the raw-materials or workers required to build a tight knit work-place community are hard to find. Workers do not want (and can not afford) to get too involved or identified with a single organization, otherwise they risk hurting their value as *free agents*. It also is not smart for them to pledge long-term commitment to a single organization, because they could find themselves downsized without any options or alternatives. Finally, workers have to continually look for new opportunities and guard against new competition.

Although the idea for concertive control and community-based management is still attractive, it cannot work in an environment without trust and identification—two aspects of organizational life that have been challenged during the past few years. It seems as if it is no longer practical for some firms to maintain long-term commitments to all of their employees. Organizations need to be flexible and able to respond to market changes. As one corporate executive explained, it is now detrimental to think of your organizational membership as family. In this fast-paced and competitive environment, firms need to be able to adjust their workforce quickly and "you can't fire family."

Open, free-flowing communication can also be compromised in the current system because workers are not made to feel safe and cannot afford to take risks. They are not always able to rely on organizations and co-workers to be loyal, so communication from and between workers may be stifled. Likewise, organizations cannot necessarily trust workers to be tightly identified and make organizationally appropriate decisions, so a more top-down managerial approach may be used to make decisions. At all levels, participation seems to suffer, preventing normative models of control from being effectively applied.

Organizations and individuals that recognize this change in the environment seem to be more successful than those who try to hang on to the old ways of doing things. In a recent study, Heckscher (1998) noted that organizations may no longer be competitive if they hold to the old workplace community system. Heckscher examined 14 companies in order to find distinctions between firms that seemed to be successful in the new era of organizational downsizing and international competition and those that were having difficulty. Whereas organizational theorists have presumed that a committed and loyal workforce is important and beneficial to organizations, Heckscher found that companies with some of the most loyal employees were also experiencing some of the greatest difficulties. He explained that this might be due to managers and organizations holding on to antiquated definitions of organizational life that are no longer appropriate in our modern economy. The old definitions of loyalty were based on the ideas that "we are all in this together, for the long haul." This is no longer the case. Heckscher equated our retrogressive desire for workplace community to our nostalgia for small-town America: We like the idea, but don't really want to live there. Organizations need to find an alternative to the closed, tight-knit community, one in which everyone is willing to take part and will provide some of the control benefits of the old system without the commitment requirements or flexibility restrictions.

An additional challenge to the normative, community-based management strategies that we have known is posed by the increasingly independent and autonomous knowledge workers. *Free agents* and *knowledge workers* are defined by their skills and professional identities rather than their organizational memberships. As we note earlier, these workers are specialists who travel from job to job, wherever the work and money are available. One of the few constants in their life may be their professional identities. As Cheney (1983) explained:

[A]s we move toward a postindustrial society populated largely by professionals in high technology and service firms, Galbraith anticipates—and fears—an even greater blending of individual and organizational goals, with some individuals identifying most strongly with *particular* employers and others with "industries," professions, or even technology itself. (pp. 157–158)

The worker does not need the long-term support or identity benefits of the formal organization if their professional ties are strong. These ties weaken management's control and influence on the individual worker, creating yet another friction point in the workplace. The organization seems to still want the worker to identify and find community within the system, but the worker has other influences and affiliations that weaken the bonds to the organization.

If the values and decisional premises of different professional groups are internalized and invoked by the worker in order to maintain his or her identity as a member of the profession, such premises may contradict with those of the specific organization.

> Professions then are seen as trans-organizational loci of culture that interpenetrate organizations through the ideologies and values enacted by individuals as they make concrete decisions. These values may or may not contradict organizational values. This is the point at which consistencies and contradictions among organizational rhetors is acted out. (Barker & Cheney, 1994, p. 85)

As these disconnected workers become more prevalent in our society, organizations will need to determine how they will overcome the control challenges of having multiple decisional premises at work in the system. A dominant set of decisional premises can no longer be assumed; this change in the work force also seems to threaten the effectiveness of concertive control methods.

Problems With the Rational Model for the Current Workforce

Even as organizations may be unable to maintain a normative control system, they also seem to resist moving to a purely rational model. The growing significance of the free agent or knowledge worker prevents organizations from effectively managing them in a rational, top-down manner. With an extremely specialized workforce comprised of independent knowledge workers, an environment is created that is too multifarious for any single manager or system to effectively monitor and control. As Mulligan (1991) described the situation, "Other things being equal, within any structure greater complexity makes it harder to effectively impose control from above .... Control ceases to be a resource that is held by some and exercised over others but becomes embedded within the structure, as a means of adapting and of meeting goals" (p. 57). Unlike previous workforces, knowledge workers do not need a significant amount of supervision, training, or outside resources to do their work, they are largely self-sustaining. Traditional superior-subordinate relationships are difficult to apply to this group of workers because it is unlikely that the organization will have someone qualified to supervise them. Drucker (1992) noted that:

> [B]ecause the modern organization consists of knowledge specialists, it has to be an organization of equals, of colleagues and associates. No knowledge ranks higher than another; each is judged by its contribution to the common task rather than by any inherent superiority and inferiority. Therefore, the modern organi-

zation cannot be an organization of boss and subordinate. It must be organized as a team. (p. 101)

The steep hierarchy traditional in rational forms of control will not be effective here; thus, traditional rational forms of control are seemingly ill-suited to manage this group effectively. Workers also seem to resist the idea of going back to a strict system of rational control, even the disconnected *knowledge workers* or *free agents* appreciate the benefits that workplace communities provide and want to have membership in some sort of workplace system. Becoming isolated individuals within the organizational system is not a desirable option. In order to keep ahead in their professional lives, workers need some sort of interaction that will enable members to build on and develop each other's ideas.

Innovation takes place when members can share information with each other freely and easily. This direct contact is not something that can easily be replicated or replaced with other forms of communication. Workers need to have informal interactions and a sense of workplace community to gain these advantages. Periodic or mediated interaction does not seem to be a replacement for community.

One of the great myths of the Information Age is the idea that technology will create collaboration... It doesn't happen this way. Common work issues and a desire to learn from one another are the drivers behind these communities, not technologies. To put it another way, "No one has yet invented a technology that replaces a pitcher of beer." (Stamps, 1997, p. 34)

In order to ensure that organizational members are learning and working to the best of their ability, organizations need to ensure informal interactions between them. They cannot afford to totally abandon workplace communities or push them outside the control system.

PROJECT-BASED CONTROL

Workers and managers want the benefits of a tight-knit organizational community without the corresponding constraints that such systems require. The solution might be to merge normative and rational control strategies in order to create a project-based (rather than organizationally based) system of control. This system of control would create temporary work groups by joining together individuals with commitments and organizations that have a mission. Organizations, ... no longer [are] looking for loyal employees, but for people with the right skill sets who view their commitments as temporary and project focused (Gould et al. (1997, p. 13). New organizational forms have " ... manifested a form of community different from that of loyalty, one built around a common *purpose* rather than a common history" (Heckscher, 1995, p. 123). Under this system, group members are together for a specific task and are not expected to give any sort of long-term membership commitment. The commitment is limited to the lifetime and needs of the project. Communication channels are primarily limited to the project group because each group is largely self-sustaining. The organization's and workers' interests are joined together to achieve a common goal—but the commitment does not extend beyond the project. As we will now illustrate, this sort of control strategy enables firms to blend both normative and rational approaches within the same system.

Normative Control Elements

The ability to work in a project-based work group (rather than a nameless, faceless hierarchy) allows workers to form temporary bonds and a short-term workplace community with their other group members. Workers do not want to depend on organizations but also don't want to be isolated *free agents*. They want to create temporary communities to facilitate cooperation and working together (Heckscher, 1995). Thus, the project groups can potentially achieve many of the communicative benefits and personal growth opportunities that previous normative organizational models offered workers. Communication codes and trust can be developed between these workers for the duration of their project. These systems can be highly participatory within the group boundaries and can therefore allow a flatter organizational structure. The close contact also allows the workers to learn from each other to grow (and be more marketable) in their professions. The opportunity to work in multiple project groups, rather than a single organization, keeps the workers fresh and flexible. While the project groups fail to provide the workers with job security, they do provide a way for them to sustain short-term connections with others.

The temporary nature of these project groups might also foster a greater degree of worker identification than might otherwise be obtained. The project-group members have a common purpose that allows them to form a shared identity. Although they may all have independent professional identities that dominate their decision-making process, the fact that they were selected to work together should indicate the compatibility between their decisional premises and that of the organization for the specific project. Additionally, because these groups have a limited time commitment, the members can form an independent "group identification" rather than have to identify with the whole organizational system. The more immediate contact and mutual understanding involved throughout the duration of the relationship might make this sort of identification easier to bear for *free agents* who do not want to be too tied down for too long.

Indeed, identification with the group purpose rather than loyalty to the entire system may be a more successful approach for some contemporary workers and organizations. According to Heckscher's (1995) study of downsizing firms, the ones that were more successful were those in which members weren't necessarily loyal or identified with the organization, but were identified with their project group.

> There seemed to be a sense not so much of being *in* this together as of *working* together toward a common purpose, one based on a collective definition of strategy and of the demands of the environment. It is a far more contingent and voluntaristic form of community than the old; some might say it is colder and less fair. But it can also be seen as less paternalistic, more capable of responding to and developing individual capacities. (pp. 11–12)

This sort of identification and worker commitment allows workers to be independent and think for themselves, while still working together with their teammates.

Rational Control Elements

Project-based management also has important features of the rational model of control which make it effective. Because of a lack of a highly identified or committed workforce, it is difficult to be able to empower workers to make decisions about the direction or focus of the organization. Managers cannot presume that workers are all using the appropriate decisional premises if trust and loyalty have been eroded, or if a significant portion of the workforce is made up of contingent (nonemployee) laborers. Thus, decision making and worker control might need to become more centralized and hierarchical in nature. The project-based control system allows for this because managers are defining the nature of the task, allocating the resources, and selecting the workforce. Although the project group has flexibility in how the task is completed, the important organizational decisions and ultimate oversight of the group is more top-down in nature.

Rational models of control also tend to be faster than normative's diffused, participatory management techniques. In a hierarchy, there are specific people who collect the information and make decisions for the entire system. Communication throughout the organization is limited so it can be efficiently managed by a small group of people. Oversight and control is simplified by isolating project-groups into self-sufficient units. In this competitive era, there is a need for quick reaction time and organizational flexibility. A more structured, rational, decision-making process might better serve organizations in this environment. In the project-based system, each group is relatively autonomous and is not involved or necessarily tied to others. Managers can quickly add or delete groups, without having to impact or consult the rest of the organization.

Additionally, by allowing the project groups to foster their own limited organizational communities, this obligation is removed from the general management, and they can focus more on organizational task and design issues. Each group can form a distinct culture that does not necessarily have to agree with other groups. The organization's management no longer needs to ensure that the whole culture and all of the members work together—only that they work at a local level. This shifts the normative control efforts to the group level and allows the organization to manage the entire system with a more rational control style.

Limitations of Project Control

Although project-based control provides members with a sense of identification and common purpose and provides managers with flexibility and autonomy, there are still several challenges that it poses to organizational control efforts. Tompkins (1993) described some of the problems and advantages of project-based management from his study of NASA during the Apollo project. NASA was run with a matrix structure, with work teams that were assembled from permanent divisions. Tompkins found that there was high-member cohesion within the work teams but also high degree of conflict between the groups. Additionally, there was a decreased level of communication between the project teams and the disciplinary divisions.

In their 1994 study of permanent work teams, Barker and Tompkins noted that participation in these teams potentially threatened the worker's identification and loyalty to the organization as a whole.

> Because the identification process is so strong in the teams, the work group becomes, in a way, an irresistible force that attracts members' identification at the expense of the larger organization and other targets.... The team competes with the organization for the worker's loyalty and identification. (pp. 226)

Barker and Tompkins also found that worker identification with the goals and objectives of their specific work team could inhibit the organization from effectively managing the worker: Although identified members of the team might use the work group's decisional premises to make choices, these may not always be in line with the goals of the organization. For example, workers might do things that would advance the cause of their own work group, at the expense of another. Additionally, when there are points of contention, Barker and Tompkins (1994) found that workers might support the team's perspective over that of management.

The Tompkins (1993) and Barker and Tompkins (1994) studies both deal with permanent members of an organization rather than people who only had a short-term commitment to the system. It is important to note that current temporary project groups are qualitatively different from permanent organizational teams or project teams assembled from permanent organizational members. Although all three may seem self-sustaining and may have a fair degree of self-management, temporary project groups have a temporal boundary to them that the others do not. Project group workers only enter the organization after a task has been identified and their group is disassembled once the task is complete. The project group workers may try to stay within the organization, but they have no guarantee that there will be a place for them. The group itself is only is existence for the duration of its task.

The control problems found with permanent teams might be exacerbated in the short-term project structure. Edmund Burke noted that the strongest source of identification and loyalty is the "little platoon" to which we belong. In the new work environment, the *knowledge workers* only have their individual project groups. The temporary project communities, "don't require or ensure worker loyalty. There is also no guarantee of worker obedience because things are more negotiable and people are loyal to their specific project" (Heckscher, 1995, pp. 174–175). Reliance on temporary project groups might actually decrease horizontal communication between organizational units even more than other models of control. The project group members live and die by the success of their task and not the overall success of the organization. Thus in-fighting between groups and communication breakdowns might create significant problems for organizations using this strategy. Organizations need to consider that such a situation may be a potential challenge to this type of control.

CONCLUSION

Workplace communities can be an important source of control in organizations. Informal interactions between workers can be directed to support the formal organizational goals—creating an identified and tightly controlled system. However, as we have shown, organizations must ensure that the proper conditions exist for these communities to flourish and work. Communities are collections of people whose relationships are based on trust, allegiance, fealty, and responsibility. For organizations to harness workplace communities as control mechanisms, these sorts of relationships must be able to be established. Current trends in the work environment have made this difficult for some firms to accomplish.

Despite the challenges, organizations have not abandoned the concept of workplace community. Both workers and managers, for different reasons, seek the benefits of community membership (open communication, productivity, identification, control, and security) to do their jobs. Because everyone seeks them and because of current organizational realities, the challenge is to find new forms of community for the work environment. For firms unable to sustain an organization-wide community or workers unable to commit to a single organization, the project-based community might be a solution—a temporary sense of community may be better than none at all.

REFERENCES

Barker, J. R. (1993). Tightening the iron cage: Concertive control in self-managing teams. *Administrative Science Quarterly, 38,* 408–437.

Barker, J. R., & Cheney, G. (1994). The concept and the practice of discipline in contemporary organizational life. *Communication Monographs, 61,* 19–43.

Barker, J. R., & Tompkins, P. K. (1994). Identification in the self-managing organization: Characteristics of target and tenure. *Human Communication Research, 21,* 223–240.

Barker, L. J. (1998). *Real people, real interaction—even onnamoo: The discursive construction of virtual community on Lambdamoo.* Unpublished doctoral dissertation. University of Colorado, Boulder.

Barley, S. R., & Kunda, G. (1992). Design and devotion: Surges of rational and normative ideologies of control in managerial discourse. *Administrative Science Quarterly, 37,* 363–399.

Barnard, C. I. (1968). *The Functions of the executive.* Cambridge, MA: Harvard University Press.

Braverman, H. (1974). *Labor and monopoly capitalism: The degradation of work in the twentieth century.* New York: Monthly Review Press.

Burke, K. (1937). *Attitudes Toward History.* Berkeley: University of California Press.

Butterfield, B. D. (1995, December 31). Pink slips and profits: In 1995, layoffs were an all-too-familiar routine (p. 55). *Boston Globe:* p. 55.

Carbaugh, D. (1996). *Situating selves: The communication of social identities in American scenes.* Albany, NY: SUNY Press.

Cheney, G. (1983). The rhetoric of identification and the study of organizational communication. *Quarterly Journal of Speech, 69,* 143–158.

Deal, T. E., & Kennedy, A. A. (1982). *Corporate Cultures: The Rites and Rituals of Corporate Life.* Reading, MA: Addison-Wesley.

Deetz, S. (1996, September). "Stakeholder conceptions of organizations and the forces of participation". Lecture given at the University of Colorado, Boulder.

De Tocqueville, A. (1966). *Democracy in America.* New York: Harper & Row.

Drucker, P. F. (1994, November). The age of social transformation. *The Atlantic Monthly, 274,* 53–80.

Drucker, P. F. (1992, September/October). The new society of organizations. *Harvard Business Review,* 95–104.

Durkheim, E. (1933). Introduction: The problem. In G. Simpson (Ed.), *On the division of labor in society.* New York: Macmillian.

Gossett, L. M. (1993). *The evolution of the Kittredge honors program: An analysis of the between formal and informal structures within organizations.* Unpublished General Honors Thesis. University of Colorado at Boulder.

Gould, S. B., Weiner, K. J., and Levin, B. R. (1997). *Free agents: People and organizations creating a new working community.* San Francisco: Jossey-Bass.

Heckscher, C. (1995). *White-collar blues: Management loyalties in an age of corporate restructuring.* New York: Basic Books.

Miller, J. (1995). *Organizational commitment of temporary workers: A combined identity theory and psychological contract perspective.* Unpublished doctoral dissertation. University of Colorado, Boulder.

Mulgan, G. (1991). *Communication and Control.* New York: Guilford Press.

Nisbet, R. (1988). *The present age: Progress and anarchy in modern America.* New York: Harper & Row.

Novak, M. (1997). *The fire of invention: Civil society and the future of the corporation.* Lanham, MD: Rowman & Littlefield.

Oakeshott, M. (1975). *On human conduct.* Oxford: Oxford University Press.

Parker, R. E. (1994). *Flesh peddlers and warm bodies: The temporary help industry and its workers.* New Brunswick, NJ: Rutgers University Press.

Pearce, J. L. (1993). Toward an organizational behavior of contract laborers: Their psychological involvement and effects on employee co-workers. *Academy of Managment Journal, 36,* 1082–1096.

Peters, T. J., & Waterman, R. (1982). *In search of excellence: Lessons from America's best-run companies.* New York. Harper & Row.

Reich, R. B. (1991). *The Work of Nations*. New York: Knopf.

Rose, R. (1994, October). Temporary job. *The Wall Street Journal*, A4.

Sias, P. M., Kramer, M. K., & Jenkins, E. (1997). "A comparison of the communication behaviors of temporary employees and new hires." Paper presented at the 1997 NCA conference, Chicago, IL.

Simon, H. (1976). *Administrative behavior: A study of decision-making processes in administrative organizations*. New York: Free Press.

Stamps, D. (1997, February). "Communities of practice: Learning and work as social activities." *Training, 34*(2), 34.

Taylor, B. C. & Trujillo, N. (in press). Qualitative research in organizational communication. In F. Jablin & L. Putnam (Eds.), *The new handbook of organizational communication*. Newbury Park, NJ: Sage.

Tompkins, P. K. (1993). *Organizational communication imperatives: Lessons of the space program*. Los Angeles: Roxbury.

Tompkins, P. K., & Cheney, G. (1985). Communication and unobtrusive control in contemporary organizations. In R. D. McPhee & P. K. Tompkins (Eds.), *Organizational Communication: Traditional themes and new directions* (pp. 179–210). Newbury Park, NJ: Sage.

Wolf, W. B. (1982). *The basic Barnard: An introduction to Chester I. Barnard and his theories of organization and managment*. Ithaca, NY: Cornell University Press.

Zemke, R. (1996, March). "The call of community: Creating a sense of community in the workplace." *Training, 33*(3), 24.

7

Forms of Connection and "Severance" in and Around the Mondragón Worker–Cooperative Complex

George Cheney
The University of Montana–Missoula, USA
and *The University of Waikato, Hamilton, NE*

CONNECTION VERSUS SEVERANCE
IN CAPITALIST DEMOCRACY

What are we to make of today's market with regard to questions of democracy and community? In answering this question, I would like to turn briefly to both Karl Marx (1977, 1983), who said a great deal about the market of his day, and Max Weber (1978), the great theorist of bureaucracy. Marx and Weber are frequently posed in opposition to one another, in terms of their analyses of organizational and work-related phenomena. Marx, after all, interpreted most issues of the workplace in terms of one overriding theme: shifting control over the means of production. Specifically, he decried the various ways in which workers were alienated or separated from the very products and processes of their own labor, as he observed the factories of mid-19th century England. Weber, on the other hand, benefitted from a later birth date than Marx, in that he was able to respond to his predecessor's works, thereby choosing to give greater emphasis to the social arrangements around which production is accomplished. Weber saw as his foundational principle the social "logic" of an organization or those systematic features that literally hold the organization together and make certain kinds of authority relations possible. This type of bureaucratic life, for Weber, meant that democracy would be difficult to achieve and maintain at work, although the bureaucratic ideal of nonarbitrariness may be thought to be something of a democratic impulse.

As sociologist Derek Sayer (1991) explained, both Marx and Weber were keenly aware of the antidemocratic trends manifest in the modern organization. For Marx, these disturbing trends took the form of removal of control from the literal hands and pockets of the workers, as the craft system of production was radically replaced by mass production in factories, along with the ways in which surplus capital was generated and controlled from without. And, as is often not mentioned, Marx saw this sort of situation, especially the overthrow of craft production, as amenable to the widespread development of bureaucratic organizational structures.

What really unites Marx and Weber according to Sayer (1991), is the theme of *severance*. Severance, a term we unthinkingly associate with the pay one receives when leaving an organization (especially nonvoluntarily), really refers to "cutting or separating, divorcing or pulling apart." Severance pay is for "severed" employees. What Marx and Weber each did so well was to highlight the various kinds of *social severance* that had come to characterize the modern organization and economy. These include, from Marx's viewpoint, the ways owners are removed from workers, the ways products are alienated from their producers, and the ways capital is extracted and abstracted from "local" situations—each of these cases often performed without regard for the dignity of human labor or the interests of the community. For Weber, too, severance was built into the model of bureaucracy: the separation of work from home, the removal of the "whole person" from work and the substitution of role, an emphasis on the replaceability of the employee within a machine-like organization, and the distribution of control away from individual persons and toward an entire system (of presumably fair and reasonable rules, regulations, habits, procedures, etc.). "Severance" is perhaps a more vivid and incisive term than the traditional sociological concept of alienation.

As suggested by the title of this essay, severance should be seen in counterpoint to "connection," with the latter referring to connections between and among people, to work, to land, and in community. However, I must caution that such a distinction cannot be used simplistically or cleanly. For instance, new communications and computer technologies simultaneously afford opportunities for new kinds of connections even as their use contributes to the loosening of other social ties (see, e.g., the reviews by Cheney et al.1998; Harrison, & Falvey, in press). In the domain of material possessions and derived senses of identity, we may observe both processes of commodification and ways in consumption and exchange themselves can be sacralized in human interaction (see, e.g., Belk, Wallendorf, & Sherry, 1991). Thus, any assessment about progressive alienation or detachment must take in account interpretive and experiential diversity (e.g., consider how the term "consumption" has a range of meanings and has been transformed over the course of the 20th century). Still, however, drawing from the central insights of Marx and Weber about modernity, we can identify persistent ways in which modern institutions are deeply alienating. Thus, the concepts of severance and connection are offered here in a heuristic and provocative spirit.

Let's fast forward to the present day. Although bureaucracy has indeed developed in much the way Weber saw it solidifying in the early 20th century, the marketization of society has surpassed even what Marx envisioned for the future. Despite praise for budding "postbureaucratic" organizations, the rationalized, hierarchical structure is very much with us today—especially in larger organizations (see, e.g., Heckscher & Donnellon, 1994). There are, of course, some countertrends—such as the return of some paid work to the home through "telecommuting." Today's market is far more global and much more fueled by consumers' desires than anything Marx quite imagined. The entire marketing industry, for example, adds a new dimension to the market under the presumption of *democratization*: giving people what they presumably want, when they want it, and how they want it—or so it seems (see Laufer & Paradeise, 1990).

The two great thinkers, Marx and Weber, have alerted us to the possibilities for severance—severance, perhaps, in the names of free trade, restructuring, consumer service, and globalization. Each of the general trends I've mentioned here has its democratic face or side: free trade argues for a reduction of parochial-seeming boundaries around the economic activities of a community, nation, or region. Indeed, this is the guiding principle of the European Union. Restructuring argues for a "flattening" of hierarchy with the goal of distributed responsibilities among employees of a firm. The reign of the consumer is based on the idea that each person can get what she wants through the unending abundance and unceasing adaptation of the marketplace, and as such, represents perhaps the most prominent current expression of democracy. Finally, the term *globalization* suggests one world—although a world conceived of more in markets than in nations, in that economic discourse about globalization has come to overshadow political, social, and cultural discourses (see, e.g., Gray, 1998; Kuttner, 1997).

In various ways, these trends include some tendencies of severance: severance of people from one another—in any authentic sense of community and democracy; severance of control over business from its people—as in the subordination of employees' interests to the concerns of often very distant consumers or investors; and severance of people from "place"—in the sense of devalued connections with community, locale and land. All this is true although, of course, new types of social bonds are being forged through the marvels of information technology and computer-mediated communication (see Castells, 1996). For example, in a feminist critique of the current market economy, Gibson-Graham (1996) wrote:

Ultimately, capitalism is unfettered by local attachments, labor unions, or national-level regulation. The global (capitalist) economy is the new realm of the absolute, not the contingent, from which social possibility is dictated or by which it is constrained. In this formulation economic determinism is reborn and relocated, transferred from its traditional home in the "economic base" to the international space of the pure economy (the domain of the global finance sector and of the all powerful multinational corporation). (p. 9)

If Gibson-Graham is substantially correct in her observation, then the trends she lamented ought to be apparent worldwide and even in areas and institutions known to have strong social traditions to the contrary, as in the case of Mondragón.

THE PARTICULAR AND GENERALIZABLE CASE OF THE MONDRAGÓN COOPERATIVES

A Selective History

As is well-known within the world of so-called "alternative organizations," like co-ops and collectives, Mondragón is one of the oldest and most successful cases of worker ownership and self-governance. Founded in 1956 through the efforts of a quiet but charismatic Basque Priest, José María Arizmendiarrieta (or Arizmendi), along with five young engineers from a traditional steel mill, these industrial cooperatives have grown in size to include over 150 distinct co-ops with more than 33,000 employee-owners ("associates" or "socios;" see Cheney, 1999). Arizmendi saw the co-ops as representing a "third way"—between the excesses of either unbridled free-market capitalism or centralized state socialism.

Today the co-ops are represented by two different corporations. The largest of the two, the Mondragón Cooperative Corporation (MCC), ranks as the tenth largest private firm in Spain, with total sales in 1999 exceeding eight billion U.S. dollars. The other corporation, Grupo ULMA, consists of five co-ops that broke away from MCC in early 1992 over issues of corporate reorganization. ULMA, with 1,200 employee-owners, is among the top 25 private firms in the Basque Country.

The Basque County has been significantly industrialized since the mid-to-late-19th century, which is the historical context out of which the Mondragón cooperatives developed. The largest number of its cooperatives are in the industrial sector, making products that range from machine tools to auto parts to packaging and warehousing systems. For example, one of the largest single cooperatives, FAGOR-Electrodomésticos, is the leading manufacturer of refrigerators in Spain. The single largest co-op today is Eroski, MCC's huge supermarket chain, now the largest of its kind in Spain.

In addition to the individual co-ops, there is a large superstructure of "second-tier" cooperatives. After studying the rise and fall of many Utopian communities and worker cooperatives in 19th-century Britain and United States, Arizmendi gathered support for the creation of a cooperative bank, the Caja Laboral Popular, in 1959. Later, the system came to include its own health care services, provisions for social security, and a complete educational system (which now features a technical university). In the view of Arizmendi and his cofounders, a degree of financial and institutional autonomy would be essential to the cooperatives' long-term survival.

The cooperatives of Mondragón do not sell outside stock; equity is held almost entirely by associates. Typically, 70% of profits go in individual capital accounts, to accrue dividends for employees, to pay out salaries, and to be held until employees end their association with the co-ops. Roughly 20% of the firms' profits are socialized in the form of investments in joint or intercooperative projects (including training and marketing), and approximately 10% of the money is used to support community endeavors (especially Basque-language schools). Today, the intercooperative projects are taking on greater importance, especially as the two corporations each try to respond to the market with a single voice. The co-ops employ a complex system of direct and representative democracy, whereby each co-op elects a president and a governing council. The council in turn appoints a manager. Each cooperative also maintains a social council, which is designed to counterbalance the economic concerns of the governing council and management with a social vision. Typically, social councils focus on issues such as safety, hygiene, and rewards. In the practical day-to-day decision making of a cooperative, it is the governing council, acting together with management, that holds the most power of any organ or body. In some of the co-ops, participation through the social councils is vigorous and independent-minded; in others, one finds social councils that are ineffectual and without much practical authority.

All of the individual co-ops that belong to MCC combine to create a cooperative congress, in which there is proportional representation according to the size of each cooperative. While being economically resilient for more than 40 years, the Mondragón cooperatives underwent a great deal of organizational change, including a widening of the wage differential scale, centralization of strategic control in a managerial superstructure, sectoral restructuring, and the emergence of a thoroughly customer-driven firm. The pace of these and other changes was greatly accelerated in the 1990s, particularly after the end to most trade barriers between and among members of the European Union (EU) in 1992.

Reasons for Success and Longevity

Although opinions vary widely on the reasons for Mondragón's longevity and success, I would like to highlight the three most important explanations here. Indeed, these factors are important to understanding the challenges and changes at Mondragón today, especially for an analysis of shifting work and other social practices. The first explanation for Mondragón's achievement is the *cultural factor*. Simply put, a number of the early analyses of Mondragón emphasized the system's uniqueness and how it drew its values and energy from Basque culture (see the extensive commentary in Whyte & Whyte, 1991).

Even more compelling in this respect, though, is the linkage between the concept of *solidaridad* (or solidarity) that exists among the larger Basque and Spanish cultures and the several meanings of solidarity within the cooperatives (Cheney, 1997). The culture there displays a dual stress on self-reliance and collaboration. Thus, Basques often appears to outsiders as both staunchly independent—as individuals, as well as in their collective nationalistic interests—and as highly interdependent with one another. In this way, to the extent that we may generalize about Basque culture, we can imagine both isolated shepherds and examples of group ingenuity as being emblematic of the society. *Solidaridad* (in Spanish) symbolizes Basques' commitment to one another as well as their connections to the land and the region in which they live.

Solidarity is a strongly evocative concept for many Basques, bringing to mind not only their attachments to their immediate loved ones, neighbors, and their nationalistic pride, but also their powerful sentiments about their locales. One Basque engineer, who was working temporarily as a quality and participation expert in ULMA-Forja (a forge that manufactures pipe fittings for the oil industry), told me that he could no longer feel good about his "long commute" or about living during the week in the town of Oñati, where Forja is located. "I need to return to my place," he told me—to a town just 30 kilometers away. (Recent opinion polls in the Basque Country and in Spain generally reveal an emerging openness toward job mobility, however.)

Solidaridad is written into the constitution of the co-ops; it is one of the famous 10 principles, all of which became fully articulated and approved by the First Cooperative Congress of the Mondragón cooperatives in 1987. These principles were inspired by those of the Rochdale Pioneers in 19th-century Britain and they are largely consistent with the recent Statement on the Cooperative Identity by the International Cooperative Alliance (1995). MCC's 10 official principles are: Open Admission, Democratic Organization, Sovereignty of Labor, The Instrumental Character of Capital, Self-management, Pay Solidarity, Group Cooperation, Social Transformation, Universal Nature, and Education.

Importantly, the last five principles incorporate some notion of solidarity, although the term is mentioned explicitly only once and in that case with respect to salary and wages. The broader notion of solidarity includes: (a) maintaining a relatively narrow salary range between highest paid and lowest paid employees; (b) "intercooperation," or the sharing of resources by cooperatives in the same groupings within the larger cooperative; (c) union with the larger communities in which the cooperatives operate; (d) identification with social-justice movements elsewhere; and (e) training focused on the next generations. In addition, I should mention informal employee-to-employee solidarity, which was clearly emphasized in many of my interviews.

The stress on solidarity persists today, although in its several senses it is threatened by the internationalization of the cooperatives as well as by the sharper focus on efficiency, as shown later in the chapter.

The set of structures and relationships at Mondragón features solidarity; even more importantly, it includes second-order or second level cooperatives such as the Caja Laboral bank, a social security system, and an educational system. These institutions figure prominently in what I call the *economic autonomy and infrastructure factor*. In other words, the cooperatives of Mondragón have been able to achieve both longevity and success in large part because of their own means of "buffering" themselves from the ebbs and flows of the larger market and society—at least until quite recently.

Especially important in terms of maintaining a buffer between the co-ops and the larger environment has been the role of the Caja Laboral bank. From the time of its creation in 1959, the Caja Laboral has provided not only low-interest loans for the development of new cooperatives but also an array of support services.

The superstructure of support services at Mondragón, especially the Caja Laboral and LKS, the Bank's Entrepreneurial Division, have played roles in the development and growth of the cooperatives that are difficult to exaggerate. These institutions help to protect the co-ops from many of the fluctuations of the larger market, granting them opportunities for economic risk, offering social security (in both the literal and the figurative senses), and providing for a managerial center of cooperative activity. There is yet another cluster of factors in Mondragón's success story. The *internal dynamism and adaptability* that have resulted from a complex system of direct and representative democracy must be considered.

Although the structure of each co-op is fairly traditional below and apart from the bodies mentioned earlier, I must stress the ways in which this dual governance–management structure grants social vitality as well as organizational effectiveness to the cooperatives. While granting exceptions in the cases of particular organs in certain co-ops that function only weakly, it was evident to me that the fact of the existence of these various organs and the expectations associated with them produced a strong democratic awareness in most of the co-ops I visited. That is to say, even when worker-members were complaining about the performance of their governing bodies or the persons holding the top positions in the co-op, their criticism was almost always couched within a recognition that the governing bodies ought to be enlisting significant participation, consulting widely with the co-ops' membership, and making informed decisions or at least offering credible recommendations for decisions. A middle-level manager in MAPSA co-op, a manufacturer of aluminum automobile wheels in the bull-running city of Pamplona, was quite passionate when he said to me: "To participate in the governance of the business is a privilege that carries with it weighty responsibilities. The organs give us legitimate means for expression ourselves, but it's up to us to take on the roles of true *socios* through vigorous involvement in the whole." In this way, a central part of the rationale for employee participation at Mondragón has been a valuing of democratic process for its own sake (see the classic article by Dachler & Wilpert, 1978).

Today's Challenges: Impetus for Research and Reflection

Issues of relationships, identity, and place are strikingly relevant to the present and future Mondragón cooperatives. As MCC's corporate house organ, *Trabajo y Unión* (Work and Union) attested, There are obvious tensions between the "cooperative culture" and the "corporate culture." In a 1996 article in that publication, one of the founders of MCC, Jesús Larrañaga, argued that the old cooperative values of the organization (e.g., participation and social solidarity) must be reframed in terms of "globalization" of the economy; that is to say, profit and efficiency must become foremost, although they must be based in the direct engagement of the worker-member-owner in the management of the firm. In this light, Larrañaga spoke of a kind of *neo-cooperativism* that casts participation not so much as a right or a privilege but as a demand to serve the customer in ever more efficient ways. For Sharryn Kasmir, author of *The Myth of Mondragón* (1996), the tension between economic and social values had already been lopsidedly resolved in favor of the corporate culture. For her, the path of Mondragón is going only one way: toward multinational corporate capitalism. "In situating the Mondragón cooperatives within the global economy, one lesson becomes clear. Worker-owners are not shielded from the forces of the global market" (p. 194). Indeed, this view is based on and consistent with what some representatives of the quasi-union within the co-ops, KT (or "Cooperative Groups"), told me in April of 1994, "The management of MCC is now very distant from our heritage; they have violated some of our most enduring principles, such as solidarity" (personal communication). For other observers, such as the former President of MCC, Javier Mongelos, these two domains are not inherently incompatible. As he told me in an interview in May, 1994, "Far from seeing employee participation on the decline, we are encouraging and witnessing its resurgence." Still, others, such as leaders and many workers in the ULMA group of five co-ops that broke away from MCC in 1992, there are ways to maintain important ties within the context of progress in the market. The former President of the ULMA group, José Antonio Ugarte, told me in early 1994, "that we saw separation from MCC as the only way to preserve our commitment to the community, the land and local autonomy" (personal communication). Yet still for others, such as some of the *socios* in MCC's Otalora Training Center, the maintenance of the organization's core values can well continue, even within the current phase of globalization. MCC's house sociologist, Mikel Lezamiz, was clear in saying to me in 1994 and again in 1997, that there remained many opportunities for revitalizing the cooperative spirit of MCC. This diversity of opinion compels further investigation, even allowing for the fact of multiple organizational cultures within the cooperative complex (see Young, 1989).

In terms of this part of the overall research project, the following general research question emerges: "What is the nature and extent of severance at Mondragón with respect to the system's founding values, local control, and authentic worker participation?" More specifically, I examine areas where a sense of community may well be deteriorating: (a) within the context of workplace participation in the co-ops, (b) with respect to the co-ops' interorganizational solidarity, (c) in the sense of local linkages and identities, and (d) in terms of a possible transformation in the prevailing understanding and practices of citizenship.

To address these questions, I draw on a variety of sources of data from the more than seven-year study. All told, I spent more than 6½ months conducting fieldwork at Mondragón, including visits in 1992, 1994 and 1997. With unfettered access to the co-ops, I conducted more than 125 interviews (all in Spanish), carried out more than 200 hours of workplace observation, attended over a dozen goverance meetings, collected hundreds of corporate documents, participated in more than 20 hours of training workshops, conducted one survey of changing values in three cooperatives, and made repeated visits to three midsized (100–300 employees) cooperatives (two of which were also covered in the survey). My research within the cooperatives themselves was complemented by more than 300 conversations with people in the surrounding communities. The broad scope of these activities enabled me not only to delve deep into the work experience and structural changes within the co-ops but also to consider the relationship between changes at work and in the larger society during the 1990s. In fact, it was the realization in early 1997 that the image of the consumer was coming to reshape both the internal affairs of the co-ops and activities external to them that widened the analysis of my project, making it possible to consider some surprising and disturbing trends with respect to community in an around the co-ops.

AREAS OF DIMINISHED COMMUNITY

Employee Participation and Relations in the "New" Organization

In all instances of the implementation of new programs for quality, participation, and customer responsiveness in the co-ops, common structural elements occur: the reduction in importance of first-line supervision, the use of functional and cross-functional teams, the creation of tighter feedback loops in communication between top management and employees at lower levels of the organization, the bringing of the lower level employee closer to the customer, the creation of new channels for suggestions from below, and the development of sophisticated analyses of production based on frequent reporting from various areas of the plant. The impact of all this organizational change on employee participation can be seen through an examination of total participative management (TPM) in a manufacturing co-op in Pamplona—a maker of aluminum wheels that was converted from a traditional capitalist firm to a cooperative in 1991 and 1992 and currently employs about 200 persons (one of the three co-ops where I conducted in-depth interviews with a stratified random sample of employee–owners or *socios*).

In 1997, the TPM program in MAPSA was being directed by a combination of experts from another of MCC co-op's personnel and quality departments, who worked together with MAPSA's newly installed top management. The program is based on a careful diagnosis of MAPSA's production processes and the implementation of a model of Total Quality Management (although, in this case, under the heading of TPM). Elias Pagalday, Director of Quality for the consulting co-op and the chief overseer of TPM's implementation in MAPSA, explained to me the basic characteristics of the program. The program's overall slogan is, "Client Consciousness + Employee Involvement + Profitability of the Firm = A Stable Future." Under that banner, specific areas of work were targeted for the introduction of TPM, including the foundry, mechanization (or calibrating and finishing), painting, and the offices, although the thrust of the program was clearly directed primarily at line, rather than staff functions.

The program was well underway by mid-1997, with several work areas already being reorganized according to the principles and techniques of TPM, guided by a general ethic of "customer-focused" management. Tight feedback loops were being put in place in the work areas previously mentioned, as well as others, so that immediate and regular information about production output would be available to supervisors and directors above them. Within this system, all employees are expected not only to fill out an array of charts at the end of each shift but to send suggestions upward, as part of the practice of constant improvement (*Hobekuntza,* in Euskara, the Basque language, or *Kaizen*, in Japanese). According to Pagalday, groups would not really be expected to make decisions, despite the use of the term *autonomous* for describing their organizational niche. Although the role of the supervisor, in terms of formal authority, was being diminished on the one hand, the need for the supervisor's frequent communication with those above him was being reinforced. And, a comprehensive communication process was being established for regular cross-functional meetings at all levels of the firm, including making plans for eventually holding weekly meetings between the Management Council and all workers on each of the three shifts.

One of the cornerstones of this new system lay in the statistical analysis of efficiency and quality. Specifically, an efficiency index was applied in MAPSA, as in a number of other MCC co-ops, for the standardization of the assessments of production levels. The index is calculated by a five-step process, beginning with the 8 hours that a machine or a larger work station is theoretically in operation for one entire work shift. From those 8 hours, time is then deducted for such things as start-up, breaks, machinery maintenance, "micro-stops" (for one reason or another), and defective pieces. The resulting time period is the actual percentage of time a machine or a work station is engaged in the production of acceptable products, and this proportion is, in turn, equated with quality production. From this statistic, an employee's (or a work team's) added value can be calculated. I found that this sort of language was creeping into managerial discourse in the cooperatives, representing an important shift from even 10 years ago when added value (or *valor añadido*) was more likely to refer to the advantages for an employee of working in a cooperative as opposed to a standard *sociedad anónima* (or "Inc."; see the discussion in Greenwood & González, 1989). As du Gay (1996) observed, all sorts of organizations are coming to define in a very explicit way, the "worth" of an employee (or a work team) in terms of the incremental gains in productive efficiency represented by that employee's (or that group's) work. Being a better employee can thus be rather narrowly defined within such management programs (cf. Halal, 1996).

In this process, and in the discourse surrounding it, the attention of the organization and presumably the workers is focused almost exclusively on a single and measurable idea of efficiency and quality. "Because the *Kaizen* system of 'continual improvement' requires a program of standards which are measurable and reproducible, work tasks become meticulously regulated and enforced in a manner which is indistinguishable from scientific management" (Boje & Winsor, 1993, p. 61). Ironically, despite the widespread praise of new "post-bureaucratic" organizations, the New Workplace may feature bureaucratic standardization in the form of the close monitoring of work processes and production (Alder & Tompkins, 1997; Barker, 1999; Sewell, 1998).

As I talked further with Pagalday and with others in MAPSA, it became evident to me that one risk with such an overwhelming emphasis on this model of participation was that social factors could easily be lost in an obsession with efficiency. This is what Taylor (1994) calls the overtaking of the rhetoric of the social firm by the rhetoric of the economic firm. In Taylor's view, as well as my own, the devaluing of the social dimension of work serves not only to "objectify" the individual employee but also to minimize the importance of employee relations that are not in the direct and measurable service of productivity and efficiency.

It is not that efficiency in the use of physical resources and labor energies of the employees can be ignored; my caution concerns what might be lost in the process of narrowing the vision of work processes so much. It is a short step from this sort of efficiency index, taken as a master indicator of organizational success, to the treatment of employees more as instruments than as shaping contributors to the organization itself. The organization can be blinded by its own definition and practice of efficient production, thus diminishing the very possibility of seeing or enacting the business as a community. The advancement of the self as well as the larger group or cooperative becomes chiefly or wholly tied up with added value for the customer, thereby reducing the significance of or completely disregarding employee relations for their own sake (cf. Dachler & Wilpert, 1978).

In fact, two top managers in MAPSA acknowledged that they shared my concern for the potential loss of social energy in the firm, and they wanted to see what they could do to establish a broader base of participation within the cooperative. As of late 1998, MAPSA was continued to create autonomous groups, aimed at reducing the distance between indirect and direct involvement in production processes and "the assumption of responsibilities for work processes at the lowest hierarchical levels of the organization possible" (according to MAPSA's internal documents). In 1997, Maria Jesús Zabaleta, Director of Finance and interim Director of Personnel at MAPSA, expressed the hope that work teams could become autonomous in meaningful ways so as to make some of their own decisions about how best to maximize production (e.g., in the control of stocks and in safety and hygiene). And, the General Manager, Juan Ramón Iñurria, emphasized his desire that despite the overwhelming emphasis on efficiency and client or customer service in the TPM process, MAPSA would have "space for participation with concern for the social values that make it a cooperative."

To address some of these deficits, MCC is now implementing a comprehensive communication plan; however, in its first phase, it has an overwhelming emphasis on the top-down transmission of information. In ULMA, the comprehensive communication plan is less developed as of this writing, but it is also seen as less pressing due to the physical proximity of the cooperatives in one valley and because of their comparatively small scale (with a total of 1,200 employees, as opposed to 42,000 for MCC). However, the general manager of ULMA-Forja, a forge that makes pipe fittings and flanges, stressed to me in 1994 and again in 1997 the need to make communication as transparent or clear as possible, not only within the five individual cooperatives of ULMA but also within the larger corporation or Grupo. General Manager Fernando Recalde added, "the identities of each cooperative and of the Group as a whole need to play a part in the communication process as well as being reinforced by it."

In both MCC and ULMA, I heard frequent acknowledgment of the deterioration of informal group relations—the ones that existed, for example, over lunch, in the break room, after work—a cultural change attributed mainly to the general speed-up in lifestyle, although due also to the specific work demands within the cooperatives. And, the July, 1994 issues of MCC's corporate house organ, *Trabajo y Unión* included an article that highlighted the need for "fluid" communication in all directions: descending, ascending, and horizontal. However, in my conversations in both systems, I sensed that most leaders and managers were at a loss for exactly how to revitalize what ought to be (and what once was) a spontaneous and vital part of the social dynamics of these organizations. For this reason, in offering some conclusions from my case studies to the managers and elected representatives of each of the three co-ops on which I focused my attention, I underscored the need to provide more forums, within the context of work, for the informal exchange of ideas and for general relationship building. This need seemed to be crucial at the level of individual cooperatives, where there was, in every case I studied, a sense of distance between the shop and the offices. (As will be discussed shortly, this sense of distance is exacerbated by new categories of employment that involve non- or temporary status with respect to the ownership of the firm.) The gap was also apparent at the level of sectors in the case of MCC and the level of the Group or Corporation in the instance of ULMA. Thus, the evolution of the two communication plans, and particularly their allowance for the creative exploration of new ways to revitalize daily work interaction in the cooperatives, will be important to observe in the next ten years.

Intercooperative Restructuring and Local Solidarity

The issue of sectoral reorganization, previously mentioned, is an important one in the Mondragón cooperatives and it brings to mind the larger question of intercooperative relations in MCC and in ULMA. As I saw in the course of my three visits, there are really three dimensions to these interrelations: financial, structural, and sociocommunal. The financial aspects to intercooperation have a long history in the Mondragón cooperatives, dating back to their founding. Over the years, these relations have become further specified and legally codified in the form of provisions for the socialization of gains and losses within groups of cooperatives. Simply put, there are collective funds established within groups of cooperatives for the purpose of offering financial support to those *cooperativas de base* that are in need.

Also, as defined in the acts of MCC's Third Cooperative Congress of 1991, additional centralized accounts aimed at educational and promotional projects of MCC's cooperatives (e.g., more vigorous marketing efforts at an international level and collective investments in new technologies) have been created, as determined by the General Council of the Cooperative Congress (1991). The existence and management of these accounts within MCC officially represent a commitment to intercooperative solidarity, in addition to the mechanisms already existing at the levels of sectoral and residual regional groups.

Financial intercooperation is thus defined as a means of solidarity between and among individual cooperatives. At the same time, however, there are implications for the autonomy of individual cooperatives. Cooperatives that are the strongest in their sectoral groups, in the case of MCC, or within the ULMA Group as a whole, can be subject to resentment toward the benefactors of their sound financial positions. Indeed, this was one of the chief reasons for some profitable cooperatives' hesitation in joining MCC in 1992, according to a number of my interviewees. The former President of the cooperative, José Ignacio Gandarias, related to me, in

1994, the story of MAIER, a highly successful manufacturer of plastic auto parts, in the ancient Basque capital of Gernika:

> MAIER's stance regarding full participation in MCC was critical because of the co-op's negative history with a regional group of co-ops. We were each different kinds of companies. MAIER was always the strongest. Then, each of the other three in the group disappeared. We didn't have any projects together, and our functions were quite distinct. So, MAIER wasn't used to having any important industrial links with other co-ops.

This type of solidarity, then, can be viewed positively or negatively, depending on the financial position that a cooperative is in at a particular point in time. Solidarity can logically be seen as a threat to autonomy for the co-op that is repeatedly asked to share its resources. As an engineer at MAIER told me in 1994, "We are the leaders [in our *agrupación*], so naturally people want us to share out benefits. If we are on top of the group and another co-op is way at the bottom, we should help them out. But, of course, a lot of people do not understand this" (personal communication).

The structural dimension of intercooperative solidarity also implicates a so-cial–communal dimension. I mean this in the sense that the structural (re)organiza-tion of the cooperatives has relevance both to the prescribed organizational relationships between and among them and to the sense some *socios* have of hav-ing their fates linked with those members of other individual co-ops.

The reorganization of MCC in the direction of sectors, or by function, in late 1991, was not problematic for the majority of cooperatives. As former Vice President of MCC's Automotive Division, Rafael Leturia explained to me in 1994, "There are *comarcal* [regional] groupings [of the 15 total that were gradually created] that never really jelled, so their disappearance didn't cost anything." But, as he hastened to add, "Contrariwise, there are groups like FAGOR that are finding it difficult for the *comarcal* bonds and groups to disappear or become less important. It is particularly difficult in the case of FAGOR because of their strong sense of economic solidarity with the *comarca* [of Alto Deba, the "county" around the town of Mondragón]."

Indeed, the transformation from an emphasis on regional groupings of cooperatives to one based on function and market niche became an issue in the case of both the old FAGOR group in the Mondragón Valley and the ULMA co-ops in the Oñati Valley, just 12 kilometers to the north of the Mondragón Valley. In fact, this policy shift, which came into effect with the close of the 1991 Cooperative Congress, became a central point of contention in the growth of KT (the quasi-union, called in Basque or Euskara, "Cooperative Groups") as an oppositional voice within FAGOR and the subsequent departure of the ULMA Group of co-ops from the formal organizational structure of MCC. KT was founded in 1982–1983, in fact, because of organizational changes initiated within the cooperatives—particularly centralization of policy direction.

In the case of KT, the issues of FAGOR's identity, solidarity and autonomy as a group of cooperatives are highly emotional and related indirectly to their view of equality as an unwritten, but important principle of the cooperatives' tradition. A powerful image of community pervades KT's formal and informal discourse. In an interview in 1994, two of their representatives, Mila Larrañaga and José Angel Echebarria, described the issue for themselves and the KT group in these terms:

> We think today that we are changing the fundamental pillars of cooperativism. We do not want to break with the *grupo comarcal* [of FAGOR]. Frankly, we do not see the [competitive] advantages that MCC is suggesting. What we see is an MCC that is losing the philosophical principles on which the cooperatives were founded. These are the principles that we use as points of reference: the right to vote, solidarity, equality, and everything the involves direct participation of the members.

The question of internal restructuring raises the broader issue of business expansion and internationalization.

Internationalization and Regional Commitment

Consistent with the analysis of organizational values here, the issue of growth can be understood on two levels. The first is the effect of increased size on such aspects of the organization as coordination, cohesion, and communication. The second concerns the arguments advanced in favor of growth. Both are important to a full understanding of the dynamics of size in organizations, and each calls for reflection. This is as true in mainstream organizations as it is in so-called alternative ones. Clearly, each organization should decide *why, when, and how* it needs to grow, recognizing that growth in itself may change the fundamental character of the organization as well as altering in substantial ways the organization's relationship to the environment. Many an organization has been seduced by the illusion that there are no social costs to growth, only benefits to be gained in terms of material success. However, as the cases in Rothschild and Whitt's (1986) book *The Corporate Workplace* show, some organizations see their small size as in some way constitutive of who they are, choosing to take a very cautious and deliberate policy toward growth and the changes it inevitably brings.

The visibility of the FAGOR brand of home appliances, the presence in most Basque communities of larger Eroski supermarkets, the Caja Laboral's move toward becoming a separate institution in its own right, and the rapid multiplication of Mondragón's international delegations and factories (now in nearly 20 other countries), are several of the most important signs that the cooperatives have now far exceeded any of the expectations of their founders in terms of financial success, resources, geographic reach, and power. And, given this tremendous expansion, one could hardly expect the cooperatives to have the same organizational character that they did, say, 15 or 20 years ago. Despite the economic downturns of the early 1980s and early 1990s, each causing a severe drop in overall employment levels for the Basque Country and Spain, the cooperatives of Mondragón have emerged with greatly expanding sales, tremendous financial reserves, and a conservative corporate strategy that strongly prefers conversions of existing noncooperative corporations in the region over new cooperative start-ups.

One of the key justifications I heard at Mondragón for policies of growth was the need to maintain a commitment to employment—to generate and maintain employment—especially in the Basque Country proper. In this vein, MCC signed a historic agreement with the Basque Parliament in 1997 that officially made the cooperatives one of the key instruments in the achievement of the employment policies of the Department of Justice, Economy, Labor, and Social Security. What exactly this agreement means in practice is still unfolding as of this writing. However, the agreement does call for MCC to work systematically and vigorously toward the creation of more than 8,000 new jobs by the end of 2000. Of course, the capacity of a single organization to generate fully new employment remains a contested issue in economics, with many analysts insisting that only macroeconomic forces and policies (e.g., monetary programs or national-level industrial projects) can effectively alter broad employment patterns. Nevertheless, both MCC and ULMA have played demonstrably important roles in the economies of their respective communities, and each corporation tends to express its solidarity with the larger environment in terms of a commitment to full employment. The fact that unemployment rates for these communities have generally been lower than for the whole of Basque Country or for the nation of Spain, even in times of severe economic recessions, is often used as a confirmation of the linkage of cooperative management policies to employment patterns.

The full-employment justification for expansion is particularly interesting because it can be used as a transcendent goal—with an implicit utilitarian ethic—expressed in effect like this: "Ultimately what counts is the *existence and preservation* of jobs for us and for our children; so whatever we can do to achieve that goal is warranted." The editorial policy of *TU* magazine, as well as the opinions of many managers around Mondragón, increasingly reflected this position as the 1990s wore on.

Concern here is warranted especially because much corporate expansion is taking place through the hiring of nonowning employees and employee-owners who are on a fixed schedule (e.g., for 3-year periods). Both within the co-ops around Mondragón and in those abroad, these new categories of employees are seen as a threat to social solidarity because they will cause many employees will have a diminished status in terms of pay, benefits, and job security. As revealed by my interviews, this is a growing concern at all levels of the cooperatives, even with the recent economic upturn.

Of course, it is important to note, as already discussed, that much of the actual growth of the cooperatives in recent years has been outside their well-spring communities and beyond the borders of the Basque Country. Even more important here is the fact of *how* the case for employment policy is made. In MCC, especially, the general argument about expanding employment is offered as an expression of solidarity even as the corporation is reorganizing along sectoral rather than regional lines and is extending itself globally. Thus, for some employees and especially those in the quasi-union KT, these corporate messages appear to be in conflict with one another. As one representative of the group in FAGOR Electrodomésticos told me in 1994, "We hear MCC talking about its commitment to employment here, but we also see them breaking with the solidarity that defines us and binds us with the community." Regardless of one's perspective on the wisdom of this cluster of co-operative policies, the coherence of the policies is for many *socios* not self-evident. Again, the market-oriented justifications being used to undergird the cooperatives' new policies may represent an internal drive as much as a set of responses to actual market pressures.

The Consumer Society and Participation by Wise Consumption

If the market symbol is to mean anything of substance when we probe its depths, it must represent the accumulation of transactions and relationships. At base, the market is a deeply social enterprise, despite the fact that it is typically treated as a great abstraction in much of today's popular discourse (cf. Daly & Cobb, 1994; Polanyi, 1955; White, 1981). Schmookler (1993) explained well the disjuncture between the intended purpose of the market and its actual workings when he said, albeit aphoristically, that the market is a whole lot less than the sum of its parts. What he meant is that the market—and perhaps even more importantly our talk about the market—discourages us from seeing the larger picture, the wholeness of our connections in society, and the fabric of relations that might constitute some genuine form of community. In Schmookler's words, "The market is exquisitely sensitive to the needs we have as 'social atoms,' and it disregards the needs we have as a social community" (p. 62). *The market is therefore a narrow substitute for a wider array of human relationships.* Thus, the individual person or *consumer* is encouraged to think only about the highly immediate, personal, and local contexts for his or her decisions: "I feel like driving to work today, rather than taking the bus"; "Should I buy this cosmetic product or that one?" and so forth. These decisions and others are pulled out of their larger social matrix or context just as "the market" being abstracted from people. "[This] creates a social order wherein economic language ... exhaustively describes our world, hence *becomes* our world" (Turner, 1994, p. 121).

On this expansive market landscape, *one of the most democratic promises routinely held out to people today is participation through consumption.* Not only is the citizen most often described *as* a consumer, but the act of consuming is also widely touted as the principal means for democratic decision making and *citizen* participation in today's society (see Laufer & Paradeise, 1990). In other words, through "voting with your dollars" at the local shopping mall, individual persons are declaring their preferences for this or that and thereby influencing not only what corporations choose to offer consumers but also the general course of the society's development. As Schmookler (1993) succinctly put it, "The market is often likened to a democracy, in which we all vote with our money. Each time we spend, it is as though we have put our vote in the ballot box of this economic democracy" (p. 46).

The *socios* of the Mondragón co-ops, along with citizens of that region in general, are coming to describe themselves more and more commonly as "consumers." And, in this way, each *socio* who adopts such a view becomes a message to the co-ops about broader cultural change. In this sense, the analysis of the health of community within the cooperatives must be carried out with great attention to broader cultural patterns around the co-ops. For an area with a strong tradition of various forms of citizen participation, we can rightly wonder how the emergent expressions of consumerism will modify the culture of these cooperatives or be appropriated in ways specific to the dominant culture already present.

For example, younger generations of co-op and community members, most of whom describe themselves as more career minded and more materialistic than their parents, may come to see themselves as *active* consumers with certain rights at work as well as in the marketplace (see Gabriel & Lang, 1995; cf. Derber & Schwartz, 1983). Interestingly, the supermarket chain Eroski has its own promotional activities, including extensive consumer education programs for adults and children. These activities may well be having a double effect on the communities in which the co-ops operate: the increase of Eroski's own clientele and the reinforcement of the idea that the most appropriate means of citizen participation today is what Eroski called in its corporate magazine "appropriate consumption" (see Kasmir, 1996). Thus, the cooperatives may have a new sort of social movement orientation toward the larger community as they support the ideals of consumerism as key to participation in the larger society. Eroski's Director of Consumer Education, Arantza Laskurain, explained to me in early 1998 that the co-op was interested in teaching consumers to make the best possible kinds of decisions. This program of consumer education will be important to watch in the next 10 years, not only for its own measure of success but also in giving a reliable reading of the extent to which Basque citizens are coming to substitute the culture of consumtion for more traditional forms of community participation. Thus, the particular forms that consumer advocacy and consumer behavior take in the Basque Country will have a shaping influence not only on the cooperatives but also on other social institutions there, including the family, politics, religion, and so forth. A key question then remains: To what extent might the benefits of great participation in the practices of consumption at the same time mean a displacement of other forms of community engagement?

Cofounder of the Mondragón cooperatives, Alfonso Gorroñogoitia, admitted to me in the summer of 1997 that the consumer movement had two sides for the culture of the area around Mondragón: It fueled demand for products and services, thus benefitting the cooperatives, and also contributed to an attitude of entitlement focused on material acquisition. In his view, it is ironic that solidarity must now be legislated and actively promoted in the co-ops, when in the past "we simply *had* solidarity."

CONCLUSIONS AND EPILOGUE

Just as Marx and Weber may be brought together under the same heading of concerns about severance in the modern world, so we must look long and deep at the interrelations of the market and organizational practices today. What does the market mean for the possibilities for a humane, democratic, and healthy workplace? This question is especially salient at Mondragón because of the cooperatives' tradition of devotion to democratic values, but the same concerns can be raised about all sorts of organizations that comprise our larger societies. If the market is to continue to be privileged in the complex of social, political, and economic relations of modern life, then it surely deserves our scrutiny in terms of the values being pursued in the market's name (Cheney, 1998b). And, just as my own investigations of workplace democracy have necessitated an analysis of the market as both a context for and a reference point of the Mondragón co-ops, we may look to the market as we ponder questions about democracy's future. If it tuns out that a democratic organization such as Mondragón cannot survive in the contemporary market economy—if its value commitments prove to be ephemeral rather than enduring—then the viability of community in senses deeper than that of a "community of consumers and investors" (Weisberg, 1998) is threatened. A recent front-page article in *The Wall Street Journal* (Langley, 1998) stated the question plainly using the words of a nun who directs one of the largest hospital chains in the United States: "no margin, no mission." But the obverse of this question is just as important: If an organization like Mondragón survives and prospers only to lose its soul, then what value is continuance? In this respect, the matter of Mondragón's evangelism is crucial. By this I mean the degree of MCC's interest in spreading the ideals of cooperativism and engaging the larger market. This issue is, in fact, causing a profound division within the cooperatives of MCC just as it is beginning to be debated in the emerging multinationalism of UMLA.

With respect to the relationship between communication and community, the theme of this book, several important observations can be made from the past, present and future Mondragón experience. First, community, like the related term "democracy," should be understood both in terms of the specific practices and criteria thought to constitute it (e.g., certain types of deep relationships) and of how it is *framed* as an issue or set of issues. At Mondragón, as elsewhere in the world today, a single-minded focus on the market has implications that go far beyond the public discourse and may well serve to penetrate the way interpersonal relationships are conducted at work. In response to my analysis of change at Mondragón, the engaged reader might distinguish between and among: (a) discursive transformations (e.g., the substitution of the consumer for the citizen) that operate on the mere surface of a complex of social relationships, (b) discursive patterns that are appropriated by users in a particular setting or area (as the idea of consumption being playfully treated), and (c) the case in which fundamental change is taking place within a variety of institutions in a culture that are subjected to or that endorse a particular rhetoric (e.g., "marketization"). Although I would not answer an unqualified "yes" to the commonly asked question, "Has Mondragón sold out?" I would say that the economic benefits of marketization may come to be matched or superseded by losses in the social realm—and that those losses, in turn, could perhaps jeopardize future economic success (see Moye, 1993).

Second, with respect to community building and maintenance, the Mondragón experience clearly points to these conclusions: (a) that community building works best when it is built on a solid foundation of culturally held values, especially some values that privilege commitment to the collective along with the sacredness of individual rights; (b) that any attempts to promote participation and solidarity (at work or in the political sector) need to be revisited over time, lest they become a mere shell of involvement; and (c) that each new generation of workers or citizens will, to some extent, redefine what community means for them—in fact, their creative engagement is essential to the ongoing life of the community.

I would not go so far as to offer a recipe for "good community," recognizing the diversity of meanings for it and the fact that any strong community can be oppressive for certain members who feel in some way disenfranchised by the core or dominant group. However, I close this discussion by saying that to the extent that the market story for participation and success in today's world has no vocal and compelling competitors, genuine opportunities for community building inside and outside of the workplace are undermined.

ACKNOWLEDGMENTS

This chapter is part of a much larger project (see, e.g., Cheney, 1995, 1997, 1998a, 1999) conducted from 1992 through 1999. The author owes thanks to many people for help and support, all of whom are mentioned in the book, *Values at Work* (Cheney, 1999). Here, I would like to thank especially Yudit Buitrago (co-author of chapter three in that book) for her help, encouragement, and insights. Also, I express gratitude to the Department of Management Communication at the University of Waikato, Hamilton, New Zealand, for research support during the second half of 1998, when much of this essay was written.

REFERENCES

Alder, G. S., & Tompkins, P. K.(1997). Electronic performance monitoring: An organizational justice and concertive control perspective. *Management Communication Quarterly, 10,* 254–288.
Barker, J. R.(1999). *The discipline of teamwork: Participation and concertive control.* Thousand Oaks, CA: Sage.
Belk, R. W., Wallendorf, M., & Sherry, J. F., Jr. (1991). The sacred and the profane in consumer behavior: Theodicy on the odyssey. *Highways and byways: Association for Consumer Research, 59–98.*
Boje, D., & Winsor, D. (1993). The resurrection of Taylorism: Total quality management's hidden agenda. *Journal of Organizational Change Management, 6,* 57–71.
Castells, M. (1996). *The rise of network society.* Malden, MA: Blackwell.
Cheney, G. (1995). Democracy in the workplace: Theory and practice from the perspective of communication. *Journal of Applied Communication Research, 23,* 167–200.
Cheney, G. (1997). The many meanings of 'solidarity': Negotiation of values in the Mondragón worker–cooperative complex under pressure. In B. D. Sypher (Ed.), *Case Studies in Organizational Communication, II* (pp. 68–83). New York: Guilford.
Cheney, G. (1998a, May–June). Does workplace democracy have a future? *At Work,* 15–17.
Cheney, G. (1998b). "It's the economy, stupid!" A rhetorical–communicative perspective on today's market. *Australian Journal of Communication, 25,* 25–44.
Cheney, G. (1999). *Values at work: Employee participation meets market pressure at Mondragon.* Ithaca, NY: Cornell University.
Cheney, G., Straub, J., Speirs-Glebe, L., Stohl, C., DeGooyer, D., Whalen, S., Garvin-Doxas, K., & Carlone, D. (1998). Democracy, participation, and communication at work: A multidisciplinary review. In M. E. Roloff (Ed.), *Communication yearbook, 21* (pp. 35–91). Thousand Oaks, CA: Sage.
Dachler, H. P., & Wilpert, B. (1978). Conceptual dimensions and boundaries of participation in organizations: A critical evaluation. *Administrative Science Quarterly, 23,* 1–39.
Daly, H. E., & Cobb, J. E., Jr. (1994). *For the common good.* Boston: Beacon Press.

Derber, C., & Schwartz, W. (1993). Toward a theory of worker participation. *Sociological Inquiry, 53*, 61–78.

du Gay, P. (1996). *Consumption and identity at work.* London: Sage.

du Gay, P., & Salaman, G. (1992). The cult(ure) of the customer. *Journal of Management Studies, 29*, 615–633.

Gabriel, Y., & Lang, T. (1995). *The unmanageble consumer.* Thousand Oaks, CA: Sage.

Gibson-Graham, J. K. (1996). *The end of capitalism (as we knew it).* Oxford, UK: Blackwell.

Gray, J. (1998). *False dawn.* New York: New Press.

Greenwood, D., & González, J. L. (1989). *Culturas de FAGOR.* San Sebastián, Spain: Editorial Txertoa.

Halal, W. E. (1996). *The new management: Democracy and enterprise are transforming organizations.* San Francisco: Berrett-Koekler.

Harrison, T., & Falvey, L. (in press). Democracy and new communication technologies. In W. Gudykunst (Ed.), *Communication yearbook 23.* Thousand Oaks, CA: Sage.

Heckscher, C., & Donnellon, A. (Eds.). (1994). *The post-bureaucratic organization: New perspectives on organizational change.* Thousand Oaks, CA: Sage.

International Cooperative Alliance. (1996). *Statement on the cooperative identity.* Madrid, Spain: Confederación Española de Cooperativas de Trabajo Asociado.

Kasmir, S. (1996). *The myth of Mondragón: Cooperatives, politics, and working-class life in a Basque town.* Albany, NY: State University of New York Press.

Kuttner, R. (1997). *Everything for sale: The virtues and limits of markets.* New York: Knopf.

Langley, M. (1998, January 7). Nuns' zeal for profits shapes hospital chains, wins Wall Street fans. *The Wall Street Journal,* A-1.

Laufer, R., & Paradeise, C. (1990). *Marketing democracy.* New Brunswick, NJ: Transaction Books.

Marx, K. (1977). *Capital* (Vol. 1). (B. Fowkes, Trans.). New York: Vintage. (Original work published 1865–1872)

Marx, K. (1983). *The portable Karl Marx* (E. Kamenka, Trans.). Harmondsworth, UK: Penguin.

Moye, M. A. (1993). Mondragón facing 1992: Adapting co-operative structures to meet the demands of a changing environment. *Economic and Industrial Democracy, 14*, 251–276.

Polanyi, K. (1955). *The great transformation.* Boston: Beacon Press. (Originally published 1944)

Rothschild, J., & Whitt, J. H. (1986). *The cooperative workplace: Potentials and dilemmas of organizational democracy and participation.* New York: Cambridge University Press.

Sayer, D. (1991). *Capitalism and modernity: An excursus on Marx and Weber.* London: Routledge.

Schmookler, A. B. (1993). *The illusion of choice: How the market economy shapes our destiny.* Albany, NY: State University of New York Press.

Sewell, G., (1998). The discipline of teams: The control of team-based industrial work through electronic and peer surveillance. *Administrative Science Quarterly, 43*, 397–428.

Taylor, P. L. (1994). The rhetorical construction of efficiency: Restructuring and industrial democracy in Mondragón, Spain. *Sociological Forum, 9*, 459–489.

Turner, J. (1994). Economic nature. In D. Clow & S. Snow (Eds.), *Northern lights* (pp. 113–136). New York: Random House.

Weber, M. (1978). *Economy and Society* (2 vols.). G. Roth & C. Wittich (Eds.). Berkeley: University of California Press.

Weisberg, J. (1998, January 25). United shareholders of America (pp. 29–31). *The New York Times Magazine.*

White, H. C. (1981). Where do markets come from? *American Journal of Sociology, 87,* 517–547.

Whyte, W.F., & Whyte, K. K. (1991). *Making Mondragón: The growth and dynamics of the worker cooperative complex* (2nd ed.). Ithaca, NY: Cornell University Press.

Young, E. (1989). On the naming of the rose: Interests and multiple meanings as elements of organizational culture. *Organization Studies, 10,* 187–206.

III

Media, the Public, and Community

8

Revising Communication Research for Working on Community

Eric W. Rothenbuhler
University of Iowa

This chapter is an essay in reconceptualization, aimed at realism. It begins with a review of the literature of communication and community, showing that community is predominantly conceived as a unitary object, good, built on commonality, and distinct from individuals, who have varying relations to it. Communication is conceived as one of the devices of the relation between individuals and community. Communication and community are both presumed to be based on commonality and to be good. This leaves us able to describe degrees of happiness in communities, and the contribution of communication to that, but mostly unable to offer any advice for improving them.

Following a critical review of the communication and community literature, I offer an alternative model based on presumptions of difference and difficulty rather than commonality and happiness. In the alternative model community is a social accomplishment rather than an existing entity. In that model, communication is a means for the accomplishment of community rather than a medium of relation to it or information about it. Furthermore, because community in that model is fractious, so too will be the communication.

By way of introduction, here is a schematic example of the problems in the existing literature and the solutions to which this chapter is addressed. Predominantly the literature is concerned with the contributions of different kinds of communication behaviors (e.g., reading newspapers or talking with neighbors) to degrees of information that people have about their communities, their involvement in the community, identification with it, and affection for it. Communication and community are both seen as good things that reinforce each other with happy results. This is implicitly a normative model, an ideal standard. A more realistic model would allow researchers to account for, and hopefully to participate productively in, communities' efforts to improve the happiness of life within them. That requires recognition that the actualities of communities vary from their ideals and that communication is often about those differences. Furthermore, communication can then be seen as participating in the process of constructing community, allowing us to identify how hopes, dreams, plans, debates, disagreements, negotiations, self-delusions, disappointments, and frustrations all participate equally with happiness and commonality in the substance of the communication of community.

THEORETICAL POSITIONS ON COMMUNICATION AND COMMUNITY

The theoretical literature on communication and community is more inspiring than informing. With only small degrees of misrepresentation, it can be sorted into three categories: the pessimistic, the optimistic, and the critical.

The first category, the pessimistic position on communication and community, begins with worries over the viability of community under the conditions that exist in urban, industrial societies and mass mediated cultures. Here the differentiation of the urban social structure and industrial economic order, and the ubiquity of made-for-profit, mass-distributed communication and culture are identified as threats to community, which is conceived (often implicitly) as a native or natural phenomenon dependent on primordial commonality and kept alive in face-to-face communication networks (Bellah, Madsen, Sullivan, Swindler, & Tipton, 1985; Meyrowitz, 1989; Stein, 1960). Tönnies's (1988) *Gemeinschaft und Gesellschaft* has often been interpreted as a classical source for this thinking.

In Tönnies's writing, *Gemeinschaft* and *Gesellschaft* are contrasting models for types of social relations. Whereas the ideal-type of *Gemeinschaft* is the family and household system of a premodern European peasant village, the ideal-type of *Gesellschaft* is the exchange of buyer and seller in the modern market place. In *Gemeinschaft,* social relations are built on commonality of land, blood, and mind, with such relations growing out of shared history. People's whole concrete identities are relevant in interaction in that relations are seen as being between particular individuals, not between roles, functions, or types of people. In *Geselleschaft*, social relations are built on the functionality of differences. The stasis of commonality of land, blood, and mind is replaced by the mobility of differences, activity, and exchange. People's concrete identities are irrelevant to their functionality in *Geselleschaft*; interactions occur between abstractly defined roles, rather than concretely defined, whole, and particular people. Tönnies's use of historical examples introduced ambiguity into his text, with the result that *Gemeinshaft und Gesellshaft* has often been interpreted as a theory of the transition to modernity, rather than an analytical model of types of social relations. The historical interpretation, then, is that the transition to market economies, industrial labor, and the dominance of urbanization and technologies of mass production, distribution, and communication are a threat to community, in that they replace *Gemeinschaft* with *Gesellschaft*. This position is not without research support, though interpretation of research along these lines has engendered controversy (e.g. Vidich & Bensman, 1968).

The second category of theory on communication and community, the optimistic position, shares the idea with the pessimistic one that community depends on commonality but is strikingly different in analytical position and evaluative tone. These optimistic essays take their inspiration from the common etymological origins of communication and community, and emphasize the idea of commonality (e.g., Dewey, 1966). Within them, communication and community are taken to be both expressions of commonality and the means by which commonality is created and sustained. Communication is taken to be both a phenomenon of community, and the primary means of its sustenance. This conceptual position has a sophisticated rationale, but it also often appears in rather more muddled, if not naively idealistic forms. The result of such thinking can be that any means or instance of communication may be taken as evidence of community (e.g., Aspen Institute, 1995). Such idealism may be a natural result of this conception because when pushed to its logical conclusion, the idea that communication produces community because both depend on commonality and also expresses and creates it, implies that systems of telecommunication can create community independent of place (Webber, 1963). Each new medium has been examined in its turn, for the possibility that it could sustain a community of pure communication, unencumbered by place or other material concerns. From 19th-century discussions of the newspaper and public opinion by de Toqueville, Tarde, and Tönnies among others, through mid-20th century hopes for mass communication, cybernetics, and consensus, new media have been believed to hold the promise of greater human connection. The Internet is only the latest medium to show itself as not quite able to sustain the hope of community independent of place (e.g., Jones, 1995). Complications aside, this optimistic idea that communication and community are associated because they are both based on commonality, is a natural rallying point for communication scholars, and often serves as a beginning point for communication research, even when that research goes on to document quite different phenomena, such as conflict and struggle (e.g., Phelan, 1988).

The third category of theory in regard to communication and community is concerned with these as themes of intellectual history; for want of a better term, we can call this the critical position. This literature addresses the connection of ideas of communication and ideas of community in the history of Western philosophy (Nisbet, 1982), in implicit logics in the history of sociology (Kreiling, 1989; Quandt, 1970), or the appearances of these ideas in American literature, culture, or politics (Strauss, 1968; Tinder, 1980; White & White, 1962). Collectively, these works of intellectual history make the point that any logical connection of communication and community has as much to do with how we think as it does with what we have observed.

The pessimistic and the optimistic positions on communication and community share fundamental ideas: that community is based on commonality, that communication is important to community, and that community and communication are good. The pessimists, however, regard mass communication, telecommunication, and culture-producing industries as suspect—as forms of false communication and culture. Mass communication and commercial culture may give rise, in their eyes, to false community. The antidote would be the true social relations found in interpersonal communication. The optimists, on the other hand, see mass communication and the associated culture-producing industries as important supplements to interpersonal communication and local social organization. These larger communication systems represent an opportunity to integrate the huge numbers of people in modern societies into a great community, larger and more diverse than the small town. The critics and intellectual historians, help us to understand the social circumstances conducive to these divergent ideas, and ultimately portray them as matters of literature and authorship. So any transcendence, synthesis, moderation, or specification of the two positions (i.e., pessimism and optimism) or reconnection of the history of ideas with present social conditions has been left to empirical workers. In that literature of empirical research, we find that the relations of communication and community vary with the means of communication, the community, the larger social structure, the historical era, the circumstances of individuals, and other contingencies.

EMPIRICAL STUDIES OF COMMUNICATION AND COMMUNITY

The relation of communication and community became a topic for empirical research within the Chicago school of sociology in the early decades of this century. That work appeared as a response to worry and skepticism about the viability of community in modern societies, especially under urban conditions. These ideas could be traced to the European sociological inheritance—as interpreted for the purpose of studying the American social setting (e.g., Loomis & McKinney, 1988; Redfield, 1960)—and had a vital presence in the thought and work of the progressives (e.g., John Dewey, Jane Addams, Josiah Royce), who were so important for the Chicago school (Quandt, 1970). Importantly, this work too begins with the idea that community and communication are inherently linked on the basis of commonality; the question is whether that commonality had survived the transition to industrialization, urbanization, and modernity.

The Chicago studies found their answer. Neighborhoods, voluntary associations, and local institutions were shown to be locations of *Gemeinschaft* within the *Gesellschaft* of the larger city. Important to later research, communication processes and systems within these settings were shown to be essential to communal processes, with the outcome that social networks, organizational participation, residency, and mobility appeared as meaningful patterns rather than alienated structures (Bulmer, 1984; Burgess & Bogue, 1964; Hatt & Reiss, 1957; Kurtz, 1984; Short, 1971; Whyte, 1955; Wirth, 1964).

Although the Chicago work was devoted to the urban setting, more recent research has shown that interpersonal interaction and a supportive social network are necessary to feelings of communal attachment to the place one lives, whether in an urban setting or small town. The primary differences between communities are in the resources and contingencies that are relevant to the construction of social networks and the dynamics underlying communal feelings (see Baldassare, 1983; Brown, 1993; Campbell & Lee, 1992; Cuba & Hummon, 1993; Fischer, 1975, 1982; Fischer et al., 1977; Freudenburg, 1986; Gans, 1962; Goudy, 1990; Guest & Lee, 1983; Howell & Frese, 1983; Hummon, 1986, 1990, 1992; Hunter, 1975; Kasarda, 1974; Kasarda & Janowitz, 1974; Rivlin, 1982; Sampson, 1988; Stinner, Loon, Chung, & Byun, 1990; Street, 1978; Suttles, 1984; Tsai & Sigelman, 1982; Wellman, 1979.) This research has continued, especially as applied in rural settings (Beggs, Hurlbert, & Haines, 1996), and as concerned with various outcomes, such as provision of social support (e.g., Wellman & Wortley, 1990), household economic decisions (e.g., Cowell & Green, 1994) or patterns of mental health (e.g., O'Brien, Hassinger, & Dershem, 1994).

An important part of the Chicago school research was concerned with the newspaper. Park's (1922) *The Immigrant Press and Its Control* and Janowitz's (1967) *The Community Press in an Urban Setting* each documented the unique contributions of newspapers and newspaper reading to communities. Later research has continued this work, documenting the role of the newspaper in the formation and maintenance of people's feelings of attachment to the places they live (reviewed in Stamm, 1985). This research literature has grown considerably in the last decade, and attention has turned to more complex models, including other media (Finnegan & Viswanath, 1988; Jeffres, Dobos, & Lee, 1988; Neuwirth, Salmon, & Neff, 1989; Rothenbuhler, Mullen, DeLaurell, & Ryu, 1996; Viswanath, Finnegan, Rooney, & Potter, 1990), longitudinal processes and data (Chaffee & Choe, 1981; Shim & Salmon, 1990; Stamm & Guest, 1991; Zhu & Weaver, 1989), and issues of measurement, causal order, and analytic technique (Becker & Fredin, 1987; Collins-Jarvis, 1992; Jeffres & Dobos, 1984; Jeffres, Dobos, & Sweeney, 1987; Rothenbuhler, 1991; Rothenbuhler et al., 1996). Despite the differences, one set of general findings from this literature is clear. Feelings of attachment, identification, and involvement in a community are associated with communication, especially reading the newspapers and talking with neighbors, friends, or co-workers, with being more settled in the community (e.g. having lived there long, owning a home), and with being more active in the local area (e.g. working, shopping, sending children to school, or attending church in the local area).

Research on community has been marked by a conceptual transition since the late 1970s or so. Having answered the question about the viability of community in modern society, researchers have moved on to concern with analyzing the underlying dynamics of "community ties"—bonds between the individual and community (e.g., Gerson, Stueve, & Fischer, 1977; Kasarda & Janowitz, 1974; Stamm, 1985). People's feelings of attachment to their communities, their involvement in local affairs, their identification with their community, and the patterns of behavior that keep people in the locality, have come to be identified as types of ties to the community. These ties were initially seen as evidence of the continued viability of communities; they have come to be seen as the outcome variables that researchers need to explain. The more recent research is dominated by analyses of the causes and correlates of community attachment, involvement, identification, and activity. The community tie has thus become an outcome variable, predicted by such phenomena as dense local social networks, local newspaper reading, conversations about local affairs, time and attention given to local affairs and activities, home ownership, and length of residence.

For the sake of contrast, consider Putnam's (1995a; 1995b) provocative articles on "bowling alone." Putnam's work was not motivated by a concern with community attachment, per se, nor with community ties as an outcome, but with bonds between neighbors and neighborhood, citizens and civil-setting, as a form of social capital useful to the good health of a democracy. No matter what the merits of the research—and there are indeed reasons to question the evidence and inferences (Galston, 1996; Portes & Landolt, 1996; Schudson, 1996; Skocpol, 1996; Valelly, 1996)—the motivating questions of Putnam's work remind us of larger concerns.

An interesting and inevitable result of the empirical research on community—whether the focus is on community ties as outcome variables, or community processes as contingencies for some larger issue of concern—is the generalization that community membership varies. Because the empirical literature tends to define membership in terms of types of ties, such as attachment and involvement, which are operationalized as measures of individual proclivities, then it naturally follows that community membership varies across individuals. One interpretation of this record of empirical variance in community membership, is that people's devotion of time, energy, and resources to community may be a quasi-rational response to their circumstances, producing what Janowitz (1967) called the community of limited liability. The idea is that like limited liability participation in a corporation, people's willingness to devote time, energy, and resources to a community is proportional to what they expect of the community; they will quickly withdraw if the community needs more of them than they are willing to commit. Other research has found patterns supportive of this idea. Fischer (1982) argued that personal networks and activities as people construct "personal communities," reflect a balance of constraints and resources (cf. Campbell & Lee, 1992). To the extent that community is thus reduced to a quasi-economic phenomenon, subject to people's calculations of cost and benefit, there would be serious limits on the capacity of any community to motivate its members to action in difficult times (Rothenbuhler, 1995).

SUMMARY AND IMPLICATIONS

The theoretical literature on communication and community asserts that the two are connected in important ways, that both are based on commonality and both are good, but that mass communication in modern society may have deleterious results for community. The empirical literature indicates that people vary in the nature and degree of their community ties: involvement, identification, affection, and so on. Studies consistently show that communication behaviors are positively associated with these ties to community. Apparently, if we wanted to increase the prevalence and strength of community ties, we would induce greater participation in community-oriented communication. Studies also indicate some prevalence of quasi-economic thinking about the places people live, a sort of limited-liability approach to community. Hence, there would be a danger that efforts to increase community involvement would be received as undue demands, decreasing the attractiveness of the community.

PROBLEM DIAGNOSIS

The communication and community literature can offer us little in the way of advice about how to work on community because of unidentified limits in its concepts and operationalizations. These limits inhibit understanding of key aspects of the reality of communication and community.

First the presumption of commonality disables us in regard to the reality of differences. Real communities are made up of different individuals, in different positions, with different backgrounds, different interests, possessing different resources, and facing different contingencies. Communities are made out of these differences. They are, then, social accomplishments, and our attention should be directed toward the work that makes communities real, rather than the myth of commonality that makes them appear to generate spontaneously. Similarly, communication is not something based on commonality. Some means of connection, such as a common language or common attention to the same media, may be necessary for communication. Fundamentally, however, communication is based on difference; it is where *differences* exist that communication arises (see Peters, 1994, 1995, 1999; for a theory of communication founded on this principle).

Second, community is almost always either conceived as, or endowed with the connotations of, "the good life" (cf. Williams, 1983). The good life, of course, is defined differently by everyone who uses the phrase, but no one is against it. Other than a small strain of American fiction devoted to the stifling character of small-town life and some quips from misanthropic philosophers (Hobbes assessed life as short, nasty, and brutish; Sartre said hell is other people) community is always treated as a good thing. Community is then a valued ideal; that ideal guides the research literature. There is nothing wrong with that per se, but the way in which that unquestioned ideal combines with other characteristics of theory and research on communication and community creates problems.

Third, community is usually conceived as an existing thing, separate from individuals. Obviously, a neighborhood or town, thought of as a settlement structure, can sensibly be conceived of as an existing thing separate from the individuals who may move in and out of it. But even when community is conceived as a type of relation, social process, or social network, it is still often treated as if an object that existed separate from individuals. There may be good reasons for this intellectual approach in some cases, or it may be a habit of thought, carrying structural thinking from studies of geographical communities over to studies of communal relations, communal attachments, and so on.

Note what happens when we combine these three attributes of the conception of community: Communities that are based on commonality, are good, and already exist separate from individuals, require us not to evaluate the communities, but to evaluate individuals' relations to them. This is exactly what the research literature has done, studying individual variance in types and degrees of relation to community (e.g., community ties, identification, or attachment). The unanalyzed optimism of the conception of community has blinded us to the multidimensional and highly varied reality of people's relations to the places in which they live (note the effort to separate questions of community from questions about locality by Hummon, 1992, and Kirby, 1989). Simultaneously the conception of community as a unitary, already existing object has led us away from investigation of community as performance and accomplishment, away from investigation of people's actions in building their communal relations, constructing and operating their social networks.

Consider this as an example to clarify both some of the implications of these results, and how unintended results such as these must surely be. For instance, if "community" is indeed measured by such variables as local interaction and involvement, then a grumpy old man who has lived in the neighborhood longer than anyone, but who is isolated from his neighbors and uninvolved in local affairs, would be identified as a marginal or non-member of the community. Though no one would be expected to actually draw this conclusion, it would follow that the community that is so measured could be equally improved by the elimination of the old man as by efforts to increase his inclusion.

These conceptual problems are exacerbated by characteristics of the most common operationalizations in the empirical literature. The literature is mostly based on positives, ignoring most negatives and absences. Some of this is necessary in a methodological sense because empirical work must be based on observables. But the imagination applied to rendering things observable has been rather limited, focusing on already present and mostly positive attributes. Ties to community may be considered positives in that they are measured as presences, and in that they are usually interpreted as good things. For example, structural ties such as home ownership and local employment may be interpreted as phenomena that inhibit moving, but usually they are interpreted as phenomena that build community. Affective, cognitive, and behavioral ties are all things that people feel, think, or do and all are interpreted as things that build community. There is in the literature little or no attention to the things that people do not feel, think, or do, (other than in the form of variance, that some people rate higher on our scales and indexes than do others). There is also no attention to the things people feel, think, or do that hurt community in one sense or another. The result is that the empirical generalizations that can be based on this literature are mostly about degrees of satisfaction amongst mostly happy people who mostly like the places in which they live.

Combining these problems we discover that having presumed consensus, and having mostly studied degrees of satisfaction, we know almost nothing about the processes required to build communities, solve problems, or to deal with unhappiness and badness. Even deeper, presuming community is good, and based on commonality, we implicitly defined difference as a threat to community and therefore bad. What advice, then, could a publicly supported expert, such as a professor at a state university, offer a realistically diverse community that was trying to better its group life? Little or none.

A FRESH START

The remainder of this essay is a thought experiment, based on an alternative model of communication and community. The alternative model presumes difference and difficulty rather than commonality and happiness. It reverses the presumption of the externality of community—community as something separate from individuals, to which they must be related—by emphasizing the centrality of individual experience of community. In the place of implicit idealism, the new model is explicitly idealist in regard to the hope for community, and realist in regard to the social processes of living together. In a world of difference and difficulty, of tension and contradiction between individuals and others, ideals and actualities, community is a social accomplishment rather than an existing entity. Communication in this new model is one of the means for the accomplishment of community. So communication will often be addressed to the differences that make up the community, including the differences between the ideals of community and the particular realities of the community in question. The discussion begins with fundamentals, and builds up to a workable model.

There is no more intimate experience than that which each individual has of his or her own body. This experience is intimate in its immediacy and in its privacy—and it is a condition on experience in general, and on social relations in particular.

A subjective and an objective existence, a being for self and a being for others, a consciousness of one's own self and a consciousness of other things, are in truth given to us immediately, and the two are given in such a fundamentally different way that no other difference compares with this. About himself everyone knows directly, about everything else only very indirectly. This is the fact and the problem. (Schopenhauer, 1969, Vol. 2, p. 192)

Individuals' lived-bodies are the origins of their consciousness and action in the world, radically conditioning and distinguishing one individual's experience from that of others (Merleau-Ponty, 1978; Stewart & Mickunas, 1974, pp. 65–66, 96–99). Yet we are all born to an already existing world, and the individual's consciousness, although centered in the particularity of a body, is also structured by the background assumption, sustained in everyday interaction, that this world exists for other individuals too (Schutz & Luckman, 1989). This intersubjective world is composed of material forms, objectifications of ideas, meanings, and emotions in cultural forms, and patterns of human response. Language, culture, tradition, logic, accepted fact, reasoning, meaning, emotion, belief, aesthetic response, and the rest of the ideal phenomena that define human experience, have an intersubjective structure that transcends individual experience (Dilthey, 1976). These elements of the ideal world, and even of the inner experience of individuals, are collectively structured and sustained through social processes (Durkheim, 1965). Collectively structured ideal phenomena have an objectivity; they are robust to the individual, an element of the social environment to which the individual must be adapted. Such intersubjective realities can only be built and sustained through systems of communication (Berger & Luckmann, 1967; Schutz & Luckmann, 1989).

The transition from immediate experience of the individual's own body, through systems of communication, to more or less adapted participation in an intersubjective world is a movement from biological to human being. This transition is not only the fundamental dynamic of childhood socialization but also a necessary feature of the phenomenology of everyday social interaction. We are and remain biological beings just as we are and can only understand ourselves as socialized human beings. We remain within our bodies, just as we devote the greatest part of our cognitive capacity, time, and energy to socialized thought, to communication and interaction. There is a drive, and a pressure, to be humane. Human beings are called to be civilized, to act as they should, to connect with others, to empathize, to feel awe and inspiration, to entertain and be entertained, to evaluate, to argue and reason, to rise above their circumstances, to imagine, to plan, to hope, and to try. In these and all such examples of human effort, the contrast of the particular experience within one's own body and being versus a socialized ideal is fundamental. This is a tragedy of human being: The one thing we know most intimately, our sensate being, is a limit on our efforts toward what defines us as human beings, that is, participation in an intersubjective world. The one type of knowledge to which we have truly privileged access, experience within our own body, is a pressure opposed to adaptation to the intersubjective systems of our environment. This is why Ricoeur (1981a) pointed out that phenomenology presupposes hermeneutics, and vice versa. As Schutz and Luckmann (1989) structured their argument, everyday experience gives rise to the distinction "between one's own and something Other" (p. 105); this distinction arises not only in material forms that afford us no choice in their appearance but also as signs and texts of other consciousnesses requiring interpretation, elucidation, and efforts of understanding. This fundamental problem is clearly evident in everyday efforts to communicate. Peters (1994) said that communication is the experience of our own finitude, that it is precisely in knowledge of our finitude, and the fundamental gap between self and others, that the drive to communicate is born. We discover the difference between self and others in communication, just as we strive to overcome it.

Community is the same; it is an ideal of connection, born of the experience of disjunction, a tragic ideal, as Tinder (1980) put it. Community is the desire and the effort to contain in a vision of commonality, what so obviously distinguishes us, to act so as to create a container of differences. Community has this in common with communication: "The basic units of communication are the attempts at junction" (Peters, 1994, p. 132). Similarly the basic units of community are attempts to make it so. Community appears in simple acts of human will, which, upon reflection have a tragic–heroic dimension. People choose to contain differences, to expend efforts at overcoming gaps and disparities. No collection of individuals is one; they are not each the same. The place in which they live is not all that they would choose; it is not their ideal. Yet they can choose to act as a "we," to accept the contingencies of the place as contingencies on the self.

Imagine the world as the phenomenologists do: It presents itself to my consciousness as a system of relevancies in light of my projects (e.g. Schutz, 1970). Upon reflection, the world must present itself to you and the others differently as a system of relevancies in light of your projects and their projects. Community, then, is an effort to unify these systems of relevancy. The ideal of community is one in which your relevancies, my relevancies, and their relevancies are the same; the world would present itself to us each the same way, as our world, a single system of relevancies. Short of that ideal, and even short of that phenomenological assumption of us each as radically individual consciousnesses, community is still an effort to contain the differences among individuals, within a single social project.

Community as an outcome, differences contained, is an actualized ideal; it is an intention, a hope, and a preference, that has become real by being acted on. In Dilthey's (1976) language, it is an objectification, a construction of the historical world. Community achieved, then, is an ideal that has taken on objective existence in the world of human being. The vision of differences contained becomes an actual container of differences in human action, as the vision is presumed by and enacted by people's choices of action. In the dynamic of interaction and communication, when the presumption passes—whether by taking it for granted, as a matter of shared belief, as a compromise, as an effort in the face of disconfirming evidence, or due to inattention—when it passes, community is functionally accepted as a presently relevant reality. In community, within the container of differences, the first person-plural is factually as well as grammatically correct. Although "we-ness" remains an unverifiable truth claim, it can pass and social life can be based on its having done so.

Community as a container of differences is an accomplishment, the result of an effort. At times it may be happily taken for granted, a presumption of whatever actions "come natural." At other times community can only be accomplished by a determined disregard of the radical difference between ideal and setting. The unity of projects presumed by community can be taken for granted, based on faith, or based on consciously willful effort. The fact that community cannot always, perhaps not even usually, be taken for granted, is evidence enough that even when it can be, it is because community is sustained by intentionality. Community exists where people choose to make it so; making it so is work. That work of community constructs a relation between person and people, and between people and environment. Those relations contain the differences between self and other, preference and performance, and ideal and actuality.

Communication in the New Model of Community

What are the functions of communication in this new model of community? Communication is the primary mechanism by which ideals become social realities;

thus communication is the major tool for the accomplishment of community. This works in two distinguishable ways: through efforts to communicate and through the communicative capacity of action in general. Sometimes we are engaged in explicit messages for or about community, and sometimes we are engaged in actions whose implicit communicative value is to model a social world in which some things are normal, some things are preferable, and some things are not done. The former can be called messaging communication, the latter ritual communication (Carey, 1988; Geertz, 1980; Goffman, 1959, 1967, 1976; Rothenbuhler, 1998).

Among the necessary conditions for any action to work communicatively, is that it articulates internal and external experience, individual and collective orders (Rothenbuhler, 1996, 1998; Shepherd & Rothenbuhler, 1991). A result of this is that any bit of communicative action will have the effect of altering a social space, at least partly, according to the contingencies of an individual will. When we speak, play a song, turn up the volume, schedule a TV show, change the channel, gesture, or dance, we impinge ourselves on a world, even if minimally, still undeniably giving shape to an environment that gives shape to the experience of others. But because in communication the internal–external dynamic never operates without the individual–collective one as well, that shape that the will gives to the environment has also been shaped, in-formed, by collective contingencies such that it is readable, in the terms of one prominent metaphor (Ricoeur, 1981b). In other words, everything that people do that may count as communication may count as such in part because it can be seen to have a shape (form) that is interpretable by others as coded. A meaningful syntax (shape, form) is a result of material activities that are recognizably responsive both to individual experience and collective code, convention, and structure.

Any act that involves communicative function creates a bit of social order (in the broadest sense) according to the contingencies of an individual will guided by various collective orders, both internal and external (i.e., both ideal and material collective orders, e.g., language on the one hand and architecture and roadways on the other). So every bit of communication creates a bit of social order that is, as social orders go, unusually responsive to individuals. Communication is, then, a resource by which one individual can create part of the social reality in which other individuals operate. Because their own exercises of will are guided by the social orders in which they live, communication is a device in-forming the choices and activities of others (cf. Peters & Rothenbuhler, 1989; Shepherd, 1993).

The most obvious place these activities show up is in rhetoric, argument, and persuasion. Of course the activity of using communication to give shape to the social reality of others also appears in complaint and threat, on the one hand, and in promise, entreaty, and seduction on the other. Equally so, it appears in ordinary conversation, in broadcasting, reading the newspaper, and playing the stereo. These examples could be multiplied endlessly, for the point is that every bit of communication, not only those that are intended to affect others' thoughts or actions, has some of this function. The other side of this is that every individual action is taken in a world that is already partially shaped by a local history of the communicative actions of others.

If community is an effort to construct a container of differences, and communication is a mechanism for the construction of such social realities, then "community" should appear in disagreement as much as in agreement, in disappointment as much as in satisfaction. Researchers can learn about community by studying people who disagree or are unhappy, but who nevertheless remain in relationship with each other or the place. How can people be wedded to disagreeable others and disappointing places? Often the important factors are economic constraints and other structural variables (e.g., Fischer, 1982; Rossi, 1956). But when the disagreement or unhappiness is contained in a relationship, then a history of communication must be an important element. Researchers will find, in such cases, that the communicative function of social action is prevalent. People read each other; they watch for what each other "says" by what they do. In such situations, the fabric of acts creates a social order of relationships independently of whatever else may be expressed or accomplished. This is achieved through communication ritual (Goffman, 1959, 1967).

There is always a ritual power to communication. It may be hardly noticeable and is usually not the intended function of communication (the ritual aspects of communication in general should not be confused with the specific category of rite and ceremony; Grimes, 1990; Rothenbuhler, 1998). Because of the articulation of internal and external, individual and collective, every communicative act functions ritually to identify an individual will with a social order. Any action that has a communicative function also has this additional ritual function, so that it does something, says something, and commits the actor to something. If I do something nice or something mean, then I create a nice or mean social space, make available a message about myself, the social world, and the value I place on the others with whom I am interacting, and I commit myself to being that person, living in that world, with that relationship to those others (Rothenbuhler, 1995). This is because communicative action, as a ritual performance, inherently involves both the "inside" and "outside" of the individual, tying the performer to the meanings and implications of the action by both symbols and indices. Although certain aspects of the meaning of a ritual performance are sustained by symbols and thus may be undone or held in abeyance by such internal experiences as doubt, the social implications of the performance, that is the results of the ritual, are sustained by indices that the required behavior was indeed performed (Rappaport, 1979; Rothenbuhler, 1998). Thus, in the aftermath of a communication ritual, having done it, there is no denying it; hence, no shirking of responsibility for whatever are the results.

Identifying this ritual element of communication clarifies how realities are byproducts of choices of action, how those byproducts then become the contingencies on which other choices of action are based. So the communicative element of social action is always modeling a social world that is in fact becoming (Carey, 1988; Geertz, 1980). That social world may be one we would call community.

REVISING RESEARCH

Under the guidance of this altered vision of communication and community, how should we alter our research practices? First, to the extent that community is performed in communication, we need to be studying communicative performances.

Second, to the extent that community is a location of differences and problems, we need to be studying them as well. Neither of these are deep insights, but elucidation may provoke some research ideas.

The most obvious way to study communicative performances of community would be ethnographically, following the example of the established literature on the anthropology of performance (e.g., Bauman, 1977; Bauman & Briggs, 1990; Ben-Amos & Goldstein, 1975). It should be expected that community would be performed differently in different places, times, and social roles. These differences would appear as matters of communication style and substance, following the norms of different places, times, and roles. The communicative performances of a city council meeting, for example, follow different norms and enact different visions of community than do the daily interactions of neighbors. Within the council meeting, the roles of the council member, citizen, and reporter are performed differently and enact different parts of the community constructed in the meeting. Reading the local paper and talking about it with neighbors or co-workers enacts community, although in different ways and with different entailments.

One issue it would be profitable to observe more carefully is the way in which communication is used to bind time and space. Social life in general, and certainly community, is not made up of discrete moments and events; it is made up of meaningfully integrated experiences, and communication is often used to enact, construct, or encourage that integration. Sigman (1991) showed that in moments of separation and reunion, as at the beginning and end of a workday, the talk of couples is marked by references to past and future moments, here and other places. In this way they bind the moments and places of their separation meaningfully to the experience of their union. Just as the couple's relationship is performed in talk that binds times and places, so will community be performed in time- and place-binding talk among neighbors, merchants, newspaper reporters, bankers, politicians, children, teachers, and so on.

The fact that some talk is devoted to time- and place-binding is a clue that other instances of communication may be motivated by it or may presume it, even if not explicitly devoted to it. There are traces of the performance of community in memory, meaning, presumption, identity, knowledge, and emotion. These traces can be rendered observable and analyzable by a variety of interpretive methods. Among promising recent efforts are studies of collective memory and community (see Zelizer, chap. 9, this volume), studies of the community as a built environment and local culture of artifacts and actions (e.g., Drucker & Gumpert, 1991, 1996; Suttles, 1984), studies of community as it appears in verbal accounts, images, and narrative structures (e.g., Hummon, 1988; Maines & Bridger, 1992), and quasi-biographical techniques (Hummon, 1990).

As we move from the most to the least observable, we should not forget the importance of what does not happen, what is not done. Community is a normative construction. When it is enacted, that not only means that community is done, it also means that things that are not community are not done. Methods are needed to make observations out of the fact that in communicative performances and in interviews, histories, and biographies, certain things are not said, certain things are not observed. The certain things of concern would be those that would be received by members of the community as damaging to the community. Identifying such norm violating actions would be aided by observing community conflict, or by quasi-experimental field techniques that involved the systematic violation of norms. In addition to observing communicative enactments of community (and their traces and nonpresent opposites), we need to be observing the differences on which community is constructed and the problems endemic to its being worked out. Again I start with the most obvious and easily observable and move toward the most latent and easily overlooked.

First we should be studying controversies and publicly recognized community problems. Whenever there is a scandal, an argument, a controversy, or a disagreement amongst groups and interests, then public meetings, newspapers, talk radio, lunchroom chatter, and neighborly visiting is characterized by differing enactments of differing visions of community. In this work we can be usefully guided by the tradition of rhetorical studies, where there is a great body of work and much experience with controversy and advocacy. The ritual elements of communication are of at least equal concern. Not all of the relevant talk is advocacy explicitly; the advocacy elements of the talk are not always the most important. Often what people say is less important than how they say it—what is presumed, what pronouns are used, what shared knowledge is enacted, what is left out, what emotional tone is used, and so on. From the performance point of view, the roles that are adopted and offered in the communication are the key issues (see Goffman, 1959, 1967).

Second, in our study of performances of community we need to be ever aware of the range and prevalence of interpretations. For example, use of the pronouns "we" and "our" presume whole worlds. Sometimes their use in a moment of controversy elicits objections, sometimes it does not. When it does not, it may be because others share the presumption, because they believe they share the presumption, because they figure they share enough of the presumption, because they do not want to be impolite, because they do not think it is important, or because they did not think about it at all—and to some degree it is probably different for every one of the others present. The complexity of this example pales in comparison to what is faced by a researcher in the field.

WORKING ON COMMUNITY

What advice, then, could a publicly supported expert, such as a professor at a state university, offer a realistically diverse community that was trying to better its group life?

Research devoted to community as an activity, as a striving for an ideal in which finitude is overcome and differences are contained, as something worked on through communication, has great hope of contributing usefully to the construction of community and the improvement of life in the places we live. It should not be difficult for us to help community leaders understand the complications of these processes, to help them see past their own presumptions and engage in realistic analyses. We should be able to offer policy and strategy advice. One can even imagine writing a sort of primer for the communication of community, not unlike

Aristotle's *Rhetoric*. But the conventionally impartial stance of the expert observer is not sufficient.

The analysis of this chapter supports the conclusion that community is more a matter of effort and faith than behavior, cause, and effect. The work of which community is constructed is motivated by the tension between ideals and actualities, as community lives in the on-going effort to make it so. As experts, we should expect a certain sort of failure to be inevitable as community members work together, trying to better their group life, as they are inevitably trying to bring about ideals in an actual world. Yet we know too, that the only hope of a better group life is in the process of continuing to try. If we want to help, we must adopt a more sermonic mode of communicating and of being in our communities. This will not come easily to those of us trained in the social sciences. Among other things, problems of axiology that our professional discipline has been designed to avoid, are inevitable. Our role as professional experts, therefore, is not enough; it must be validated by participation in our communities as members.

If community is enacted in communication, rather than existing separately from it, then we can go to work on community by performing it. When we act as good neighbors, we are being good neighbors, saying something about neighboring, and committing ourselves to that relationship in this neighborhood. If there is a communicative element to all acts and an actual element to all communication, both of them having ritual effectivity, then in acting out community we are saying things about it, and in engaging in community-oriented communication we are acting it out; both are real and both are effective. We contribute to community, when we go to work on community, not as experts, but as members.

ACKNOWLEDGMENTS

My thanks for comments, suggestions, and encouragement from Carey Adams, Dudley Andrew, Walter Carl, Francesco Cassetti, Wade Davis, David Depew, Herb Dordick, Dan Emory, Kathleen Farrell, Kristine Fitch, David Hingstman, Brent Malin, Robert Newman, John Peters, Michael Sáenz, Greg Shepherd, and Barbie Zelizer. An early draft was presented as "Ideals and actualities, wills and futures: The communication of community" at the 1994 Speech Communication Association convention. A late draft was presented at the Departmental Seminar, Department of Communication Studies, University of Iowa, October 13, 1998; the discussion in that setting was helpful in clarifying some points and in rewriting the conclusion. The idea for this chapter originated in my summer with the social workers in the 1993 Faculty Research Seminar at the Center for Advanced Studies, University of Iowa; my thanks for the Obermann Fellowship that supported that work.

REFERENCES

Aspen Institute. (1995). *The future of community and personal identity in the coming electronic culture*. Washington, DC: The Aspen Institute.

Baldassare, M. (Ed.). (1983). *Cities and urban living*. New York: Columbia University Press.

Bauman, R. (1977). *Verbal art as performance*. Rowley, MA: Newbury House.

Bauman, R., & Briggs, C. L. (1990). Poetics and performance as critical perspectives on language and social life. *Annual Review of Anthropology, 19*, 59–88.

Becker, L. B., & Fredin, E. S. (1987). *The mass media, knowledge and evaluation of community*. Paper presented to the Annual Convention of the Association for Education in Journalism and Mass Communication, San Antonio, TX.

Beggs, J. J., Hurlbert, J. S., & Haines, V. A. (1996). Community attachment in rural settings: A refinement and empirical test of the systemic model. *Rural Sociology, 61*, 407–426.

Bellah, R. N., Madsen, R., Sullivan, W. M., Swidler, A., & Tipton, S. M. (1985). *Habits of the heart*. New York: Harper & Row.

Ben-Amos, D., & Goldstein, K. S. (Eds.). (1975). *Folklore: Performance and communication*. The Hague: Mouton.

Berger, P. L., & Luckmann, T. (1967). *The social construction of reality: A treatise in the sociology of knowledge*. New York: Anchor Books.

Brown, R. B. (1993). Rural community satisfaction and attachment in mass consumer society. *Rural Sociology, 58*, 387–403.

Bulmer, M. (1984). *The Chicago school of sociology: Institutionalization, diversity, and the rise of sociological research*. Chicago: University of Chicago Press.

Burgess, E. W., & Bogue, D. J. (Eds.). (1964). *Contributions to urban sociology*. Chicago: University of Chicago Press.

Campbell, K. E., & Lee, B. A. (1992). Sources of personal neighbor networks: Social integration, need, or time? *Social Forces, 70*, 1077–1100.

Carey, J. (1988). *Communication as culture: Essays on media and society*. Boston: Unwin Hyman.

Chaffee, S. H., & Choe, S. Y. (1981) Newspaper reading in longitudinal perspective: Beyond structural constraints. *Journalism Quarterly, 58*, 201–211.

Collins-Jarvis, L. (1992). A causal model of the reciprocal relationship between community attachment and community newspaper use. Paper presented to the Association for Education in Journalism and Mass Communication Annual Convention, Montreal, Canada.

Cowell, D. K., & Green, G. P. (1994). Community attachment and spending location: The importance of place in household consumption. *Social Science Quarterly, 75*, 637–655.

Cuba, L., & Hummon, D. M. (1993). A place to call home: Identification with dwelling, community, and region. *The Sociological Quarterly, 34*, 111–131.

Dewey, J. (1966). *Democracy and education*. New York: Free Press. (Original work published 1916)

Dilthey, W. (1976). *Selected writings* (H. P. Rickman, Ed., & Trans.). Cambridge: Cambridge University Press.

Drucker, S. J., & Gumpert, G. (1991). Public space and communication: The zoning of public interaction. *Communication Theory, 1*, 294–310.

Drucker, S. J., & Gumpert, G. (1996). The regulation of public social life: Communication law revisited. *Communication Quarterly, 44*, 280–296.

Durkheim, É. (1965). *The elementary forms of the religious life* (J. W. Swain, Trans.). New York: Free Press. (Original work published 1912)

Finnegan, J. R., & Viswanath, K. (1988). Community ties and use of cable TV and newspapers in a midwest suburb. *Journalism Quarterly, 65*, 456–463, 473.

Fischer, C. S. (1975). Toward a subcultural theory of urbanism. *American Journal of Sociology, 80*, 1319–1341.

Fischer, C. S. (1982). *To dwell among friends: Personal networks in town and city.* Chicago: University of Chicago Press.

Fischer, C. S. (with Jackson, R. M., Stueve, C. A., Gerson, K., Jones, L. M., & Baldassare, M), (1977). *Networks and places: Social relations in the urban setting.* New York: Free Press.

Freudenburg, W. R. (1986). The density of acquaintanceship: An overlooked variable in community research? *American Journal of Sociology, 92,* 27–63.

Galston, W. A. (1996). Won't you be my neighbor? *The American Prospect, 26,* 16–18.

Gans, H. J. (1962) *The urban villagers: Group and class in the life of Italian-Americans.* New York: Free Press.

Geertz, C. (1980). *Negara: The theatre state in nineteenth-century Bali.* Princeton, NJ: Princeton University Press.

Gerson, K., Stueve, C. A., & Fischer, C. S. (1977). Attachment to place. In C. S. Fischer et al., *Networks and places: Social relations in the urban setting* (pp. 139–161). New York: Free Press.

Goffman, E. (1959). *The presentation of self in everyday life.* New York: Anchor Books.

Goffman, E. (1967). *Interaction ritual: Essays on face-to-face behavior.* New York: Anchor Books.

Goffman, E. (1976). *Gender advertisements.* New York: Harper & Row.

Goudy, W. J. (1990). Community attachment in a rural region. *Rural Sociology, 55,* 178–198.

Grimes, R. L. (1990). *Ritual criticism: Case studies in its practice, essays on its theory.* Columbia: University of South Carolina Press.

Guest, A. M., & Lee, B. A. (1983). Sentiment and evaluation as ecological variables. *Sociological Perspectives, 26,* 159–184.

Hatt, P. K., & Reiss, A. J., Jr. (Eds.) (1957) *Cities and society: The revised reader in urban sociology.* Glencoe, IL: Free Press.

Howell, F. M., & Frese, W. (1983) Size of place, residential preferences and the life cycle: How people come to like where they live. *American Sociological Review, 48,* 569–580.

Hummon, D. M. (1986) City mouse, country mouse: The persistence of community identity. *Qualitative Sociology, 9,* 3–25.

Hummon, D. M. (1988). Tourist worlds: Tourist advertising, ritual, and American culture. *The Sociological Quarterly, 29,* 179–202.

Hummon, D. M. (1990). *Commonplaces: Community ideology and identity in American culture.* Albany, NY: State University of New York Press.

Hummon, D. M. (1992). Community attachment: Local sentiment and sense of place. In I. Altman & S. M. Low (Eds.), *Place attachment* (pp. 253–278). New York: Plenum.

Hunter, A. (1975). The loss of community: An empirical test through replication. *American Sociological Review, 40,* 537–552.

Janowitz, M. (1967). *The community press in an urban setting: The social elements of urbanism* (2nd ed.). Chicago: University of Chicago Press. (Original work published 1952)

Jeffres, L. W., & Dobos, J. (1984). Communication and neighborhood mobilization. *Urban Affairs Quarterly, 20,* 97–112.

Jeffres, L. W., Dobos, J., & Lee, J. (1988). Media use and community ties. *Journalism Quarterly, 65,* 575–581, 677.

Jeffres, L. W., Dobos, J., & Sweeney, M. (1987). Communication and commitment to community. *Communication Research, 14,* 619–643.

Jones, S. G. (1995). Introduction: From where to who knows? In S. G. Jones, Ed., *Cybersociety: Computer-mediated communication and community* (pp. 1–9). Thousand Oaks, CA: Sage.

Kasarda, J. D. (1974). The structural implications of social system size: A three-level analysis. *American Sociological Review, 39,* 19–28.

Kasarda, J. D., & Janowitz, M. (1974) Community attachment in mass society. *American Sociological Review, 39*, 328–339.

Kirby, A. (1989). A sense of place. *Critical Studies in Mass Communication, 6*, 322–326.

Kreiling, A. (1989). The Chicago school and community. *Critical Studies in Mass Communication, 6*, 317–321.

Kurtz, L. R. (1984). *Evaluating Chicago sociology: A guide to the literature, with an annotated bibliography.* Chicago: University of Chicago Press.

Loomis, C. P., & McKinney, J. C. (1988). Introduction. In Ferdinand Tönnies, *Community and society [Gemeinschaft und Gesellschaft]*. New Brunswick, NJ: Transaction Books. (Original work published 1957)

Maines, D. R., & Bridger, J. C. (1992). Narratives, community, and land use decisions. *The Social Science Journal, 29*, 363–380.

Merleau-Ponty, M. (1978). *Phenomenology of perception* (C. Smith, Trans.). London: Routledge & Kegan Paul. (Original work published 1962)

Meyrowitz, J. (1989). The generalized elsewhere. *Critical Studies in Mass Communication, 6*, 326–334.

Neuwirth, K., Salmon, C. T., & Neff, M. (1989). Community orientation and media use. *Journalism Quarterly, 66*, 31–39.

Nisbet, (1982). *The social philosophers: Community and conflict in western thought* (concise edition, updated). New York: Washington Square Press.

O'Brien, D. J., Hassinger, E. W., & Dershem, L. (1994). Community attachment and depression among residents in two midwestern communities. *Rural Sociology, 59*, 255–265.

Park, R. E. (1922). *The immigrant press and its control.* New York: Harper.

Peters, J. D. (1994). The gaps of which communication is made. *Critical Studies in Mass Communication, 11*, 117–140.

Peters, J. D. (1995). Beyond reciprocity: Public communication as a moral ideal. In E. Hollander, C. van der Linden, & P. Rutten (Eds.), *Communication, culture, community: Liber amicorum James Stappers* (pp. 41–50). Houten, Netherlands: Bohn, Stafleu, van Loghum.

Peters, J. D. (1999). *Speaking into the air: A history of the idea of communication.* Chicago: University of Chicago Press.

Peters, J. D., & Rothenbuhler, E. W. (1989). The reality of construction. In H. Simons (Ed.), *Perspectives on the rhetoric of the human sciences* (pp. 11–27). London: Sage.

Phelan, J. M. (1988). Communing in isolation. *Critical Studies in Mass Communication, 5*, 347–351.

Portes, A., & Landolt, P. (1996). *The American Prospect, 26*, 18–21, 94.

Putnam, R. D. (1995a). Bowling alone: America's declining social capital. *Journal of Democracy, 6*, 65–78.

Putnam, R. D. (1995b). Tuning in, tuning out: The strange disappearance of social capital in America. *Political Science and Politics, 28*, 664–683.

Quandt, J. B. (1970). *From the small town to the great community: The social thought of progressive intellectuals.* New Brunswick, NJ: Rutgers University Press.

Rappaport, R. A. (1979). *Ecology, meaning, & religion.* Berkeley, CA: North Atlantic Books.

Redfield, R. (1960). *The little community and peasant society and culture.* Chicago: University of Chicago Press.

Ricoeur, P. (1981a). Phenomenology and hermeneutics. In P. Ricoeur, *Hermeneutics and the human sciences* (J. B. Thompson, Ed. & Trans.); (pp. 101–128). Cambridge: Cambridge University Press. (Original work published 1975)

Ricoeur, P. (1981b). The model of the text: Meaningful action considered as a text. In P. Ricoeur, *Hermeneutics and the human sciences* (J. B. Thompson, Ed. & trans.); (pp. 197–221). Cambridge: Cambridge University Press. (Original work published 1971)

Rivlin, L. G. (1982) Group membership and place meanings in an urban neighborhood. *Journal of Social Issues, 38,* 75–93.

Rossi, P. (1956). *Why families move.* Glencoe, IL: Free Press.

Rothenbuhler, E. W. (1991). The process of community involvement. *Communication Monographs, 58,* 63–78.

Rothenbuhler, E. W. (1995). Understanding and constructing community: A communication approach. In P. Adams & K. Nelson (Eds.), *Reinventing human services: Community- and family-centered practice.* New York: Aldine de Gruyter.

Rothenbuhler, E. W. (1996). Commercial radio as communication. *Journal of Communication, 46*(1), 125–143.

Rothenbuhler, E. W. (1998). *Ritual communication: From everyday conversation to mediated ceremony.* Thousand Oaks, CA: Sage publications.

Rothenbuhler, E. W., Mullen, L. J., DeLaurell, R., & Ryu, C. R. (1996). Communication and community attachment and involvement. *Journalism and Mass Communication Quarterly, 73,* 445–466.

Sampson, R. J. (1988). Local friendship ties and community attachment in mass society: A multilevel systemic model. *American Sociological Review, 53,* 766–779.

Schopenhauer, A. (1969). *The world as will and representation* (3rd ed.). (Two vols; E. F. J. Payne, Trans.). New York: Dover. (Original work published 1859)

Schudson, M. (1996). What if civic life didn't die? *The American Prospect, 25,* 17–20.

Schutz, A. (1970). *Reflections on the problem of relevance.* New Haven, CN: Yale University Press.

Schutz, A., & Luckmann, T. (1989). *The structures of the life-world* (Vol. II); (R. M. Zaner & D. J. Parent, Trans.). Evanston, IL: Northwestern University Press.

Shepherd, G. J. (1993). Building a discipline of communication. *Journal of Communication, 43*(3), 83–91.

Shepherd, G. J., & Rothenbuhler, E. W. (1991). A synthetic perspective on goals and discourse. In K. Tracy (Ed.), *Understanding face to face interaction: Issues linking goals and discourse* (pp. 189–203). Hillsdale, NJ: Lawrence Erlbaum Associates.

Short, J. F., Jr. (Ed.). (1971). *The social fabric of the metropolis: Contributions of the Chicago school of urban sociology.* Chicago: University of Chicago Press.

Shim, J. C., & Salmon, C. T. (1990). Community orientations and newspaper use among Korean newcomers. *Journalism Quarterly, 67,* 852–863.

Sigman, S. J. (1991). Handling the discontinuous aspects of continuous social relationships: Toward research on the persistence of social forms. *Communication Theory, 1,* 106–127.

Skocpol, T. (1996). Unraveling from above. *The American Prospect, 25,* 20–25.

Stamm, K. R. (1985) *Newspaper use and community ties: Toward a dynamic theory.* Norwood, NJ: Ablex.

Stamm, K. R., & Guest, A. M. (1991). Communication and community integration: An analysis of the communication behavior of newcomers. *Journalism Quarterly, 68,* 644–656.

Stein, M. R. (1960). *The eclipse of community: An interpretation of American studies.* New York: Harper & Row.

Stewart, D., & Mickunas, A. (1974). *Exploring phenomenology: A guide to the field and its literature.* Chicago: American Library Association.

Stinner, W. F., Loon, M. V., Chung, S., & Byun, Y. (1990). Community size, individual social position, and community attachment. *Rural Sociology, 55,* 494–521.

Strauss, A. L. (1968). *The American city: A sourcebook of urban imagery.* Chicago: Aldine.

Street, D., & Associates. (1978) *Handbook of contemporary urban life.* San Francisco: Jossey-Bass.

Suttles, G. D. (1984). The cumulative texture of local urban culture. *American Journal of Sociology, 90,* 283–304.

Tinder, G. (1980). *Community: Reflections on a tragic ideal.* Baton Rouge, LA: Louisiana State University Press.

Tönnies, F. (1988). *Community and society [Gemeinschaft und Gesellschaft].* (C. P. Loomis, Trans; new introduction by J. Samples). New Brunswick, NJ: Rutgers University Press. (Original work published 1887).

Tsai, Y., & Sigelman, L. (1982) The community question: A perspective from national survey data—the case of the USA. *British Journal of Sociology, 33,* 579–588.

Valelly, R. M. (1996). Couch-potato democracy? *The American Prospect, 25,* 25–26.

Vidich, A. J., & Bensman, J. (1968). *Small town in mass society: Class, power and religion in a rural community* (Rev. ed.). Princeton: Princeton University Press.

Viswanath, K., Finnegan, J. R., Jr., Rooney, B., & Potter, J. (1990). Community ties in a rural midwest community and use of newspapers and cable television. *Journalism Quarterly, 67,* 899–911.

Webber, M. W. (1963). Order in diversity: Community without propinquity. In L. Wingo (Ed.), *Cities and space: The future use of urban land* (pp. 23–54). Baltimore: Johns Hopkins University Press.

Wellman, B. (1979). The community question: The intimate networks of East Yorkers. *American Journal of Sociology, 84,* 1201–1231.

Wellman, B., & Wortley, S. (1990). Different strokes from different folks: Community ties and social support. *American Journal of Sociology, 96,* 558–588.

Williams, R. (1983). *Keywords: A vocabulary of culture and society.* (Rev. ed.). New York: Oxford University Press.

White, M., & White, L. (Eds.). (1962). *The intellectuals versus the city: From Thomas Jefferson to Frank Lloyd Wright.* Cambridge: Harvard University Press.

Whyte, W. F. (1955). *Street corner society* (2nd ed.). Chicago: University of Chicago Press.

Wirth, L. (1964). *On cities and social life: Selected papers* (A. J. Reiss, Jr., Ed.). Chicago: University of Chicago Press.

Zhu, J., & Weaver, D. (1989). Newspaper subscribing: A dynamic analysis. *Journalism Quarterly, 66,* 285–294, 337.

9

Collective Memory as "Time Out": Repairing the Time–Community Link

Barbie Zelizer
University of Pennsylvania

For those who reflect periodically on what it means to be a member of a community, it will come as no surprise to know that communities are constituted in time. As Giddens (1979) claimed, all reflections of social structure depend on a "virtual time-space," rendering social practices the outcomes of the time-space intersections in which they are situated. Community membership is no exception to Giddens' observation, and time and space remain two primary background variables that explain how communities constitute and maintain themselves.

This chapter considers community membership and the temporal dimension of this time-space intersection. Communities have always been framed partly on the basis of their temporal positioning. From small communities like families to large-scale groups such as nation-states, time remains one of the supporting beams through which communities make sense of themselves. Where would the Amish be without their shared history? How have feminists used the evolving status of women over time to forward their claims? How do political groups change and realign themselves in conjunction with mistakes of the past? How does the 25th of December differ for Christians, Jews, or Moslems? Questions such as these suggest that in different ways the constitution and maintenance of communities depend on how communities relate to time. Members of communities develop temporal practices that have to do with the content of time, the form of time, the high points and low points of time, and the context surrounding time.

Time depends on communities too. Although the familiar and systematic invocation of discrete units in temporal measurement—such as eras, hours, years, and decades—emphasizes time's primarily objective dimensions, we know that the subjective dimensions of time are as active as their objective cousins. Scholarship in various quarters of the academy (Brandon, 1965; Hall, 1959, 1976; Zerubavel, 1981) has been particularly valuable in delineating how time takes on different shapes according to context, ethnicity, institutional procedures, and an array of other intervening variables. "Being late," to use a commonly-cited example, has different valences in Latino or Mediterranean culture than it possesses in Nordic cultures. The difference of one-tenth of a second means very little to two people meeting for lunch but has enormous significance to an Olympic swimmer. In short, we understand time through cues from the environment that make it meaningful to us in different ways.

This chapter argues that time and community exist in a symbiotic relation with each other. It contends that time is as dependent on community for meaning as community is on time. By implication, this chapter also suggests that neither time nor community is able to exert itself fully without undoing the other. Collective memory is proposed as a corrective to the time–community link, harnessing both within manageable dimensions. For if pushed to their logical limit, both time and community will undermine the other. Each will push the other to exhaustion, depleting them of all meaning. Collective memory offers a stop–gap measure for this process, furnishing a time-out that offsets the potential exhaustion of the two.

Time as a Feature of Community

We can consider time first as a feature of community. Time is a central factor in a community's ability to constitute itself. Time is defined as the "continuum in which events occur in apparently irreversible succession from the past through the present to the future" (Webster's II New Riverside University Dictionary, 1984; p. 1210). Whereas time's counterpart—space—gives a picture of how communities work at one point in time, providing us with visual maps of communal interaction, function, and dysfunction that are frozen within a given time frame for reasons of analysis, by contrast the temporal dimension of communities provides a depth and array of resources that, by definition, fluctuate over many points in space and time. Temporal analysis allows analysts to see process, motion, and the movement of community from one point to another. This different kind of validity suggests that the interface connecting communities over time may have a powerful impact on our understanding of how communities stay together despite tremendous fluctuations in their constituent parts.

What is time's relation to community? Time provides a backdrop against which communities constitute themselves. As Lynch (1972) maintained long ago, "time is a mental device to give order to events, by identifying them as coexisting or successive. Moments do not exist in themselves. They are classes of events in which there is no need to distinguish one event as occurring before the other" (p. 120).

Although different types of societies develop their own time cultures, the ability of community members to engage in collective activity depends on their cooperative action in time. Time has many effects on communities and community members, in that it shapes, constitutes, and defines them, "Societies exist in time and conserve images of themselves as continuously so existing. It follows that the consciousness of time acquired by the individual as a social animal is in large measure consciousness of his society's continuity" (Pocock, 1971, p. 233).

Time not only gives community members a way to structure relations between activities but it also provides a way to conceptualize those activities as well. Early research by Evans-Pritchard (1940) on the *Nuer*, in which he distinguished between ecological and structural time in this North- African people, is an oft-cited example, but more recent scholarship has demonstrated how integral time is to the everyday functioning of a wide array of groups, communities, and collectives (Back & Gergen, 1963; Gurvitch, 1964; Lewis & Weigert, 1981; Zerubavel, 1987).

Although the Durkheimian school was the first in sociology to address the communal dimensions of time (Durkheim, 1965/1912), an early article in the United States by Sorokin and Merton (1937) elaborated on time's inherently social dimension. That work produced a wide range of scholarship that demonstrated the extent to which collective action depends on time (Bergson, 1988/1908; Bloch, 1977; Fabian, 1983). Time functions "as a context for anchoring the meaning of social acts and situations" (Zerubavel, 1981), and communal activities as broad as holidays, work schedules, and mourning rituals or as confined as mealtimes, television programming, and newspaper delivery all depend on time.

What is important here is the idea that communities, when seen through a temporal lens, are never static but need continuously to be defined and redefined. Constitution work never ends but rather works in a kind of race with the timepieces that pace its progression. This means that, ultimately, time undoes its ability to shape communities by virtue of its never being able to stop shaping them. Somewhat like the experience of being on an unstoppable treadmill, times loses some of its cogency by virtue of its ever presence.

Community as a Feature of Time

Community's relation to time exhibits similar patterns to those seen in time's relation to community. We can consider what communities do with time and how they constitute themselves temporally. In that time exceeds the life span of the normal human being, community boundaries in time cannot depend on communal members. That is to say, if a community dies with its members, the community ceases to exist. By definition, then, the community must exceed the life of the social group if the community is to survive. This creates a need for devices that extend the individual's experience of time beyond the normal horizons of everyday experience, to a past and future that transcend the individual.

Such devices are at the core of ongoing temporal work on the part of community members. In most cases, this work takes the shape of reorganizing time. One such example is freezing time, exemplified in the celebration of holidays or other ritual moments. Museums, fashion shows, and television retrospectives provide additional ways of positioning certain times above others. Even the cyclical arrangement of a family's week—the time reserved for family hours, homework, bedtime reading—depends on a consensual reorganization of time. When we speak of "time immemorial" or "time out of time," when we tell stories of "the olden days" or the activities of "once upon a time," or even when we call a "time out," we are reorganizing time.

In all these cases, the community reorganizes to accommodate a break in the so-called normal time by stopping the flow of the everyday. Whether it be grandparents' tales of the days of yore, autobiographical accounts of the glorious days of a profession, or commemorative language used in religious ceremonies, rearranging time through language and practice is an instrumental part of maintaining community identity in ways that make sense for its present and future members.

When circumstances change, and the folklore of a given community no longer works, then the accounts of the community change too. Each of us has witnessed history being rewritten—family lore told from different vantage points, institutions that lay different claims to reality as they experienced it, national histories that offer varying accounts of the past in accordance with the hyphenated existences that constitute a nation. One of the most legendary examples involved the ways in which statues of Lenin were replaced with busts of Stalin so as to accommodate changes in the former Soviet regime (Tumarkin, 1987). In each case, language and practice rearrange earlier rearrangements of time. This suggests that temporality rests on a fundamental instability of communal lore. That instability is worked and reworked to the community's advantage, in ways that consolidate it.

This means that communities necessarily upset temporal patterning and chronological sequencing. They reorient time, making it tool through which community members maintain and extend the life of the collective. Community becomes predicated on a dissociation between the act of remembering and the chronological sequencing of time. Time becomes a social construction, the target of strategic reshaping by the group. Here too, then, if taken to extreme, the practice can undo the entity. For if time becomes so subjectified that it is no longer able to realistically ground the community in a shared past linked with real-life events, the community runs the risk of undoing itself as well.

Collective Memory: Correcting the Time–Community Link

How do communities and time move beyond the undoing of each other? For both time and community, the ongoing and often exhaustive nature of the link between them has different repercussions. For time, the question becomes one of addressing how time stops long enough to measure itself. For communities, the issue is one of how communities use time to unite rather than separate. It is here that notions of collective memory come into play. Collective memory reigns within the space of the time–community link, providing a viable way for collectives to lend meaning to the past. Collective memory frames the time–community link in a way that allows community members to understand and recognize time as meaningful, and it does so in ways that uphold the collective.

Ever since the writings of Proust gained popular appeal, the self was seen as a way of organizing temporal events. *Collective memory*—a term that gained popular contemporary resonance through the work of French scholar Maurice Halbwachs—extends the connection with identity. Seen as a way of constituting the past within the present (Halbwachs, 1992), it is a process "not of retrieval but of reconfiguration [that] colonizes the past by obliging it to conform to present configurations" (Hutton, 1988, p. 314).

Collective memory offers a way of welding the passage of time and community together in a mutually meaningful fashion. Both are integral and necessary components for collective memory to function. This suggests that, together, community and time exist in an oscillating relationship. They provide a seesaw of ground and figure—when one takes over the foreground of attention, the other fades to the background, and vice versa.

Community as Ground, Time as Figure

Without community, collective memory has no foundation or infrastructure against which to fashion its interpretations of the past. Community functions as the backdrop or the ground of collective memory. This is because memory temporally organizes experience only if it is socially supported. Collective memories rest within the lore of collectives—whether they be families, nationals, ethnic groups, or members of professional associations. In each case, interpretive communities arise that choose to make certain points in time salient, unimportant, contested, or uniformly received (Zelizer, 1993; also Schudson, 1992). But without some resonance within a community, such choices are irrelevant.

We can consider, as an example, ongoing interpretations of the Holocaust. Collective memories of the atrocities of World War II have undergone waves of recollection, where specific time periods have fashioned collective interpretations of what happened in conjunction with other events contemporaneous to the moment of interpreting or remembering. Since 1945, remembering the Holocaust has, at different moments, been shaped as collective amnesia, as targeted remembering that forces attention to what happened, exemplified in statements like "Never Again," and as a muted, less directed kind of memory work that no longer produces a consensual linkage between the parallels between then and now, seen in debates over links between the Holocaust, on the one hand, and contemporary atrocities in both the Balkans and Africa, on the other. This has happened regardless of the community engaged in the memory work: Even Holocaust survivors, for instance, refrained from sharing their wartime experiences during the amnesiac period that extended for the first few decades after the war (Zelizer, 1998).

Time as Ground, Community as Figure

A similar patterning characterizes situations in which community becomes the figure to time's ground. Time is the material that collective memories use to shape shared interpretations of the past. Collective memory approaches time as a raw material to be constituted—and reconstituted—in accordance with the aims and goals of a community's members. Because accounts of the past become a way of collectively fashioning existence in the present, collective memory uses temporality not only to establish community but to challenge and reconstitute its own boundaries over time. In this sense, time functions as the figure in collective memory work, nudging up against the ground of community, to shape interpretations of the past.

But collective memory has not depended on an invocation of time in its expected form. Rather, collective memory dissociates the act of remembering from time's primarily linear sequencing. Chronology, dismissed by Lowenthal (1992) as "history-book time" (1985, p. 221), takes on value here only insofar as it contrasts the interrupted nature of memory. Time's *re*creation becomes so central that nonsequential temporal patterning is often heralded as a constituting feature of shared memory. In short, time becomes a social construction, the target of strategic rearrangement. Because "every relic exists simultaneously in the past and present…what leads us to identify things as antiquated or ancient varies with environment and history, with individual and culture, with historical awareness and inclination" (Lowenthal, 1985, p. 241).

Examples by which community and time come together in the shaping of collective memory are boundless: When the Berlin Wall came down, national communities on both sides needed to reconstitute memories of the past so as to better live together in the future. Native Americans challenge dominant construction of the U.S. frontier narrative in a way that upholds their community amidst the ruins of earlier recollections that they did not even partially own. Sometimes communities link strange bedfellows—as in the children of Holocaust survivors from different nations. Governments, educational systems, and religious organizations all actively work to make certain that collective accounts of the past fit the present. The media here are a key tool in helping large groups interpret the past in similar fashion. Through these institutions and others, collective memory gives time and community a frame in which to interact. It holds them at abeyance from each other, thereby assuring their effectivity. Collective memory allows the group to use time in a fruitful way at the same time as it allows time to function to the group's benefit. Collective memory thereby repairs the excesses built in the time–community link.

Thus, the past of the British empire was crafted in order to fill voids that existed in collective understandings of the past (Hobsbawm & Ranger, 1983). The belief that Vietnam era protesters were "anti-troop" was employed 20 years later during the Persian Gulf War, although it had no consonance with the actions surrounding the earlier conflict (Beamish, Molotch, & Flacks, 1995). Abraham Lincoln was recalled by subsequent generations of Americans in ways that invoked what was important at the time of remembering, producing early images of a folksy Lincoln giving way to a portrait of a remote and dignified individual (Schwartz, 1990). Memories of the Holocaust were adjusted to fit the national agendas of different generations of Europeans (Judt, 1992; Miller, 1990).

Elsewhere, I discussed some of the practices by which the time–community link is managed by collective memory (Zelizer, 1995). *Retrospective nominalization* is one such practice, used in reference to the renaming of events, issues, or places in accordance with later events, issues, or places. For instance, World War I stopped being called the Great War only once World War II came into collective consciousness. The Holocaust became known as the Holocaust only during the 1970s, some 30 years following the events that motivated that name. This means that at the same time as the use of the old secures and solidifies the new, the new helps assign and reassign meaning to the old. Time—and its concomitant traits of sequentiality, linearity, and chronology—are used as resources for the establishment and continued maintenance of memory in its social, collective form. Such an understanding of memory is based on a far more cyclical and nonlinear relation to time than has been traditionally assumed.

Another practice by which time is rearranged is by *collapsing commemoration.* Here, commemorative dates or holidays are used to remember more than one event at the same time. In Valensi's (1986) discussion of Jewish memory, for instance, she demonstrated how one date on the Jewish calendar—the 9th of the month of Av—has come to commemorate many events ranging over hundreds of years in Jewish history, including the destruction of the First Temple, the destruction of the Second Temple, the fall of the Jewish kingdom of Palestine, and the Bar Kochba revolt. In memory, these events were collapsed into the same day. Similarly, the patterning of holiday time, by which religious or magical rites are repeated in similar temporal circumstances, makes us able to predict the placement of holidays on a grid connecting the four seasonal quadrants (Santino, 1994). Still another example surrounds the erection of the tombs of the unknown soldier, which were set in place following World War I. As Gillis (1994) pointed out, these tombs offered a way to remember everyone "by remembering no one in particular" (p. 11). In this case, as in others, memory work succeeded over time by undoing the activity with which it had traditionally been associated.

What does all of this suggest? It suggests that collective memory redefines both constituents of the time–community relationship: It takes what is most risky about each element and neutralizes the risk by framing it with the other. Time becomes not only a way to subjectively thread the past to the present, but a way for communities to consolidate their identity. Community becomes a reflection of a strategic decision to highlight certain aspects of identity over others, often forging unexpected connections; yet these connections depend on time to gain meaning.

Conclusion: Collective Memory as "Time-Out"

What does this tell us about the continued functioning of the time–community link, and its continued maintenance through collective memory?

Two features are most salient about this relationship. One concerns the work involved in community building and maintenance, which in effect never ends. Community maintenance depends on a constant look backward, to the previous life of the community members, so as to constitute them as a collective in the present day. This, by definition, makes temporal analysis necessary, for without it, the analysis of communities would deny consideration of all the fluctuations through which community members maintain their links with each other. In turn, this makes a simultaneous consideration of time and community necessary for understanding how each works.

But a second issue is also important here. It concerns the ability of collective memory to give communities and time a shared and mutually advantageous way in which to relate. Collective memory keeps the time–community link within reasonable limits, allowing both to flourish but not knock each other off the map in doing so. In this way, it functions somewhat like a time-out in athletic competitions, allowing for the kind of breathing space that keeps both competitors thrashing and ready for the next round.

Both of these points suggest that in considering the issue of building community, we need not focus simply on the entity produced. Rather, we must examine its production by focusing on processes of collective remembering. In the building and maintaining of community, only rarely does memory work cease. It is time we captured it at its core and celebrated it for what it gives our understanding of time, of community, and of the link between them.

ACKNOWLEDGMENTS

I thank Teodor Florea and Susan Nasberg for research assistance on this chapter. I also thank Eric Rothenbuhler for his careful eye and infinite patience and Gregory Shepherd for spearheading the collective effort of which this is a part.

REFERENCES

Back, K. W., & Gergen, K. (1963). Apocalyptic and serial time orientations and the structure of opinions. *Public Opinion Quarterly, 27,* 427–442.

Beamish, T. D., Molotch, H., & Flacks, R. (1995, August). Who supports the troops? Vietnam, the Gulf War and the making of collective memory. *Social Problems, 42*(3), 344–360.

Bergson, H. (1988). *Matter and memory.* New York: Zone Books. (Original work published 1908).

Bloch, M. (1977). The past and the present in the present. *Man, 12,* 278–292.

Brandon, S. (1965). *History, time and deity: A historical and comparative study of the conception of time in religious thought and practice.* New York: Barnes & Noble.

Durkheim, E. (1965). *The elementary forms of the religious life.* New York: The Free Press. (Original work published 1912).

Evans-Pritchard, E. (1940). *The Nuer.* London: Oxford University Press.

Fabian, J. (1983). *Time and the other: How anthropology makes its object.* New York: Columbia University Press.

Fraser, J. T. (Ed.). (1966). *The voices of time.* New York: George Braziller.

Fraser, J. T. (1975). *Of time, passion and knowledge.* New York: George Braziller.

Fraser, J. T., Haber, F. C., & Miller, G. H. (1972/1975). *The study of time* (Vols. I–II). New York: Springe-Verlag.

Giddens, A. (1979). *Central problems in social theory: Action, structure, and contradiction in social analysis.* Cambridge: Cambridge University Press.

Gillis, J. (Ed.). (1994). Memory and identity: The history of a relationship. In *Commemorations: The politics of national identity* (pp. 5–30). Princeton, NJ: Princeton University Press.

Gurvitch, G. (1964). *The spectrum of social time*. Dordrecht-Holland: D. Reidel.

Halbwachs, M. (1992). *On collective memory*. Chicago: University of Chicago Press. (Original work published 1951).

Hall, E. (1959). *The silent language*. New York: Anchor.

Hall. E. (1976). *Beyond culture*. New York: Anchor.

Hobsbawm, E., & Ranger, T. (Eds.). (1983). *The invention of tradition*. Cambridge: Cambridge University Press.

Hutton, P. (1988). Collective memory and collective mentalities: The Halbwachs-Aries connection. *Historical Reflections [Reflexions Historiques], 15*(2), 311–322.

Judt, T. (1992, Fall). The past is another country: Myth and memory in postwar Europe. *Daedalus*, 83–118.

Lewis, J. & Weigert, A. (1981). The structures and meanings of social time. *Social Forces, 60*(2), 433–462.

Lowenthal, D. (1985). *The past is a foreign country*. Cambridge: Cambridge University Press.

Lynch, K. (1972). *What time is this place?* Cambridge: MIT Press.

Miller, J. (1990). *One, by one, by one*. New York: Touchstone Books.

Pocock, J. (1971). *Politics, language and time*. New York: Atheneum.

Santino, J. (1994). *All around the year*. Urbana, IL: University of Illinois Press.

Schudson, M. (1992). *Watergate in American memory: How we remember, forget and reconstruct the past*. New York: Basic Books.

Schwartz, B. (1990). The reconstruction of Abraham Lincoln. In D. Middleton & D. Edwards (Eds.) *Collective remembering* (pp. 81–107). Beverly Hills: Sage.

Sorokin, P., & Merton, R. (1937). Social time: A methodological and functional analysis. *American Journal of Sociology, 42*(5), 615–629.

Tumarkin, N. (1987). Myth and memory in Soviet society. *Society, 24*(6), 69–72.

Valensi, L. (1986). From sacred history to historical memory and back: The Jewish past. *History and Anthropology, 12*(2), 283–305.

Zelizer, B. (1993). Journalists as interpretive communities. *Critical Studies in Mass Communication, 10*, 219–237.

Zelizer, B. (1995, June). Reading the past against the grain: The shape of memory studies. *Critical Studies in Mass Communication*, 214–239.

Zelizer, B. (1998). *Remembering to forget: Holocaust memory through the camera's eye*. Chicago: University of Chicago Press.

Zerubavel, E. (1981). *Hidden rhythms: Schedules and calendars in social life*. Berkeley: University of California Press.

Zerubavel. E. (1987). The language of time: Toward a semiotics of temporality. *The Sociological Quarterly, 28*(3), 343–356.

10

Virtual–Online Communities: How Might New Technologies be Related to Community?

Howard E. Sypher
University of Kansas
Bart Collins
University of Louisville

The days of an Internet dominated by stereotypical computer nerds are quite over. According to a mid-1998 survey by Ziff-Davis's Technology User Profile, almost one third of the United States' 103 million households have Internet access (Niccolai, 1998). Given the relatively quick time in which this level of Internet diffusion has developed, the popular and academic literature can barely keep track of the social, psychological, political, and economic ramifications of this new wave of computer mediated communication (CMC) technologies. One of the difficulties associated with monitoring the effects of Internet use is that technologies associated with the Internet change rapidly. Whereas e-mail has been around, largely unchanged, since the 1960s, the World Wide Web did not exist until 1991. In between e-mail and the web are a whole host of obsolete, emerging, and hybrid protocols and technologies designed to make it easier for a person and a computer to interact with each other as well as to interact with other persons and computers on the network. It is not uncommon to hear people make reference to the fact that many of us live in a networked world, and, by implication, if one is not connected to the network, one is simply not connected at all. The unconnected are out of the loop, socially and otherwise.

Although many of us, and pretty soon most of us, have access to the Internet, to what extent can we really say we are more connected to others as a result? In the GVU's ninth Internet survey, 45.3% of more than 12,000 respondents reported that

"Since being on the Internet, I have become more connected with people like me" (Georgia Tech's Graphics, Visualization & Usability Center, 1998). Only 2.7% of the respondents reported being less connected.

Does having access to new communication technologies actually increase the quality of our communication with others? Are we more social creatures as a consequence of logging on to the Internet? Or, consistent with the theme of this volume, does access to these new technologies encourage or discourage the development of community? This is not a particularly easy set of questions to answer, and this brief chapter does not pretend to answer them. However, one can begin to sketch out the conceptual landscape of what might be required to begin answering these questions. In other words, how might access to CMC technologies contribute to our social well-being and sense of community with others?

Scholarship in this area is quite divided. For some, CMC technologies will inevitably function to reconnect our isolated and fragmented social ties (Healy, 1997; Lockard, 1997). For others, the expectation that an activity as solitary as sitting in front of a computer monitor can do anything other than further isolate us from others is ridiculous (Stratton, 1997). For the former, individuals like Howard Rheingold (1993) very passionately argue for the benefits of a world dominated by CMC. Rheingold, in his groundbreaking work, *The Virtual Community: Homesteading on the Electronic Frontier*, said: *See Rheingold*

> My direct observations of online behavior around the world over the past ten years have led me to conclude that whenever CMC technology becomes available to people anywhere, they inevitably build virtual communities with it, just as microorganisms inevitably build colonies.

> I suspect that one of the explanations for this phenomenon is the hunger for community that grows in the breasts of people around the world as more and more informal public spaces disappear from our real lives. (p. 6).

On the other side of the equation, we have the voice of those like Stephen Talbot (1995), who in his work, *The Future Does Not Compute: Transcending the Machines in Our Midst*, responded to those technological utopians who might argue that "Net connections to the socially isolated will at least tend to lead them out of their isolation in happy ways" (p. 65). Talbot responded, "It's a stunning leap of faith … Did the telephone—bringing with it the ability to call anyone in a city of five million people—move the city toward more intimate community, or has it merely enabled us to hunker down within our separate castles, talking, perhaps, to more and more people while cut off from community more than ever before" (p. 65). Although the battle over the relationship between community and communication technologies is well underway, most everyone agrees that we are sorely in need of stronger community ties. The question is whether the Internet and related technologies will help or hinder our attempts at reconnecting with others. Charting the social effects of Internet use is difficult. One way one might do it is by following the lead of people who study traditional media effects. For instance, the negative social and community effects of television have been reasonably well documented (see Putnam, 1995). Like television, the Internet can be viewed as a medium that encourages a particular use of our time that, while using it, prohibits our engagement in other, more social, activities. Unlike television, however, the Internet not only allows for passive reception of information, but active engagement in social activities of its own kind. We can use the Internet to interactively communicate with others, regardless of any arguments about the quality of the interactions. The Internet, itself, refers to a whole slew of mechanisms by which we can gain access to information or communicate with others, whereas the television represents a relatively singular sort of activity that is largely noninteractive. In this regard, it is much easier to make sense of research that points to the relation between television use and any other social effect than it might be to make sense of research that relates Internet use to particular social effects. Internet use, relative to television use, is much more nebulous and ambiguous.

As an example of the problems this sort of ambiguity causes, consider the recent work of scholars from Carnegie Mellon who found very small, but negative, correlations between Internet use and social well-being. In this longitudinal study, 93 families in Pittsburgh, Pennsylvania were assessed on a variety of variables, including social involvement. Subsequently, they were all given free access to the Internet. One to 2 years later, subsequent testing on the same variables indicated that measures of social involvement were lower as a function of the amount of time people spent on the Internet. Of particular note was the positive relationship between loneliness and time spent on line. Though the effects were small and hovered right at the edge of statistical significance, the report received substantial media attention for a study in the social sciences and heralded the damaging social effects of using the Internet. The ultimate conclusion drawn by the authors of the study (Kraut et al., 1998) stated:

> Both as a nation and as individual consumers, we must balance the value of the Internet for information, communication, and commerce with its costs. Use of the Internet can be both highly entertaining and useful, but if it causes too much disengagement from real life, it can also be harmful. Until the technology evolves to be more beneficial, people should moderate how much they use the Internet and monitor the uses to which they put it.

Thus, the Carnegie Mellon scholars leave the impression that the Internet is a paradoxical technology. It is paradoxical in the sense that a presumably social technology should not result in asocial or nonsocial behavior.

How should we respond to these data? Should we be worried about our access to the Internet in the ways that the Carnegie Mellon data suggest we should? Our response is that their conclusions are overstated. Not only because the observed effects were quite small but because the ways this scholarship presupposes a certain conceptualization of what constitutes positive social interaction. The relation that was found might have been expected; it is our general contention that CMC, in fact, can both enhance and degrade our participation in larger notions of community. This is primarily so because community and its relation to technology can be construed in very many different ways. To enhance one's participation in one type of communal relation with others may indeed detract from one's ability to participate in others.

The Carnegie Mellon study highlights this issue very clearly by looking only at how the use of the Internet is related to non-Internet related social activity. This particular conceptualization does not necessarily yield a paradox. What could be considered paradoxical would have been data suggesting that Internet use leads to a decline in Internet-related social activity. Of course, we cannot think of any set of conditions that would lead to the observation of such a relation.

One major part of this problem is that Internet-based relationships and interactions are assumed to be much more cold and distant than are possible in analogous face-to-face interactions and relationships. This particular orientation usually follows from what is known as the "cues filtered out" approach (Walther & Burgoon, 1992), which highlights the observation that interacting through computers limits the types and numbers of socially relevant cues that are available for processing in any given interaction. This lack of social information, as in much nonverbal behavior, possibly produces a more egalitarian environment by promoting anonymity but presumably makes the development of social relationships more difficult. One commonly used cited ramification of this is the phenomenon of "flaming," where individuals can easily engage in uninhibited, negative, or rude social behavior. The cues filtered-out perspective basically operates under the assumption that online environments, because of their deindividuating effects, are much more likely to operate outside of standard norms and rules that might govern social- or community-enhancing behavior (Sproul & Kiesler, 1991).

However, how norms and rules emerge and are enforced within online community groups has been the subject of substantial research and is often discussed in research that looks specifically at various types of online discussion groups (see Baym, 1995). Norms and rules governing interaction always form within any set of relationships if those relationships hope to remain stable over time. Communities, as organized sets of relationships, need mechanisms for limiting the potential for destructive activities on the part of its members. In highly formal communities, these may take the form of laws that determine specific consequences for specific infractions, and certain members of the community have legitimate power to enforce the community laws. In less formally constructed communities, informal norms and rules often develop in which, basically, the members police themselves. In online communities, both formal laws and informal rules and norms are often created to insure to the ability of the community to maintain itself over time. Network administrators or discussion group moderators often have the power to formally limit the ability of a particular person to contribute to discussions by simply canceling their subscription to a service. In contrast to this extreme sort of enforcement, online activities are often loosely governed by what is called Internet etiquette or "netiquette." For instance, members who deviate from established norms of online behavior may be attacked by others. One common technique might be to flood the offender's personal e-mail account with information, the goal of which is to exceed the storage capacity of the offender's account and render it inoperable. Most Internet "how to" books contain sections on generally observed rules of etiquette for new participants (e.g., Krol, 1992). Even within the same kind of online communities, norms for behavior vary greatly. For example, Baym (1995; 1999) pointed out that different news groups employ very different normative models of conduct and etiquette. For example, in soap-opera news groups, Baym (1995) argued that there is a taboo on flaming, yet in Star Trek news groups flaming and contentious e-mail is common.

From a social psychological perspective, Postmes and his colleagues (Postmes, Spears, & Lea, 1998) adopted the Social Identity model of Deindividuation Effects model (SIDE; Reicher et al., 1995) from Steve Reicher's work on crowd behavior. Reicher provided an alternative explanation for so-called "deindividuation effects" by arguing that deindividuation is not best characterized as a loss off the sense of "self" or personal identity (Postmes & Spears, 1998). The SIDE model states that factors that may cause a sense of deindividuation, such as the combination of anonymity and group immersion, or the dissociating experience of interacting via a computer network, can actually reinforce group salience and conformity to group norms. Thereby, the SIDE model predicts conformity to norms associated with the specific social identity of the group, rather than conformity to any general norms.

More specifically, the SIDE model proposes that when an individual finds himself or herself in a so-called deindividuating situation (i.e., a situation in which individuating information that allows effortless identification of others and oneself is relatively scarce), this person will be tempted to explain events and make sense of the situation by looking for contextual cues as to what is appropriate and desirable behavior in that context. Normally, in an individuating setting, such a person may be more tempted to seek personal guidance, and to pay relatively less attention to the (social) context. In a deindividuating CMC session, the cues that may guide a person's behavior will mostly be sought in the social relationships between communicators because of the very social nature of communication itself. In other words, group members may become depersonalized, which means that a person will no longer address each person in the group as an individual but rather as a member of the social group (see Postmes et al., 1998, for a complete discussion).

The influence of factors in the social sphere may be felt in CMC, especially when people are dissociated and deindividuated. This idea has some implications for community in CMC environments. CMC, according to this line of thought, is not necessarily the cold and heartless medium it is so often made out to be and that the work of Kraut and his associates suggests. Rather, the medium can be perceived as warm and welcoming, if only communicators share a common identity or have a common bond.

One other possible criticism of the cues filtered out perspective is that it must basically assume limited technological development. However, the expansion of technology to incorporate more and more features of face-to-face interaction is occurring at an incredible pace. Multimedia-enhanced interactions, including audio and video with compelling virtual environment are more and more commonplace.

Even so, much like Rheingold's experience would suggest, many people seem to form positive social relationships and develop strong community ties even in text-only computer environments.

This new orientation, therefore, operates from a different construal of what ought to be the relation between community and technology. It is one that argues community need not only be one that exists outside of mediation through some sort of network. It can also be created and maintained online. The value of the Internet is not in its ability to rebuild traditional community, but to accent it with alternative virtual forms of community that fill gaps in the lives of people longing for communities they do not have. After all, interaction with others, whether through news groups, e-mail, chat, and so forth, is easy to find on the Internet.

"The Well" is probably the first recognized example of a community electronic network. The Well, which had its origins in Berkeley California during the 1960s, was started by Stewart Brand. It was consciously designed as an experiment in community and communication, was countercultural in orientation and relied on volunteers to build its data base, provide the hardware and software, and was only marginally successful by most measures. More contemporary and ambitious efforts at community building are those by America Online and GeoCities' online neighborhoods. Even more currently, typical Internet search engines and subject directories, such as Yahoo! and Excite, are developing online chatrooms and discussion groups for people to join, ostensibly under the assumption that these are alternative ways to participate in "communities." Perhaps an even better and more recent example of a commercial attempt at building electronic community building can be found at *theglobe.com*. This site has chat and communication as its central focus.

There are other possible relations that linger somewhere between these two positions, as well. Because of technologies like the Internet, existing traditional communities can turn to the Internet as a way of helping maintain participation in the community and attracting new members to the community. These are often referred to as public electronic networks (see Rogers & Allbritton, 1997). One of the most well-known and probably most written about public electronic networks is Public Electronic Network (PEN) in Santa Monica, California. PEN's major objectives include enhancing awareness of city programs and facilitating the delivery of public services, providing an alternative means of communication for residents to convey their needs and preferences to their local government and to other residents, providing an electronic forum for discussion of issues and concerns of residents in order to promote an enhanced sense of community; extending to the community the opportunity to understand computer technology, and providing access to the hardware and software to learn to communicate via an electronic network. These objectives are pursued by providing access to the electronic network to all citizens via libraries and other public buildings.

PEN services include e-mail to city departments, council members, community organizations, and all other PEN users. PEN also provides online forms and transactions such as recreation class registrations, business license renewals, petty theft reports, job interest applications, bus itinerary requests, consumer complaints, library card registrations, and so forth. PEN posts over 250 menu items of information including city jobs, bus schedules, school district news, public safety, building projects, neighborhood information, youth programs, library events, pets for adoption, pier and theater events, public safety bulletins, and much more. PEN also provides searchable databases including the Municipal Code, a City Services Guide, and archives of past City Council and Planning Commission business; computer conferences hosting on-going discussions on education, crime, development, youth issues, homelessness, neighborhood organizing, rent control, public art, the environment, etc; and dial-up access to the library catalogue provides searches by title, author or subject, tells if a book is checked out or not, and allows holds to be placed on books.

With PEN, City Hall is available to residents at their convenience. The use of electronic communication with city officials reduces car trips to government facilities, reduces waits at city service counters, reduces staff time spent responding to walk-in and telephone inquiries, and enables staff to provide more thorough responses to e-mail inquiries. PEN facilitates the process of communication between residents and local government, particularly when more than one city organization is involved. Unfortunately, PEN-like entities are still relatively unique, but PEN does provide a good example of how an electronic network might support and supplement the traditional civic channels of a community. Many other city governments are attempting to use electronic networks to enhance civic access and participation (Scottsdale, Arizona and Oakland, California are other good examples). Indeed these efforts are generally taking place all over the world. In most cases, however, these efforts have not been well documented or rigorously investigated by scholars. One recent exception to the general lack of research in this area is the extensive documentation of Ishida (1998) in an edited collection focusing on community computing in Kyoto, Japan. Unfortunately an overview of their activities and activities in other cities is beyond the scope of this chapter.

Larryville.com in Lawrence, Kansas probably is pretty typical of many of the new digital community networks, and this online effort offers a clear contrast to PEN and its goals. Most sites like Larryville.com are not affiliated with official community or city electronic gateways, and rather offer an alternative to the official channels of information. For the most part they are often antigovernment and tend to attract input from individuals who feel their viewpoints are not well represented on city commissions, in the local news media, or the business community. They typically employ threaded discussions and community bulletin boards that post opinion pieces. As with many MOOs and other similar electronic way-stations they reflect the personality of the people who created and maintain the site and in many ways are closer to The Well with what they are trying to accomplish in their form of community building. *Larryville.com*'s motto is "Community Happens." Obviously, we feel it's a bit more complicated than that: Community takes work, online or offline.

These examples serve to illustrate that there are many ways in which we might expect technology and community to be related to one another. The relation need not be between Internet use in general and social well-being in general. Community potentially can exist entirely in mediated form. We can also see evidence of existing traditional communities using the technology as a way of adding value to the existing community structure. This is not to say, however, that any specific effort to establish or enhance community through the use of CMC will be successful.

Aside from any particular definitional constraints one might place on the idea of community, online or otherwise, the technology is likely here to stay. Given this state of affairs, our goal is centered on how to make the best possible uses of the technology, either to prevent it from destroying whatever hopes for real community are left, or to allow it to foster new forms of community in real and meaningful ways. How we meet this challenge of harnessing the technology can be approached from a variety of directions, with a range of perspectives. However, two points seem plain: First, access needs to be easy and available. Like all technologies, unless its use is automatic and natural, little community benefit can develop. When members of a nation or state are shut out to decisions because they do not have the same technological access, important issues develop. Technology needs to provide clear solutions to real problems, not create its own set of problems. If a city government web site does not provide access to important city information then the result can be detrimental to efforts to build or enhance a sense of community. Additionally, people should feel that there are real consequences associated with their participation, that they are losing valuable social contact when they do not participate, and that the payoffs of participating actively are great.

Second, questions regarding bandwidth must be addressed. E-mail, voicemail, telephones, faxes, and the Internet all have the capacity to provide new mechanisms for establishing or maintaining interpersonal interactions. Yet all these electronic means of connecting still pale beside the richness of face-to-face interaction. Multiple mediums enhance the experience of all. Our general assumption is "the richer the medium, the better." People interact differently, have different communicative needs, and can make contributions in different ways. Mediums that restrict how people can participate force them to choose whether to participate at all.

Following from these points and illustrations, the relation between technology and community can take on various forms. The technology can function to replace or displace traditional community or social activity much like any other activity. It can also function to provide people with alternative communities that only exist by virtue of the technology—forms of community that do not exist in unmediated environments. Finally, it can provide traditional communities with new mechanisms by which members can participate and interact, creating hybrid social environments and communities that coexist in traditional and mediated forms. From what we can see, there is ample evidence that all of these factors are at work when examining the relation between the use of technology and the development or enhancement of community. Depending on how one operationalizes community, what values one places on the relative merits of mediated or unmediated relations, and how one goes about assessing the success of the technology at creating or maintaining these networks of social relationships, the relationship between the use of technology and subsequent membership in a community is still very much up in the air. Given that the technology is here and that it is quickly reaching or has already reached critical mass in its diffusion throughout society, our goal ought to be binging the use of the technology to the service of community, in whatever forms that community might take.

Researchers can do some things to help, rather than hinder, our ability to see issues of community in online environments. Obviously, researchers need to clearly identify their theoretical and methodological biases. For instance, what, for a given researcher, constitutes use of the medium (surfing, chatting, etc.), and what constitutes community or social interaction (online or traditional, etc.)? Additionally, research can be enhanced by contextualizing treatment of technology and community within the framework of analogous research on other mediums, such as television, telephone, print, and so forth. In other words, what makes computer-mediated environments so unique and special that they deserve specific treatment? Very few of the issues are new. Other mediums for expression and interaction have struggled with many of the same problems that computer mediated interaction also raises.

We do not think there are any clear answers to the questions associated with the extent to which online communities can be mapped over traditional face-to-face communities. We do know that we live in a world of wireless telephones where we are accessible almost anyplace and time, where e-mail is now used more than traditional letter writing, where online discussion groups get extensive use, and where the World Wide Web allows us to learn more about other peoples and their cultures. These new features of our environment help us maintain old relationships and sometimes develop new ones. But do these ways of communicating work because they are layered over more traditional means of communication and community adding weak ties to an already existing network of strong personal ties? Or, can real community exist where an electronic network is the only means of social interaction? Will technological advances eventually bring us to the point where the bandwidth available in traditional face-to-face interactions is not significantly different from that in electronic interaction? At the moment there are clear quantitative and qualitative differences, but the gap is narrowing.

REFERENCES

Baym, N. (1995). The emergence of community in computer-mediated communication. In S. G. Jones (Ed.), *CyberSociety: Computer-mediated communication and community*, pp. 138–163. Thousand Oaks, CA: Sage.

Baym, N. (1999). *Tune in, log on: Soaps, fandom and the on-line community*. Thousand Oaks, CA: Sage.

Georgia Tech's Graphics, Visualization & Usability Center (1998). GVU Center's ninth WWW user survey. (Available, *http://www.gvu.gatech.edu/user_surveys/survey-1998-04*).

Healy, D. (1997). Cyberspace and place: The Internet as middle landscape on the electronic frontier. In D. Porter (Ed.), *Internet culture* (pp. 55–71). New York: Routledge.

Ishida, T. (1998). (Ed.). *Community computing: Collaboration over global information networks*. West Sussex, England: Wiley.

Kraut, R., Lundmark, V., Patterson, M., Kiesler, S., Mukopadhyay, T., & Scherlis, W. (1998). Internet paradox: A social technology that reduces social involvement and psychological well-being? *American Psychologist, 53,* 1017–1031.

Krol, E. (1992). *The whole Internet: User's guide and catalog.* Sebastopol, CA: O'Reilly.

Lockard, J. (1997). Progressive politics, electronic individualism and the myth of virtual community. In D. Porter (Ed.), *Internet culture* (pp. 55–71). New York: Routledge.

Niccolai, J. (1998). Internet population continues to grow. *PC World Today* (Available, *http://www.pcworld.com/cgi-bin/pcwtoday?ID=9009*).

Putnam, R. (1995). Bowling alone: America's declining social capital. *Journal of Democracy, 6,* 65–78.

Postumes, T., Spears, R., & Lea (1998). Breaching or building social boundaries? SIDE-Effects of computer-mediated communication. *Communication Research, 25,* 689–715.

Reicher, S. D., Spears, R., & Postumes, T. (1995). A social identity model of deindividuation phenomena. In W. Stroebe & M. Hewstone (Eds.), *European review of social psychology,* Vol. 6 (pp. 161–198). Chichester: Wiley.

Rheingold, H. (1993). *The virtual community: Homesteading on the electronic frontier.* New York: Addison-Wesley.

Rogers, E. M., & Allbritton, M. M. (1997). The Public Electronic Network: Interactive communication and interpersonal distance. In B. D. Sypher (Ed.), *Case studies in organizational communication 2: Perspectives on contemporary work life* (pp. 249<@150). New York: Guilford.

Sproul, L., & Kiesler, S. (1991). *Connections: New ways of working in the networked organization.* Cambridge: MIT Press.

Stratton, J. (1997). Cyberspace and the globalization of culture. In D. Porter (Ed.), *Internet culture* (pp. 55–71). New York: Routledge.

Talbot, S. L. (1995). *The future does not compute: Transcending the machines in our midst.* Sebastopol, CA: O'Reilly.

Walther, J. B., & Burgoon, J. K. (1992). Relational communication in computer-mediated interaction. *Human Communication Research, 19,* 50–88.

11

Building an Electronic Community: A Town–Gown Collaboration

Teresa M. Harrison, James P. Zappen,
Timothy Stephen, Philip Garfield,
and Christina Prell
Rensselaer Polytechnic Institute

The Internet has generated a number of innovative and exciting social phenomena; among the most engaging of these are *virtual communities*, which are created when individuals meet in online interactional environments, bond together as a group, perceive a sense of shared identity, and maintain cooperative social ties over time. In 1993, Rheingold drew national attention to the appearance of virtual communities, underscoring their importance as one of the compelling ways that Internet technology is helping to create new connections between people. Pointing to contemporary yearnings for community that have followed in the wake of anemic urban areas and disconnected suburban enclaves, Rheingold argued that interaction online could reinvigorate feelings of community among people by drawing on shared interests and common concerns that transcend culture, time, and space. The notion of Internet-based virtual communities has turned the attention of many community seekers away from the neighborhood and in the direction of cyberspace. But what has not been generally recognized is that Rheingold's original virtual community, The Well, in San Francisco, had a strong foundation in geography. New friends that were discovered in cyberspace ended up meeting one another in physical space, as new face-to-face relationships were born in the local community.

Although virtual communities in cyberspace have generally commanded significant media coverage, relatively little attention has been focused on ways the

Internet can be used to strengthen traditional geographic communities. This, despite of the appearance of the now burgeoning numbers of geographically oriented community networks; nearly 400 currently exist or are planned (Schuler, 1996) and most of these with a home page on the World Wide Web. Despite their relative lack of publicity, these networks are the locus for a significant grassroots effort aimed at reinvigorating traditional local communities.

Many of the first community networks began as the hobbies of computer enthusiasts operating their own electronic bulletin-board systems (Cisler, 1993). However, a significant number of them have developed into "free-nets" and are now organized as 501(c)(3) nonprofit organizations. Other networks are the ongoing projects of city governments, libraries, foundations, or universities (Harrison & Stephen, 1999). Regardless of their origins, a significant number of community networks have received support from the Telecommunications Information and Infrastructure Assistance Program, a funding program sponsored by the National Telecommunications and Information Administration, which is a branch of the Department of Commerce, charged with making information technology infrastructure available to communities.

Community networking projects are undertaken for a variety of reasons, but perhaps the most common has been to provide public access to the Internet and information on the World Wide Web for those who would otherwise not be connected (Carter, 1997; Law & Keltner, 1995). This motivation implicitly draws on the theme of "information democracy" (Doctor, 1992), which suggests that the ability to participate meaningfully in democratic decision making—by becoming knowledgeable about and formulating preferences among choices—rests on the citizen's ability to access information and acquire the resources required to do so. Thus, information is here seen as a vital precondition for exercising one's role as a citizen in a democracy.

Community networking has also been viewed as a site for significant reinvigoration of democratic practices at the level of community involvement and participation (Schuler, 1994). Since the earliest days of the Internet, theorists have been alive to the potential for computer-networking technology to be used to support or extend certain kinds of liberal democratic processes, such as serving as a means for quickly assessing public opinion or for enabling citizens to communicate with their representatives (Abrahamson, Arterton, & Orren, 1988; Barber, 1984; Hiltz & Turoff, 1978/1993). One of the first and most famous community networks, the Santa Monica Public Electronic Network Project, has provided free access to the network and to the technology for accessing the network for city residents, enabling even the homeless to access city government information and to discuss topics of pressing community interest with city council members (Law & Keltner, 1995; Rogers, Collins-Jarvis, & Schmitz, 1994; Schmitz, Rogers, Phillips, & Paschal, 1995). As Bertelsen (1992) pointed out, much of the optimism about the democratic potential of computer networking has focused on its interactive capabilities and the prospects for participatory democracy that such capabilities make possible. Both theorists and practitioners interested in fostering deliberative democratic practices have grasped the potential for community networks to be the locus for conversation and discussion in community-wide social gatherings (see, e.g., Doheny-Farina, 1996; London, 1997).

Although they represent an application of Internet technology with significant democratic potential, there is no question that community networks are fragile sociotechnical systems with many practical hurdles to overcome. Beyond gaining the acceptance and support required to serve as legitimate sites for civic interaction, they must also overcome economic challenges to their viability (Schuler, 1995). Most networks so far are sustained by inexperienced volunteers with little agreement on their missions or how to go about achieving them. In this context, it is not insignificant that the National Public Telecomputing Network, founded by Tom Grundner to serve as an umbrella support organization for networking projects fashioned as free-nets—a computer networking equivalent of the Corporation for Public Television—has recently declared bankruptcy. One response to the need to provide additional support to the movement has come from Douglas Schuler (1997), perhaps the nation's most active proponent of community networking. He has called on academic researchers to work together with community networking practitioners to design and develop networking projects and to create a knowledge base that will enable practitioners to become more aware of the factors that are important to success. This chapter describes a project that originated in part as a response to his call.

In this chapter we describe the efforts of a group of faculty, staff, and students at Rensselaer Polytechnic Institute to create the technological and social foundations for a community- networking enterprise in Troy, New York. Rensselaer is the oldest technology-oriented institution of higher education in the United States; however, its information technology projects have rarely involved the surrounding community. In early 1997, a group of faculty and staff submitted a proposal to an institutional research funding program to create a demonstration project that would illustrate—to Rensselaer and to Troy—the value of using information technology to enhance the quality of life in the local community. That proposal received modest funding and subsequently some in-kind contributions of computer equipment and software.

What follows is a report of our efforts to create a collaborative venture, marrying the technical and theoretical skills of Rensselaer students and employees with the local knowledge of Troy citizens to produce community-oriented information to be accessible through the World Wide Web and through local computer kiosks. More specifically, we discuss our particular commitments to a collaboration between the university and the community that was designed to build community, by creating what democratic theorist Robert Putnam (1993) called "social capital." We then describe the genesis of the project and the particular focus that it acquired in its early instantiation. The next major section of the chapter considers our efforts to work with Rensselaer students to develop community-oriented content for the project. In this section, we describe our course, Web Design for Community Networking, which was designed to provide a service-oriented component to the education of students who are pursuing technologically oriented degree programs. One of the goals of this course was to encourage students to work with members of the Troy community to develop web-based projects; we describe the mechanisms that we adopted to achieve this goal. Finally, we reflect on what we have learned from the project and discuss our future efforts.

BUILDING COMMUNITY THROUGH
THE DEVELOPMENT OF SOCIAL CAPITAL

Licklider and Taylor (1968), who developed the technology leading to the Internet and who were among the first to envision social outcomes of computer networking, predicted that computer-mediated communication would lead to the creation of online communities based on commonality of interests. What they did not envision at the time was that the very same communication capabilities could also draw on common interests to strengthen traditional geographically based communities. The earliest community networkers, such as David Hughes in the 1980s, used their personal computers as bulletin-board systems to make citizens aware of local political issues affecting the common good and to create the opportunity for mobilizing community action on such issues (Rheingold, 1993).

In 1993, with the establishment of the U.S. Advisory Council on the National Information Infrastructure, community activists saw the potential to develop a broad policy that would spell out how national information infrastructure could serve as the foundation for community development. Proponents of civic networking (see, e.g., Civille, 1993; Civille, Fidelman, & Altobello, 1993; Fidelman, 1994; Sharp & Beaudry, 1994) advocated the development of a national strategy for using information technology to revitalize both economic and civic institutions in local communities, which would lead to a revitalization of the American economy and civic culture in general. This vision of civic networking, articulated by Civille, Fidelman, and Altobello (1993) and representing the Center for Civic Networking, advocated broad public access to, and individual use, of networked information for the purpose of stimulating economic development; it advocated reducing the costs of government services, health care, pollution, and layoffs; it advocated improving education; and it advocated reviving civic institutions and public discourse.

But just as the social connections made possible through information technology do not necessarily produce community (Jones, 1995), simply using networking technology to access information does not automatically achieve the economic and civic advantages that proponents hope to realize through community networks (Friedland, 1996). Although social connections, information, and the tools for accessing information are important prerequisites, Friedland (1996) suggested that the development of more concrete social uses of the technology will determine the extent to which networking is an effective tool for civic activism. What computer networking makes possible is the opportunity to forge new patterns of association between actors in the community, develop cooperative relationships, and create the basis for mutual trust. Such qualities are essential to the concept of social capital, which Putnam (1993, 1995) argued is the basis for effective democratic governance and for an engaged and participatory citizenship.

Putnam (1995) was not optimistic about the democratizing potential of electronic networks because he doubted that meetings between citizens in electronic forums created the kind of mutual engagement typically fostered through face-to-face relationships. However, Friedland (1996) argued, based on his analysis of community networks and other forms of Internet-based civic activism, that electronic networks provide the opportunity for citizens to build new networks of relationships, create new norms for sharing and reciprocity, and erect new foundations for trust. These are the very qualities that comprise social capital, which is best conceived as a communal, rather than an individual or group asset, such as economic capital. It is social capital that enables "participants to act together more effectively to pursue shared objectives … " (Putnam, 1996, p. 31). Within the context of geographically situated community networks, the associations that originate online can transfer easily to face-to-face contexts and vice versa. It is also important to note that even attempts to organize and build a community network may similarly have the effect of creating new patterns of sustained associations, thus presenting the potential to build community.

Background and Commitments of our Project

Our efforts to design a project that would illustrate the benefits of a community network have been motivated by the value we saw in the development of new networks of relationships between members of the Rensselaer community and members of the Troy community. This motivation stemmed from our assessment of the existing level of integration or, rather, lack thereof. Although the two communities have worked closely with each other at times over the course of 175 years of shared history, more recent relations between the city and Rensselaer had grown distant and cool. Rensselaer sits on a commanding bluff overlooking the eastern bank of the Hudson River where the city of Troy is situated. The vertical geo-physical distance between the university and the town has seemed to be matched by the social distance between the actors in each community.

Troy had been the site of significant technological innovation earlier in its history; indeed, some have called it the "Silicon Valley" of the 19th-century industrial revolution (Carroll, 1997). But during the decades of the 20th century, the city had undergone hard times financially, losing much of its manufacturing and industrial base and nearly going bankrupt in the early 1990s. A significant portion of the downtown district was rebuilt following a fire in the late 19th century; thus city buildings present models of Victorian architecture attractive enough to be chosen as the settings for major motion picture period films such as the *Age of Innocence*. However, many blocks of the downtown area have also undergone substantial deterioration, with a corresponding decline in the number of retail businesses and customers. Students at Rensselaer had come to possess negative attitudes toward the neighbor city and were reluctant to patronize businesses, restaurants, and bars in the downtown area. An eroding tax base meant that city schools were no longer competitive with school districts in the surrounding region; thus Rensselaer's faculty and staff frequently chose to live elsewhere, exacerbating the lack of integration between the university and the city.

Although we were committed to the idea of building collaborative associations between citizens of Troy and members of Rensselaer, we were also convinced that the community should retain ultimate ownership over any community-networking project that might be organized as a result of our demonstration project. One of the dangers of university-sponsored networking projects is that, on the basis of superior technical expertise, university personnel will overwhelm community representatives, building the system "for" the community, instead of with them. As a result, community members may have little sense of ownership for the project and little idea of how to use, maintain, or significantly alter their own web-based information or services. We have made a number of efforts to avoid this type of outcome.

First, we were guided by the admonitions of networking theorists and practitioners, such as Schuler (1996), who warned that failing to actually involve the community in favor of professional guidance is one way to "kill" a community network. Similarly, Gygi (1996) warned that project developers who "are concerned with building democratic institutions will need to ensure that their decision-making processes are participatory and collaborative" in order to achieve their objectives. We describe our efforts to involve the community in the planning and implementation of the demonstration project in the following sections.

Second, we were also motivated by the need to educate members of our community in using Internet and World Wide Web technology. Community organizations need ultimately to be responsible for updating and maintaining the materials that were developed to represent them on a World Wide Web-based community network. We believed that such materials must function positively if they were to support the mission of the organization in order to be considered valuable and that, to do so, they needed to be designed and maintained by individuals who understood how they worked. Thus, members of these organizations needed to be equipped with some degree of expertise to undertake these duties.

The development of Web pages relies on a certain level of computer literacy extending beyond that of using a word processor; thus, members of community organizations need to acquire specific computer-related skills to successfully maintain web-based materials. For example, they need to learn HTML, a scripting language that converts text documents to formatted web pages, making edits or changes to a web page very different from edits or changes made to a word processed text document. People cannot simply type in words and print a new version of the file as if they were using word processor. Also, because successful web pages need to be regularly updated to accurately reflect the ongoing activities of an organization, they need to be equipped to make those updates to better insure that their materials are useful and contribute significantly to the mission of their organization. Taken together, community organizations need to be able to perform a certain number of computer-related tasks if they are to maintain and truly own their web-based materials and the community network as a whole.

We knew that we would not be able to undertake extensive training programs for community organizations in our planning for the design of our demonstration project. However, we were sensitive to the need to plan for training on a more long-term basis to be able to extend and build upon the project. Furthermore, we also were sensitive to the need to build a demonstration project that would excite and motivate community members to seek the training that would enable them to maintain their own networking materials on a community Web site.

Origins of our Approach

In the Spring of 1997 our group, originally comprised of six faculty and one staff member from Rensselaer, received funding for the development of a demonstration information technology project focused on the community of Troy. Although we were sure we wanted the project to center on the development of a community-wide networking service, we were unsure about what particular approach the project should take. Thus, we embarked on a series of conversations with representatives of the community that took place over the summer and into the fall.

Over the course of several months, members of our group met with representatives from the Mayor's office, leaders of community-based organizations such as the United Way of Northeastern New York, the President of the Troy Downtown Merchants Association, members of the Troy Cultural Council, leaders of several arts organizations, and the Executive Director of the Hudson-Mohawk Industrial Gateway, who also oversees the management of the Troy RiverSpark Visitors Center. At that time, we received an endorsement from the Mayor's Office and expressions of enthusiasm and support from others for our project.

While these conversations were underway, the Albany (N.Y.) *Times Union* newspaper also published two articles that were seen as highly relevant to our project. One of these reported on the difficulties that boaters on the Hudson River were experiencing in finding restaurants and services in downtown Troy, only three blocks from Troy's city marina. Later research taught us that a significant number of overnight boaters traveling north on the Hudson River choose to spend the night in Troy, prior to heading west on the Mohawk River toward the Great Lakes because Troy provides the last opportunity to service a boat for the run to the Great Lakes. Merchants and city government leaders were very interested in attracting these travelers to town. The second article reported on the dissatisfaction felt by Troy merchants because Rensselaer students did not patronize downtown businesses.

These articles established the desirability of a Web site that would serve the purpose of introducing audiences to the commercial attractions of downtown Troy and that would help visitors and short-term residents find their way there. We thus decided to design the Web site centering in part on the idea of a visitor-oriented on-line map that would serve as an interface to information about particular commercial, cultural, and historical institutions and organizations in downtown Troy.

Additionally, representatives of community organizations consistently expressed the need for a centralized community-events calendar for the Troy region, because they were unable to know when events they sponsored were likely to conflict with other events drawing on the same audience. Furthermore, there appeared to be a generalized need to publicize the numerous cultural and social events taking place in the Troy area.

Following our early research, we worked with the United Way of Northeastern New York to organize a focus group consisting of leaders of community organizations whom we brought to a computer lab on campus and told about our plans and aspirations for a community network that would include a centralized community-events calendar. We also further showed this group a series of online community network materials and asked for their comments. The conversation that ensued provided us with the criteria that we would use in selecting the software to carry out the essential functions of a calendar. For example, these representatives made it clear that the calendar would at first need to be updated by a trained individual in one community office and that only later, with more extensive training, could it be operated by representatives of community organizations.

By the middle of the fall, 1997, the nature of the project had become clear, and its direction solidified in the name by which we referred to our undertaking: "The Troy Map-Calendar Project."

Organizing the Organizers

By late Autumn of 1997, the project's founding group of six faculty and staff had grown to involve 15 people, including several graduate students and three representatives from the Troy community who had shown a great deal of early interest in the project. We referred to ourselves as the Rensselaer Coalition for Community Networking (RCCN). In late autumn, we articulated our mission in the following statement: "To assist Troy organizations to realize their purposes by developing usable, sustainable, accessible information and information-delivery systems."

In order to realize this mission, we sought to design, develop, build, and launch a web-based information system that would center on a map of Troy as well as centralized community calendar that would serve to promote the community and the commercial, historical, social, and cultural organizations that comprise downtown Troy. In direct response to the issues we heard from community members, we established the primary purposes of the map–calendar project: (a) to develop a mechanism that would help stimulate economic, cultural, and social development in Troy, (b) to empower and amplify the voices of community organizations, (c) to entice visitors and short term residents into Troy to spend money, and (d) to provide a central information resource for Troy.

Two project subgroups formed: one to design the site—its information architecture and interface—and the other to design and develop the software supporting it. Other members of the RCCN designed the database that would store business, community, and calendar information; they researched cartographers, aerial photographs, and artists in order to make decisions about what the map would look like; they demonstrated menuing and online calendaring applications; they interviewed graphic designers; they digitally photographed each business in the downtown Troy target area; and secured tax parcel maps from the county.

With the technical aspects of executing a project of this sophistication under way, two members of this group undertook the development of extended content for the Troy map–calendar project. In addition to the centralized calendar and map-driven searching capabilities of the site, we thought it would be useful to provide visitors to the site with information on the history, culture, and present-day features of the city of Troy, if the community was to be portrayed as an attractive place to visit, shop, study, and live. Toward this end, two of us worked together to create a senior-level course at Rensselaer that became the occasion for extended contact with members of the Troy community in designing content for the community Web site.

WEB DESIGN FOR COMMUNITY NETWORKING

In Spring 1998, we offered an undergraduate course titled Web Design for Community Networking to provide an opportunity for Rensselaer students to develop in-depth web presentations on Troy's considerable social, cultural, historical, and commercial resources. Rensselaer has large numbers of engineering, science, computer science, and Electronic Media, Arts, and Communication (EMAC) students, and we anticipated that these students would bring to our course high levels of technical competence, including professional web-design experience, computer-programming skills, and expertise in visual and graphic design. We believed that in order to motivate these students to do their best work, we would have to permit them to develop projects that matched their abilities and interests. At the same time, we hoped and expected that they would develop projects that would be perceived as interesting and valuable to members of the Troy community. Put simply, we wanted to ensure both student and community ownership of these projects in the short- and long-term.

To achieve these goals, we created an advisory board that included Rensselaer faculty and technical staff and members of the Troy community, we identified prospective clients in the community, and we organized the course much as we would organize a professional web-design project, with time and opportunity for students to develop their ideas, to develop a storyboard for their projects, to construct a prototype, and to complete their projects. We also included a requirement that students present their group projects and solicit feedback from the advisory board and clients and that they interview them for their particular projects and respond to their suggestions. In some instances, we engaged additional students outside of our course to establish supportive relationships with clients in order to sustain projects that required long-term maintenance.

Advisory Board

Prior to the start of Spring term, we created an advisory board for class projects and invited members of the RCCN and members of the Troy community who had expressed interest in the Map–Calendar Project to serve as members of the Board. We also invited representatives from Troy city government, Rensselaer county government, the Chamber of Commerce, local businesses, not-for-profit organizations, and community volunteers and activists to be a part. We asked members of the advisory board to be available to offer us advice on the map–calendar project and to give their time on one or more occasions during regular class meeting times to respond to our students' projects. More than 24 people from Rensselaer and Troy consented to serve on the board and to contribute actively to our project in their role as advisors.

Clients From the Troy Community

Prior to the Spring term, we also identified some potential clients familiar with the Troy community and its history and invited them to make presentations at the beginning of our course, both to provide context and background about Troy and to explain their own interests in community networking. These potential clients represented civic, commercial, tourism interests in Troy, and they significantly influenced the design and outcomes of our course. They included Dr. William St. John, former Director, Rensselaer County Market Block Incubator Program, and former Executive Director, Rensselaer County Regional Chamber of Commerce; Dr. P. Thomas Carroll, Executive Director, Hudson Mohawk Industrial Gateway; and Joe B. Fama, Executive Director, Troy Architectural Program, and Staff Director, City of Troy Waterfront Commission. Their participation inspired several of the major projects in our course and direct engagement with people in the Troy community.

Organization of the Web-Design Course

To ensure that we used our advisory board and clients effectively, we organized our course as we would a professional design project, as a sequence of steps or milestones, with feedback at each of these steps. The steps included development of the initial project ideas; design of a flowchart or storyboard to map out the major components and the flow of information of each project; the construction of a working prototype to enable potential users to get a good sense of the "look and feel" of the information and navigation system, and a formal presentation of the final projects to a real audience of clients and potential users in the community. To ensure a variety of responses and to avoid overburdening our advisory board and clients, we invited different groups to respond to our students at different times. For example, we invited the advisory board and clients for a presentation of the initial project ideas; faculty, technical staff, and selected advisory board members for the storyboards; individual clients as scheduled with their individual groups; and all participants for the presentation of the completed projects.

Individual Projects

The individual student projects developed during a long period of generating and testing project ideas and another long period of developing the informational and design components of the projects, the latter task was complicated and enriched enormously by the feedback from the advisory board and clients, most of which was directed toward engaging both Troy community members and prospective users in the electronic recreation of the life and activity of the community. These projects included recreations of Troy's rich history and culture, commercial and entrepreneurship information, informational and service components, and support for not-for-profit agencies.

Several projects presented historical and cultural information about Troy for both local residents and visiting tourists. These projects included presentations of Troy's architecture, its history, including its place in major-league baseball, its role in filmmaking, and its women, both past and present. For example, one of these projects presented Troy's history and culture in the form of virtual postcards. The Troy architecture project offered a gallery of original photographs illustrating the various styles of glasswork, ironwork, and stonework throughout Troy, organized on a map of the downtown area. Inspired by Dr. Carroll's visit to our class, the Troy history project established a rich repository of historical vignettes accessible by either time (precolonial–colonial, early industrial, late industrial, and post-industrial) or subject (education, society–culture, industry–economy, and disasters) categories. The Troy history project also included a quiz and a slide show originally prepared for Troy's RiverSpark Visitor Center and rendered accessible on the Web via RealPlayer.

Several other historically and culturally oriented projects addressed particular themes or activities. Created by two baseball enthusiasts, the Troy baseball project captures Troy's moment in history as a major league baseball team, the Troy Trojans, later to become the New York and San Francisco Giants. Titled "Hollywood on the Hudson," the Troy filmmaking project tells the story of major films shot on location in Troy, including *The Age of Innocence*, *The Bostonians*, and portions of *Ironweed* and *Scent of a Woman*. The filmmaking project also included a virtual tour of film locations, recollections of the filmmaking by Troy residents, and information about prospective film locations. The Troy women's project recounted the accomplishments of influential women in Troy, both historical and contemporary. Finally, the virtual postcard project permitted visitors to send virtual postcards of scenes from Troy's history, its riverfront and parks, and its educational institutions.

Another project, guided and encouraged by Dr. St. John, presented entrepreneurship information as a way of promoting commercial enterprises in Troy and ensuring their success through careful planning and management. The entrepreneurship project included information about how to successfully launch a new business venture, whom to contact in Troy, and the special advantages of starting a business in Troy.

Some other projects provided information about basic services available in Troy. One project includes contact information for emergency services, including fire, police, hospital, and transportation information. Another project, directed primarily toward travelers who arrive in Troy by boat via the Hudson River, included information about boating and boating safety, map and travel information, and information about nearby restaurants, hotels and motels, grocery stores and pharmacies, shops and theaters, and the like.

Finally, a few of the projects offered web-page development support for not-for-profit organizations in the community, including the local United Way and Unity House, a local social-service organization.

Feedback From the Advisory Board and Clients

Feedback from the Advisory Board and clients provided useful information about the design of the projects, especially suggestions on how to make the web pages more dynamic and interactive, and encouragement to include members of the Troy community and their activities as informational components of the web pages. In response to this feedback several groups added interactive elements to their projects, such as quizzes or virtual tours of the city. The "Hollywood on the Hudson" group also added information about prospective film locations and stories by residents who had participated in the filmmaking, by playing roles as "extras" or by providing services to the filmmakers, such as meals or lodging. This information had the effect of highlighting particular businesses in the downtown area.

Interviews with clients brought these clients' perspective to the design of the webs and encouraged students to include components of immediate interest and use to potential visitors to the web materials, such as prospective investors and tourists. The entrepreneurship group, for example, included information about available building space in Troy, in response to a request from Troy's deputy mayor, both to promote commercial activity and to disseminate useful information about available space for sale or rent to the widest possible audience. The emergency services group added information about transportation as a result of a visit to the police department, in response to a police request for information to assist travelers who frequently (mis)direct their inquiries about travel arrangements to the police. The waterfront group added information about nearby services when they learned that boat travelers frequently arrive in Troy in search of groceries, medicine, liquor, and cigars, and even Internet connections in order to plug in their laptops and check their e-mail.

Presentation of the Completed Projects

As the finale to our web-design course, we required that our students present their completed projects formally to members of the advisory board, their clients, and other representatives from the Troy community, a total of about 35 participants. We also presented our students' work to a variety of other groups, including Troy's Community Presence organization, the Rensselaer County Leadership Council, a local women's educational sorority, and faculty and graduate students from Syracuse University. These presentations provided both positive responses and constructive criticisms on our own and our students' work.

OUTCOMES AND CONCLUSION

When we wrote this chapter in the summer of 1998, we were still in the process of completing the development work on the Web site that was to house last semester's student projects; we anticipated completing it by September, 1999. At this point, the demonstration project, originally funded by Rensselaer and oriented toward illustrating the benefits of information technology for the local community, will also have been completed. However, we are acutely aware that the larger project of building a community computer network for Troy has only just begun. We believe that our demonstration project will also serve as a valuable foundation for this future work and that our collaboration has generated some measure of social capital that will fuel its future development. Furthermore, we have learned some interesting lessons in the process that will add to the resources that we now bring to this work.

There is no question that members of our team have now established some valuable new relationships that are continuing to enmesh members of the Troy and Rensselaer communities in collaborative activities. Some of us have joined with a group of Troy citizens to continue to develop plans for a community network. We meet regularly to select the activities that will be encompassed by the network and to decide how to involve a wide array of community organizations, including neighborhood associations, social-service organizations, youth organizations, cultural organizations, and business and industry. Our efforts have already secured the endorsement of the mayor and the participation of a representative of the Troy city government. Furthermore, other collaborative activities involving community organizations and the use of Internet technology have been stimulated by our work, including web training that several of us are providing for local organizations.

Although we did not encounter resistance or hostility to this project, over the course of the last academic year we did meet with some suspicion on the part of Troy residents about our motives and concerns about the longevity of the efforts. We were reminded by several residents that, in the past, people from Rensselaer had come to the community "to do good" and disappeared relatively quickly. Indeed, members of the Troy community that served on our advisory board may have been motivated initially more by curiosity than by trust in what our collaboration would accomplish. Rather than trying to organize large numbers of people, we have chose to cultivate those who were interested enough to come to class meetings, this in the hope that the development of a shared history, in which we could all see what the project was progressively accomplishing in material and social terms, would overcome any initial reservations. This hope has been redeemed. Because some of the individuals that were initially curious, but a little suspicious, are now working with us to develop the network, we expect these individuals to help us create the additional social capital that will be required for future progress.

Similarly, we learned that stimulating students to collaborate with clients and other members of the Troy community was not a completely straightforward task. Although the course enrolled 24 students, who all heard about the course expectations on the first day of class, and although members of the current generation of students are ostensibly more community oriented than the prior generation (Mitchell, 1998), our students were initially quite reticent about calling on Troy business people and community leaders and discussing their projects with them.

Toward this end, it was essential to bring members of our advisory board and clients to campus to make initial introductions. The first meeting between the class and the advisory board, in which students laid out their ideas before any development work had begun, turned out to be a crucial one. Here, members of the board became genuinely excited by the projects that the students had proposed and responded by showering praise and numerous suggestions for improvement. Their feedback was motivating and stimulating to the students, who then quickly appreciated that board members could be valuable resources. The second meeting, in which students presented the storyboards for their projects to board members and clients, resulted in an even more pronounced feedback effect as Troy residents began to realize that the students' projects were becoming a reality. At the presentation of the final projects, it became apparent that the students' projects had inspired an outpouring of community pride among those who attended, an effect of their work that our students, mostly computer scientists, systems engineers, and electronic-media majors, had never experienced.

We are currently in development of some ideas about how to involve members of community organizations in web-technology training. The need for community training has been inspired by our commitment to community ownership of the network. Too frequently community networks contain web materials for community organizations that are never updated because they were initially developed by someone else, who either donated time or was paid for the work. Several members of our group have thus begun to involve community organizations in probono web-technology training. Although these activities have not been extensive, a couple of key ideas are beginning to emerge. For example, it is becoming apparent that training activities need to take place within the context of developing an organization's web materials and that such materials should be the major focus of training. Furthermore, it appears that such training needs to be task oriented, enabling learners to accomplish particular goals with their web materials in a short period of time. These approaches contrast generic web-training courses that focus on HTML and are designed to teach a wide variety of topics within HTML. Our approaches seem advantageous for learners who initially do not have a lot of time to devote to web activities and are not yet convinced of their usefulness for their organizations' missions. We expect that we may need to revise these ideas with different kinds of community members, such as school-age children. Clearly there is much more to learn about how to diffuse information about web technology in our community.

Volumes are now being written about the potential for computer networks to reinvigorate the spirit of community and to enhance the practice of democracy in its many forms; nearly as much is being written about the potential for the technology to further dissipate both community and democracy. The technology makes it plausible to move in either direction; the disagreement is over what individual users—current and potential, practitioners and academics—will actually choose to use the technology to do. It is obvious that these issues are still very much in the process of being resolved. Academic researchers participate in creating the future, whether they simply place their bets on an outcome or take action to realize them.

More than anything else, we learned that social capital is not only or most importantly an individual asset but an asset held in common by members of a community working together to achieve their common purposes. Academic researchers cannot create social capital by themselves; but, in collaborating with practitioners in our communities, and through the social capital that such interactions can yield, we hope to realize a vision of the future of community and democracy that is closer to our preferences.

REFERENCES

Abrahamson, J., Arterton, C., & Orren, G. (1988). *The electronic commonwealth: The impact of new media technologies on democratic politics.* New York: Basic Books.

Barber, B. (1984). *Strong democracy.* Berkeley, CA: University of California Press.

Bertelsen, D. (1992). Media form and government: Democracy as an archetypal image in the electronic age. *Communication Quarterly, 40,* 325–337.

Carroll, P. T. (1997). Interview. *Troy United Newsletter, 6*(2), 3.

Carter, D. (1997). Digital democracy or information aristocracy: Economic regeneration and the information economy. In B. D. Loader (Ed.), *The governance of cyberspace* (pp. 136–152). London: Routledge.

Cisler, Steve, (1993). Community computer networks: Building electronic greenbelts [Online]. Available: *http://bcn.boulder.co.us/community/resources/greenbelts.txt.*

Civille, R. (1993). *The Internet and the poor* [Online]. Available: *gopher://nic.merit.edu:7043/00/conference.proceedings/network.communities/intern.*

Civille, R., Fidelman, M., Altobello, J. (1993). A national strategy for civic networking: A vision of change [Online]. Available: *gopher://gopher.civic.net:2400/00/ssnational strat/national strategy.txt.*

Doctor, R. D. (1992). Social equity and information technologies: Moving toward information democracy. In M. E. Williams (Ed.), *Annual Review of Information Science and Technology, 27,* 43–96.

Doheny-Farina, S. (1996). *The wired neighborhood.* New Haven: Yale University Press.

Friedland, L. (1996). Electronic democracy and the new citizenship. *Media, Culture, and Society, 18,* 185–212.

Gygi, K. (1996). Uncovering best practices: A framework for assessing outcomes in community computer networking [Online]. Available: *http://www.laplaza.org/aboutlap/archives/cn96/gygi.html.*

Fidelman, M. (1994). Life in the fast lane: A municipal roadmap for the information superhighway [Online]. Available: *http://civic.net/fastlane.html.*

Harrison, T., & Stephen T., (1999). Researching and creating community networks. In S. Jones (Ed.), *Doing Internet Research* (pp. 221–241). Newbury Park, CA: Sage.

Hiltz, S., & Turoff, M. (1993). *The networked nation.* Cambridge, MA: MIT Press.

Jones, S. (1995). Community in the information age. In S. Jones (Ed.), *CyberSociety.* Newbury Park, CA: Sage.

Law, S. A., & Keltner, B. (1995). Civic networks: Social benefits of on-line communities. In R. H. Anderson, T. K. Bikson, S. A. Law, & B. M. Mitchell (Eds.), Universal access to e-mail: Feasibility and societal implications [Online]. Available: *http://www.rand.org/publications/MR/MR650/mr650.ch5/ch5.html.*

Licklider, J. C. R., & Taylor, R. W. (1968). The computer as a communication device. *Science and Technology,* 21–31.

London, S. (1997). Civic networks: Building community on the net [Online]. Available: *http://www.west.net/~insight/london/networks.htm.*

Mitchell, M. (1998). *A new kind of party animal.* New York: Simon & Schuster.

Putnam, R. (1996). The strange disappearance of civic America. *Policy: A Journal of Public Policy, 12*(1), 31–43.

Putnam, R. (1995). Bowling alone: America's declining social capital. *Journal of Democracy, 6*(1), 65–78.

Putnam, R. (1993). *Making democracy work: Civic traditions in modern Italy.* Princeton, NJ: Princeton University Press.

Rheingold, H. (1993). *The virtual community.* Reading, MA: Addison-Wesley.

Rogers, E., Collins-Jarvis, L., & Schmitz, J. (1994). The PEN project in Santa Monica: Interactive communication equality, and political action. *Journal of the American Society for Information Science, 45,* 401–410.

Schuler, D. (1994). Community networks: Building a new participatory medium. *Communications of the ACM, 37,* 39–51.

Schuler, D. (1995). *Creating public space in cyberspace: The rise of the new community networks* [Online]. Available: http://scn.org/ip/commnet/iwdec.html.

Schuler, D. (1996). *New community networks: Wired for change.* Reading, MA: Addison-Wesley.

Schuler, D. (1997). Community computer networks: An opportunity for collaboration among democratic technology practitioners and researchers [Online]. Available: http://www.scn.org/ip/commnet/.

Schmitz, J., Rogers, E., Phillips, K., & Paschal, D. (1995). The Public Electronic Network (PEN) and the homeless in Santa Monica. *Journal of Applied Communication, 23,* 26–43.

Sharp, M., & Beaudry, A. (1994). *Communications as engagement: The Millennium report to the Rockefeller Foundation.* http://www.cdinet.com/Millennium.

12

Of What Use Civic Journalism: Do Newspapers Really Make a Difference in Community Participation?

Keith R. Stamm
University of Washington

Newspapers have rediscovered an old journalism model and given it a new name: *civic journalism*. The model argues that journalists need to make more concerted, systematic efforts to involve people in community affairs, if the media are to make a contribution to community participation (Denton & Thorson, 1998). At the same time, it is hoped that the reward for these efforts will be increased readership and circulation. This is not altogether a new idea. Sociologists and mass-communication scholars have been theorizing about the role of newspapers in community integration since the early work of Park (1937). Decades of research spawned by this model (i.e., the community integration model), has produced a considerable body of evidence linking newspaper use with a variety of individual–community relationships, called *community ties* (Stamm, 1985). Unfortunately, little or no effort has been made to bring these two related areas together.

The purpose of this chapter is to explore what these models have in common and to ask what has been learned from community integration research that is of potential relevance to developing more effective civic journalism and hence developing more active community participation.

MORE EFFECTIVE CIVIC JOURNALISM

What would make civic journalism more effective? Some civic journalism advocates posit that improving the content of media, such as newspapers will suffice to make a difference in community participation, whereas others argue that media must go further and provide the avenues for citizen involvement. Improving content may entail a change from news as a form of knowledge to news as a form of civic discourse (i.e., a medium for conversation among citizens [Anderson, Dardenne & Killenberg, 1994]). Parisi (1997), echoing Dewey (1946), called for a *public journalism* in which the newspaper becomes the community's social narrator or moderator, organizing a wider range of views than the community itself produces. Going beyond these types of content changes, Denton and Thorson (1998) proposed more innovative mechanisms, such as town-hall meetings and educational efforts that show citizens how public affairs affect them and how they can in turn impact public affairs. Thus, on one hand, media would serve as a forum for the exchange of views among citizens of a community, and on the other hand, media would construct the forum and provide tools for participating. In both cases, the hope is that the media can find new ways to make a difference in the ability of a community to operate more democratically.

The complement to this view is evident in theorizing about community integration, in which authors beginning with Park (1937) and Janowitz (1952) have posited that *exposure* to the content of newspapers is the mechanism by which the individual is integrated in the local community. More recently, this view has been most clearly stated by Bogart and Orenstein (1965) who concluded that "residents of suburbia inevitably acquire a sense of identity with the people and institutions of nearby towns because of day-after-day, month-after-month exposure to the news minutiae of a particular nearby town through reading its newspaper" (p. 180).

It should be noted that these authors were addressing the contribution of newspaper reading to a sense of identity, rather than to community participation. But a sense of identity may be an important step toward participation (e.g., an awareness of the community and a feeling of belonging might need to come first, with participation coming later in the process of community integration). If we conceive of community integration as a process in which different kinds of ties are formed sequentially, then we are led to ask which ties come first and which ties normally need to be formed before the kind of citizen participation sought by civic journalism is likely to happen. In other words, does civic journalism "put the cart before the horse" when it asks citizens to do things for the community before they have formed significant ties to the community?

Civic journalism does indeed put the cart before the horse, according to one of its leading advocates, Jay Rosen. Rosen (1992) asked, to what avail are the contributions of civic journalism if no public exists? He described the experience of the Columbus, Georgia *Ledger-Enquirer*, which presented the community with a remarkably complete and sophisticated portrait of itself only to be greeted with a brief period of chatter followed by silence and inaction. Initially, the newspaper's civic journalism effort failed to spark community participation. There was no public out there, only an audience, said Rosen, and an audience is not a public. The newspaper's efforts were rewarded only after it was realized that a public needed to be formed first. That is, they had to provide a mechanism that would serve as a starting point for citizen participation. This was in accord with the process conception of community integration, which posits that the relationship between citizen and community develops in stages.

The need to form a public was recently recognized in a public journalism project called "We the People/Wisconsin" conducted by media in and around Madison, Wisconsin. (Denton & Thorson, 1998). This project sought to involve citizens in the gubernatorial and senatorial campaigns not only through media coverage, but through holding town hall meetings, and staging debates with questions from town-hall participants. A study of the project provided evidence that this did increase interest in the elections and encouraged people to vote, but provided no direct evidence that community involvement had been affected.

CRITERIA FOR EFFECTIVENESS

If there is a shortcoming in the civic journalism model, it is the tendency is to focus on the behavior of the individual rather than the behavior of the community. For example, the current model treats "citizen participation" as individual behaviors such as voting in elections and interest in community affairs. Neither of these features take into account such community behavior as thinking and working together on a community problem. Thus, the question is not only what does the individual do as a consequence of public journalism, but what does the community do?

In this regard, it should be helpful to think about the objectives of civic journalism from the perspective of what it takes to produce community. As Parisi (1997) pointed out, civic journalists tend to objectify community. They tend to treat it as a thing already produced and thus see the problem as getting individual citizens to become more active. Community theorists, however, have sometimes viewed community more in terms of process than object. From this process perspective it seems unlikely that community can be produced in the absence of commitment and willingness to work together. Civic journalism may need to do something about commitment and willingness before community participation becomes a realistic objective. If people are not committed to the idea of working collectively, and are unwilling or unable to work together then they can have no community in which to participate (cf. Rothenbuhler, chap. 8, this volume). Perhaps civic journalism would be well advised to make an investment in creating these preconditions for community participation instead of investing all its efforts in participation. In the Columbus, Georgia example, it was necessary that the newspaper organized a series of town meetings that provided the avenue for commitment and willingness to be developed (Rosen, 1992).

RESEARCH QUESTIONS

There are two questions about community ties that are relevant to the concerns of civic journalism. The first concerns whether people are actually ready for the kind of community activism envisioned by civic journalism: Is there sufficient evidence of citizen involvement in community processes to suggest this readiness? In particular, is there commitment and a willingness to work together? To the extent there is evidence of such involvement, we might then ask, secondly, whether, and under what conditions, such involvement is related to the exposure to newspaper coverage of community affairs.

RESULTS OF RECENT RESEARCH

Recent research on the role of newspapers in their communities has touched on individuals' relationships to community as a process. These are the kinds of ties most relevant to the concerns and objectives of civic journalism. This chapter draws from a number of studies of such ties, particularly from a recent study conducted in Mobile, Alabama, and a new, unpublished study conducted in Seattle, Washington.

The Mobile study (Stamm, Emig, & Hesse, 1997) was based on a probability sample ($n = 432$) of a demographically diverse population. It included a measure of community involvement based on four kinds of involvement: (a) *attending*—following what goes on in local government and public affairs, (b) *orienting*—having ideas for improving the community, (c) *connecting*—getting people together to discuss the community's needs, and (d) *taking action*—working to bring about change in the community.[1]

The Seattle study was based on a probability sample ($n = 149$) of riders on the state ferry system.[2] Although the sample was small, this study had the advantage of incorporating more detailed and exhaustive measures of community involvement than most previously published studies. This is particularly important, because the questions dealt extensively with kinds of involvement we have suggested might be antecedent to participation. The ferry population was a key to this kind of measurement development, because the number of items included made telephone administration impractical. The study incorporated 44 questions directed at different aspects of commitment to community and willingness to work together as a community. Thirty-two of these items combined to yield a four-factor solution with eigenvalues greater than one and based on a minimum of six items (Table 12.1). Factor 1 was identified as a community commitment factor (alpha = .87, 10 items); Factor 2, willingness to work together (alpha = .84, 9 items); Factor 3, community

---

[1]This same measure is employed by McLeod et al., 1996 (see Table 12.6).

[2]Conducted by School of Communication graduate students at the University of Washington, May, 1996. Special recognition is extended to Jan Aune, Robin Bush, Zahna Caillat, Brennon Martin, and Vilma Rajaraman.

TABLE 12.1

Factor Loadings for Dimensions of Community Involvement

	Commitment	Work Together	Responsibility	Tolerance
Commitment shared				
In this community people get together socially—e.g., fairs, picnics, & games.	.83			
This is the kind of community where people turn out for public meetings.	.78			
In this community we're able to work together to maintain quality of life.	.71			
People here are willing to make sacrifices to help out others.	.67			
Even if I could get a better job somewhere else, it wouldn't be easy to give up living in this community.	.65			
If I were having trouble and needed help, there's no place I'd rather be.	.63			
I'm always proud to tell my friends in other parts of the country about my community.	.61			
This community is an easy place to make friends in.	.52			
I don't worry about my house when I'm gone because I know my neighbors watch out for me.	.49			

(continued on next page)

TABLE 12.1 (continued)

Factor Loadings for Dimensions of Community Involvement

	Commitment	Work Together	Responsibility	Tolerance
If I run out of something or need a special tool, I can borrow it from a neighbor.	.46			
Willingness to work together				
Write a letter to the editor of the local newspaper.		.77		
Write a letter to an elected official in the community.		.73		
Hold an office or a position of leadership within your community.		.71		
Show up for meeting on issues that affect the community.		.65		
Speak up publicly when something needs to be brought to community's attention.		.64		
Seeks signatures for a petition concerning the community.		.64		
Help raise money for a community project by asking others to contribute.		.59		
Keep informed on matters affecting the community.		.55		
Display a bumper sticker promoting the community.		.47		

TABLE 12.1 (continued)
Factor Loadings for Dimensions of Community Involvement

	Commitment	Work Together	Responsibility	Tolerance

Responsibilities

Vote for a bill that would cost you money but would help others.			.65	
Be more willing to reach out and help people who need it.			.63	
Donate money on a regular basis to community causes.			.59	
Do volunteer work for a community organization.			.57	
Clean up a park in the community.			.55	
Would feel badly if I didn't do my part to help out the community.			.52	

Tolerance for Diversity

A member of a minority group can get along as easily as anyone else.				.81
You can be different and people treat you like anyone else.				.77
Members of minority groups are appreciated for what they contribute.				.69

(continued on next page)

TABLE 12.1   (continued)
Factor Loadings for Dimensions of Community Involvement

	Commitment	Work Together	Responsibility	Tolerance
When major decisions are made, usually agree with the community.				.65
People think it's important to listen to those who have different views.				.59
People can usually agree on what's best for the community.				.55
Eigenvalues	9.38	3.50	2.31	1.84
% variance	25.4	9.50	6.20	5.00
alpha	.87	.84	.76	.76

responsibility (alpha = .76, 6 items); and Factor 4, tolerance of diversity (alpha = .76, 6 items).

Results of the Mobile and Seattle studies show that community involvement is highly variable, depending on the kind of involvement. In Mobile the more demanding forms of involvement occupied a relatively small minority of citizens (Table 12.2). However, the more detailed Seattle study suggests that commitment to community was fairly widespread (Table 12.3), as was willingness to work with others, and community responsibility (Table 12.4). Tolerance of diversity also appeared fairly widespread although, interestingly, tolerance of different kinds of people was more common than tolerance of different ideas (Table 12.5). These general trends hold up remarkably well over a variety of items tapping each kind of involvement.

The Seattle findings would seem to bode well for the idea that the community compact is indeed alive and well, at least in the communities from which this sample was drawn. This, in turn, suggests that substantial numbers of citizens are ready and willing to do things for their communities. However, the Mobile findings lead to questions about how readily these expressions of commitment and

TABLE 12.2
Percent of Involved Mobile Residents by Levels of Involvement (*n* = 417).

	Low			High
Involvement Level	1	2	3	4
Following local government	7.6	10.7	31.1	50.6
Ideas for improving	8.2	35.5	30.0	26.4
Getting people together	35.9	35.4	19.0	9.7
Working for change	25.8	40.3	20.5	13.3

willingness can be converted into forms of involvement that are closer to participation (e.g., the number agreeing goes down with the shift from expressions of willingness to reports of behavior).

Given the evidence that substantial numbers of people appear to be involved in communities in a variety of ways, the second question regarding newspaper's relationship to community involvement is relevant. Any observed relationship between newspaper use and community involvement is subject to a variety of interpretations (e.g., that newspaper use makes a difference in community involvement, or that community involvement makes a difference in use of newspapers). The first of these two is preferred from the perspective of civic journalism, but neither can be ruled out.

Table 12.6 reports correlations between newspaper reading and a variety of community involvement measures, from several pertinent studies. These particular studies were chosen because they employed measures of community involvement as such, rather than indices that combine measures of involvement and its correlates, such as length of residence, home ownership, and various group memberships (a strategy some researchers use to increase reliability at the risk of confounding validity). All of these measures, with one exception, were positively related to some measure of community newspaper readership. Clearly there is a relationship here, which in these studies is taken as evidence that newspapers make a difference in community involvement. We should also notice that most of the correlations, although statistically significant, are modest in strength. Among the more modest correlations are those in which the measure pertains to some form of participation, for example, working for change $r = .22$), attending a community forum $r = .20$), participation in local organizations $r = .13$). The low correlations cannot be considered as due to low reliability of the involvement measures. Even the

TABLE 12.3
Percent Committed to Community (n = 149)

Commitment Item:	Disagree	Neutral	Agree
Get together socially	11.7	22.1	66.2
Turn out for meetings	21.8	25.4	52.8
Work together for community	16.7	27.8	55.6
Make sacrifices for community	15.2	35.9	49.0
Would miss community	11.7	22.1	66.2
Help for trouble	22.8	32.4	44.8
Proud of community	10.3	17.9	71.7
Easy to make friends	13.1	24.1	62.8
Neighbors watch out	16.0	16.0	68.1
Borrow from neighbors	14.5	13.8	71.7

highly reliable indexes constructed in the Stamm, et al. (1997) and Rothenbuhler et al. (1996) studies yielded no correlations greater than $r = .26$.

Considering that these findings are consistent across a number of studies and a number of different measures, the evidence indicates that newspapers may make some contribution to community involvement, but the size of the contribution is not large. This leaves plenty of room for contingencies (e.g., newspapers may make more of a difference during periods when the individual's community relationship is being actively constructed. One important class of contingencies identified by previous research involves the processes of engagement and disengagement as people move in and out of communities (Stamm & Guest, 1991). Some people are not ready to participate in a community at all—the commitment, willingness, and feeling of responsibility are not yet there. Others may be in transition, previously committed and willing, perhaps active as well, but now in the process of disengaging from the community and moving on to a different one.

TABLE 12.4
Percent Willingness to Engage in Community Activities ($n = 149$)

	Disagree	Neutral	Agree
Items From Work Together Factor			
Write to local newspaper	13.5	17.0	69.5
Write to officials	8.6	16.4	75.0
Hold a community office	33.6	28.0	38.5
Show up for meetings	14.6	23.6	61.8
Speak up for community	14.3	20.7	65.0
Circulate community petitions	25.7	21.4	52.9
Raise money for community	23.9	26.1	50.0
Keep informed about community	6.4	14.2	79.4
Display community sticker	47.5	17.0	35.5
Items From Responsibilities Factor			
Vote to raise taxes	10.6	19.9	69.5
More willing to reach out	10.6	19.7	69.7
Donate money to community	13.4	27.5	59.2
Volunteer for community organization	8.3	25.0	66.7
Clean up community park	8.4	16.1	75.5
Would feel badly	13.1	21.4	65.5

The point is that communities, just like newspapers, have a turnover problem. Any given community has both stable members and those who are moving in or out. To achieve a community of active participants, the turnover problem needs to be dealt with. People have to be brought into a community before they can become active participants. An opportunity to participate might be the basis for bringing some people in, but the kind of opportunity offered needs to take into account that these people are not yet committed to the community, and are probably not sure whether they want to do anything collectively.

TABLE 12.5
Percent Tolerant of Community Diversity (n = 149)

Diversity item	Disagree	Neutral	Agree
Get along with minorities	30.6	14.6	54.9
Free to be different	28.3	15.2	56.6
Appreciate minority contribution	23.6	24.3	52.1
Usually agree with community	28.0	35.7	36.4
Listen to different views	16.7	35.4	47.9
Agree on best for community	27.3	34.3	38.5

Newcomers, people just arriving in a local community from somewhere else, are an important but seldom-studied group. They are an important group because they represent a critical juncture in the process of community involvement, the point at which these people need to be brought into the community. What happens in the first few months may well leave a significant imprint on the kind of community relationship that will evolve. Many newcomers experience severe dislocation (Stamm, Jackson & Bowen, 1977). Things are very different in the new community, and people have great difficulty making the connections they need to make (e.g., finding the right neighborhood, getting children in the right schools, locating needed services, even finding a job). Settling in a community takes a lot of communicating, yet in most communities, newspapers do not treat newcomers any differently than those who are already established in the community. There is no special edition of the paper tailored to newcomers, no special effort to bring them into the community. Still, research shows that certain kinds of newspaper use—home-related, neighborhood-related, and community-related—increase with the severity of dislocation (Stamm, Jackson & Bowen, 1977).

The individual's movement in and out of local communities has also been represented in a stage model based on length of residence in the community, both past and future (Stamm & Weis, 1986). Length of residence, past or future, may be

TABLE 12.6

Correlations of Newspaper use With Measures of Community Involvement

Source	Involvement Measure	r	p <	n =
Brown & Daves (1979)	Political involvement	.20	.01	299
Cobbey (1980)	Participation in local organizations	.13	.01	400
Stamm & Weis (1986)	Participation in community groups	.26	.01	500
McLeod et al. (1996)	Local political interest	.49	.01	394
	Institutional activities	.36	.01	
	Attending community forum	.20	.01	
	Community involvement	.39	.01	
Rothenbuhler et al. (1996)	Community attachment	.17	.001	386
	Community involvement	.20	.001	
Stamm, Emig, & Hesse (1997)	Attending to community	.49	.01	432
	Ideas for improving	.20	.01	
	Working for change	.22	.01	
	Getting people together	.22	.01	
	Total index score	.41	.01	
Stamm & CMU 513 (1996)	Community commitment	.26	.01	149
	Willingness/Factor 1	.24	.01	
	Willingness/Factor 2	.25	.01	
	Tolerance for diversity	.06	ns	

short—less than 5 years, or *long*—5 years or longer. Based on length of past and future residence, four stages have been distinguished: *drifting*—short past and short future; *settling*—short past and long future; *settled*—long past and long future; *relocating*—long past and short future. Research employing this model shows that individuals begin to get more involved in a community during the settling stage (Table 12.7). At this stage, the proportion identifying with the community is higher than the drifting stage, and there is also an increase in involvement as measured in a variety of ways. The research also shows that identification and involvement tend to decline in the relocating stage (e.g., for those individuals who are on their way out of the community). If newspapers were to become more concerned about the process of involving people in communities, then it would appear they should focus on people in the drifting and settling stages. The questions still have to be asked: What is it that makes a difference in these people's commitment, and in their willingness to get involved? If newspapers carry more news about local politics and government, will that help initiate involvement in communities?

Examining the relationship between newspaper use and community ties within the settling and drifting stages provides evidence that newspapers may be making a difference within these two critical stages. The Mobile study found that newspaper use was more strongly related to "working for change" within the drifting and settling stages than the settled and relocating stages (Table 12.8). Curiously, newspaper use was most strongly correlated with "ideas for improving" in the relocating stage, perhaps because this is the stage when people focus on what is wrong with their present community. If that is so, then we must wonder whether the focus on what's wrong comes before the decision to leave or afterward. The difference here is important because in the first case we would question whether the newspaper's focus on community problems provides an impetus to leave the community; in the second, the newspaper would only be helping to supply the rationalization for a decision already made.

The most recent Seattle study also found fairly strong relationships, within the drifting stage, between community newspaper use and both willingness to work together and tolerance of diversity (Table 12.9). These correlations were stronger than those found in either the settling and settled stages, suggesting that newspapers may play some role in the transition from drifting to settling. Interestingly, the strongest correlation between newspaper use and commitment to community was found in the settling stage, whereas the evidence of a newspaper contribution to "willingness" and "tolerance," present in the drifting stage, had all but vanished. This provides further evidence of the importance of the residence stage as a contingency in the contribution of newspaper reading to community involvement.

SOME IMPLICATIONS FOR CIVIC JOURNALISM

From the perspective of a community integration model, should civic journalism, in its concern with community participation, be more broadly concerned with a process of forming community ties? Research suggests that other kinds of community ties may be important antecedents to participation (i.e., commitment, willing-

TABLE 12.7

Readiness for Community Participation by Stage of Residence

Readiness to Participate	Stage of Residence					
	Drifting	Settling	Settled	Relocating	X2/F	p <
Identify with community[a] (%, N = 470)	54%	64%	76%	64%	9.04	.03
Community involvement[b] (mean, N = 432)	9.79	10.87	11.60	10.89	5.86	.01
Commitment[c] (mean, N = 149)	4.37	5.17	5.15	4.51	6.34	.01
Willingness[c] (mean, N = 149)	4.51	5.15	4.67	4.59	2.69	.05
Responsibility[c] (Mean, N = 149)	4.89	5.47	5.26	5.06	2.57	.06
Tolerance[c] (mean, N = 149)	4.20	4.53	4.16	4.30	1.04	ns

[a]Stamm & Fortini-Campbell (1983).

[b]Stamm, Emig, & Hesse (1997).

[c]Washington ferry study (1996).

ness, and involvement). As Rosen (1992) and Denton (1993) recognized, civic journalists need to be concerned with bringing people into communities, not only with getting them to participate once they are in. The situation is analogous to teaching a child to swim—you have to get them in the water first. The evidence we have from community ties research suggests that many people are ready to participate, to the extent that they share commitment, willingness to work with others, and community responsibility. There is also evidence that newspapers are making at least some contribution to producing this readiness, with or without the additional communication efforts entailed in civic journalism. It is also clear that many people are not ready to participate, so we must question whether efforts to encourage participation from these people are premature.

Because the community integration model presents some additional objectives for civic journalism, it should also raise questions about how to conduct civic journalism. How can we more effectively bring people into communities? Is sponsoring a community conversation about local problems and issues the best way to do it? We might at least ask, "what else brings people into communities?" The community ties research suggests that addressing the communication needs of new-

TABLE 12.8.
Correlations of Newspaper use With Community Involvement
by Residence Stage (n = 417).

Involvement As	Drifting	Settling	Settled	Relocating
Attending to community	.46**	.55**	.46**	.50**
Ideas for improving	.25	.13	.16**	.38**
Getting people together	.27	.29*	.17**	.30
Working for change	.48**	.44**	.09	.30
N =	39	61	275	41

Note. Italicized coefficients differ from nonitalicized coefficients in that row by more than one standard error. Standard error of the correlation coefficient equals 1/sqrt of n.

*$p < .05$. **$p < .01$

comers to a community (those in the drifting and settling stages) would be one place to start. What could newspapers do that would support their first steps toward community integration? Town meetings and public forums may not be the best approach for all, especially those who are in the early stages of community integration and have yet to achieve the community commitment and responsibility that participation in such meetings may require. Future research on the efficacy of such public journalism efforts would be wise to investigate the relationship between participation in these community activities and the measures of community involvement described in community integration research. Addressing the largely unmet need for effective community involvement presents a substantial opportunity for development. We ought to consider civic journalism as a working hypothesis—the best basis that we have at the moment for building more effective communication processes on behalf of more effective communities. Civic journalism, in that sense, represents what we need to know about the relationship between communication and community, not only what we already know. Learning more about this relationship is as essential to the future of communities as it is to the continued survival of newspapers.

The essential question about this relationship was stated over 50 years ago (Dewey, 1946), yet remains essentially unanswered: Can the city become more than a vast prison of unconnected cells in which people of different occupations, color, class, and creed fail to understand one another on the basic issues of human life? By helping to build stronger and more inviting community processes, civic journalism can help shape future communities in which people more effectively share their perceptions of problems and a collective vision of what their communities could become.

TABLE 12.9

Correlations of Community Newspaper Attention With Community
Involvement Factors by Residence Stage

Involvement As	Residence Stage			
	Drifting	Settling	Settled	Relocating
Commitment	.22	.41**	.19	-.03
Willingness/Factor 1	.50**	-.03	.28	.40**
Willingness/Factor 2	.37*	.03	.46**	.34*
Tolerance of diversity	.33*	.10	-.05	.24
N =	32	40	41	29

Note. Italicized coefficients differ from nonitalicized coefficients in that row by more than one standard error. Standard error of the correlation coefficient equals 1/sqrt of *n*.
*$p < .05$. **$p < .01$

ACKNOWLEDGMENTS

Conducted by School of Communication graduate students at the University of Washington, May 1996. Special recognition to Jan Aune, Robin Bush, Zahna Caillat, Brennon Martin, and Vimla Rajaraman.

REFERENCES

Anderson, R., Dardenne, R., & George Killenberg, G. The conversation of journalism. Westport, CN: Praeger.

Bogart, L., & Orenstein, F. (1965). Mass media and community identity in an interurban setting. *Journalism Quarterly, 42,* 179–188.

Denton, F., (1993). Old newspapers and new realities: The promise of the marketing of journalism. In F. Denton & H. Kurtz (Eds.), *Reinventing the newspaper* (pp. 3–58). Twentieth Century Fund Press.

Denton, F., & Thorson, E. (1998). Effects of a multimedia public journalism project on political knowledge and attitudes. In E. Lambeth, P. Meyer, & E. Thorson (Eds.), *Assessing public journalism* (pp. 158–178). Columbia: University of Missouri Press.

Dewey, J. (1946). *The public and its problems.* Chicago: Gateway.

Janowitz, M. (1952). *The community press in an urban setting.* Glencoe, IL: Free Press.

Parisi, P. (1997) Toward a philosophy of framing: news narratives for public journalism. *Journalism & Mass Communication Quarterly, 74,* 673–686.

Park, R. E. (1923). The natural history of the newspaper. *American Journal of Sociology,* *29,* 273–289.

Rosen, J. (1992, Winter). Forming and informing the public. *Kettering Review,* 60–70.

Rothenbuhler, E. W., Mullen, L. J., DeLaurell, R., & Ryu, C. R. (1996). Communication, Community attachment, and involvement. *Journalism & Mass Communication Quarterly, 73,* 445–466.

Stamm, K. R. (1985). *Newspaper use and community ties.* Norwood, NJ: Ablex.

Stamm, K., Emig, A., & Hesse, M. (1997). The contribution of local media to community involvement. *Journalism & Mass Communication Quarterly, 74,* 97–107.

Stamm, K., & Guest, A. (1991). Communication and community integration: An analysis of the communication behavior of newcomers. *Journalism & Mass Communication Quarterly, 68,* 644–656.

Stamm, K., Jackson, K., & Bowen, L. (1977). *Antecedents to newspaper subscribing and using.* ANPA Research Reports, No. 6.

Stamm, K., & Weis, R. (1986). Testing the community integration hypothesis. *Communication Research, 13,* 125–138.

13

The Limits of Community in Public Journalism

Christopher R. Martin
University of Northern Iowa

The choices they give us are these: Forfeit your integrity and betray your coworkers by crossing the picket line, or forfeit your job. So much for different voices. And so much for the stated commitment for making bad things better.

—Laurie Bennett, a striking Detroit Free Press reporter, on receiving notification from the newspaper that her job will be given to a nonunion replacement worker unless she returns from the strike. —Bennett (1995)

Public journalism is about making bad things better. The bad things in this case are public life and journalism itself. Over the last century, the practice of U.S. journalism has adopted an objective style of reportage that, "is, above all, a journalism that justifies itself in the public's name but in which the public plays no role, except as an audience—a receptacle to be informed by experts and an excuse for the practice of publicity" (Carey, 1995, pp. 391–392). Thus, journalism has failed to provide a public forum, acting more as a site for institutional monologue than of community dialogue.

The problem is not lack of information, but a crisis in meaning. Social critic Neil Postman (1995) argued that communication media have created a useless glut of information: "Information comes indiscriminately, directed at no one in particular, in enormous volume at high speeds, severed from meaning. And there is no loom to weave it all into fabric. No transcendent narratives to provide us with more guidance, social purpose, intellectual economy" (p. 35).

That much of the public seems disengaged from journalism is tacitly admitted by newspapers. In 1997, the National Newspaper Association began its first ever advertising campaign on behalf of more than 1,600 newspapers in North America. The Association's president (1997) said that the $5.7 million television ad campaign's strategy, "is to create advertising that adds excitement and momentum to newspapers," and to, "showcase newspapers as a vital, vigorous and valued medium" (p. C6). The initial wave of celebrities to promote newspaper reading in the 3-year campaign included former Presidents George Bush and Jimmy Carter, Barbara Bush, Norman Schwarzkopf, John Elway, and L. L. Cool J.

From a public journalism perspective, the ad campaign is a sign of journalism's problem—addressing community members as consumers (or potential consumers) and not citizens (Austin, 1997). What ails journalism the most is its disconnection from citizens and public life. What public journalism seeks to do, according to one of its leading advocates, Jay Rosen (1997), is

> to make journalism whole again by stressing those things that have been left out, neglected, or not allowed to shine in the busy environment of the American newsroom: things like civic participation, deliberative dialogue, cooperative problem solving, taking responsibility for the place where you live, making democracy work. (p. 7)

In other words, public journalism attempts to construct a more cohesive, civic-based master narrative out of stories that have been traditionally treated as unrelated, "objective" bits in a never-ending news stream.

Public journalism (also often referred to as civic journalism or community journalism) emerged in the late 1980s as a response to journalism's "Old News" irrelevancy and the challenges of the "New News" outlets such as music, movies, and the Internet (see Katz, 1992). In a number of local experiments with public journalism across the country, newspapers "moved beyond cool neutrality and detachment, acted as if they belonged where they were and cared about that place, began treating people as citizens rather than consumers, risked the approbation—if not condemnation—of many of their peers, and helped make things better" (Merritt, 1995, p. xvi).

One of the earliest efforts was led by *Wichita Eagle* editor, Davis "Buzz" Merritt, who has become the nation's most noted practitioner of public journalism. Disgusted by the vacuous image- and soundbite-based 1988 presidential campaign and its news coverage, Merritt decided to test a new issues-based approach to election coverage. For the 1990 Kansas gubernatorial campaign, the *Eagle* developed the "Your Vote Counts" project in order to shift the focus of the coverage from candidate driven to issues driven. The issues tracked during the 8-week project, which was given a high profile in the *Eagle* and on a local television station, were recognized through voter surveys. Merritt reported that due to the project, voter turnout was up and issue cognizance was "strikingly higher in the *Eagle* readership area, compared to the rest of the state" (p. 82).

After the encouraging results of the Wichita project and another early project in Columbus, Georgia in which the newspaper sponsored public meetings (Rosen,

1994), public journalism efforts have since been conducted in dozens of American cities and regions, including Portland, Maine; Cape Cod, Massachusetts; St. Paul, Minnesota; Charlotte, North Carolina; Akron, Ohio; Spokane, Washington; Madison, Wisconsin; a consortium of six newspapers and National Public Radio (NPR) affiliates in Florida, and a national project by NPR. The majority of public journalism projects have covered issues such as children and families, community planning, crime, economic development, education, elections and government, environment, and race relations. One of the biggest forces in public journalism is the Pew Charitable Trusts, a Philadelphia-based foundation that established the Pew Center for Civic Journalism in 1993 with a $3.6 million grant, and refunded it with an additional $4.3 million in 1996 for 3 more years. The center funnels grants to newspapers and other journalism outlets to pay for things like consultants, polls, and town meetings to facilitate discussions covered for public journalism projects (Knecht, 1996).[1]

A number of public journalism projects have been undertaken at newspapers owned by Knight-Ridder, America's second-largest newspaper chain. Knight-Ridder was an early proponent of public journalism: the *Wichita Eagle* and the Columbus (GA) *Ledger-Enquirer* are both properties of the chain, and the Pew Center for Civic Journalism's $25,000 James K. Batten Award for Excellence in Civic Journalism was named after the chairman of Knight-Ridder, who died in 1995. The chain received more than $1 million from the Pew Center to fund 14 civic journalism efforts between 1993 and 1996 and vowed to continue to internally fund civic journalism initiatives afterward ("The James K. Batten Award," 1995, p. 3; "Knight-Ridder to Fund," 1997, p. 11)

A much-lauded public journalism project at a Knight-Ridder newspaper was the "Children First" campaign at the *Detroit Free Press*. The *Free Press*, managed through a Joint Operating Agreement with Gannett Co.'s *Detroit News* since 1989, is Knight-Ridder's fourth largest newspaper property, after the combined *Philadelphia Inquirer* and *Philadelphia Daily News*, the *Miami Herald*, and the *San Jose Mercury News*.

The *Free Press*' public journalism initiative began in 1993 as a proactive follow-up to the newspaper's 1992 series on violence against children in the metro area. The Children First campaign included a 24-page pullout section that publicized summer recreation needs for disadvantaged youths. This "Summer Dreams" effort raised $500,000 and benefitted more than 5,000 children. According to *Free Press* managing editor Robert McGruder (personal communication, May 20, 1998), by the spring of 1998, nearly $3 million had been raised, with the help of matching grants from a foundation. The newspaper also sponsored a forum on violence against children, which drew an audience of 1,100 parents, educators, and juvenile justice officials. The *Free Press* buttressed the Children First project with a special team of four reporters assisted by a youth panel and advisory committee and devoted a weekly Sunday Children First col-

---

[1]Other foundations working to support public journalism include the Kettering Foundation, the Poynter Institute for Media Studies, and the John S. and James L. Knight Foundation, which helped to establish the Project on Public Life and the Press at New York University.

umn to youth issues. The newspaper also permitted newsroom staffers to use up to 2 hours of their work week to volunteer in public schools (see Charity, 1995; "Civic Journalism," 1995, p. 4; Rosen, 1999).

One of the *Free Press'* most successful follow ups, according to the Project on Public Life and the Press, was:

> a column about a child who suffered third-degree burns in a bathtub [that] was packaged with an offer of water-temperature gauges, a coloring book for pre-schoolers on burn prevention and a tip sheet on accident prevention developed by an area university and a local hospital. More than 1,000 of these kits were mailed to readers. (Austin, n.d.)

Dale Parry (1995), features editor for the *Free Press*, said that his newspaper regularly tried to provide many of its stories with proactive follow-up information in sidebar boxes. Parry argued that readers hate "no exit" stories that report a problem but do not supply any information to address it (personal communication, June 27, 1995).

The Bias of Public Journalism

The Children First project of the *Free Press* is certainly a noble cause. Some critics, however, have charged that public journalism imposes an inappropriate advocacy role on journalists, surrenders news coverage to public opinion, and operates mainly as a marketing gimmick (see Campbell, 1998, 408–410). Public journalism supporters often acknowledge such criticisms (which usually defend journalism's traditional style and philosophy of objectivity) and offer thoughtful responses that generally defuse these points (see, e.g., Merritt, 1996; Shepard, 1994). However, other recent critiques are more substantial, and identify significant limits in the philosophy and practice of public journalism.

First, Parisi (1997) argued that the monikers civic and public journalism should represent different things. The current movement is a civic journalism that tries to engage citizens in civic life by asking them to help define local news agendas. Unfortunately, the scope of civic journalism is limited to local resources and solutions, leaving "established structures of political power and economic interests as unexamined as do mainstream narratives of strategy and conflict" (p. 682), thus providing little change from current journalism practice. Parisi explained that "civic journalism, with its optimistic sense that all problems will yield if local folks just roll up their sleeves, is in this sense an extended exercise in normalization" (p. 680) because it refuses to discuss issues that exceed local boundaries, lines of authority, and dominant thought. Thus, broad socioeconomic problems like global environmental degradation just don't fit into civic journalism's narrow pattern of framing.

A better journalism—Parisi (1997) called it a "public" journalism—would build on the present dialogue opened by civic journalism enthusiasts, but place the journalists as a central "social narrator/moderator" responsible for airing issues that stretch beyond local systems. Public journalism accounts would include local voices to legitimize and ground discussion, but would also include the broad range of sources necessary to provide full social and economic context for the issue. Moreover, a public journalism would not be afraid to break free of traditional journalistic conventions and dominant ideology in order to provide a fuller exploration and explanation of issues, in the hope of serving the public good.

Parisi (1997) concluded his challenge of the existing public journalism by asking whether "the institution of journalism genuinely seeks reform" (p. 682). Hardt (1997), in his review of several publications on public journalism, said no. He argued that this movement in journalism does little to change the basic relationships that inform journalism work:

> There are limitations to the new definition [of journalism], which does not encourage the pursuit of public interest journalism under new forms of ownership and public participation, or a new understanding of professionalism that frees journalists from editorial controls and acknowledges their professional independence. Instead, it remains ideologically committed to journalism as a business that relies on the satisfaction of its particular consumer-community, redirects journalistic practices accordingly, and offers a recipe for temporary relief from the symptoms of a deeper social and economic crisis. (p. 104)

Thus, although some practices of journalism change in a public journalism-oriented newsroom, the underlying relationship of journalism to the community does not change.

Indeed, an article by Ed Fouhy (1997), then Executive Director of the Pew Center for Civic Journalism, illustrated the shortcomings of public journalism as a solution to the journalism problem. Fouhy reminisced about the Boston of his youth, which had seven daily newspapers, and his cousin Bob, the city editor of one of them. Bob lived in the Boston neighborhood where he was raised, married a local girl, served in the Army, had kids who were sent to neighborhood schools, attended a local church, and conversed regularly with neighbors from his front porch. Thirty years later, Fouhy lamented, Boston has only two dailies and newsrooms are filled with elite college graduates who are distanced from the rest of the community by their large salaries, suburban refuges, private schools, and rejection of churchgoing. Moreover, big media companies move editors around so much that few newsroom leaders have roots in their communities.

Fouhy (1997) concluded his essay, "Somewhere along the line, the sense that a newspaper represents the interests of the citizens of a community has been lost. Perhaps one reason why civic journalism has taken hold in so many newsrooms is the conviction that it's time to get that connection back" (p. 2). Fouhy's reasoning has the veneer of common sense, but the problems he outlined—the suburbanization of a city, the professionalization of journalism, the decline of church attendance, and the rise of media conglomerates—are enormous social, cultural, and economic phenomena that are not likely going to be reversed through local public journalism efforts alone.

Like Fouhy, Rosen (1994), and Merritt (1995) also cited the increasing corporatization of journalism outlets gobbled up by media chains as a rationale for embracing public journalism. But again, although public journalism does call for a change in the practice of journalism at the level of reporters and editors, it does not call for a change in the practices of the corporate institutions that own and operate the journalism organizations, or those institutions' relationship to the community. So, public journalism ultimately tends to address issues that do not upset local systems of power, or challenge the news audience. As Robert McGruder (1998), managing editor of the *Free Press,* noted about his paper's Children First project, "I believe in an agenda, in the bias to improve children, but that's the community agenda, too. We're not trying to sell something to the community that the community doesn't already feel" (personal communication, May 20, 1998).

It therefore is not surprising that as the *Free Press* worked to maintain the Children First project through the mid-1990s, they avoided creating a broad public dialogue on one of the biggest stories to hit Detroit in years: a 19-month strike at the *Detroit News* and *Free Press.* The Detroit newspaper strike began July 13, 1995 and lasted until February 1997. Six unions led nearly 2,500 workers—reporters, editors, drivers, mailers, engravers, and press operators—to walk out on the *Free Press* and *News* after the unions charged that management refused to bargain fairly in contract renewal talks. The newspapers hired replacement workers to fill most of the positions, allowing the publication of the *News* and *Free Press* to continue throughout the strike.

During the strike, the focus on the Children First project lessened, with only one principal reporter assigned to the initiative by the time the strike ended (R. McGruder, personal communication, May 20, 1998). The big story was the newspaper strike, a strike that the National Labor Relations Board declared had "high national and international visibility" (Fitzgerald, 1997), which AFL-CIO President John Sweeney (1996) called "the most important strike we have in our country today" (as cited in Frank, 1996, p. 19), and which a labor specialist at Detroit's Wayne State University asserted was "the single most important strike confrontation in Detroit in the last quarter century" (Trimer-Hartley, 1995, p. 6). Although the strike had a clear connection to the public lives of metro Detroit residents, it was shut out of the *Free Press'* civic activism. According to the *Free Press'* McGruder, "we thought the strike needed to be settled at the negotiating table, and not in public forums" (personal communication, May 20, 1998). However, if public journalism is about journalism and its disconnection from public life, then the Detroit Newspaper strike points to the underlying causes of what ails journalism, and why public journalism, as practiced, will have limited impact on communities.

Public Journalism, Private Business Operations

By 1997, there were 120 newspaper chains owning 1165 daily newspapers, about 77% of the nation's dailies. The newspaper chains controlled about 81% of the nation's weekday circulation and 87% of the Sunday newspaper circulation (Morton,

1997). The same trend of increasing consolidation has been occurring in local radio and television news outlets as well.

Whereas public journalism seeks to strengthen the connection between local news media outlets and their communities, the corporate owners of the news companies often manage from afar, disconnected from the community and its culture. Moreover, journalism is just part of the product mix for many of these corporations, which also count billboards, business information services, and security systems among their product lines.

The *Detroit Free Press* is one of the many U.S. newspapers owned by a distant corporate firm. Knight-Ridder Inc., headquartered in Miami, Florida, is the parent corporation of the *Free Press* and owner of more than 30 newspapers, such as the *Philadelphia Enquirer,* the *Philadelphia Daily News,* the *Miami Herald,* and the *San Jose Mercury News.*[2] Since 1989, the *Free Press* has worked under a Joint Operating Agreement (JOA) with the *Detroit News,* whose parent corporation is Gannett Co. Inc., of Arlington, Virginia, owner of *USA Today* and more than 90 other daily newspapers. Gannett and Knight-Ridder are the two largest newspaper chains in America (Newspaper Association of America, 1997).

According to the JOA, the *Free Press* and *News* share all business, production, and distribution operations under the Detroit News Agency, a corporation owned in equal shares by Knight-Ridder and Gannett (although Gannett has a 3–2 voting advantage over Knight-Ridder). The two newspapers operate independent editorial offices, publishing separate daily editions Monday through Friday, and combined their editorial content into one newspaper for Saturday and Sunday editions, which run under the *Detroit News and Free Press* masthead.

Although most newspapers and other news outlets try to maintain an impermeable firewall between editorial operations and business operations, it is clear that in cases of serving the public interest and improving public discourse, there are often competing goals. For example, the "Guiding Principles" articulated by Knight-Ridder management (Ridder & Fontaine, 1996) in the company's 1995 Annual Report expressed an emphasis on stock value, a request for greater employee productivity, and a commitment to journalistic content that is high quality, but consumer-oriented:

1. We will increase the value of this company for the shareholders. We will do so by being more market-driven and customer-focused.
2. We will meet our challenge by relying on the talents of Knight Ridder's people, whom we need to perform at a higher standard than before.
3. We will build on the strength of our valuable content because, at our core, we are a content company with an unwavering commitment to high-quality journalism. We will deliver that content however, wherever and whenever customers want it.

---

[2] By early 1998, Knight-Ridder, Inc. dropped the hyphen and "Inc." portions of its corporate name for a new branding and logo campaign, making the corporation henceforth known as

Guiding Principle 3 might come closest to articulating a commitment to public journalism but sounds more like a pledge to follow market research.

Of course, it is no secret that news operations want to make money, and, in fact, profit is necessary to their survival. But, what is a reasonable amount of profit, and how is that reconciled with public journalism? Meyer (1995), a journalism professor and former 23-year Knight-Ridder employee, argued that newspapers need to adjust to profit margins lower than the 20% to 40% that have been possible in the monopoly markets that dominate the daily newspaper business (Editor & Publisher, 1997). Meyer explained that, "a business whose product has high turnover and consequently huge revenues can do nicely with a low profit margin" whereas "a low turnover product needs a high margin" (p. 40). Supermarkets are an example of a high-turnover business and do quite well with 1% to 2% profit margins, most retail businesses average 6% to 7% in profit margins, whereas low-turnover businesses such as yacht and luxury sedan sellers need much higher profit margins. Daily newspapers, Meyer said, are "more like supermarkets than yacht dealers," (p. 40) and need to learn to live with lower profits.

Merritt (1995) noted that when newspapers are acquired by publicly traded corporations, maintaining high profit margins is paramount, and profits are often held steady or increased by cutting costs, which can affect news quality. Doing good journalism does cost more money. According to McManus (1994), passive news gathering (e.g., working from press releases, video news releases, wire services) is less expensive, but does not serve the public interest as well. Conversely, more active discovery (e.g., attending meetings, sifting through data, investigating tips), which better serves public interests, is more expensive. In his study of medium, large, and very large local television stations, he found pretax profits ranging from 15.8% to 39%—similar to the newspaper industry—and argued that these stations could devote more of their resources to active news gathering and still make reasonable profits.

"As more and more newspapers have been acquired by public companies," Merritt (1995) said, "operating those companies has become a delicate balancing act between civic responsibility and hard fiscal realities" (p. 41). But, in the case of the *Free Press* and the Detroit newspaper strike, the act entails little delicacy, for the balance is clearly weighted on the business end of the enterprise.

It was not always this way for the *Detroit Free Press*. In the local culture, the *Free Press* had the reputation as the higher quality newspaper in town, a "writer's paper" with a pro-union tradition that distinguished it from the conservative, pro-business *News*. Striking urban affairs reporter Bill McGraw (1995) wrote, "the *Free Press* once was one of the most liberal big-city dailies in America." But just a few weeks into the strike, the *Free Press* had already forfeited its carefully cultivated public profile. The most obvious harbinger that the newspapers' corporate officers were prevailing was their hiring of replacement workers to coerce striking workers to return. As recently as a year earlier, *Free Press* editorials had called for legislation banning permanent replacement workers (see Bennett, 1995; McGraw, 1995).

Knight-Ridder's corporate partner in the strike standoff was Gannett, the largest newspaper chain in America. Gannett, especially under the leadership of former CEO and chairman, Al Neuharth, earned a reputation for acquiring monopoly-market newspapers across the country, and then extracting wildly high profit margins from them. Although Gannett publicly pursued an image as a great protector of free speech to woo independent papers, after purchases it regularly cut back staff and local news content and quality, hiked advertising rates, and often lost some local circulation, all the while reaping greater profits for the corporation (Bagdikian, 1992; McCord, 1996).

Gannett bought the *Detroit News* in 1986, and teamed up with Knight-Ridder to apply for a Joint Operating Agreement, claiming that years of fierce competition threatened to put the then-smaller *Detroit Free Press* out of business, leaving the *News* as the sole major newspaper to serve the sixth largest newspaper market. On the grounds of saving a failing city newspaper and preventing cities from becoming one-newspaper towns, federal JOA legislation essentially grants a two-paper monopoly. Under such an agreement, the newspapers' editorial offices remain independent, but advertising, production, and distribution departments are combined to save the two papers by taking them out of competition with each other. The proposed JOA was fought by many in Detroit, and even the antitrust division of the U.S. Attorney General's office and a federal administrative law judge concluded that the losses claimed by the two papers in their case to win a JOA constituted a deliberate strategy to gain a JOA and increase profits by eliminating the competitive environment. The judge ruled against the JOA, but then embattled Attorney General Edwin Meese granted a 100-year JOA to Knight-Ridder and Gannett—one day before he left office (Frank, 1996; McCord, 1996). Neuharth later admitted in court that before Gannett purchased the *News*, he had conspired with the owners of the *Free Press* to apply for a JOA (McCord, 1996).

With the JOA approved in 1989, Knight-Ridder and Gannett, comanaging their newspapers through the Detroit News Agency, raised newsstand prices and advertising rates, intending to cash in on the now-noncompetitive Detroit market. But, with rising newsprint costs, a recessionary economy, and awful mismanagement (Gonyea & Hoyt, 1997), this "sure thing" Detroit newspaper monopoly failed to bear profits for 4 years. McCord (1996) charted the first evidence of how the newspapers' profit-minded strategy seriously misread the community:

> Grown cynical during the highly suspect and highly publicized JOA drive, readers and advertisers alike declined to swallow the sharp hike imposed on them. Circulation at both papers plummeted, with the fall at the Gannett-owned *News* by far the most precipitous. From a pre-JOA average daily circulation of 690,422, the *News* dropped to just 359,057 by mid-1994. Over the same period Knight-Ridder's *Free Press* fell from 626,434 to 551,650 (p. 272).

Even with declining circulation in Detroit, the parent corporations had done well. In 1994, Gannett's newspaper group had a 23.1% profit margin, the highest of any other major chain, whereas Knight-Ridder's newspapers earned a healthy 16.4% margin (Meyer, 1995). In that same year, things turned around for the Detroit News Agency (DNA), with $56 million in profits. But the margin was not high enough for Gannett and Knight-Ridder, who, based on their other operations, had envisioned profits in the 20% range from the Detroit franchise. In 1995, union contracts were up for renegotiation, and in a time of improving profitability, the DNA pushed for further cuts.

An Objective Business

One of the public journalism movement's greatest criticisms of mainstream journalism is the news style of objectivity, in which newswriters distance themselves from their subject and act as if they do not exist within the moment, but are merely observing, recording, and reporting the scene. Merritt and Rosen argue for journalists to drop the feigned invisibility and reconnect themselves to the community. The news outlets that have adopted the strategies of public journalism have tried to do this and have directed their reporters and editors to change their everyday manner of doing news work.

Although news workers are imagined as figures who are part of public life, the news institution itself—the media business that operates the newspaper, television station, or radio station—seems to have escaped public journalism's philosophy and practice. So, although the method of news reporting may change with public journalism, there are no demands that the corporate office rethink its business practices to the benefit of the community. In many ways, the business side of journalism acts as if it is invisible, as if its actions are objective, with neutral impact on the community. Yet, as the case of the *Detroit Free Press* demonstrates, the business operations of a news organization have a profound effect on the community the news medium serves.

Although the *Detroit Free Press* had been experimenting with public journalism and Knight-Ridder had taken a leading role among newspaper chains in supporting public journalism years before the 1995–1997 strike, the civic lessons of connection, fair-minded participation, and democratic deliberation were absent from the newspaper's coverage and corporate operations during the strike (see Fitzgerald, 1996a). The 19-month Detroit newspaper strike that began in 1995 was not the first strike ever involving a newspaper, or even the first newspaper strike in Detroit. Veteran Detroit journalists remembered the 9-month strike of 1968. But, this more recent strike had a different, meaner tone. Susan Watson, a *Free Press* columnist until she went on strike and was later locked out, said "Nineteen sixty-eight didn't have the bitterness. It wasn't the same at all.... You didn't have the fear like you do now" (Jones, 1996, p. 1C).

There was a feeling from many that the DNA was out to cripple the newspaper unions (Frank, 1996; Gonyea & Hoyt, 1997; Jones, 1996). When strikers tried to stop shipments of the lucrative *Detroit News and Free Press* Sunday edition from the Sterling Heights, Michigan printing plant, the trucks drove full speed at picketers (West, 1995). Later, the DNA employed helicopters to airlift enough newspapers out of the plant to deflate the efforts of strikers. The most surprising tactic was the DNA's payment of about $480,000 to the city of Sterling Heights to subsidize police overtime to guard the plant. When Sterling Heights city-council members found out about these payments, they forced the city manager who accepted the payments to resign, and voted to ban the payments, which many regarded as a payoff to court the favor of the police (McCord, 1996; West, 1995). These actions, plus the DNA's quick addition of replacement workers—many of them careerist management trainees shipped in from other Gannett newspapers (Horowitz, 1995)—helped the *News* and *Free Press* to not miss a day of publication.[3]

Management of the Detroit newspapers claimed victory for not being shut down by striking workers, but the standing of the papers in the community greatly suffered. A boycott by readers and advertisers created huge losses during the strike, costing the Detroit newspapers more that $200 million in losses (Bernstein, 1997) and a circulation slide of 35% (Fitzgerald, 1996c). Yet, from the Wall Street perspective, fending off the unions was good news. After workers ended their walkout, the *Detroit News* proudly reported that, investors ... didn't flinch, with Gannett stock gaining 48.85% and Knight Ridder shares jumping 40 percent during the strike (Howes, 1997).

Although stock value increased for both corporate chains, the long-term relationship of both newspapers with the community withered. An early indication that some readers would be dropped in favor of new distribution practices occurred shortly after the 1989 JOA, when the Detroit newspapers ended delivery to readers living in outlying areas with high-circulation costs and few advertisers (McCord, 1996). During the strike, the corporate office was willing to forfeit even more readers, particularly those who were less valuable to upscale advertisers and the bottom line. Frank Vega, CEO of the Detroit Newspaper Agency, told the *Chicago Tribune* that losing one-fourth of the circulation of the Detroit newspapers was not fatal: "A lot of people stopped taking the paper, and they may have been union members. But I'm not sure how many union members shop at Neiman-Marcus. Most of them shop at Sam's Warehouse" (as cited in Frank, 1996, p. 22).

Even after striking union members agreed to unconditionally return to work on February 14, 1997, the DNA vowed to keep its replacement workers and hire back the original workers only when positions became available. The effect was a lock-out of the original employees, allowing the conflict to linger. Gonyea and Hoyt (1997) observed the extensive criticism the Detroit newspapers received from civic and religious leaders throughout the labor dispute: "There is no way to put a dollar figure on the intangibles—credibility and goodwill ... Some working-class neighborhoods are still dotted with lawn signs reading NO NEWS OR FREE PRESS WANTED HERE and cars all over the roads still bear bumper stickers reading NO SCAB PAPERS." Although the Detroit newspapers' strategy yielded quick cost-cutting for Wall Street and may have discouraged future union actions for long-term labor savings, Meyer (1995) explained that 80% of a newspaper's value is its good will—its standing in the community. Thus, in terms of

---

[3]From the beginning of the strike until September 18, 1995, the *News* and *Free Press* published a single combined daily edition.

good will—an element that is not measured by Wall Street—the Detroit newspapers' performance has been dismal.

Public journalism advocate Merritt (1995) acknowledged that excessive profits influence journalism quality but sees no way out: "There is no intrinsic reason why newspaper companies could not operate on a much smaller margin, even single digits, particularly when technology is reducing basic production costs and the entry fee. But today's newspaper companies are captives of their affluent, and often penurious, history" (p. 41).

Public journalism is not entirely incompatible with profit-seeking. Capitalism is flexible enough to incorporate popular movements and ideas. But newspapers must commit their whole enterprise to work toward the public interest and must be motivated by more than just fishing for short-term profits.

Susan Watson, the locked-out *Free Press* columnist, asked of the Detroit newspapers, "where do they draw the line of responsibility in a civil society?" (personal communication, May 27, 1998). For the *Free Press*, the scope of responsibility was much too narrowly defined. Whatever good will and community connections that might have been gained through the Children First project, many times that amount has been lost through the *Free Press'* business practices. The case of the *Detroit Free Press* demonstrates this: If public journalism is to be a serious movement, its theory and practice must be extended holistically, from the newsroom to the boardroom—not just in projects, not just in day-to-day journalism, but in all elements of the newspaper operations.

Other Journalisms, Same Community

Is there a better way for news organizations to connect with their communities? Eliasoph (1988) suggested that for generating alternative news frames (one of the goals of public journalism), the news form itself (i.e., news gathering done with traditional journalistic conventions) is not as important as the institutional structure of the news organization. She argued that alternative news narratives would be more common, "if news organizations could exist which were not so beholden to corporate and commercial interests, and which employed noncareerist reporters with different ideologies themselves, and which had different relations to both their audiences and the social movements on which they reported" (p. 330).

Thus, news organizations may first need to rethink their economic structures rather than their reporting formulas in efforts to transform their reporting. Weekly newspapers and alternative newsweeklies offer models for how dailies might structure themselves to operate in the public interest.

Although daily newspapers have been the major focus of the public journalism movement (along with some efforts that include local radio and television news), America's weekly newspapers argue that they have been connected with their communities all along—reporting on school-board activities, zoning meetings, and senior citizen center lunch menus that broadcasters and big dailies typically disdain (Sheppard, 1996). The growth of weeklies has been impressive, too, with total weekly circulation increasing from 20.9 million in 1960 to 56.7 million in 1993 (Newspaper Association of America, 1997).[4]

About two-thirds of weekly newspapers are owned by small chains, but Sheppard (1996) noted that profit margins are lower, ranging from 5% to 15%. With lowered profit demands, "many chain-owned weeklies don't face the pressure to perform for next quarter's stockholder report that dailies do ... most weekly executives interviewed said that they're committed to long term instead of short term dividends." (p. 34)

Alternative press newspapers occupy a special niche of weeklies that characteristically tend to emphasize local news, arts, and entertainment and include such papers as the *Boston Phoenix*, the *Denver Westword*, and the *Iowa City-Cedar Rapids Icon*. Alternative newsweeklies are generally distributed free to readers, and have an attitude that's informed by the counterculture, says Richard Karpel, executive director of the Association of Alternative Newsweeklies (personal communication, May 21, 1998). Daily papers have been quite influenced by these alternatives, and have often imitated their design and extensive listings in entertainment sections. But, the imitations are mostly cosmetic—the AAN bans membership to weeklies affiliated with dailies to maintain the organizational credibility of alternative newsweeklies (Giman, 1997). Alternative newsweeklies are a $300 million-a-year business in North America, have doubled circulation in the last 6 to 7 years, and continue to grow 10% every year, Karpel noted. The structure of ownership gives the alternatives more freedom, Karpel said: "None of our companies are publicly traded, with stockholder demands. This makes a lot of difference. When Wall Street gets involved, you have a lot less control."

The elements of difference that have popularized weekly newspapers and alternative newsweeklies include not only their commitment to community (which public journalism preaches), but also alternative business structures that see the community as something to invest in, rather than extract profits from (something public journalism doesn't address). Media activist Michael Albert (1997) outlined the tenets of such alternative media structures:

> An alternative media institution (to the extent possible given its circumstances) doesn't try to maximize profits, doesn't primarily sell audience to advertisers for revenues (and so seeks [a] broad and non-elite audience), is structured to subvert society's defining hierarchical social relationships, and is structurally profoundly different from and as independent of other institutions, particularly corporations, as it can be. (p. 53)

---

[4]The *Detroit Sunday Journal* was an award-winning weekly that served many of the readers who stopped buying the *News* and *Free Press*. With financial and advisory help from other unions and organizations, the *Journal* published for 4 years with a steady weekly circulation of nearly 40,000 papers. The *Journal* ceased publication in 1999, as staff members were increasingly being called back to their former jobs at the *News* and *Free Press* or pursued other careers. (Fitzgerald, 1996b; S. Watson, personal communication, May 27, 1998; Watson, 1999).

What news organizations can gain by moving toward such organizational changes is the freedom to actually achieve the community connectedness and democratic deliberation that public journalism proposes, without the obvious contradictions that business operations can create. As Carey (1997) reminded us, "Community names a way of life where something more and other than the values of the market—'the almighty dollar,' in common expression—holds sway" (p. 1).

However, if market values are what ultimately inspire the news media, the hope of communities is this: With the growing popularity of weeklies and the threat that the Internet and alternative news systems will slowly eat away at revenues, big dailies, like all news organizations, may finally realize that their primary assets are their public credibility and good will. In order for daily newspapers to remain credible institutions in their communities—and vital, vigorous, and valuable—public journalism as currently practiced is not enough. A better form of public journalism happens when the primary value of the *entire* news organization is to operate more fully in the public interest.

The news media are fundamentally based on facilitating communication within a community. And active, democratic communities are based on accessible communication that provides a public forum for the people who live there. But the lessons of public journalism tell us that good communication intentions alone can not overcome the limits a news organization creates when it treats its community like mere consumers. For the health of themselves and their communities, news organizations must think of themselves primarily as a medium for public exchange, and secondarily as a medium for commercial exchange.

REFERENCES

Albert, M. (1997, October). What makes alternative media alternative? *Z Magazine, 10*, 52–55.

Austin, L. (n.d.). *Public life and the press: A progress report.* New York: Project on Public Life and the Press.

Austin, L. (1997). Public journalism in the newsroom: Putting the ideas into play. In J. Rosen, D. Merritt & L. Austin (Eds.), *Public journalism theory and practice* (pp. 36–47). Dayton, OH: The Kettering Foundation.

Bagdikian, B. H. (1992). *The media monopoly* (4th ed.). Boston: Beacon Press.

Bennett, L. (1995, August 7). Groping for choices we can live with. *Detroit Sunday Journal* [Online]. Available: *www.rust.net/~workers/features/sj8.htm.*

Bernstein, A. (1997, August 4). 'Disaster' for Motown papers? *Business Week*, 38–40.

Campbell, R. (1998). *Media and culture.* New York: Bedford/St. Martin's.

Carey, J. (1995). The press, public opinion, and public discourse. In T. L. Glasser & C. T. Salmon (Eds.), *Public opinion and the communication of consent* (pp. 373–402). New York: Guilford.

Carey, J. (1997). Community, public, and journalism. In J. Black (Ed.), *Mixed news: The public/civic/communitarian journalism debate* (pp. 1–15). Mahwah, NJ: Lawrence Erlbaum Associates.

Charity, A. (1995). *Doing public journalism.* New York: Guilford.

Civic journalism … what's happening. (1995, June). *The Civic Catalyst, 4*, 6.

Editor & Publisher (1997). *Editor & Publisher International Yearbook.* New York: Author.

Eliasoph, N. (1988). Routines and the making of oppositional news. *Critical Studies in Mass Communication, 5*, 313–334.

First national ad campaign by newspaper association (1997, September 12). *New York Times*, p. C6.

Fitzgerald, M. (1996a, March 16). Strike coverage. *Editor & Publisher, 129*, 15, 44.

Fitzgerald, M. (1996b, March 16). Voice for strikers. *Editor & Publisher, 129*, 14, 41.

Fitzgerald, M. (1996c, September 28). Feeling the effects of the strike. *Editor & Publisher, 129*, 11, 36.

Fitzgerald, M. (1997, July 12). Strikers get another victory. *Editor & Publisher, 13*, 13.

Fouhy, E. (1997, April). Elite journalists and their communities: The gap has widened. *The Civic Catalyst, 2*.

Frank, T. (1996, November 25). Killing news in Detroit. *The Nation, 263*, 19–23.

Giman, W. (1997, July 26). AAN maintains ban on papers with daily affiliation. *Editor & Publisher, 130*, 11.

Gonyea, D., & Hoyt, M. (1997, May 15). Fallout from Detroit: From a brutal strike, bitter lessons and lasting losses. *Columbia Journalism Review, 36*, 36–41.

Hardt, H. (1997). The quest for public journalism. *Journal of Communication, 47*(3), 102–109.

Horowitz, R. (1995, November). A portrait of a Gannett scab. *Labor Notes, 5*, 14.

Howes, D. (1997, February 16). Analysis: Back to work offer reflects strike's reality. *Detroit News* [Online]. Available: *detnews.com/1997/metro/9702/16/02160088.htm*.

The James K. Batten Award. (1995, June). *The Civic Catalyst*, 3.

Katz, J. (1992, March 5). Rock, rap and movies bring you the news. *Rolling Stone*, pp. 33–35, 40, 78.

Knecht, G. B. (1996). Why a big foundation gives newspapers cash to change their ways. *Wall Street Journal*, pp. A1, A14.

Knight-Ridder to fund civic journalism projects. (1997, April). *The Civic Catalyst, 11*.

McCord, R. (1996). *The chain gang: One newspaper versus the Gannett empire*. Columbia, MO: University of Missouri Press.

McGraw, B. (1995, August 25). A bond broken, a trust betrayed. *Detroit Sunday Journal* [Online]. Available: *www.rust.net/~workers/features/striker25.htm*.

McManus, J. H. (1994). *Market-drive journalism: Let the citizen beware?* Thousand Oaks, CA: Sage.

Merritt, D. (1995). *Public journalism & public life: Why telling the news is not enough*. Hillsdale, NJ: Lawrence Erlbaum Associates.

Merritt, D. (1996, July–August). Missing the point. *American Journalism Review*, 29–31.

Meyer, P. (1995, December). Learning to love lower profits. *American Journalism Review*, 40–44.

Morton, J. (1997, July–August). Chains swallowing other chains. *American Journalism Review*, 52.

Newspaper Association of America (1997). *Facts about newspapers 1997*. Vienna, VA: Author.

Parisi, P. (1997). Toward a "philosophy of framing": News narratives for public journalism. *Journalism & Mass Communication Quarterly, 74*(4), 673–686.

Postman, N. (1995, July–August). Currents. *Utne Reader*, 35.

Ridder, T., & Fontaine, J. (1996, February 1). Letter to shareholders. *Knight-Ridder 1995 Annual Report* [Online]. Available: *www.kri.com/fn_li/fn_ar_04.html*.

Rosen, J. (1994). Making things more public: On the political responsibility of the media intellectual. *Critical Studies in Mass Communication, 11*, 362–388.

Rosen, J. (1997). Public journalism as a democratic art. In J. Rosen, D. Merritt & L. Austin (Eds.), *Public journalism theory and practice* (pp. 3–24); (Occasional paper) Dayton, OH: The Kettering Foundation.

Rosen, J. (1997). *What are journalists for?* New Haven, CT: Yale University Press.

Shepard, A. C. (1994, September). The gospel of public journalism. *American Journalism Review*, 28–34.

Sheppard, J. (1996, July/August). The strength of weeklies. *American Journalism Review*, 32–37.

Trimer-Hartley, M. (1995, December). The battle of Detroit: Newspaper unions vs. media monoliths. *Agenda*, 4–6.

Watson, S. (1999, November 21) Journal for 4 years, but solidarity forever. *Detroit Sunday Journal*, 4.

West, J. (1995, November). Unions focus on advertiser/circulation boycott as Detroit newspapers reject peace offer. *Labor Notes, 5,* 14.

14

Why Localism? Communication Technology and the Shifting Scales of Political Community

Andrew Calabrese
University of Colorado

We have inherited, in short, local town-meeting practices and ideas. But we live and act and have our being in a continental national state. —(Dewey, 1927, p. 113)

Dewey's (1927) observation, written at a time when the pace of technological change within the means of communication was not nearly as frenzied as today, still rings true, with one exception: The connection between widespread aspirations for democratic politics at the local level, and the scale on which "we live and act and have our being," seems by most contemporary accounts to be more mismatched than ever. Familiar laments about the decline of community, and about our lack of a sense of place, increasingly highlight how the steamroller of capital mobility and globalization has left in its wake less hope than ever for the national state to serve as the main guarantor of democratic life on a local level. Nevertheless, within the voluminous and exponentially growing body of published work on the subject of globalization, some writers have attempted to explain, if not promote, countertrends. Depending on one's perspective, subgenres of "globalization talk" can reflect on nationalism, fundamentalism, identity politics, tribalism, and localism. Although few writers might argue that globalization should be seen as a primary cause of these trends, it is a recurrent theme to be sure. How localism in particular fares today, and a rationale for the role of communication technology in this context, is my main concern here.

In this chapter, I examine how the concept of localism relates to the discourse about communication technology. However, in doing so I step back a bit from the exigencies of current media policies and practices and, instead, focus on the meaning, possibilities, and limitations of "the local" in a contemporary world in which "the tyranny of distance" is seen as a thing of the past. Why should we care about local culture, local knowledge, or local politics when innovative uses of communication technology seem to enable us to escape the parochial confines of the local? Indeed, it is not uncommon to encounter refrains that a preoccupation with the local in political practice or social policy is a regressive stance. In this trope, the local equates to atavism or impotence. It is antiuniversalist, even tribal, and it certainly is not good Leftism because it accepts "a principle of merely local or marginal opposition to the real movement of society," and thus represents "the abdication of the global" (Martin, 1995, pp. 99, 107). This Manichean depiction of the local–global nexus implies that no sensible and progressive response to globalization could be anything but grandiosely global, as if to say that political engagement on any smaller scale is not only ineffectual but counterproductive to the extent that it poses a distraction to the real movement of society.

Of course, there are good reasons for taking an ambivalent stand toward localism, particularly to the extent that local mobilizations categorically oppose state power, as Amin (1990) warned. But this does not seem to be the only course, and there are good reasons to conclude that local action should be seen as a necessary element of effective strategies of political engagement. In the context of the United States, the risk is too great to concede the rhetoric of localism to America's pseudocommunitarian politics of resentment that have led to a program of welfare reform that is punitive toward the poor and that turns a blind eye toward corporate welfare (Issac, 1995). In sum, a political strategy of localism need not, and should not, be viewed as inherently myopic and insular. This point is particularly meaningful when discussing the connection between localism and communication technology and related policy making.

It seems that we can either abandon localism and local participation as a core value in a social policy that is aimed at democratic communication, or we can redefine and defend it in order to enliven its historical relevance. In the following analysis, I argue for the latter position with two goals in mind: to develop a rationale for communications policy governing media localism that is based on democratic theory and, from within that framework, to recommend redefining the political concepts of localism and local participation. Although my arguments are in many ways grounded in the context of media industries and policies of the United States, I believe that there is broader relevance to such an analysis, particularly in light of the global influence exerted by U.S. media industries and policies, both directly and by example.

There are serious deficiencies in how the concept of localism has been deployed in the context of U.S. communications policy, particularly stemming from tensions between expectations that broadcasters be responsive to the culture and politics of specific geographic communities, versus the commercial imperatives of broadcast networks to span many such communities and intentionally produce for the largest possible market in order to enjoy economies of scale. Often, the term *localism* has been used to refer to a geographic space of a size and scale that constitutes, to borrow a term from Williams (1974), a "knowable community." However, as quickly became the case in the evolution of broadcasting in the United States, the term localism has been used to designate little more than the fact that specific programs are produced by individual broadcast and cable stations, with little accompanying effort to be responsive to the specificities of a particular geographic area, whether it be a large metropolitan area or a small market.

PAST AS PROLOGUE: VISIONS OF LOCALISM IN U.S. MEDIA POLICY

The T.V.A. [Tennessee Valley Authority] experience demonstrates the folly of identifying technical projects with the creation of democratic community. As contemporary rhetoric is doing with electronics, T.V.A. rhetoric coupled ideas about electrical sublimity with attitudes concerning contact with nature and saw in the merger the automatic production of democracy. (Carey & Quirk, 1970, p. 237)

U.S. communications policy has always been nominally committed to the idea of localism as a Jeffersonian-style means of promoting decentralized public discourse about matters of social and political consequence. Indeed the statutory basis for this public interest mandate can be found in the Communications Act of 1934, at least as far as broadcast licensing is concerned.[1] Pursuant to this mandate, the Federal Communications Commission (FCC, 1987) "established a scheme for distributing radio service in which every broadcast station is assigned to a community of license with a primary obligation to serve that community." In both the case of broadcasting and cable television, an ethos of small-town democracy has constituted the underlying mythology, if not the reality, of localism in U.S. communications policy. This rhetoric for the "automatic production of democracy" has fostered aspirations to sustain public discourse that is tied to the culture and politics of particular places. In the case of cable television in the U.S., and now more recently of computer-mediated community networks, the concept of localism also has been tied to aspirations for direct access to the means of communication and participation in public discourse. In retrospect, we may, with good reason, conclude that efforts to realize such aspirations have been largely frustrated by commercial imperatives, and we may thereby conclude that there is no good reason to have high expectations for a renewal of an ethos

---

[1]The Communications Act of 1934 states: "In considering applications for licenses, and modifications and renewals thereof, when and insofar as there is demand for the same, the Commission shall make such distribution of licenses, frequencies, hours of operation, and of power among the several States and communities as to provide a fair, efficient, and equitable distribu-

of local participation, in light of the present wave of industrial and technological restructuring in telecommunications.

The basic goals of a broadcast localism policy in the U.S., as the National Telecommunications and Information Administration (NTIA) observed in its report entitled *Globalization of the Mass Media*, have been "to promote the provision of local broadcast service to as many communities as practical and to ensure that broadcasters provide programming that meets the needs of their local communities" (U.S. Department of Commerce, NTIA, 1993, p. 217). In a chapter on the relation between localism and globalization, the NTIA concluded that, "the availability of broadcasting services in a community would seem to promote the availability of local news and information in that community" (p. 226). However, the evidence weighs against, concluding that the broadcast localism mandate has been effective, and the track record of cable, despite its celebrated channel capacity, is hardly any better.

The legacy of localism as a U.S. broadcast-policy mandate is a weak one. Localism has been a linchpin of public interest policy discourse from 1927 to the present, but in practice, as Robert Horwitz (1989) wrote, it has been an, "often ambiguous policy goal underlying many Commission decisions," resulting in, "a kind of mushy policy foundation to which subsequent decisions, conflicts, and controversies had to adapt" (p. 155). The localism mandate, he noted, was "a surprisingly conscious policy" that evoked images of a Jeffersonian pastoral ideal of small-town America, rural wholesomeness, and grassroots democracy, "within the bounds of commercial ownership, of course" (p. 174). In the balance between this seductive democratic vision and the dictates of market competition and performance, the spirit of localism has been more valuable for selling policies favoring commercial broadcast network inroads at the local level than it has been for developing strong locally originated media. Whatever the good intentions underlying legislative and regulatory policy, Horwitz concludes, this "fiction of the local broadcaster" (p. 192) has served, "only to veil the actual practices and consequences of a commercially organized, national system of network broadcasting" (p. 194). In the NTIA's U.S. Department of Commerce, 1993) report on globalization, it concluded that the broadcast policies for localism "need not be altered. The need for them continues in today's global marketplace" (p. 227). This recommendation is commendable as far as the symbolic support for what little there is of mandated local broadcast production, but it has proven to be a somewhat toothless proclamation.

The problematic relation between localism and commercialism is not limited to the broadcasting industry, as the history of the younger cable industry demonstrates, and indeed cable's evolution has helped only to sustain the localism mythology. Cable access has been characterized by the industry as a financial burden and an infringement on cable operators' First Amendment rights. Nevertheless, public access to cable television has managed to survive, at least up to the present, as a sort of sacred cow in federal policy, albeit in a progressively more weakened condition. Despite its image as a cheap refuge where social misfits can talk among themselves, public access cable lends value to the official rhetoric of localism, up through the present mandate, that public, educational, and government access channels can be included in the basic tier of cable service.

From its early days of commercialization, the cable industry has been subject to access requirements, the result of an enthusiastic vision that cable technology could become a democratizing force in a grassroots transformation of the American U.S. public sphere (Sloan Commission, 1971). However, the history of public-access cable policy in the United States reflects a basic conflict between commercial interests and publicly imposed demands for the subsidization of noncommercial television production and distribution resources. The most fertile period of public-access advocacy was one in which the citizen pressure for access was the effort of a loose coalition of moderately left-progressive visionaries whose goal was to channel the power of television from a commercial tool to for manipulatives a passive consumer culture to a forum for a local civic culture of participation (Engelman, 1990). The beginning of the era of the metamorphosis of cable television from a community antenna toward a vertically integrated, multibillion dollar industry also was an era of widespread political activism. Localism, with its ring of authenticity and grassroots democracy, was among the causes motivating media-policy activism, and access was central to that ethos. As Horwitz (1989) noted:

> Cable appeared to offer the opportunity for direct access to television to those left out by conventional television: seniors, minorities, nonprofit organizations, local arts groups. Local government and community meetings could be carried live. Schools and hospitals would be interconnected for teaching purposes. In short, the embrace of cable as a potentially participatory medium reflected the participatory utopianism of the grassroots citizens movement itself. (p. 251)

In the name of localism, the U.S. Supreme Court maintained in 1972 that the FCC could require cable operators to originate television programming that was responsive to local community needs.[2] At about the same time, the FCC promulgated rules that were designed to relieve cable operators from the obligation to originate local programming and instead required them to provide access channels to the local community.[3] In 1979, the FCC's access rules were defeated on the basis that they wrested editorial control from cable operators and thus exceeded the lim-

---

[2] Midwest Video Corporation (*Midwest Video I*), v. United States, 406 U.S. 649 (1972).

[3] These rules required cable operators in the top 100 television markets to provide at least one channel each for public, educational, local governmental, and leased commercial access. In addition, facilities for the production of local programs were to be provided by the cable operator free of charge to public, educational, and local governmental groups. 36 FCC 2d 143, on reconsideration, 36 FCC 2d 326 (1972). Subsequently, the access rules were modified to apply to all cable systems with 3,500 or more subscribers, and four separate access channels no longer were required if fewer channels would serve a market's access demands. 59 FCC 2d 294 (1976).

its of the FCC's jurisdiction over cable.[4] Thus, a federally guaranteed right of direct public access to cable was seen as a violation of the First Amendment rights of cable operators, and it was not until the passage of the Cable Communications Policy Act of 1984 that Congress decided to impose the less demanding access requirement that is in effect today. As amended, that legislation reads:

> "A franchising authority may in its request for proposals require as part of a franchise, and may require as part of a cable operator's proposal for a franchise renewal ... that channel capacity be designated for public, educational, or government use.[5]"

Whether local public-access cable makes a difference in a community is a matter of disagreement. Certainly, the criteria for judging the success of such efforts can not be the same as those applied to judging commercial cable channels, or even public television with its small but national audience and its far more integrated pool of production, distribution, and programming resources. Rather, it is more reasonable to view public access as a public-meeting room or town hall where gatherings are held and ideas are shared by and for members of a community. As Aufderheide (1992) stated, "access does not need to win popularity contests to play a useful role in the community. It is not surprising if people do not watch most of the time" (p. 59). Nevertheless, some access centers are thriving models for the far greater number of cable markets in which access either does not exist or plays an insignificant role in the local community.

The fact that our commercially oriented media audiences historically have been minimally socialized to treat television as a participatory medium is not an inherently good reason for abandoning the goal, particularly in an era in which there is rapid development and diffusion of the technological capabilities that radically increase individual and group opportunities for producing and disseminating video. As with the history of cable to date, the future post-channel world is likely to be one in which noncommercial interests will struggle, as I argued elsewhere (Calabrese & Borchert, 1996). Certainly the traditional financial base of public access cable loses its justification as the likelihood of local competition among multichannel delivery systems (including high-speed Internet service) increases, thereby calling to question the present rationale for municipalities to draw revenue from cable operators alone, if from any of these sources, to fund access channels.

---

[4]The court concluded that cable systems should not be treated as common carriers, because to do so would negate "the editorial discretion otherwise enjoyed by broadcasters and cable operators alike." Basing its decision on an interpretation of "Congress' stern disapproval" of taking editorial control away from cable operators, the Supreme Court affirmed the Eighth Circuit's decision to vacate the access rules, discouraging what appeared to be a movement by the FCC toward a common carrier-type approach to cable regulation. FCC v. Midwest Video Corp. (*Midwest Video II*), 440 U.S. 708 (1979).

[5]47 U.S.C. 531(b). Available at: http://law2.house.gov/us

The utopian visions for cable access were bound to fail. They were too techno-logically deterministic—too focused on the technology to the neglect of a coherent social, cultural, and political rationale—and reflected too little awareness of insti-tutional inertia and the structural causes of civic discontent and apathy. Excessive faith, not a lack of faith, in the ability of national policy to engineer local, direct de-mocracy is a principal root of the disillusionment about the information society's ability to deliver the democratic goods. As Streeter (1987) suggested, policy mak-ers are, among other things, story tellers, and localism is a useful plot device.

If the government's purpose is to secure the public interest, then government must be responsive to changes in the conditions in which those interests can be realized, and to the threats to such realization. My point is not that more govern-ment is better: A responsive and proactive government is not necessarily a more meddlesome one. The laudable, democratic spirit of localism that guided early media-policy development in the United States, and that refuses to vacate me-dia-policy discourse today, lags far behind the economic and technological reali-ties of a largely U.S. and West European government-induced era of rapid media-industry restructuring on a global level. As well, that democratic spirit re-flects the prevailing ahistorical tendency in progressive media activism, which has posed little more than minor stumbling blocks in this new era of wild capital-ism in telecommunications.

The original goal of the advocates of media localism was to invigorate a politi-cally and culturally involved community life at the local level. Today, the goal is the same, but because the focus of public life has long been disconnected from spe-cific localities, a commitment to local participation must not only be a commit-ment to community life within specific geographic locales, but also to community life at a grassroots level that transcends locale. Any meaningful concept of local-ism would of course need to reflect such an understanding of how the local and the translocal are related. Before discussing a rationale for thinking about localism in connection with translocalism, I present a more general foundation for defending localism in political terms.

AN ARGUMENT FROM PARTICIPATION

A meaningful concept of media localism must be tied to means of strengthening direct access to the means of communication. This is not to imply that we should distrust representative forms of expression, but rather it is to agree with those who have argued that democratic representation is strengthened through the active ex-ercise of political participation. Indeed, there is a well-reasoned heritage in west-ern political thought that favors participation as the most authentic means of sustaining and enriching democratic public life. Awareness of that legacy is valu-able as a point of departure for further consideration of the question "Why local-ism?" in the arena of media policy today.

Discussion of a contemporary philosophical rationale for connecting local-ism and participatory democracy profits from consideration of the contributions and limitations of the political–moral philosophy of Jean-Jacques Rousseau.

Rousseau's (1762/1968). search for a model of a just and virtuous civil society led him to admire elements of the political organization of the city–state of ancient Greece. He opposed representative government on the principle that representation deprives the public of its right to exercise its will by placing authority and control to the hands of an elite that was elected by majority vote. For Rousseau, majority voting does not necessarily reflect the general will, as he described it, but it is at best a poor surrogate for the expression of that will. The only consolation Rousseau took in the practical necessity of majority voting is based on his assumption that, in principle, voting should follow a prior consensus: "The law of majority-voting itself rests on a covenant, and implies that there has been on at least one occasion unanimity" (p. 59). From this position, Rousseau accepted representative government, not as an expression of the general will, but rather as a means of delegating authority: "the sovereign, which is simply a collective being, cannot be represented by anyone but itself—power may be delegated, but the will cannot be" (p. 69).

It should be noted that Rousseau, who has been praised as a founder of the modern western democratic tradition, also has been vilified for the inspiration his ideas have given to totalitarianism (Masters, 1991), although this is a matter of dispute. In defense of Rousseau, he feared that what he termed "the general will," or what we might now term "the public interest," is undermined if it becomes possible for a group to be powerful enough to exercise its private interests as though they reflect a general consensus. Writing ambivalently in Rousseau's defense, Durkheim (1892/1960) noted, "In this theory we discern the horror of all particularism, the unitary conception of society, that was one of the characteristics of the French Revolution" (pp. 107–108). Durkheim was not writing here in defense of the royalists, but rather he was evoking the example of the French Revolution to refer to the "Reign of Terror" (1793–1794) that emerged in order to repress the counterrevolution by force. It is estimated that about 40,000 persons were killed by "the Terror," and hundreds of thousands were arrested or detained (Palmer & Colton, 1971). Durkheim cited this period to illustrate an extreme danger of polluting the meaning of "the public interest" by way of particularism. Perhaps he would have used the reign of Stalin, instead of Robespierre, had he lived to witness that later period of terror. Less charitable toward Rousseau was Arendt (1963), who made observations similar to Durkheim's that particularism under Robespierre was elevated to the status of the general will, but who also argued that the seeds of this extreme are planted deeply in Rousseau's own thinking. This remains a matter for dispute for reasons that are paralleled in claims that the Soviet Gulag necessarily was the logical outcome of Marx's thought.[6] Offering a more recent basis for seeing participatory democracy as not being without risks, Carole Pateman (1970) noted that,

---

[6]For example, in an interview given several years before the end of the Soviet Union, Foucault (1980) argued that it is important to question not how the texts of Marx and Lenin were betrayed under Stalin, but rather to question "all these theoretical texts, however old, from the standpoint of the reality of the Gulag. Rather than of searching in those texts for a condemnation in advance of the Gulag, it is a matter of asking what in those texts could have made the Gulag possible, what might even now continue to justify it, and what makes it intolerable truth still accepted today" (p. 135). This is slippery post hoc reasoning, because by Foucault's standard it is impossible for a political doctrine to exist that did not contain seeds of destruction or inhumanity.

he collapse of the Weimar Republic, with its high rates of participation, into fascism, and the post-war establishment of totalitarian regimes based on mass participation, albeit participation backed by intimidation and coercion, underlay the tendency for 'participation' to become linked to the concept of totalitarianism rather than that of democracy. (p. 4)

Rousseau (1762/1968) feared that factionalized interests would vie for power and falsely claim the moral authority to represent the public interest. But his concern with the dangers of interest group politics to the point of rejecting them did not properly address the problems and the possibility of developing and sustaining participatory structures in large, complex societies.[7] Similar to Rousseau's fear of the potential for majority rule to devolve to factionalism was that of James Madison (1996). However, unlike Rousseau, Madison favored representative government and majority rule rather than limit his vision of democracy to the scale dictated by Rousseau's view that true democracy was possible only in sparsely populated peasant societies. In his famous statement on the dilemma of factions in representative government, Madison observed the same fundamental tension between liberty and justice in 1787 that had preoccupied Rousseau, but concluded that the greater evil would be to suppress the opportunities for groups to contend in the public sphere.[8]

Of course, concerns about factionalization and social fragmentation still preoccupy many U.S. intellectuals and public servants today, leading to a (perhaps inaccurately nostalgic) view that there once was a time in this nation's history in which the imagined unity existed. Another social and political theorist, Alexis de Tocqueville (1830/1945), praised the fact that the social order in the United States rested heavily on participation in voluntarily formed civil associations. de Tocqueville was fascinated with the impulse he found among Americans to organize around any number of interests, as he knew nothing comparable in the Europe of his time. In Volume 2 of *Democracy in America*, de Tocqueville noted:

---

[7]In *The Social Contract*, Rousseau (1762/1968) tended to avoid the problems of realizing his vision of direct democracy except in lands where he perceived a sufficient degree of simplicity among the people and a sufficiently small population. In short, despite his living and writing in a Europe in which modernization, population growth, bureaucratic complexity, and urbanization were beginning to accelerate all around him, Rousseau's primary hope for participatory democracy was with relatively premodern societies. Thus, he had hopes for Corsica as an ideal testing ground for the enactment of his vision of democracy because of the relative economic equality among the peasantry.

[8]Madison (1966) wrote the following in what is perhaps the most famous of *The Federalist Papers* (#10): "Liberty is to faction, what air is to fire, an ailment without which it instantly expires. But it could not be a less folly to abolish liberty, which is essential to political life, because it nourishes faction, than it would be to wish the annihilation of air, which is essential to animal life, because it imparts to fire its destructive agency" (p. 43).

I met with several kinds of associations in America of which I confess I had no previous notion; and I have often admired the extreme skill with which the inhabitants of the United States succeed in proposing a common object for the exertions of a great many men and inducing them voluntarily to pursue it ... Thus the most democratic country on the face of the earth is that in which men have, in our time, carried to the highest perfection the art of pursuing in common the object of their common desires and have applied this new science to the greatest number of purposes. Is this the result of accident, or is there in reality any necessary connection between the principle of association and that of equality? (pp. 114–115)

As he noted, associational life in the United States was neither limited then, nor now, to matters directed solely toward private affairs. Rather, de Tocqueville (1830/1945) saw the exercise of the right of *political* association as a means by which citizens managed to participate directly in the expression of their interests and opinions:

There is only one country on the face of the earth where the citizens enjoy unlimited freedom of association for political purposes. This same country is the only one in the world where the continual exercise of the right of association has been introduced into civil life and where all the advantages which civilization can confer are procured by means of it. (p. 123)

Furthermore, de Tocqueville (1830/1945), saw participation in local government as a means of enabling individuals to become effective participants in a national polity: "Town meetings are to liberty what primary schools are to science; they bring it within the people's reach, they teach men how to use and how to enjoy it" (p. 63).

In an effort to move the discussion about participatory democracy forward to the late 20th century by assessing the concept's strengths and weaknesses in the present context, Pateman (1970) began her analysis with a critical explication of a position that dominates contemporary democratic theory, namely, that participation is impractical and unwarranted, and should be limited to voting for representatives. The basis on which this position was advanced is reflected in how the public is characterized. As Pateman noted, there is a powerful tendency in recent political thought (little has changed since 1970 in this regard) to treat the public as a "mass" that is "incapable of action other than a stampede" (Schumpeter, 1943), that is apathetic (Berelson), whose lower socioeconomic groups tend toward authoritarianism (Dahl, 1956), and whose increased participation would threaten to undermine political stability (several authors). Little needs to be said about the low regard that this perspective, and the political action it informs, holds for average citizens. This view of citizens is mirrored in many ways by the dismissive manner in which citizens are regarded in mass-society theory (Brantlinger, 1983), from which much of mass-media theory was derived. Another claim that was widespread within this line of thought, Pateman noted, was that these theories were value free.

In contrast to these theorists, Pateman (1970) examined the contributions of Rousseau and Mill to democratic theories of participation. Unsatisfied with Rousseau's perspective on the possibilities for participation in large, complex societies, Pateman looked to Mill. Drawing from Mill's (1958) *Considerations on Representative Government*, she argued that:

> if individuals in a large state are to be able to participate effectively in the government of the 'great society' then the necessary qualities underlying this participation have to be fostered and developed at the local level. Thus, for Mill, it is at local level [sic] where the real educative effect of participation occurs, where not only do the issues dealt with directly affect the individual and his everyday life but where he also stands a good chance of, himself, being elected to serve on a local body. (pp. 30–31)

While Pateman (1970) revealed her lack of faith in Mill's (1958) integration of participatory functions in representative government, she concluded that the educative function "might give scope for direct participation in decision making" (p. 33). The problem with Mill's view, however, is that the educative function is geared toward the development of *critical deference*. As Pateman stated, "The whole argument about the 'critical deference' of the multitude rests partly on the suggestion that participation aids the acceptance of decisions and Mill specifically points to the integrative function of participation" (p. 33). This critique is consistent with contemporary critiques of management-organized industrial quality circles and their usefulness in stemming labor unrest through co-optation that favors management objectives to the disadvantage of labor. Instead of advocating an educative function for participation that is geared simply toward the development of critical deference, Pateman moved beyond Mill at this point and argued that the true aim of participation should not be deference, but civic competence. In this respect, Pateman was truer to de Tocqueville's (1830/1945) understanding of civic education than she is to Mill's. Civic education, and the capacity for competent public judgment, are derived experientially, and the feasible opportunity to participate in public life is a necessary precondition to that end.

Pateman's (1970) argument can be summarized as stating that participation in political and nonpolitical settings at local levels, where greater opportunities for participation are available, engenders a competent citizenry at representative levels. As she argued:

> The ordinary man might still be more interested in things nearer home, but the existence of a participatory society would mean that he was better able to assess the performance of representatives at the national level, better equipped to take decisions of national scope when the opportunity arose to do so, and better able to weigh up the impact of decisions taken by national representatives on his own life and immediate surroundings. (p. 110)

Thus, advancing beyond Rousseau's (1968) exclusive faith in local participation, and Mill's (1958) notion that the demands of democratic representation are met through locally acquired critical deference, Pateman demonstrated the complementarity of local participation and the ability to judge the quality of political representation. These views are of central relevance to any discussion of democratic communication.

Pateman's (1970) analysis emphasized the value of local participation in the name of both participatory and representative democracy. What Pateman did not emphasize, however, was what I term *translocalism*, the direct communication that increasingly takes place between and among active participants in organizations, coalitions, and social movements that may or may not have significant memberships in a single locale, but whose collective membership across potentially great distances makes for an increasingly important form of participation. Amid all of the discussion of global culture, the information highway, and the globalization of the mass media, little is said about the persistent and increasing problems experienced at the local level by communities struggling to sustain political, economic, and cultural autonomy as capital deprives them of it with the tacit and active assistance of government at all levels (Calabrese, 1991; Castells, 1989). An examination of the opportunities and limitations for greater access to communications media is one of value in that regard.

TRANSLOCAL COMMUNITY

In its deepest and richest sense a community must always remain a matter of face-to-face intercourse. This is why the family and neighborhood, with all their deficiencies, have always been the chief agencies of nurture, the means by which dispositions are stably formed and ideas acquired which laid hold on the roots of character. Is it possible for local communities to be stable without being static, progressive without being merely mobile? Can the vast, innumerable and intricate events of trans-local associations be so banked and conducted that they will pour the generous and abundant meanings of which they are potential bearers into the smaller intimate unions of human beings living in immediate contact with one another? … There is at present, at least in theory, a movement away from the principle of territorial organization to that of "functional," that is to say, occupational, organization. It is true enough that older forms of territorial association do not satisfy present needs. (Dewey, 1927, pp. 211–212)

Talk of localism tends to evoke talk of community, understandably, because when we talk of community we tend to think of it in local, if not intimate terms. However, the idea of community has enjoyed somewhat of a renaissance in recent times, due in no small part to the technological utopianism that characterizes much of the enthusiasm toward the emancipatory prospects for geographically dispersed virtual communities. As with so many past technological utopias in America, the idea of virtual communities bears elements of visions of pastoral idealism and hopes of the technological sublime.[9] Characteristic of such visions is a concept of commu-

---

[9]Two good historical accounts of technological utopianism in the United States are by Marx (1964) and Segal (1985).

nity without friction: no oppressive hierarchy, no stifling groupthink, no destructive or regressive tendencies.[10]This ahistorical rhetoric of community grafts boundless and optimistic technological futurism on the rootstock of images of simpler and better bygone days. Such rhetoric is manifest not only in the idea of a return to rural bliss by way of high technology but also in the idea of recovering the essential elements of community in cyberspace.

To trace the intellectual origins of the sociological understanding of the idea of community, perhaps the most commonly cited touchstone is *Gemeinschaft und Gesellschaft*, by Ferdinand Tönnies (1887/1957). Unfortunately, many sociologists have overextended the use of Tönnies' concept of *Gemeinschaft*, or community, and they have tended to offer a simplistic reading of his views on rural community life (Calabrese, 1991). His ideal-typical comparison of community and society is not premised mainly on the principle of a spatial division between country and city, but rather on the nature of social relations.[11] The prevailing reading of Tönnies is that he saw the community of premodern Europe as rooted in locality. However, although he did see the rural agrarian community in contrast with urban industrial society, he also saw Gemeinschaft as actually and potentially translocal. That is, our most widely credited theorist of the concept of community was aware in his own time of the idea that communications media ("the press") were used to bind space beyond the local community (i.e., to maintain communities of interest).

Even more noteworthy is that Tönnies (1887/1957) articulated a view of *Gesellschaft* that presages today's commonplace understanding about the nature of the relationship between media and globalization, referring to nation states as "but a temporary limitation of the boundaryless Gesellschaft" (221). Thus, in his comments on the press, he wrote, "It [the press] can be conceived as [having an] ultimate aim to abolish the multiplicity of states and substitute for it a single world republic coextensive with the world market, which would be ruled by thinkers, scholars, and writers and could dispense with means of coercion other than those of a psychological nature." (p. 221)

It is unfortunate that Tönnies did not live to see the age of television and the Internet, or no doubt he would have stated a slightly different line-up of who the inheritors of global gesellschaft would be, and he most likely would have high-

---

[10]Although Williams (1983) was not writing about America, he put it well when he concluded about the term *community* that, "unlike all other terms of social organization (state, nation, society, etc.) it seems never to be used unfavorably, and never to be given any positive opposing or distinguishing term" (p. 76). Elsewhere, Williams (1979) wrote: "It was when I suddenly realized that no one ever used "community" in a hostile sense that I saw how dangerous it was" (p. 119). Of course, we should question the uncritical treatment that the idea of "community" tends to receive in cyber-talk. Sennett (1974) and Berman (1982), each in different ways, highlighted the destructive tendencies of *gemeinschaft*, laying open to doubt any social or political theory that treats the concept in strictly positive terms.
[11]In a seminal work, Pahl (1968) dismissed the rural–urban continuum as "vulgar Tönniesism" to make the point that *gemeinschaft* and *gesellschaft* relationships can be found among different groups in the same place, whether it be a rural or an urban locale.

lighted the political power of global media and telecommunications firms. Nevertheless, his message would otherwise be on target: symbolic exchange and social control "of a psychological nature" would replace coercion as first-order means to rule the world market.

Similar to Tönnies, but in reflection of the United States rather than Germany or the global Gesellschaft, John Dewey recognized a sharp distinction between the categories of *Gemeinschaft* (community) and *Gesellschaft* (society). Unlike Tönnies, Dewey (1927) sounded more of an alarm, and indeed wrote in a more prescriptive vein, in his account. In *The Public and Its Problems*, Dewey worried over whether the "Great Society" of the United States, a paragon of modernity,[12] had eclipsed the possibility of democratic public life in the context of the local community. In Dewey's view, mobility uproots community and has a destructive impact on identity. In search of a solution, he ruminated over the prospects for developing a scale of community life that could parallel that of the great society, which he aptly termed the *Great Community*. His solution to the eclipse of the public would have been to take one of modernity's greatest sets of innovations—the means of communication that sustain the great society—and make them into a sort of antivenom to recover community life. In Dewey's view, "communication alone can create a great community" (p. 142), it would also be necessary for modern means of communication to serve to strengthen rather than undermine the local community. Thus, he proposed an ethos for the great community that would not abandon the local community in a torrent of hyper-mobility: "We lie, as Emerson said, in the lap of an immense intelligence. But that intelligence is dormant and its communications are broken, inarticulate and faint until it possesses the local community as its medium" (p. 219). In this vision, Dewey wanted very much for the local community to make the means of communication a primary mechanism for maintaining its membership in the "great community."

Of course, Dewey can be dismissed for having offered a naive attempt to reinvigorate a vision of local democratic community life, one that arguably seems to have fallen even further behind in living up to the challenges of hyper-mobile modernity. The question we now must ask is whether the changing historical conditions since the time he wrote, invite a recovery of his vision. What does participatory theory tell us about localism today? Furthermore, what does it tell us about the role and potential of communication technology for the local community? Localism need not imply regressive separatism or parochialism.[13] It can mean that a politics of place should carry weight as a counterbalance to the placeless power that increasingly dominates our global political economy (Castells, 1989). In an age when capital mobility on a global scale has never been greater, and when the loyalty of capital to specific places is fleeting, Castells argued for the restoration of control over local communities through the strengthen-

---

[12]In *Gemeinschaft und Gesellschaft*, Tönnies (1887/1957) referred to the United States as "the most modern and Gesellschaft-like state" (p. 221).

[13]With perhaps good intention, there is a backlash against so-called "identity politics" in the United States that arises from a concern about the destructive potential of exclusionary group definitions that are along the lines of gender, race and ethnicity,   *(continued on next page)*

ing of networks of local governments and local grassroots nongovernmental organizations for purposes of sharing information, decision making, and forming strategic alliances. He maintained that, "active citizen participation and a nation-wide or worldwide network of local governments" (pp. 352–353) could pose a parallel, democratic power structure to match the often disruptive, mobile power of global capital. The ability to understand and to translate the significance of matters of national and global importance for a local community is likely to become an increasingly valuable set of skills and talents. For all the talk of our mobile society, the thought of being uprooted and losing a sense of place is still worrisome to many Americans. If a new politics of participation is to become relevant and vital, it will have to be a politics that can enable the members of place-bound, local communities to understand the world from a multiplicity of perspectives, part of which must be rooted in a politics of place and part of which must transcend place.

With good reason, a number of policy analyses have arrived at the conclusion that a means to link community access centers, and thus to establish translocalism as a public interest priority, would do much to invigorate and revitalize the spirit of localism that Congress and the FCC have promoted for so long. Reflecting on cable television and the prospects for networking access centers, Kellner (1990) argued, "viewers seem to be ready for more socially critical, controversial, and investigative television, thus it is probable that a public interest network would have a large and devoted following" (p. 214; see also Aufderheide, 1992).

In order to ensure the growth and health of a community network movement, it seems essential that the financial basis on which local media relies become a priority for social and cultural policy. The question of how funds should be secured will be controversial in any event. Aufderheide (1992) proposed that a "national video production fund … could be paid for in a variety of ways, such as spectrum fees; revenues from profits from sales of broadcast stations and cable systems; and charges on videocassettes, VCRs, and satellite dishes" (p. 61). Of course, television is not the only mode of communication that is of growing interest and concern in policy discourse about the changing telecommunications environment. Given the rapidly evolving processes of digitalization, high-speed transmission capacity, and multimedia convergence, perhaps it makes more sense to think in terms of some form of "bit tax" on all transmissions. This may become the most reasonable means of building a revenue base for subsidizing universal access, community media centers, and perhaps public-service media in a digital age. Although these mea-

---

[13](continued from previous page) locality, and sexual orientation. Although there is legitimacy in this concern, I also believe that the vigor of this backlash warrants suspicion. It is regrettable but believable that there are conditions under which individuals and groups take comfort by choosing to form social enclaves after becoming endlessly frustrated in struggles to overlook, or educate others about, subtle and not-so-subtle sources of prejudice, inequality, and intolerance. I find it simple-minded to categorically dismiss such choices with the trendy label *victimization*. Such language spares its purveyors from getting mired in trying to understand the complex origins of exclusionary politics in the United States, and, whether by design or default, it serves to reinforce reactionary sentiments, the latter being a cure that is at least as evil as the disease it

sures raise the specter of socialism in the minds of market ideologues who fail to consider how impure the market actually is, they also are market-oriented measures that depend on revenues from a healthy commercial system. A fee tribunal could be responsible for the collection and reallocation of funds. It is hard to see how community media in the United States can move beyond the ghettoized form they presently take unless there became such publicly guaranteed sources of funds for access, production and distribution (Calabrese & Wasko, 1992).

Of course, a major challenge is how to evaluate the success of media-access initiatives, particularly if we maintain that the legitimate means of assessing social costs and benefits of access should not be based on commercial criteria, for instance, of audience size. Indeed, whether the criteria of evaluation should be reduced to economic indicators is an important question. As Aufderheide (1992) argued, "This is a wildly speculative area of economics, because it deals with externalities such as the health of a democratic polity" (p. 63). Compounding these issues is the fact that the telecommunications and mass-media industries in the United States are undergoing significant transformations. As recent debates about the FCC's responsibilities and scope of authority pertaining to universal service and the educational and library e-rate[14] illustrate, the question of what are the essential telecommunications needs of an active citizen is subject to even further speculation. At present, there is no consensus on communication needs for effective citizenship, which may simply reflect that the tail of commercial economic development in telecommunications will wag the dog of the public interest.

In the name of translocalism that extends beyond national boundaries, comparative research about localism is vital. The effects of the globalization of the mass media are experienced differently in different national contexts, and the citizens of the United States continue to be far less subject to media influence from outside their country in comparison with most of the world's population. The United States also stands in the foreground as a target of concerns about cultural imperialism in terms of the influence of its media industries throughout the world. Although much if not most of that criticism has come from Western European intellectuals, there appears to be a shift in attention, stemming from a fear that the cultural identities within Western Europe will be swallowed up by a European at-

---

[14]Much of the current policy debate about updating universal service policies at both the federal and state levels has been focused on adapting to a telecommunications environment in which there has been and continues to be a never-ending process of industrial restructuring in local and long-distance telephone service, in digital multimedia convergence, and in the increased supply and demand for Internet service. The Telecommunications Act of 1996 mandated that the FCC and a joint federal–state board adhere to a set of universal service principles that includes increasing the availability of advanced telecommunications in classrooms and libraries (Pub. L. No. 104–104 (1996), see section 254 [b] [6]). This particular focus of the universal service mandate is now referred to as the e-rate. At present, the e-rate initiative is somewhat under siege by powerful commercial interests who are unfriendly toward having financial obligations to subsidize low-cost access to telecommunications for schools and libraries. Two useful sources for following this subject are the Washington, D.C. Office of the American Library Association (*http://www.ala.org/washoff/wonow.html*), and the Office of Education Technology of the U.S. Department of Education (*http://www.ed.gov/Technology/eratemenu.html*).

tempt to mimic an U.S. style and scale of media production and distribution. In recent years, many European intellectuals have directed their attention to what is happening in Brussels rather than Hollywood, and the concerns about the loss of cultural identity heard within Europe are just as often, if not more frequently, directed at the new Europe than at the United States. European economic integration is an effort to establish a stronger trading bloc and a more highly integrated internal market, and the media industries are a key strategic focal point in that initiative. The search for a more universal and exportable cultural idiom, many intellectuals fear, will lead to the sacrifice of the cultural variation within Europe, preserving those specificities only in the form of relics for the tourist gaze. Among the responses these concerns have generated is a call for localism (Cronberg, Duelund, Jensen, & Qvortrup, 1990; Heiskanen, 1988; Jankowski, 1998; Jankowski, Prehn, & Stappers, 1990; Lundby, 1992). At the heart of that call, a case is made for the preservation and fostering of democratic community life, local identity, and local media structures that are participatory in nature. Whether this call for localism and participation in the context of a network society is heard as loudly within the United States is worthy of study and comparison. Although there certainly are notable differences among the positions of intellectuals and their contexts for reflecting on media policies and practices, the cause in common springs from the rapidly heightening awareness in Western Europe, the United States, and many other parts of the world that a local–global tension is at the heart of political, economic, and cultural transformation, and for better and for worse, on a global scale.

Aspects of the issues raised here are now the subjects of conferences, of volumes of trade press, and of speeches by powerful public officials. Another place where such concerns arise frequently is on the Internet, where many discussion groups engage daily in debates over what the future of telecommunications will or should be like in the United States. Indeed, today's community network movement strongly testifies to the heightened and widespread conviction that telecommunications can and should be used to link communities in a fashion of what Falk (1997) referred to as "globalization from below." In the past couple of years, hundreds of local community networks have sprung up in cities and towns across the United States and in other countries with the aim of being responsive to the information and communication needs of local citizens, one need of which clearly is the ability to communicate translocally.

CONCLUSIONS

The recommendations made here reflect in part an awareness of the specificities of the past manner in which localism, local access, and local participation have been conceived as public interest mandates in the United States. They also anticipate the changing conditions, both institutionally and technologically, under which the idea of the public interest must be addressed in the field of telecommunications. The broadcast, telephone, cable, and Internet-based industries of the United States have operated under different assumptions about the public, its needs and its interests. Today, the talk of media convergence, in technological and institutional terms, leads to a new set of political questions about how the public interest will be articulated. Public service in broadcasting, public access in cable, and universal service in telephone and Internet service are all a part of a new mix of issues to be addressed together, if not converged, as these industries restructure. Telecommunications is a topic of popular culture and esoteric government, industry and academic discourse. Among the many concerns for citizens' groups is that the new media environment may cater predominantly to consumerism and that the touted prospects for expanding democratic participation for all but the educated and affluent will be left by the wayside (e.g., Calabrese & Borchert, 1996).

This chapter has attempted to advance a critical position in favor of realizing the aims of participatory democracy in modern society. Whether it appears to be quixotic or not, an argument of this type must be sustained in policy and practice, for to refuse to do so is to underestimate the intelligence and dignity of citizens and to reduce the likelihood of their commitment to an active public life. If the public interest is to provide for more than the public display of powerful private interests, as so much of our understanding of the concept suggests actually happens, then a commitment to achieving a more democratic alternative that includes a revised concept of, and renewed commitment to, localism should be central to the aims of policy making in a democratic society.

To some, the idea of localism is inherently parochial and regressive, despite its appeals to democratic participation. It is important to remember that many an awful deed has been done in the name of noble ideals, and there is no doubt that the simplicity of the appeal to an ethos of direct democracy masks the complexity of the challenge. The possibility of sowing seeds of co-optation or of undermining democratic purposes would seem to be inherent in the challenge. In this vein, we can see that a public interest policy that places a high priority on direct democracy could, or rather is likely to, lead to the participation and effectiveness of a great many groups and individuals who were far from being among the intended beneficiaries of improved quality and increased quantity of participation in the public sphere. In this sense, defenses in favor of participation must include recognition that a risk of democratic communication stems from our inability to dictate who are and are not worthy participants in an enhanced public sphere. However, arguments on the vileness or sacredness of particular values are easily defeated bases on which judgments about the structure of democracy can be made, and the alternative will always be imperfect but worth seeking. The risk of democracy, as a process, is that as a result of democratic means, we may not always like the outcome. Nevertheless, as an ideal, "democracy" should mean that we will always have the right and the opportunity to speak against an outcome and perhaps win support for its reversal.

ACKNOWLEDGMENTS

This chapter originally was presented as an essay in May 1993 at the 43rd annual conference of the International Communication Association in Washington, D.C. I am grateful for helpful comments from Pat Aufderheide and from the students in my graduate seminar on "Communication, modernity, and spatial relations" in the fall of 1993.

REFERENCES

Amin, S. (1990). Social movements in the periphery. In S. Amin, G. Arrighi, A.G. Frank, & I. Wallerstein, *Transforming the revolution: Social movements and the world-system* (pp. 96–138). New York: Monthly Review Press.

Arendt, H. (1963). *On revolution.* New York: Viking.

Aufderheide, P. (1992). Cable television and the public interest. *Journal of Communication, 42,* 52–65.

Berman, M. (1988). *All that is solid melts into air: The experience of modernity.* New York: Penguin. (Original work published 1982)

Brantlinger, P. (1983). *Bread & circuses: Theories of mass culture as social decay.* Ithaca, NY: Cornell University Press.

Calabrese, A., & Borchert, M. (1996). Prospects for electronic democracy in the United States: Re-thinking communication and social policy. *Media, Culture and Society, 18,* 249–268.

Calabrese, A., & Wasko, J. (1992). All wired up and no place to go: The search for public space in U.S. cable development. *Gazette, 49,* 121–151.

Calabrese, A. (1991). The periphery in the center: The information age and the "good life" in rural America. *Gazette, 48,* 105–128.

Carey, J. W., & Quirk, J. J. (1970). The mythos of the electronic revolution. *The American Scholar, 39,* 219–241, 395–424.

Castells, M. (1989). *The informational city: Information technology, economic restructuring, and the urban–regional process.* Cambridge, MA: Blackwell.

Cronerg, T., Duelund, P., Jensen, O. M., & Qvortrup, L. (Eds.). (1990). *Danish experiments: Social constructions of technology.* Copenhagen, Denmark: New Social Science Monographs.

de Tocqueville, A. (1945). *Democracy in America* (Vols. 1–2, Rev. Ed., H. Reeve & F. Bowen, Trans. & Eds.). New York: Random House. (Original work published 1830)

Dewey, J. (1927). *The public and its problems.* New York: Holt.

Durkheim, E. (1960). *Montesquieu and Rousseau: Forerunners of sociology.* Ann Arbor, MI: University of Michigan Press. (Original work published 1892)

Engelman, R. (1990). The origins of public access cable television, 1966–1972. *Journalism Monographs, 123,* 1–47.

Falk, R. (1997). Resisting 'globalisation-from-above' through 'globalisation-from-below'. *New Political Economy, 2*(1), 17–24.

Foucault, M. (1980). *Power/knowledge: Selected interviews & other writings, 1972–1977* (C. Gordon, Ed.); (C. Gordon, L. Marshall, J. Mepham, & K. Soper, Trans.). New York: Pantheon.

Heiskanen, I. (1988). Local media, regionalism and international economic integration. *Nordicom Review, 2,* 1–12.

Horwitz, R. B. (1989). *The irony of regulatory reform.* New York: Oxford University Press.

Issac, J. (1995, Spring). Going local. *Dissent,* pp. 184–188.

Jankowski, N. (Ed.). (1998). *Javnost/The Public, 5*(2). (Special issue on Community media: Theory and practice).

Jankowski, N., Prehn, O., & Stappers, J. (Eds.). (1991). *The people's voice: Local radio and television in Europe.* London: John Libbey.

Kellner, D. (1990). *Television and the crisis of democracy.* Boulder, CO: Westview.

Lundby, K. (1992, August). *Communication environment for local media.* Paper presented at the 18th meeting of the International Association of Mass Communication Research, Sao Paulo, Brazil.

Madison, J. (1966). The Federalist No. 10. In A. Hamilton, J. Madison & J. Jay (Eds.), *The Federalist papers* (pp. 42–49). New York: Doubleday. (Original work published 1787–1788)

Martin, R. (1995). Resurfacing socialism: Resisting the appeals of tribalism and localism. *Social Text, 13*(3), 97–118.

Marx, L. (1964). *The machine in the garden: Technology and the pastoral ideal in America.* New York: Oxford.

Masters, R. D. (1991). Jean-Jacques Rousseau. In D. Miller, J. Coleman, W. Connolly & A. Ryan (Eds.), *The Blackwell encyclopedia of political thought* (pp. 455–458). Oxford, UK: Basil Blackwell.

Mill, J. S. (1958). *Considerations on representative government.* Indianapolis, IN: Bobbs-Merrill. (Original work published 1861)

Pahl, R. E. (1968). The rural–urban continuum. In R. E. Pahl (Ed.), *Readings in urban sociology* (pp. 263–297). Oxford: Pergamon. (Original work published 1966)

Palmer, R. R., & Colton, J. (1971). *A history of the modern world to 1815.* New York: Knopf.

Pateman, C. (1970). *Participation and democratic theory.* Cambridge: Cambridge University Press.

Rousseau, J.- J. (1968). *The social contract* (M. Cranston, Trans.). New York: Penguin. (Original work published 1762)

Segal, H. P. (1985). *Technological utopianism in American culture.* Chicago: University of Chicago.

Sennett, R. (1974). *The fall of public man.* New York: Alfred A. Knopf.

Sloan Commission on Cable Communications. (1971). *On the cable: The television of abundance.* New York: McGraw-Hill.

Streeter, T. (1987). The cable fable revisited: Discourse, policy, and the making of cable television. *Critical Studies in Mass Communication, 4,* 174–200.

Tönnies, F. (1957). *Community and society.* (C. P. Loomis, Trans. & Ed.). New York: Harper & Row. (Original work published 1887)

U.S. Department of Commerce, National Telecommunications and Information Administration. (1993). *Globalization of the mass media.* Washington, D.C.: U.S. Government Printing Office. NTIA Special Publication, 93–290.

Williams, R. (1974). *Television: Technology and cultural form.* New York: Schocken.

Williams, R. (1979). *Politics and letters.* New York: Verso.

Williams, R. (1983). *Keywords: A vocabulary of culture and society* (Rev. Ed.). New York: Oxford.

Author Index

A

B

Subject Index

A

Accountability, 98–99
Advisory board, 209–210, 212, 213–214
Advisory Council on the National Infrastructure, 204
Agendas, hidden, 91
Alternative discourse communities, 83–84, *see also* Feminist organizing
Alternative model, community, 167–171
Alternative news forms, 246, *see also* Newspapers; Newsweeklies
America Online, 196
Anger, 60, 64
Anglo-feminists, 103, *see also* Feminist organizing
Antagonistic forces, coping, 79
Antisocial strategies, 44
Apollo project, 130
Aristotelian–Hegelian school, 15
Aristotle, 3–4, 10–11
Atrocities, contemporary, 185
Attitudes, 120, *see also* Downsizing
Attribution errors, 46

B

Babylon, 4
Backstabbing, 89, *see also* SAFE community
Back-stage strategies, 54, 65–67
Bandwidth, 198, *see also* Internet
Basque culture, *see* Mondragón Cooperative Corporation
Behavior, 40, 45, 194
Berlin Wall, 186
Bias, 238–240
Bill collectors, 56
Boaters, 206
Bonds, cohesive, 116–117
Boundaries, 94, 95–96, 99–100, 121
Bounded emotionality, 102
Bowling alone, 164
Boycott, 245
Breaks, 66
British Empire, 186
Broadcasting, 253–257, *see also* Localism
Bulletin boards, online, 197
Bureaucracy model, 136
Burnout, 61

C

Cable television, 253, 254–256, *see also* Localism; Television
Caja Laboral Bank, 140
Calm, staying, 60, 63
Capital mobility, 264–265
Carnegie Mellon Study, 193–194
Case study method, 57–59, 72–75
Category system, 56
Center for Civic Networking, 204
Center of consciousness, 13
Centralization, 911 services, 53
Chatrooms, 196
Chicago school, 162
    concepts of community/communication, 7, 14–19
Children First campaign, 237–238, 240

7984